THE THRILLER AND
NORTHERN IRELAND SINCE 1969

To Jim, Greta and Phil Kelly,
whose dedications are infinitely more worthwhile

The Thriller and Northern Ireland since 1969

Utterly Resigned Terror

Aaron Kelly

Studies in European Cultural Transition

Volume Twenty Eight

General Editors: Martin Stannard and Greg Walker

ASHGATE

Published by
Ashgate Publishing Limited
Gower House
Croft Road
Aldershot
Hampshire GU11 3HR
England

Ashgate Publishing Company
Suite 420
101 Cherry Street
Burlington, VT 05401-4405
USA

Ashgate website: http://www.ashgate.com

British Library Cataloguing in Publication Data
Kelly, Aaron
    The thriller and Northern Ireland since 1969 : utterly resigned terror. – (Studies in European cultural transition)
    1. Politics and literature – Northern Ireland – History – 20th century 2. Suspense fiction, English – History and criticism 3. English literature – 20th century – History and criticism 4. Political violence in literature 5. Gangsters in literature 6. Terrorism in literature 7. Politics in literature 8. Northern Ireland – In literature
    I. Title
    823'.08720932416

Library of Congress Cataloging-in-Publication Data
Kelly, Aaron.
    The thriller and Northern Ireland since 1969 : utterly resigned terror / Aaron Kelly.
        p. cm.
    Includes bibliographical references and index.
    ISBN 0-7546-3839-1 (alk. paper)
    1. English fiction – Irish authors – History and criticism. 2. Northern Ireland – In literature. 3. Politics and literature – Northern Ireland – History – 20th century. 4. Literature and society – Northern Ireland – History – 20th century. 5. Detective and mystery stories, English – History and criticism. 6. Authors, Irish – Homes and haunts – Northern Ireland. 7. Northern Ireland – Intellectual life. 8. Political violence in literature. 9. Social conflict in literature. 10. Violence in literature. 11. Crime in literature. I. Title.

    PR8891.N67K45 2004
    823'.92–dc22

                                                                            2004021831

ISBN 0 7546 3839 1

Printed and bound in Great Britain by TJ International Ltd, Padstow, Cornwall

Contents

General Editors' Preface		*vi*
Acknowledgments		*vii*

Introduction
'You Didn't Need a Reason to Kill People,
Not Here': Narrative, the North and Historical Agency   1

1   'The Green Unpleasant Land': The Political Unconscious
of the British 'Troubles' Thriller   26

2   'And What Do You Call It?': The Thriller and the
Problematics of Home in Northern Irish Writing   57

3   'New Languages Would Have to be Invented':
Representations of Belfast and Urban Space   83

4   'A Man Could Get Lost': Constructions of Gender   111

5   'It's Not for the Likes of Us to Philosophize':
The Pleasure and Politics of Thrills, or,
Towards a Political Aesthetics   140

Appendix A: Travelling With Crime Novels by Walter Benjamin   165
Appendix B: On the Popularity of the Crime Novel by Bertolt Brecht   167

Bibliography   *172*
Index   *210*

General Editors' Preface

The European dimension of research in the humanities has come into sharp focus over recent years, producing scholarship which ranges across disciplines and national boundaries. Until now there has been no major channel for such work. This series aims to provide one, and to unite the fields of cultural studies and traditional scholarship. It will publish the most exciting new writing in areas such as European history and literature, art history, archaeology, language and translation studies, political, cultural and gay studies, music, psychology, sociology and philosophy. The emphasis will be explicitly European and interdisciplinary, concentrating attention on the relativity of cultural perspectives, with a particular interest in issues of cultural transition.

Martin Stannard
Greg Walker
University of Leicester

Acknowledgments

I would like to acknowledge the financial support of the Queen's University of Belfast, whose provision of a research scholarship permitted me to undertake research for this book as a doctoral student. During my time at Queen's I benefited from the knowledge and encouragement of the staff of the School of English and in particular I would like to thank Michael Allen and Edna Longley for their guidance and generosity. I am also deeply indebted to Colin Graham of NUI Maynooth for his comments upon my work and his always thoughtful, helpful and stimulating advice. Luke Gibbons, as external examiner of my PhD, provided invaluable advice and subsequent support that has also served to guide me.

I would especially like to pay tribute to my supervisor at Queen's, Eamonn Hughes, not only for the formative and invaluable kindness, fostering and wisdom that he has shown to me, but also for the inspiration of his groundbreaking and unsurpassed work in Irish cultural criticism. The spirit and engagement of his work continually generates hope amidst what is at times a deadening and pervasive pessimism in critical accounts of the North of Ireland, and this study would have been impossible without both the warmth and the commitment of his intellect. However unworthy, this book is an offering of thanks to him.

The final version of *The Thriller and Northern Ireland* was written during my time as a Leverhulme Postdoctoral Fellow in Scottish and Irish Literature at the University of Edinburgh and I would like to acknowledge the financial support of the Leverhulme Trust and the care of Cairns Craig in his role as my mentor. I was also granted a Research Fellowship at the Institute for Advanced Study in the Humanities at the University of Edinburgh and I am indebted to John Frow and Anthea Taylor during my time there.

Much of my research was conducted at the Northern Ireland Political Collection of the Linen Hall Library in Belfast and I am thankful for the patience, assistance and good cheer of the staff there, particularly Ciaran Crossey, Yvonne Murphy and Andy White. I would also like to extend my thanks to David Torrens at No Alibis and Jim Tullerton for their kind help in tracking down many of the primary texts covered in this study. Throughout the writing of this project, Alan Gillis read through the manuscript and I am eternally grateful to him for his unfailing support, friendship and intellectual insights and would like to extend my grateful good wishes to his wife Wendy and son Vincent. Kate Nicol's love and support since my arrival in Edinburgh has been an immense encouragement, and when needed, an invaluable relief and release in completing this book.

Additionally, my editor, Ann Donohue at Ashgate has been considerate, encouraging and patient throughout and I am very appreciative of her diligent efforts in assisting the completion of *The Thriller and Northern Ireland*. I would like to thank Dr Petra Christina Hardt at Suhrkamp Verlag for her patient and generous help in securing the permissions rights for the English translations of the essays by Walter Benjamin and Bertolt Brecht which appear as the appendix to this monograph. I gratefully acknowledge, in the first instance, Suhrkamp Verlag, and Methuen and Harvard University Press, who own the first option on translations of Brecht and Benjamin's work respectively, for permitting me to translate these essays in full. Furthermore, I would like to extend thanks to Claudio Hils for granting permission to use a photograph from his work *Red Land, Blue Land* on the book cover, and to Christoph Ulrich for assisting with the digital processing of the image.

I am also beholden to the following friends or colleagues for their comments on my work, their friendship and their kindness: Nicholas Allen, Steffi Bachorz, Chris Bates, Eleanor Bell, Ester Carrillo, Noreen Doody, Alice Ferrebe, Leontia Flynn, Chris Frieze, Sarah Gamble, Peter Garratt, Stipe Grgas, Stephen Hackett, Seamus Harahan, Martin Harvey, Stephen Harvey, Patsy Horton, Keith Hughes, Bob Irvine, Mark Jamieson, Daniel Jewesbury, Jim Kelly, Michael McAteer, Seán McKeown, Eoghan McTigue, Patrick Magee, Julie Marney, Chris Martin, Shane Murphy, Lisa Power, Emily Pritchard, David Salter, Yassamin Sheel, Paul Smith, Allyson Stack, Randall Stevenson, Lindsey Watson, Stuart Watson, Richard West.

Finally, this book is for my family, Jim, Greta and Philip Kelly, for their love, sacrifices and indomitable integrity, which will stay with me forever. I only hope that I have brought even a one hundredth of their intelligence to bear on the educational advantages that have been afforded to me and which were denied to them. This book is dedicated to my family with all my love.

The idea of eternal recurrence transforms historical events into
mass-produced articles.
Walter Benjamin

Introduction

'You Didn't Need a Reason to Kill People, Not Here': Narrative, the North and Historical Agency

'In times of terror, when everyone is something of a conspirator, everybody will be in a situation where s/he has to play detective'.
Walter Benjamin, *Charles Baudelaire*

Almost four hundred thrillers have been produced over the last 35 years in response to the current phase of political upheaval in Northern Ireland. This vast popular cultural sedimentation has ensured the enthronement of the genre as the dominant fictional mode of representing the North, supposedly granting appropriate literary form to national and historical experience. This book interrogates the complicity of the enduring confrontations, conspiracies and mysteries of the thriller form with the hegemonic view of Northern Irish society as itself suspended in a recurrent and befuddling stasis. Brian Moore's *Lies of Silence* typifies such a correlation by utilizing the regurgitatory element of the crime genre to depict the conflict as 'that endless mindless chain of killings' (64).[1] In a way, then, there is a moment of ideological conflation in the application of the thriller form to Northern Ireland. Therein the conspiracies of the genre are collapsed into what Joep Leerssen has termed 'the traumatic paradigm' (1998, 37) of Irish History, in which a nightmarish model refuses dialectical transformation and reverberates ceaselessly in irresoluble crisis.[2] I want to suggest later that there is also a utopian formal politics to conspiracy in the thriller form, which actually proffers a speculative grasp of the social totality but which is conventionally masked by this traumatic paradigm. For ultimately this book seeks to redeem not only the thriller as a form but also the historical dynamics present in the North of Ireland, to affirm a potentiality that disrupts what in many of these books appears most fated, contemptuously dismissed, statically stereotyped and without hope.

---

[1] Comparably, the dust cover of Lionel Shriver's *Ordinary Decent Criminals* introduces the text as 'a piercing novel about small lives and grand minds skewered on an immovable, immemorial conundrum'.

[2] For example, in *The Devil's Own* the IRA volunteer, Rory Devaney, tells his American host: 'It's an Irish story, not an American one. In Ireland, there are no happy endings' (Newman, 191).

To this end, it is worth noting, as Edna Longley brilliantly does (1994, 88), that when a British television production crew arrived in Belfast to shoot an adaptation of Gerald Seymour's novel, *Harry's Game*, filming was disrupted for two weeks because the weather was too good and the dismal rain desired by the crew's preordained notion of Belfast atmospherics was kept at bay. In many ways, this book is about those two weeks of sunshine which signalled so vividly that even the seemingly most elemental and unchanging of forces in the North will always defeat fixated stereotyping. So this study designedly and deliberately takes as its subject a body of texts that often propagates the most despicable, unpalatable and pessimistic things about Northern Ireland, in order to expose such representations to a Marxist critique that I shall term *redemptive transcription*. The aim, then, is to find hope in texts that seem devoid of solace, and to illustrate further that such hope defeats the most reactionary of these representations. In fact, to a large degree it is precisely the North's refusal to conform to such representational constraints that precipitates much of this representational hostility and contempt. Indeed, the book as a whole will uncover the real terror in these novels not so much in their depiction of terrorism but rather in the self-referential dread of stereotyped and petrified representations of the North confronting their own incapacity to superintend the intense social change of the last thirty years.

Frederic Jameson's concept of the political unconscious provides my primary theoretical framework for achieving this redemptive transcription of the historical materials encoded in the 'Troubles' thriller. Through Jameson's method I will resist interpreting the dehistoricized stasis of the thriller's formally unresolved conflict as a direct reflection of the apparently anachronistic aberration of Northern Irish politics. Jameson's Althusserian grasp of History as an 'absent cause' does not deny the referent of History but rather seeks to do justice to its inescapable force:

> What Althusser's own insistence on history as an absent cause makes clear, but what is missing from the formula as it is canonically worded, is that he does not at all draw the fashionable conclusion that because history is a text, the 'referent' does not exist. We would therefore propose the following revised formulation: that history is *not* a text, not a narrative, master or otherwise, but that, as an absent cause it is inaccessible to us except in textual form, and that our approach to it and to the Real itself necessarily passes through its prior textualization, its narrativization in the political unconscious (1996, 35).

Put succinctly, this analysis is designed to undercut a naïve reading of the 'Troubles' thriller's content level as an authentic and organically reflective representation of the 'truth' about the North. It intimates that our formal approach to the thriller will demand its own detective work symptomatically restructuring the historical clues embedded in the text. The political unconscious insists upon an ideology of form, upon the uncovering of determinate structures of formal contradiction and antinomy, through its grasp of History not as some reified or passive object of representation but as the experience of necessity which lacerates literary production. Jameson explains:

The type of interpretation here proposed is ... grasped as the rewriting of the literary text in such a way that the latter may itself be seen as the rewriting or restructuration of a prior historical or ideological *subtext*, it being always understood that the 'subtext' is not immediately present as such, not some common-sense external reality, nor even the conventional narratives of history manuals, but rather must itself be always (re)constructed after the fact (1996, 83).

Such a model enables us to examine the problematics of textualizing History without viewing Irish History as problematical in itself. In short, it ensures that an analysis of Northern Ireland may proceed in terms, not of peculiarity and anomaly, but rather of specificity and intensity. This methodology is further demanded by the conventional critical problematization of the Irish novel, which has achieved ideological perpetuity in the reception of Northern fiction. By way of illustration, Patricia Craig argues in the introduction to her collection, *The Rattle of the North: An Anthology of Ulster Prose*, that 'it is well known that conditions in the North of Ireland, from Plantation times on, were never sufficiently settled to foster literary activity, and that the development of the novel, in particular, was consequently retarded' (1). In ascertaining, through the political unconscious and its dialectical Marxist appropriation of Freud and Lacan, how the inexorable subtext of History throws ideology into formal contradiction in the literary text, we are pursuing and interrogating, if you will, the *latent manifestos* of literary production. That is, the work of critical detection seeks the inscription of History in the text, not in the obviated corroboration of the reified reflection of content and a directly recuperable formal structure, but rather through the dialectical and symptomatic decoding of ideological distortion, absence and antinomy.

A Jamesonian understanding of the text as 'inventing imaginary or formal "solutions" to unresolvable social contradictions' (1996, 79) permits the following reformulation: the conventional reading of the closed, ahistorical continuum of the thriller as the passive reflection of the North's own interminable stasis is itself implicated in an attempt to offer more profound resolutions at deeper formal and interpretative levels to a host of historical, and thus alterable, problematics and anxieties. This book will comprehend precisely such a strategy of representational containment, which seeks jointly to manage and repress determinate historical and social materials. Our own critical-detective motto should read: crimes can be solved!

Let me first outline the dominant, reactionary interpretations of both the thriller and Northern Ireland, which I will then begin to subvert. The deep embeddedness of the conventional idea that the thriller merely offers a passive reflection of the North's degradation is exemplified by Margaret Scanlan's comment: 'the aesthetic impulse is as alien to the Shankill Road as the well-shaped plot is to the erratic behaviour of home-made bombs; a private life, in the face of repeated violations, becomes almost as inconceivable as a simple moral judgment or a happy ending' (1985, 145-146). Here, then, in the implied inaccessibility of civilized literary form, the supposed crudity of popular fiction and Northern Irish society reciprocally reinforce one another. The specific deployment of a static and dehistoricized view of the thriller's mechanisms to habituate a conventional representation of Northern Ireland's intractable depravity is indicated further by Elizabeth Bouché's review of *The Armalite Maiden* by Jonathan Kebbe: 'In the dark corners of the human heart, there's a curiosity about what passions pull triggers, and that is what allows thriller characters and plots to be almost interchangeable, no matter in what country they are set' (46).[3] Yet there is a telling contradiction in Bouché's formulation between the assuredly stock or 'interchangeable' and thus transhistorically consistent, and the somewhat more insecure 'curiosity' that impels such avowed representational certainty. I intend to expose the moments of *ideological conflation* produced by the thriller's application to Northern Ireland as more anxious moments of *ideological suture* vainly attempting to disguise historical and representational fracture.

Therefore, whilst the hundreds of thrillers written about the North over the last thirty years seemingly attest to the mutual debasement of both Northern Ireland and popular fiction, I ultimately wish to argue otherwise. At its most mechanistic, the thriller is certainly a form which attempts to suggest that there are no classes, no gender, no community or women's groups, no human agency or collective projects of emancipation, in short, nothing beyond the cyclical iteration of two tribalized, allochronic monoliths. The insistence by Colin Bateman's hero, Starkey, in *Divorcing Jack* that 'you didn't need a reason to kill people, not here' (150), epitomizes a dominant portrait of the North as an unintelligible terrain voided of human agents or historical direction, which it is the task of the crime narrative merely to superintend and regulate. Such a terminal exegesis sustains the more pessimistic accounts of the social function of crime fiction as a Foucauldian system of Panopticon regulation and control, which normalizes its power in hierarchically systematizing social otherness into a criminal and 'carceral' formation (Foucault 1991, 307). For example, Franco Moretti figures detective fiction as the apotheosis of representational coercion: 'this culture knows, orders and defines all the significant data of individual existence as part of social existence. Every story reiterates Bentham's Panopticon ideal: the model prison that signifies the metamorphosis of liberalism into total scrutability' (1988, 143). Such a formulation instigates an untenably monolithic conception of form and genre. As Raymond Williams postulates, genre 'is neither an ideal type nor a traditional order nor a set of technical rules. It is the practical and variable combination and even fusion of what are, in abstraction, different levels of the social material process that what we have known as genre becomes a new kind of constitutive evidence' (1977b, 185).

The classical and conservative account of the crime narrative can be destablized by uncovering the historical possibilities residing in the political unconscious. Crime is not defined solely by the legal apparatus, nor is the social map provided

---

[3] Such representational exploitation permeates the whole cultural and economic field: '[c]uriosity is what makes NI tick – needs a simple in depth explanation presented in a visitor friendly way' . This proviso is from Maureen Mackin et al, *The Cultural Sector: A Development Opportunity for Tourism in Northern Ireland, Summary Report*, a report prepared in January 1998 for the Northern Irish Tourist Board, the Arts Council, the Northern Ireland Film Commission and the Rural Development Council amongst others. Cited by Spurgeon Thompson, 1999. 53.

by crime necessarily a penitential one. The struggle over precisely what constitutes crime is a political struggle conducted by conflictual social agents. Nonetheless, in designating the thriller form as multicoded, I am not suggesting that this historical multiplicity of social meaning resides in some vacuous plurality or diffusion of power. It is instead a determinate political conflict. I would thus contest Jerry Palmer's static and depoliticized view of the thriller form as blank slate: 'the basic apparatus of the thriller can accommodate more or less any set of political beliefs, precisely because they constitute only a superficial layer' (1978, 67).[4] The thriller – reputedly the most throwaway of literatures – is actually the monumental form of social complexity. Of course it can house a reactionary façade of ideological defence or withdrawal but within its battlements there is also a utopian architecture of social construction and spatialization. When the critic Francine Cunningham asks – 'so now that the ceasefire has been announced, what will happen to all the Northern Ireland writers? Where will they go for their material?' (26) – there is implicit in such a question the sense that the 'Troubles' are the zero sum of all Northern Irish fiction, culture and society. Indeed, Bateman's *Divorcing Jack* distils the historical intricacy and contestation of the North into a single, configural narrative of violence: 'Life stories pondered over in courts merged in repetition after a while until you could look back and identify only one common denominator, a gelled identity of misshapen lives, depraved by politics, gunfire, bigotry, repression and poverty, with God in a supervisory capacity' (156-157). It is by taking as its subject the popular literary form, which is conventionally viewed as reducing Northern Irish society to nothing more than nor these 'Troubles', that this monograph will instantiate the historical complexity of both the North and the thriller form itself. Moreover, the general critical treatment of 'Troubles' fiction is unwilling to acknowledge both the abundance and the formal politics of the thriller, dismissing it as mere 'trash' or as a vacant superstructure simply framing an explicitly standard exegesis.

The conventional conflation of the supposed mysteries of the thriller into the traumatic paradigm of a Northern Ireland beyond solution actually seeks to mystify a more subversive formal drive (just as the enigma of other stock and interchangeable locales had sustained the Cold War thriller and international terrorist texts had arrogated the historical specifics of the Arab-Israeli conflict or Latin America). The reiterative mode of the genre also attests to a more global, late capitalist effort of detection that continually desires the renegotiation of a lost sense of society itself, which as a conceptual or alterable whole has withdrawn into

---

[4] Indeed, Palmer undercuts his own argument by continuing: '[t]he one political belief that the thriller could not accommodate is anti-individualism, for ... individualism is fundamental to the thriller' (67). Similarly, in an early essay largely devoid of the formal analysis of his later work, Jameson describes crime fiction as 'a form without ideological content, without any overt political or social or philosophical point'. 'On Raymond Chandler'. *Southern Review* 6:3 (1970). 625. The political unconscious instructs that all forms have concretely embedded ideological content. An illuminating survey of the political mechanics of the genre is provided by Stephen Knight's *Form and Ideology in Crime Fiction*. London: Macmillan, 1980.

obscurity. By way of exemplification, I shall briefly turn to Jack Higgins's *Touch the Devil*, which takes its title from the character Liam Devlin's expression 'touch the devil and you can't let go'. Devlin tells his British counterpart Ferguson: 'none of us can stop can we? No going back. Bloody undertakers the lot of us, always carrying some poor bugger out in a coffin ... the trouble is, you see, that we're not playing the game any more. The game's playing us' (1982, 74-75). Indeed, Higgins's work more generally exemplifies the inert stationing of characters in relation to the North as locale within the more mechanistic thriller. Higgins's texts often reutilize his famous and stock characters who are drawn into permanent almost necessary intrigues. Liam Devlin first appeared in Higgins's *The Eagle has Landed*, as a conspirator in a Second World War plot to assassinate Winston Churchill, but is subsequently called upon by the British state to help thwart IRA attempts to kill both Margaret Thatcher and John Major (Higgins 1982 and 1992).

Interestingly, Devlin's character, together with that of his IRA colleague, Martin Brosnan, who are portrayed as 'a couple of anachronisms from the early days of the Irish Troubles' (1982, 39), are reiteratively deployed as ideological signifiers of idealistic villainy indicting the degraded, inveterately corrupt nature of the current conflict. Ferguson, the head of British Intelligence describes them thus: 'men like Devlin and Brosnan want to be able to fight with clean hands and a little honour. Their tragedy is that in this kind of war that is just not possible' (1982, 46). Unable to alter the social corruption symbolized by one level of the thriller's formulations, to substantively change their present, these characters function only as the repositories of the lost codes of a knowable, moral world of right and wrong. Perhaps the most fatalistic staging of such petrified configurations of character and locale framing a relentless violence occurs in M.S. Power's *Children of the North* trilogy, wherein each text begins with a chapter relating the death of what will be its main protagonist. Hence, Eamonn Hughes affirms that 'the failing of the novel in regard to Northern Ireland is that, by accepting the image of the North as fated, it has not allowed for the interplay of characters, form and circumstances' (1992, 7).

So whilst acknowledging that the more conservative modes of the thriller collude with such a diffusion of human agency, I will now begin to tease out precisely how the thriller also possesses the formal apparatus to subvert such disablement. Bertolt Brecht has commented with characteristic adeptness upon the social symbolism of crime fiction:

> We gain our knowledge of life in a catastrophic form. It is from catastrophes that we have to infer the manner in which our social formation functions. Through reflection, we must deduce the 'inside story' of crises, depressions, revolutions, and wars. We already sense from reading the newspapers (but also bills, letters of dismissal, call-up papers and so forth) that somebody must have done something for the evident catastrophe to have taken place. So what then has been done and by whom? Behind the reported events, we suspect other occurrences about which we are not told. These are the *real* occurrences. If we knew these incidents, we would understand. Only History can inform us about these real occurrences – insofar as the protagonists have not succeeded in keeping them completely secret. History is written *after* catastrophes. The basic situation, in which intellectuals feel that they

are objects and not subjects of History, forms the thought, which they can display for enjoyment in the crime story. Existence depends upon unknown factors. 'Something must have happened', 'something is brewing', 'a situation has arisen' – this is what they feel, and the mind goes out on patrol. But enlightenment only comes, if at all, after the catastrophe. The death has taken place. What had been fermenting beforehand? What had happened? Why has a solution arisen? All this can now be deduced (456-457).[5]

What Brecht anticipates here is the movement away from the ideology of the single, individualized crime or murder to the age of the thriller (and ultimately its conspiratorial form). Brecht provides a method for foregrounding the move by which historical agents attempt to become not the objects but the subjects of History. That is, crime fiction and crime narratives provide imaginary or subjective resolutions to History itself, to its prior, constitutive mystery and catastrophe as such. This formulation helps explicate Althusser's otherwise incapacitating and unintelligible account of History as 'a process without a subject or goal(s)' (1993, 133).[6] Our sense of the social formation itself is now both mysterious and mystificatory, an audacious criminal extravagance goading our investigation.[7] By suggesting that crime fiction is not reducible to a Panopticon regulatory system of control, I also wish to contend that ideology is not limitable to false consciousness. Put another way, there is no authentically non-ideological map of the social, though not all (ideological) representations are of equal political value. In fact, particularly in the myopia of postmodernism, ideology can offer, in Jameson's terms, 'a possibility of knowledge' (1994, 27).

As a result, I am proposing here a more dialectical consideration of the relationship between the Real and the Imaginary, or History and the Subject, wherein the Real is reducible neither to an unknowable thing in itself nor a chain of events that we can adequately and authentically represent directly. Ideology, as with networks of crime in the thriller, becomes a necessary narrative or fantasy effort by which the subject constructs a place for him/herself in an historical

---

[5] The translation is my own. A full translation of the essay can be found in the appendix. Similarly, all translations from Walter Benjamin's *Gesammelte Schriften* are mine: they are cited as *GS* plus the volume and page numbers.

[6] The most engaged and devastating critique of Althusser's position is provided by E.P. Thompson's *The Poverty of Theory* London: Merlin, 1979. 193-397.

[7] With specific reference to the North, it is noteworthy that much 'Troubles' output deals with 'the untold story', the 'dirty war', 'covert operations' and so on. For example, Brian Rowan's journalistic account of the Peace Process is entitled *Between the Lines*. The talks process was itself quite deliberately conducted 'behind closed doors', away from the distraction of public involvement. Such a removal of the political is part of a global experience, which bespeaks the failure of representative politics. It is given a particular inflection in Ireland, I shall later demonstrate, by the failure of the intimate sequestration of Irish Nationalism and Unionism to construct a properly constituted public and thus political space.

process that is fundamentally nonrepresentable and would otherwise exclude us.[8] Consequently, there is a utopian politics to tracing a society as a cartography of crime, which functions as a site of class consciousness, and which is usually overwritten in the moment of ideological conflation in which the mysteries of the 'Troubles' thriller are conventionally collapsed into the traumatic paradigm of Irish History. Jameson comments upon the formative narrativity of ideology:

> It is rather an asymptotic phenomenon, an outer limit, which the subject approaches in the anxiety of the moment of truth – moments of personal crisis and of the agonizing political polarization of revolutionary situations; and from such an approach to the Real the subject then tends to retreat again, at best in possession of abstract or purely intellectual schemata when not of charged narrative representations. The narrative apparatus which informs ideological representations is thus not mere 'false consciousness', but an authentic way of grappling with a Real that must always transcend it, a Real into which the subject seeks to insert itself through praxis, all the while painfully learning the lesson of its own ideological closure and of history's resistance to the fantasy-structures in which it is itself locked (1979, 12-13).

Following Macherey and Althusser, Jameson suggests that 'great art distances ideology by the way in which, endowing the latter with figuration and with narrative articulation, the text frees its ideological content to demonstrate its own contradictions; by the sheer formal immanence with which an ideological system exhausts its permutations and ends up projecting its own ultimate structural closure' (1979a, 22-23). Similarly, this study of the 'Troubles' thriller is written out of an affirmative belief in the revolutionary force of History, and the inability of any ideology, no matter how ingrained, dominant or discursively self-enthroned, to survive its own textual figuration. Or more simply, no ideology can survive its own attempt to elaborate itself fully. I would, however, query the High cultural emphasis of Jameson, Macherey and Althusser. By analysing the 'Troubles' thriller, the conflicting maps of the North provided by the form – as sheer illegibility, as feminized total crime, as state formation – allegorize the broader exposition of ideology in literature. Put simply, we can witness the more reactionary of these maps expose their limitations, and ascertain the determinate aporia in their construction of place and space.

   Hence, in tracing the ideological multiplicity textualized in the political unconscious of the 'Troubles' thriller, I also hope to demonstrate that popular

---

[8] Marx famously commented in *The Eighteenth Brumaire of Louis Bonaparte* that 'men make their own history, but they do not make it just as they please; they do not make it under circumstances chosen by themselves, but under circumstances directly encountered, given, and transmitted from the past' (1977, 300). Frequently and erroneously cited as an example of Marxism's reductive determinism, this complex sense of History as the dialectical experience of Necessity and Desire informs my own attempt to synthesize Jameson's Althusserian effort to trace the absent, nonrepresentable force of History as 'what hurts' with Thompson's justifiable faith in human agency. The articulation of narrative in this introduction seeks such a dialectization of contradictory yet ultimately complementary poles of Marxist thought.

fiction cannot be dismissed as mere false consciousness or mass distraction. Rather it contains a complex and continual dialectic between ideology and utopia, between what I shall term the *repressive* and *redemptive* modalities of its imaginary, through which the text inscribes the material conditions of its production with both anxiety and hope. Thus, the dialectic of the *repressive* and *redemptive* modalities of the popular text attempt to produce what are, in effect, 'ordered dreams' (McDonald 1996, 81),[9] the articulation of collective desires and fantasies through strategic codes of symbolic containment. This book aims to effect the rupture of this political and aesthetic negotiation by affirming that the historical raw materials which the 'Troubles' thriller simultaneously strives to utilize, transform and repress, encode themselves in determinate structures of formal absence and aporia. As Jameson observes:

> anxiety and hope are two faces of the same collective consciousness, so that the works of mass culture, even if their function lies in the legitimation of the existing order – or some worse one – cannot do their job without deflecting in the latter's service the deepest and most fundamental hopes and fantasies of the collectivity, to which they can therefore, no matter in how distorted a fashion, be found to have given voice (1992b, 30).

The dialectic between the *repressive* and *redemptive* modalities of the imaginary entails the tracing of the contradictions of the optimal or dominant subject positions produced by these texts in the 'active process of making selves through reading' (McCracken, 16). In a way, the *repressive* mechanics of the text attempt what Gramsci would term a 'transformist' hegemony (58), wherein popular interests are assimilated and reworked by a dominant political subject. The utopian reading of the text necessitates an 'expansive' hegemony, which reinscribes and resituates the collective desire of the text. Tony Bennett thus contends that literary forms 'are *in* society, a part of it, actively contributing to the shaping of social relations through the ways in which they organize relations of class, community, nation and history – and one might add, gender – and inscribe their readers in those relations' ('Introduction: Popular Fictions', 4).[10]

The Marxist theoretical framework therefore requires two points of circumspection. Firstly, a refutation of the dismissal of the popular text as sheer false consciousness. Bennett saliently recognizes that the codification of popular fiction within Marxism's traditional Holy Trinity of Science, Literature and Ideology, as neither Truth nor Great Art, results in its political relinquishment:

---

[9] The term is from Ian McDonald's science fiction 'Troubles' thriller, *Sacrifice of Fools*, and refers to the collective imaginary shared by all the Shian aliens, who arrive in Northern Ireland in 2001. In a way, the Shian would be paradigmatic instances of the transformist hegemony of the optimal reading subject, bearers of a stratified and unitary fantasy.

[10] David Lloyd also asserts more generally that '[a]s a literary form, the novel is not simply the product and the reflection of certain social conditions but actively contributes to producing them as the very condition of its own reception' (1993, 131).

the *en bloc* categorization of popular fiction as a sphere of writing which contributes to the reproduction of dominant ideological formations entails that it be abandoned as a field of struggle. The only relation of political calculation it permits is that of struggling *against* popular fiction (by unmasking it, by opposing it to the knowledge of Marxism or the critical insights of Literature), rather than *within* it. It is necessary to insist, in the face of the essentialism that has blighted much Marxist discussion of the internal economy of the superstructure, that conflict and struggle take place *within* and not just *between* the different regions and spheres of the superstructure' ('Marxism and Popular Fiction', 252).

In addition, the conventional metropolitan Left's deployment of Ireland as byword for the organic collective, for the readymade and oppositional popular subject, entails a further revision. A sense of the struggle for hegemony in the popular text, the complex dialectic between the *repressive* and *redemptive* modalities of its imaginary, disrupts any seamless attachment between the text and the 'popular', for both are fractious sites of conflict. Consequently, the leftist interest in unearthing non-canonical or marginal Irish cultural materials, with which to brush the dominant literary critical and cultural approaches and narratives against the grain, deserves attention. The neglect of popular fiction is evident in such leftist accounts. The excellent work of David Lloyd has pointed out with regard to the cultural hierarchies and value systems produced by the dominant discourses within Ireland that:

> In the writings of nationalism we can observe, as it were, the anxieties of canon formation, since negation largely takes place through the judgement that a given cultural form is either too marginal to be representative or, in terms that recapitulate those of imperialism itself, a primitive manifestation in need of development or cultivation. Both judgements relegate their objects to the domain of low rather than high culture (1993, 5).

Lloyd utilizes the riotously dialogic popular tradition as 'recalcitrant' (1993, 6) to emergent nationalism and imperialism in rewriting such critical attenuation and evaluation. Contemporary popular fiction rather problematizes the recourse to such a repository given. It signals a shift in analysis from the popular as organic to the popular as populist, from organic artistic community to reading constituencies positioned in relation to the market and to the fiction industry, as well as to ideological and cultural formations, and in addition, of course, to History itself.[11]

The tendency amongst sections of the British and American Left to look for the 'auratic' (Eagleton 1998, 295) in Irish cultural production, to view Ireland as a readily accessible repository of organic, oppositional subject, is made historically inaccessible by contemporary popular fiction and its hegemonic fabric, which, rather productively, I would maintain, necessitates a revision of the very terms of

---

[11] The incompatibility of popular cultural formations with organic national affinity is illustrated by Charles Fanning, who, in his study of Irish-American fiction in *The Irish Voice in America*, disregards the 'lucrative, popular genre' of crime fiction 'because of its concern with formulaic plot, action, and resolution rather than with ethnic self-definition' (327).

this oppositional recourse to Irish culture. The thriller signifies the untenability of an organic popular or national subject and the auratic attributes of Irish culture ascribed by critics such as Terry Eagleton, following Walter Benjamin's famous essay on 'The Work of Art in an Age of Mechanical Reproduction'. The historical context of the thriller's emergence, and its announcement of the defeat of the auratic cultural product, are neatly encapsulated by a classic hard-boiled thriller, the *Maltese Falcon* by Dashiell Hammett. This wonderfully self-referential text foregrounds its own popular or mass cultural moment in centring on the frustrated quest for the auratic, for an original, authored piece of art. The text thwarts not only the characters' various claims to have 'authentic evidence of ownership' (417) but also the illusion that 'there's only one Maltese Falcon' (549) in confronting us ultimately with a duplicate, a reproduction. Mechanical reproduction disintegrates the uniqueness of a work of art through which it is imbedded in the fabric of ritual and tradition. To address a modern or postmodern Ireland and its relation to popular fiction is necessarily to reject the now historically impossible organic constitution of the popular as authentic oppositional subject through which the more pessimistic elements of the international Left have sought to override their own sense of crisis. An account of the thriller and the North is thus a rehistoricizing of Irish culture and its contemporary products, an attempt to instigate the complex, often arduous critical task of determining the historical dynamics and contestation of a specific national cultural formation within global networks of hegemony and process.

In relation to Northern Ireland, Bateman's *Divorcing Jack* offers a perhaps parodic but nonetheless telling rendering of the quest for the Maltese Falcon and its cultural significance. In the text Starkey, having initially mistaken the composer's name for 'divorce Jack', searches for a tape copy of a work by Dvořák, leading him symbolically enough to a second hand record store. The tape in question actually contains a recording of a drunken confession of terrorist involvement by Brinn, the Prime Minister elect of Northern Ireland – a curious instance of the popular cultural recodification and indeed reproduction of the Irish oral tradition so romanticized by sections of the international Left. Moreover, the lack of popular cultural awareness in regard to the North is self-referentially indicated by the text itself as Starkey often conceals himself from his pursuers through a series of aliases plucked from popular music and culture. Therefore, just as we are informed in Hammett's text that the Falcon is 'the property of whoever can get hold of it' (487), my own post-auratic investigation of the 'Troubles' thriller is designed to struggle within popular fiction, as impacted, contestatory cultural process, rather than against it as pure ideology. Given that this contemporary codification of the popular defeats the more idealized notions of the popular as natural and oppositional subject, my analysis nevertheless sets out, hopefully with historical precision, to brush against the grain the dominant ideologies informing Irish literary debate.

However, at this juncture, my application of the political unconscious to the North and my rejection of the thriller as the form of a unitary national allegory both require that attention be paid to the deficiencies of Jameson's work with regard to the national formation. But rather than using this flaw in Jameson's thought to discredit his other insights and Marxism more generally, a more rigorous application of Jameson's own methodology to modes of national representation permits a mutual specification and enhancement. Jameson's failure to grasp properly the complexity of the national could be seen as symptomatic of Marxism. As Tom Nairn puts it: 'The theory of nationalism represents Marxism's great historical failure' (1981, 329). One could equally, however, state that the theory of Marxism, or indeed any international project of human emancipation, represents nationalism's great historical failure. So how might the conflictive mappings of Marxism and nationalism be theorized and thereby resolved within a Jamesonian methodology? The mystificatory potential of the national is conveyed within Jameson's work by his homogenizing claim, in his essay, 'Third-World Literature in the Era of Multinational Capitalism', that 'all third world texts are necessarily national allegories ... the story of the private individual destiny is always an allegory of the embattled situation of the public national project' (1986, 69).[12] In a stunning critique, Aijaz Ahmad successfully destabilizes Jameson's model through the discourses of class, gender, region and religion, and stresses that 'the ideological conditions of a text's production are never singular but always several' (122). Ahmad's rebuttal does not acknowledge that a footnote in Jameson's essay beckons a

> study of the differences and similarities of specific literary and cultural texts with a more typological analysis of the various socio-cultural situations from which they spring, an analysis whose variables would necessarily include features such as the interrelationship of social classes, the role of intellectuals, the dynamics of language and writing, the configuration of traditional forms, the relationship to western influences, the development of urban experience and money, and so forth (1986, 87).

Nevertheless, the relegation of this complex methodology to a footnote, which should itself have formed the fundamental basis of the essay, indicates the adjustment of discursive emphasis mystified by Jameson's sense of the national and the post-colonial. For the nation state must be addressed by Marxism as a specific, and indeed necessary, constellation of forces upon which to ground its struggle. The challenge for Marxism, then, is to articulate the specificity of the national conjuncture without recapitulating 'the nation' as pre-ordained according to nationalist canons.[13]

A negotiation between the antagonistic mappings of the national conjuncture within a global system nonetheless necessitates not only the illumination of the

---

[12] The term 'Third World' is itself questionable for an engaged Marxism, particularly when it seems to stand outside of global capitalism.

[13] Nicos Poulantzas' account of the nation intimates that the organic unity of the national subject seeks to naturalize precise power national relationships whose re-articulation in a Gramscian expansive hegemony facilitates the reclamation of the terrain of the national as a site of struggle and contestation: '[t]he modern nation is not then the creation of the bourgeoisie, but the outcome of a *relationship* of forces between the 'modern' social classes – one in which the nation is a *stake* for the various classes' (1978, 115).

negative aspects of nationalism but also its appeal and function, if this ground is to be recovered and reinscribed with what Raymond Williams deems 'the production and the practice of possibility' (1980, 273). The national terrain in fact offers an opportunity to refine the dialectic of ideology and utopia in the thriller and its hegemonic contest in producing an optimal reading subject. Jameson himself contends that 'a Left which cannot grasp the immense Utopian appeal of nationalism (anymore than it can grasp that of religion or of fascism) can scarcely hope to "re-appropriate" such collective energies and must effectively doom itself to political impotence' (1996, 298). Given my formulation of the *repressive* and *redemptive* modalities of the text, and the formative narrativity of ideology, Marxism's task is to evaluate various levels of ideological mapping with the aim of radically subsuming and redrawing in a utopian fashion the map sketched by nationalism.[14] Jameson formulates his own faith in a Marxist analysis thus:

> To affirm the priority of Marxist analysis as that of some ultimate and untranscendable semantic horizon – namely the horizon of the *social* – thus implies that all other interpretative systems conceal a *seam* which strategically seals them off from the social totality of which they are a part and constitutes their object of study as an apparently closed object of study (1988b, vol.2, 149).

Consequently, the organizational seams of nationalism are ultimately to be mapped as mystificatory whilst Marxism facilitates a comprehensive re-articulation of disparate social layers and forms.

This book intends to map historical interstices, such as class, gender, the city and so forth, across the specific social rupture of the national formation, as mediatory vantage points from which to engage in a process that is facilitated by Jameson's own concept of *transcoding*: 'the invention of a set of terms, the strategic choice of a particular code or language, such that the same terminology can be used to analyze and articulate two quite distinct types of objects or "texts", or two very different structural levels of reality' (1996, 40). A Jamesonian transcoding, which breaks down or at the very least is subdued in his production of a national and postcolonial subject, ensures that 'we may restore, at least methodologically, the lost unity of social life, and demonstrate that widely distant elements of the social totality are ultimately part of the same global historical process' (1996, 226).

Therefore, whilst Marxism and nationalism both necessarily employ a dialectic between ideology and utopia, the resolution sought by the transcoded articulations of the former aim at the engaged mapping of a totality of determinate social and power relationalities, whilst the utopian imagination of the latter's unitary allegory strives to assuage, deflect and displace such discontinuity. Nationalist discourse is therefore a kind of negative or inverted transcoding, or metacode perhaps, an

---

[14] In tracing what he identifies as nationalism's functions of co-ordination, mobilization and legitimacy, John Breuilly posits that its 'ideology can be regarded as a sort of map. It provides people with the means to identify their own position in the world in relation to others' (365).

ideological discourse seeking simultaneously to hold together and at bay a complex chain of signification. In a way, nationalism's map is a complex fetish, which disavows the social totality that it nonetheless gestures towards. Thus, whilst John Breuilly is merely dismissive – 'nationalism is a parasitic movement and ideology, shaped by what it opposes' (380) – Alan Finlayson astutely perceives nationalism's unitary mechanisms in terms of

> an ideological process constituting subjects in a particular way always bound up with other ideological subject positions. A nationalist interpellation also includes particular political, and other, interpellations. In this way the national can become the unifying point within an ideological discourse, the category within which other categories are given and naturalised. The national becomes a popular-democratic interpellation around which the ideology of the movement is fixed (1997a, 78).

Finlayson regards the national signifier as a Lacanian *point de capiton*, a nodal point of anchorage regulating a multiplicity of meanings: 'Thus nation becomes the point which fixes down chains of ideological discourse about economy, society, morality, gender, sexuality and so forth. That is the ideological power of nation in our contemporary world – to produce those "shared values" we all believe in because in the ideological fantasy those shared values are what we are' (1996, 117). Jameson's political unconscious, therefore, proffers the means by which his own organic national text and subject may be overhauled.[15] For Marxism seeks to uncover the national as a specific constellation of social relations to be revolutionized, whereas the utopian imagination of nationalism seeks jointly to mystify and mobilize such conditions as given. In other words, the national signifier, despite its ideological surface, does not really transcend social conflict but rather seeks to dis- and re-articulate it. Marxism wills re-articulation as resolution. Therefore, when Gramsci contends that any emancipatory movement must 'nationalise itself in a certain sense' (241), the process entails not the embrace of an organic whole but rather the historical transcription of a national conjuncture onto a global dynamic in an expansive hegemonic trajectory.

   In light of my post-auratic reading of the popular text and the national *ideologeme*,[16] the hegemonic contestation of sociolects and historical materials within the thriller itself attests that the collapse of the organic is fundamental to the form. This book conveys how the organic structures many ideologies internationally, such as the New Right hegemonic projects in Britain and America,

---

[15] Jameson prefaces a 1982 essay on Joyce in the following way: 'one does not read Joyce today, let alone write about him without remembering the fifteen-year-long struggle for freedom of the people of Northern Ireland; the following, then, for whatever it is worth, must necessarily be dedicated to them'. '*Ulysses* in History' in W.J. McCormack and Alistair Stead, eds. *James Joyce and Modern Literature*. (London: Routledge, 1982) 126.

[16] By ideologeme I refer to a basic ideological mechanism designed to disavow its own position within a set of antagonistic social discourses. I am here following Jameson's definition of the ideologeme as 'a historically determinate conceptual or semic complex which can project itself variously in the form of a 'value system' or 'philosophical concept,' or in the form of a protonarrative, a private or collective narrative fantasy' (1996, 115).

but I also wish to examine the specific Irish cultural ramifications of the term. In describing both Irish Nationalism and Unionism as organic ideologies, I shall invoke Edward Said's distinction between the *filiative* and the *affiliative* (1984b, 20). The dominant ideologies in Ireland are constructed around the filiative, supposedly natural bonds and attachments, for which the family is a paradigmatic organizational unit in reproducing order, authority, and continuity. However, these ideologies are in fact designed to mystify affiliative relationalities, whether class, professional, feminist, urban etc. Such organicism is obviously strategically beneficial to the nationalist subject as *point de capiton*. In other words, the filiative ideologeme intends to disguise its hegemonic ordering of the affiliative. The national as canonically-constructed by nationalist ideology is thus a code word for the hegemonic subject. I want to formulate that hegemonic subject as *formatively interstitial*: that is, constructed across the axes of class, gender, urbanity and so on.

The confusion into which the thriller throws organic ideologies of place and identity is adumbrated by two important textual precursors that anticipate the 'Troubles' output: Liam O'Flaherty's *The Informer* (1925) and F.L. Green's *Odd Man Out* (1945). Gypo Nolan, the eponymous informer of O'Flaherty's text is alienated from the filiative community by his treachery and is prey to the following compensatory dream: '[t]hen a mad longing seized him for the protection of the environment of his youth, the countryside of a Tipperary village, the little farm, the big–red faced healthy peasant who was his father, his long-faced kind-hearted mother, who hoped that he would become a priest' (44). This dream of the rural, the familial and filiative, and the church is shored against modernity and the 'maze' (5) of Dublin. In terms of the crime, it is noteworthy that the most heinous offence is this abeyance of the filiative seam, which closes around its criminal breach. Correspondingly, *Odd Man Out* also takes as its protagonist an outsider alienated from the traditional social co-ordinates of community, religion, and filiative belonging in 'the vast bewildering dream' (62) of modernity in Belfast. Johnny is depicted in the following way: 'all the things of life seemed to withdraw from him, leaving him suspended and terribly alone. Until he recollected that he was still a fugitive, a criminal, a murderer, a dangerous revolutionary, outlawed, wounded, dying' (173). Both texts foreground the confrontation within the form of the thriller between the organic or the knowable and the illegible or the covert.

In addition to observing how the thriller demonstrates a crisis in organic ideologies of community and identity, this book will also illustrate how the form undercuts various rehearsals of the conflict as an intractable yet quarantined and ultimately extractable tumour in an otherwise ordered social body – even in texts which ostensibly attempt to represent the Northern conflict in precisely the terms of the single, removable crime afflicting a harmonious community. Perhaps the most blunt formulation of the need to extricate this sequestered blight from decent, law-abiding society is the 'terrorizing the terrorists' strategy evidenced particularly in the most elementary 'good versus evil' texts. One example thereof is Andy McNab's *Immediate Action* and its SAS hero's desire for an official Shoot to Kill policy: 'If there was, we wouldn't still be here – we'd be back home and they'd be dead. We know where they all are – if someone was giving the green light we'd just go in and take them out' (210). Such a solution to Irish terrorism as causal disruption is a strategy, which seeks in turn to validate and legitimize subsequent action of otherwise dubious legality by the hero or the state in repairing the status quo. It seemingly affirms Jerry Palmer's contention:

> What the thriller asserts, at root, is that the world does not contain any inherent sources of conflict: trouble comes from the people who are rotten, but whose rottenness is in no way connected with the nature of the world they infect. At the base of the thriller is a breath-taking tautology: 'Normally the world functions normally. Today it doesn't. Therefore something abnormal is affecting it' (1978, 87).

In relation to Northern Ireland, this tautology assists an understanding of the use of Special Powers Acts and Emergency legislation, by both the British and Irish Nation States, as avowedly temporary measures designed to combat the irruption of such abnormal intrusions in the guise of the Northern conflict. In actual fact both states and their legislation are inextricably embroiled in the production (and as products) of the very historical conditions and complex relations of social classes and forces which led to the onset of such conflict and which maintain the state in its current form. The legitimization of the Northern state on the premise of the 'Troubles' as a disruption of its ordered, normative tautology serves as a determinate historical affirmation of Walter Benjamin's formulation that '[t]he tradition of the oppressed teaches us that the "state of emergency" in which we live is not the exception but the rule' (1992, 248). In specifically grappling with the historical emergence of Fascism, Benjamin affirms that 'it is our task to bring about a real state of emergency ... One reason why Fascism has a chance is that in the name of progress its opponents treat it as a historical norm' (1992, 248-249). Benjamin's analysis intimates that it is the assignment of this study to interrogate the fixities of the status quo legitimized by the production of a sectarian state of emergency in the thriller, to undercut the account of the 'Troubles' as a cordoned, extractable problem besetting an otherwise ordered continuity.

In historicizing the 'Troubles' ideologeme, I want to undercut Palmer's account of the thriller as a perpetuation of the imaginary resolution of the sole, disentangled crime in detective fiction. Indeed, writing in the late seventies, Palmer concedes the development of what he terms the 'anti-thriller' or 'negative thriller' (1978, 43) in which the local success of the hero is insufficient to purify the social order. Palmer's standard formulation of the thriller is a progression from a conspiracy to its being scotched, so that the world is again secure and problem-free. But this is therefore replaced in his account of the negative thriller by the sense that, in Palmer's phraseology, the world is not really secure and that the evil with which the hero has dealt will recur in other forms (1978, 52). It is my contention that there is not a quantitative break between the conventional, or to use Palmer's term, 'positive' (1978, 52) thriller form and what Palmer identifies as its negative antithesis. Rather, the incommensurable insecurities, which Palmer maintains defeat the negative thriller's desired closure are constitutive of the thriller form as a whole, and are grounded in the historical conditions of its production, historical conditions which effect formal antinomy and ideological rupture in even the most optimistic resolutions of the genre. The hegemony of the thriller signals the historical untenability of the ideology of the isolated crime. In terms of critical pathways, William Aydelotte delineates, in the following summation, the unmasking and expulsion of the criminal by the society as organic community that was propagated by earlier forms of detective fiction:

> In place of the complex issues of modern existence, people in a detective story have very simple problems. Life goes along well except for the single point that some crime, usually, in modern stories, a murder, has been committed... From this act follow most of the troubles. Troubles are objectively caused by an external circumstance, the murder, which can and will be resolved, whereupon the troubles will disappear ... The mess, confusion, and frustration of life have been reduced to a simple issue between good and evil (cited by Cawelti, 81).

By reapplying Aydelotte's terminology – of the disruptive components of detective fiction as expurgated troubles – to the specifics of the representation of Northern Irish society, it is notable in dominant accounts of the conflict that the ideologeme of the 'Troubles' seeks to establish the North as a previously ordered (and potentially stabilized society in the future) once the criminal agent is removed. Such an account seeks to remove the conflict and its problematics not only from History but also by implication from its connection to the rest of this idealized, ordered society. What the social symbolism of the thriller achieves, I shall argue, is the incrimination of the whole of Northern Irish society as a totality of forces and relationships in the historical moment of the conflict. The historical irretrievability of the single, resolvable crime of detective fiction, and the ideology of an isolate Northern 'Troubles', are disclosed by the formal antinomies and fantasies of two texts, Benedict Kiely's *Proxopera* (1977) and *Victims* by Eugene McCabe (1976). These texts strive demonstrably to guard an ordered, organic society from the putatively interruptive encroachment of the figure of the terrorist.

Both texts offer haute bourgeois elegies in the midst of social disruption. Crucially, in terms of form, the Big House genre significantly yet vainly seeks, almost literally in fact, to accommodate the thriller, as in both texts haute bourgeois homes are taken over by terrorists. In the context of Irish writing, the increasing dominance of the thriller as the representational mode of the Northern conflict, and indeed, the need for Irish novelists to address or acknowledge this hegemony, is suggested by the grappling of both Kiely and McCabe, as avowedly 'literary' or 'serious' writers, with the thriller genre in the 1970s. The generic tensions of both *Proxopera* and *Victims* are, however, not merely reducible to a writerly engagement with the thriller and popular fiction as applied to Ireland, but rather, and most significantly I shall maintain, also bespeak a politics of form. Within the representational moment of the thriller, the Big House genre stands beleaguered as a sub-generic fragment attesting to a hegemony in crisis. It demarcates an ideology, whose conflagration seeks to glimmer as a fading but nonetheless incandescent beacon signalling however forlornly the desires and core values of a hierarchic social order. The original historical symbolism of the Big House genre, then, as an often apocalyptic and gothicized form confronting the dissolution of one set of social relations amidst revolutionary upheaval and land agitation, becomes rewritten and allegorically renewed in its dialectical mediation with the thriller form. It transmits a desirous, intermittent historical romance attempting to encounter and redeem the social change and hegemonic dissolution from the 1950s onwards into the Northern conflict.

In other words, the sense of an ideology of form permits the formulation of the terror in such 'Troubles' thrillers not as a direct reflection or moral assessment of the reality of terrorism or political violence, but rather as the formal enactment of the profoundest and most terminal fears of a hierarchized, organic social order in crisis. Appropriating Lenin's famous remarks on terrorism itself, it can therefore be argued that the purpose of the 'Troubles' thriller, as a literature of terror, is to terrorize: that is, simply, to indulge such ideological anxieties, even as it also seeks their resolution. Thus, the figuration of landed, propertied order in *Proxopera* and *Victims* through the Big House generic deep structure actually signifies the actuation of the recapitulative, apocalyptic instance of precisely such a social hierarchy. It provides a terror reworked by the thriller code but which ultimately discloses the inoperability of the organic ideal which both Kiely and McCabe attempt to shore against the 'Troubles'.

In *Victims*, Gallagher, the leader of the Irish Republican terrorist unit who take over the landed, Anglo-Irish house[17] of Colonel Norbert Armstrong and his family, is portrayed as a 'natural mechanism of terror and disorder. He did not, never would, want peace and harmony' (McCabe, 107). On one level, therefore, the text offers the figure of the terrorist and the 'Troubles' itself as an immemorialized source of disruption in society, the recurrent, actantial prompt necessitating the thriller narrative's move to order. Kiely's *Proxopera* equally endeavours to position both the terrorist and the ideologeme of the 'Troubles' as beyond or outside of normal, ordered society. In *Proxopera* the Binchey family are taken hostage by Irish Republicans and Mr Binchey is forced to drive a bomb into his village. This arrival of terrorism is portrayed as a fall from grace and divine perfection.[18] The overriding elegiac tone, however, both laments and belies the antinomic structural disjunction that defeats this prelapsarian organic continuity within the thriller form. In addition to the bomb plot, the discovery of a murdered body brought to the surface after a water-skiing event in the nearby lake so idealized by Binchey attempts to affirm the pervasive theme of a rural paradise sullied by human evil: 'murderers in the dark had made the sleeping lake their accomplice. The innocent lake had been forced to share the guilt. The lake, out there and fading into another dusk. The lake knew. It could never be the same again' (27). Nonetheless, modernity in the guise of the water sports does not

---

[17] The house is called Inver Hall, placing the text explicitly in the tradition of Somerville and Ross's *The Big House of Inver*.

[18] The continual representation of the leading terrorist, whom Binchey nicknames 'The Corkman', as a serpent who never speaks but merely 'hisses' (18), as with the depiction of British soldiers as 'lizards' (74), nostalgically yearns for a return to an Eden without this pure embodiment of evil. Indeed, through another mythical intertextual echo, the text beckons some latter day Saint Patrick to banish this serpentine malevolence.

notably bring with it this evil or crime but rather effects its disinterment. In short, the thriller issues a kind of return of the repressed, its terror divulging the *unheimlich* social materials which the ideological fantasy of the hierarchic paradise centred around Binchey's Big House and the 'air of aristocratic age about it' (10) designedly intends to withhold. This is enacted at a very basic textual level by the narrative motivation embroiling the aristocracy in the thrill, and indeed, the terror, of the 'Troubles'.[19]

A profound class fear of usurpation and dispossession is actuated by the terrorists' occupation of the Binchey home which impels the text to obsessively question 'who for the moment is master in this house' (19). There is a subversive formal logic underpinning such a confrontation of formerly differentiated representational and social materials. I shall argue later that this subversive formal logic is most fully enacted in the conspiratorial text and its uncovering and tessellation of the covert, secret machinations of the modern state. That is, the historical materials which democracy must seek to repress even in the very act of utilizing such materials in the supposed defence and maintenance of democracy. Nonetheless, Kiely and McCabe's deployment of the suspense or adventure thriller as repositories of symbolic containment also attempts to rationalize the terror that looms from the exudation of the *unheimlich* historical content which the 'living dream' (Kiely, 92) of Binchey's Big House cannot repress. For it is under the restructuration of the thriller that the ideological fantasy of cloistered harmony encrypted in Binchey's 'dream of the white house' (Kiely, 92) must confront its uncanny doubles. In other words, the immemorialized, aristocratic golden age – and the narrative of moral righteousness and superiority upon which it is grounded – in one set of the text's mechanics, is also exposed under the thrill of the text's real as a structure of dominance under threat. It stands demystified as the hegemonic implementation of a social totality, whose constitutive violence and inequality the aristocratic representational framework would seek both to govern and eschew.

In *Victims* this formal return of the repressed is made more explicit at the level of content. When accused of being 'sick' by the Armstrongs' daughter, Millicent, the IRA leader, Gallagher, retorts: 'Why are we sick. Come on, answer. Why?! Let's hear, any, all of you ... come on ... why?! Answer ... you know it ... you are it' (101). Again part of the thrill or the terror of the text is the radical redrawing of this aristocratic locus, and indeed, its crisis, within broader social networks. As the text's cover proclaims of the hostage-seizure: 'The victims, an Anglo-Irish family and the friends who happen to be with them, are cultured and complex people who have regarded themselves as above the battle. Now suddenly, they are dangerously involved'. McCabe's text, through the militarism of both Colonel Armstrong's

---

[19] Although the gothicization of the terrorists – '[f]or sure and certain these distorted faces are out of a nightmare' (35) – on one level strives to estrange this evil from normal society, a dialectical engagement with the return of the repressed as a formal disclosure, seeping through the underlying structural fusion and fissure of disparate social materials and generic substrata, facilitates the consideration of the terror of this thriller as the nightmare of a dominant ideology in crisis.

title and his demeanor, and the insipid sectarianism of Canon Plumm,[20] offers a more direct inculpation of this aristocratic realm with its social context than *Proxopera*. Nevertheless, there is again a twofold, and limitational, representational transaction: the class terror of a crisis in aristocratic hegemony rationalizes itself through an attachment to the terror of the thriller genre as suspense or as thrill, whilst the historical conditions of the Northern conflict are recodified reductively as an assault upon organic order in the form of the Big House.

The crisis in aristocratic hegemony is represented in very rudimentary Big House terms by the failure of Colonel Armstrong, as the ineffectual patriarch, to assert authority not only of course over the terrorists (unlike the third person rendering of Mr Binchey's superior consciousness in *Proxopera*). Additionally, the antics of his family, and in particular his drunken wife, Harriet, gesture in hackneyed gendered fashion to the decadence and impotence of this social class. Interestingly, and again in terms of gender, the most direct connection between the aristocratic hostages and their terrorist captors is the fact that the Armstrongs' daughter, Millicent, recognizes one of the terrorists, Lynam, as a former university acquaintance. Perhaps the mystery which most troubles this thriller lies in its compulsive rumination on 'indecipherable' (McCabe, 40) female identity, and the terror which this crumbling hierarchic order must encounter above all is the connection of these two young women from disparate social backgrounds through their education at Trinity. In particular, Isobel Lynam, as a woman who is a political activist and has had an abortion, becomes the primary site of this reactionary ideological fantasy. The text articulates the terror of the breakdown of traditional social alignments and positionings. Intriguingly, both texts house an intricate politics of place with regard to what Dennis Porter deems 'the landscapes of detection' (1981, 192). Porter contrasts the sequestered yet nationally symbolic locales of Golden Age British crime fiction with the infernal and labyrinthine mean streets of the American hardboiled tradition. These early 'Troubles' thrillers seem to engage both forms, shoring not only a façade of hierachic tradition but also the filiative community of Irish culture against the social figurations of the hardboiled form. With reference to English culture, Raymond Williams suggests that

> The true fate of the country-house novel was its evolution into the middle-class detective story. It was in its very quality of abstraction, and yet of superficially impressive survival, that the country-house could be made the place of isolated family of a group of people whose immediate and transient relations were decipherable by an abstract mode of detection rather than by the full and connected analysis of any more general understanding (1973, 249).

Both *Proxopera* and *Victims* evidence symptomatically the sociolectical inability of the nostalgic Big House ideologeme and its filiative community to construct a

---

[20] The naming of this rather stock character, with its echo of the murderously civil caricatures of Cluedo, perhaps points somewhat playfully to the potential social guilt of the figures in the country house.

meta-language competent to manage the social totality and its dynamics invoked by the thriller form.

Kiely's text has been conventionally regarded as more optimistic than McCabe's *Victims*. Mr Binchey defies the terrorists by resolving not to leave the bomb in the village or at the home of its prime target, Judge Flynn, but instead to drive it heroically into a nearby lake. Laura Pelaschiar posits:

> for all its pessimism and elegiac insistence that 'the world will never be the same again', *Proxopera* is one of the very few novels about the Troubles not to end tragically. At the conclusion of the book order is restored and justice is, or rather will be, done. Binchey/Kiely's traditional and highly conservative vision of the world is a manichean one: the boundaries separating good and evil are clear cut and easy to detect, and from beginning to end the three terrorists are skilfully depicted as incarnations of evil, Binchey, his family and his people as the innocent victims. Binchey's decision to stop the massacre, therefore, is the beginning of the battle between good and evil and hence, for him, not so difficult to reach, while his final resolution to reveal the names of the terrorists allows him to feel he has definitely gained the upper hand and become the moral victor of the ordeal while it also leaves the reader with the reassuring sensation that at least two of the culprits will be caught and punished (1998, 77).

Binchey is motivated to name two of the terrorists whom he recognizes from the village in a seeming affirmation of the world as knowable community. However, his son is knee-capped and his own prized Big House is burned down in retribution for the moral victory of his thwarting the terrorist plot. Subsequently, the text closes, somewhat unreassuringly, with Binchey having only resolved to reveal their names, and most crucially, without his having ascertained the identity of the most insidiously depicted member of the gang. In short, the comforting organic conclusion of social repair is forestalled and frustrated. The failure of the text's effort to frame the social and moral synthesis of its content in a definite closure betrays a stark formal antinomy. For the house which so insistently symbolizes and centres the text's social vision is uncovered as an ideological fantasy riven in its very figuration. The Big House is significantly never represented as the concrete or sustained site of moral order. We are only exposed to it, firstly, in the shape of the childhood dream of Binchey and his desire to own it, then subsequently in the nightmarish present overrun by terrorists, before it is finally burned down in Binchey's (and the reader's) absence. The Big House remains Binchey's 'living dream' (92), a textual fantasy within this thriller ultimately determined by and representing its socially symbolic generic gesture to hegemonic collapse and aristocratic apocalypse. Succinctly, then, the text's filiative ideology cannot withstand its figuration within the thriller, its affiliation to the proper historical and social levels and materials of its context.

In this sense, narrative itself, the entry into History and historical process, is the fall from grace that the text so laments. Indeed, *Proxopera* enacts two structurally incompatible stereotypes about Northern Ireland, both of which attempt to remove the North from historical process. On one level, Binchey's organic, rural community in Ireland is a haven from the nightmare of world History, which

Binchey blames the terrorists for disrupting: 'The world is in wreckage and these madmen would force me to extend that wreckage to my town below' (76). Here, therefore, stands rural Ireland as cloistered, immemorial order beyond or without History. The Northern conflict is also, however, the formulation of Ireland as too much History – as 'insoluble problem' trapped in meaningless gyration (76). Both stereotypes effect the disabling of human agency. It is very much the latter stereotype which feeds the reactionary recoil of the filiative breakdown of the text's ideology in utilizing the most pessimistic symbolic codes of the thriller form to confront, by projection, not its own impossibility, but the Northern conflict merely 'with utterly resigned terror' (70). So the most profound terror in the text is in fact a formally resigned and exhausted ideological lability.

What the organic, filiative ideologies and communities of both Irish Nationalism and Unionism encounter in the thriller, as the paradigmatic form of the state, then, are traces of their own contradictions, the breakdown of their imagined nation. In particular, the conspiratorial text provides an optimal mode for such a confrontation. In contrast to the Golden Age of detective fiction and the ideological zenith of the organic fantasy of the single, resolvable crime and criminal agent, the conspiratorial thriller demarcates historical conditions in which it is society itself, and in particular the legitimization of the social in the form of the state, that is the mystery or crime. More succinctly, then, the confrontation within earlier detective fiction of the organic community with the criminal individual, with the mystery of the self, is fundamentally overhauled and historically rewritten in the conspiratorial thriller by the confrontation of the individual with the criminal collective, the mystery of the social. In such thrillers one crime often leads not to its resolution but rather its attachment to other seemingly interminable concatenations and labyrinths of crime and conspiracy. Nevertheless, I shall assert that this conspiratorial mode also harnesses a utopian desire to uncover and trace the social totality and its complexity in however degraded or skeletal a manner through such criminal patterns and intrigues. Crime, then, in the thriller form becomes 'a connective tissue' (Messent, 1) through which to uncover concealed relationships and hidden attachments within late capitalism. Jameson observes that the ideology of the single crime has been subsumed in the era of late capitalism by 'the sense that it is society as a whole that is the mystery to be solved' (1992a, 39). Jameson comments further upon 'the "conspiratorial text", which, whatever other messages it emits or implies, may also be taken to constitute an unconscious, collective effort at trying to figure out where we are and what landscapes confront us in a late twentieth century whose abominations are heightened by their concealment and their bureaucratic impersonality' (1992a, 3).

Hence, in earlier, especially English, crime fiction the crime was supposedly disruption of the ordered, social totality, whereas the hard-boiled thriller reworked crime as precisely a means of reconnecting and mapping the social. What this recodification signifies is not so much that the ideal society of the Golden Age of detective fiction has disappeared under the degrading encroachment of modernity, but rather that this organic image of society is exposed as an ideological fantasy through its increased historical unsustainability. Which is to say that, despite its single, resolved closure, this ideological fantasy of early detective fiction cannot repress the fact that the investigation raises more questions than it answers within the knowable, organic community, and designedly so. For the crime opens up a rather anxious ideological yet also desirous space in which the whole of society or the putatively knowable community comes, almost literally, under question. It comes under an interrogatory suspicion, which the text's concluding formal solution cannot fully disperse or erase. The thriller pursues this troubled formal antinomy beyond breaking point even at the level of the text's ideological surface. It fractures the ideological mirage of the organic, knowable whole, and crime becomes a paradigmatic and mandatory means of not only expressing social insecurity but also of mapping the seemingly indecipherable reaches of the society itself and its anonymous attachments and interminable complexities.

Ann Cranny-Francis asserts that 'paradoxically, the literature of detection operates commonly as the literature of concealment, of displacement and false resolution. The "order and meaning" that the detective restores is that of dominant ideological discourses' (1990, 149). What I am arguing, is that an engaged critique of the antinomies and tenuous formal resolutions of the literary text permits the following reformulation of the emergence of the thriller in crime fiction. The imaginary resolution of the recomposition of the organic community, which informs Thomas Leitch's standard account of how 'the detective story, with its persistent emphasis on the one correct solution to a crime, is the most resolutely end-orientated of narrative modes' (475), is exposed as historically unworkable. This ideological fantasy is designed to occlude the fact that the crime and investigation raises, and seeks to conceal, more questions than answers in its interrogation of the organic ideologeme. This concealment is thus no longer repressed formal content but rather its sedimented symbolism has become consciously and historically raised to the structural level of a hegemonic generic mode, which, in turn, of course, demands its own imaginary resolutions to the historical conditions of its production. Under the utopian formulation of the conspiratorial text, there is a class allegory in the many isolated, detective figures confronting the mystery of the state. Disengaged from their organic homes within Irish Nationalism or Unionism, and indeed the British or American state, in the 'Troubles' thriller, such figures function, in their elevated yet committed contemplation of the totality of forces before them, as Sartrean 'objective traitors', as sites of class consciousness.[21]

---

[21] In *Search for a Method* and *Critique of Dialectical Reason*, Sartre provides an intellectual formulation for the assumption of historical agency, for the move from object to subject and the discovery in History of our self-alienation. What is pertinent to this introduction on the crime narrative and the Marxian dialectic of the political subject making History in conditions/conditionings not of its volition, is that, for Sartre, we do not simply impose at pattern in History but rather find or recognize one in the process of circumventing the alienation of our agency. In the crime form, the class agent recognizes a pattern and then reformulates it as narrative in producing an active, subjective entry into History. Sartre's original formulation of the 'objective traitor' was a figuration of the intellectual in 'Des rats et des hommes' (1964), so that the treachery entailed in producing this critically elevated consciousness could be viewed as a specifically bourgeois flight from the limitations of that class. Nonetheless, I am utilizing Sartre's model as the site of an encompassing class

The contestatory legal and ethical relativism of the thriller terrain, its politicized renegotiation of social co-ordinates, is intimated by the predicament of the RUC officer, Cross, in Petit's *The Psalm Killer*: 'he was no longer sure of his own moral compass. He felt lost in a grey zone, except it wasn't as easy as that. There were so many different greys, some almost indistinguishable ... he liked to think that he would have resisted corruption, but where was the line to distinguish that from canniness? (483). Indeed, the 'Troubles' thriller and its interrogation of crime, the state and the social totality, imbue Walter Benjamin's comment upon Baudelaire's Paris with renewed historical prescience: '[i]n times of terror, when everyone is something of a conspirator, everybody will be in a situation where s/he has to play detective' (1973, 40). Moreover, whilst the conventional critical account would regard the thriller form and the 'Troubles' society as blights which deserve each other, a more profound reformulation of historical relationality and applicability is possible. Given that the legitimacy of the state is one of the fundamental sites of the Northern conflict, the more utopian function of the thriller's mysteries facilitates a more subversive formal logic, which attempts to trace and confront the seemingly unfigurable complexities, and criminalities of the state, and offers itself as a paradigmatic representational mode.

With the conflictive political mappings of the form in mind, my next chapter, '"The Green Unpleasant Land": The Political Unconscious of the British 'Troubles' Thriller', examines, with specific reference to the New Right project in England, how international thriller writers use the North as an empty receptacle voided of its own historical specifics, in which to repress and resolve their own historical dilemmas. As the punning title suggests, the 'absent cause' of such representations is actually an unconscious grappling with English historical fracture, though of course the North itself is constitutive of that problematic. So, in terms of the conflictual political mappings of the thriller, these New Right texts on one level deploy the form as a system of Panopticon discourse on the North, but, on another, engage its social cartography as a mode renegotiating the British State formation. In a way, this representational bloc therefore crystallizes a Kristevan state of abjection in which the dominant subject, overwhelmed by discovering the impossible within itself, produces a thrilling representational space that is 'immoral, sinister, scheming, and shady: a terror that dissembles, a hatred that smiles' (Kristeva 1982, 4).

The following chapter, '"And What Do You Call It?": The Thriller and the Problematics of Home in Northern Irish Writing', discusses the extent to which Northern Irish thrillers collude with this dominant representational framework which dehistoricizes the North. Whilst acknowledging the hegemony of the international thriller, I resist viewing this displacement as a unitary, national subjective condition, given the determinate fracture of class and gender within both Irish Nationalism and Unionism. In contrast to the dominant discourse of 'the Two Communities', Northern Ireland is not neatly divided into self-contained and monolithic binaries; it is instead an integrated constellation of forces and

consciousness, which circumvents the delimitative maps of filiation and the *repressive* political subject.

relationalities simultaneously fractured and affiliated by the global historical dynamics of class, gender, sexuality, the city, regionality, etc. Consequently, my fourth chapter, '"New Languages Would Have to be Invented": Representations of Belfast and Urban Space', argues that the thriller's mapping of the city as a network of crime tears the strategic seams of filiative place by proffering a class allegorical figuration of the social totality. The dominant ideologies in Ireland both recoil from the dialogic, to employ Bakhtin's term, potentiality of the urban. To this end, Robert Johnstone's depiction of Belfast is revealing:

> Its dark hearts lie unexplored in my cognitive map like old charts of Africa. Terrible crimes occur obscurely in places one has no reason to visit and often every reason to avoid; civilised and measured lives carry on in unremarkable streets. Belfast is like an incorrigible extra parent or shady uncle, who shaped one's life but whose doings only filter through in news reports or rumours (1).

A specifically working-class Belfast is gothicized in the above passage and dehistoricized as some lapsed and abandoned cartography of otherness from which the thwarted ethics of the bourgeois, pastoral subject withdraws. The limitations of filiative spatiality are conveyed by Johnstone's recourse to a family model in reconciling the estrangement of the urban. Another means by which the complexity of the urban is occluded is the recurrent representation of Belfast as *femme fatale*. As a result, my fifth chapter, '"A Man Could Get Lost": Constructions of Gender', investigates how conventional gender subjectivities can function as modes of symbolic containment restricting the more utopian drive of the thriller. Nonetheless, I intend to undercut the suggestion that the genre is a securely male one and to concentrate instead on the precarious contradictions that constitute the thriller's late capitalist masculinities and femininities. As Nira Yuval observes, gender is 'a dynamic process, continuously changing, full of internal contradictions which different social and political agents, differently positioned, use in different ways' (67). My concluding chapter attempts to uncover the utopian political and aesthetic centre of the thriller form by historically rupturing its *repressive* forms of symbolic containment with what Walter Benjamin would term the *Jetztzeit* or 'time-of-the now' (1992a, 255). Ultimately the book affirms that the real terror to be found in the 'Troubles' thriller is not in its representation of terrorism but is rather, as with the 'utterly resigned terror' of Kiely's *Proxopera*, disclosed in a more profound manner by the political unconscious through the breakdown of dominant ideological positions within and about the North in the face of historical process and transition. Given the Marxist approach undertaken by the book, it closes with the full translation into English of essays by Brecht and Benjamin on crime fiction as a means of introducing these important engagements to Anglophone readerships.

Chapter 1

'The Green Unpleasant Land':
The Political Unconscious of the British
'Troubles' Thriller

'I will not cease from Mental Fight'.
William Blake, *Jerusalem*

J. Bowyer Bell discerns a correlation between the production of the thriller and broader structures of British propaganda and influence over the last thirty years: 'in some strange small way the thrillers on Irish matters may have played a part in the British campaign to restore order, if not justice, to Ulster. In bold strokes of black and white, they have painted the jolly ploughboy, the Irish rebel, the romantic gunman, as a terrorist, futile, brutal, at best, misguided, at worst a callous killer. Surely the British could ask for no more' (1978, 22).[1] However, as established in the introduction, the political unconscious of popular fiction offers a means of refuting the dismissal of popular culture as sheer mass deception, and thereby of negotiating the relationships between official propaganda or policy and the British 'Troubles' thriller in their full historical complexity. The application of a reductive Frankfurt School methodology of mass culture as self-affirmatively 'identical' (Adorno and Horkheimer, 121) to a British-Irish colonial binary[2] constitutes the subjectivity producing and superintending this body of texts as a unitary British self-presence.

Indeed, the function of gangsterism permits a brief outlining of how the dialectic of the *repressive* and the *redemptive* refutes the dismissal of the thriller as pure propaganda. Luke Gibbons posits, in accordance with Bowyer Bell, that 'the fact that the implementation of a criminalisation policy in the North in the mid-

---

[1] Similarly, writing during the Thatcher governments of the 1980s, Liz Curtis asserts that British propaganda pervades popular mediations and perceptions of the situation in the North: 'Those in positions of power, both in government and in the media, have proved most reluctant to provide a full picture of events in the North or their context, and have made considerable efforts to prevent journalists, dramatists and film-makers from exploring the situation from any angle other than that favoured by the British establishment' (1984b, 275).

[2] This binary is encouraged not only by the more basic Irish nationalist accounts of the conflict but also by the imperial trajectory informing many of the texts I shall examine, such as Kevin Dowling's *Interface: Ireland*, which posits 'Ireland was the oldest colony on earth, the first and last of the major British possessions' (38).

1970s coincided with the vogue enjoyed by the *Godfather* films handed the British authorities a valuable rhetorical weapon in their propaganda war against republicans. From then on, the leaders of Sinn Féin could be denigrated simply as 'Godfathers', and political violence similarly dismissed as 'organised crime', perpetrated by the mindless thugs of the republican mafia produced by the nationalist ghettoes' (1997, 51). Although such representation can be imbricated with the state criminalization of paramilitary prisoners, which ultimately led to the Hunger Strikes, in the *redemptive* modality of the text, the gangster is also a figure affording allegories of familial belonging, filiative communal attachment, assured masculinity and so on.

In establishing the problematics of the British identities – and by British I shall be largely referring to the 'Great Britishness' constructed by English Nationalism – produced by the 'Troubles' thriller and the function of their ideological investment in representations of Northern Ireland, I shall begin by utilizing, and to some extent questioning, the theoretical framework provided by Edward Said's *Orientalism*. Certainly the dominant fictional representation of the North by one specific genre affords a focal instance of Said's formulation of the means by which a hegemonic field of knowledge is enthroned: 'There is a rather complex dialectic of reinforcement by which the experiences of readers in reality are determined by what they have read, and this in turn influences writers to take up subjects defined in advance by readers' expectations' (1995, 94). However, in tracing the contradictions of the optimal or dominant reading positions produced by these texts across the historical interstices of class, gender, race and so on, there increasingly emerges a tension between the Gramscian and Foucauldian strands of Said's *Orientalism* that I shall seek to dissect.[3] This chapter contends that there is no homogeneous, immemorial British subject configuring a stable generic unity, but that instead the antinomies etched within and between these texts belie their implication in historical process. The most prevalent cultural force mapping such historical process in the British thriller is provided by the hegemonic project of the New Right in England. It reaches from the disenchanted maverick voices of 1970s thrillers, through the collective institutional locus provided by Thatcherism and its populist militarism, and then permeates the continuing vogue for SAS fiction in the 1990s.

Indubitably, following one line of Said's thought, Michel Foucault's concept of a 'discursive formation' (1972, 38), wherein a group of texts both produce and delimit a given mode of knowledge, does assist an understanding of the

---

[3] An interesting account of precisely this tension is provided by Dennis Porter 'Orientalism and its Problems' in Williams and Chrisman, eds. 1993. 150-161. A Foucauldian critique of Gramsci is afforded by Tony Bennett's *Culture: A Reformer's Science*. London: SAGE, 1998. Bennett maintains that Foucault's insight is that there is no singular anchorage to power and its diversity of objectives. However, I would affirm that the scope of the Gramscian concept of hegemony does encompass diversity and complexity, and most usefully, retains a sense of social struggle across that differentiality. That Bennett's Foucauldian turn is capable only of making a science out of reformism, bespeaks the limitations of such analysis.

mechanisms by which the British 'Troubles' thriller seeks to instigate and sustain a dominant representation of Northern Ireland. Foucault's models are particularly instructive in establishing the symbiotic complicity between *power* and *knowledge*: 'We should admit that power produces knowledge ... that power and knowledge directly imply one another; that there is no power relation without the correlative constitution of a field of knowledge, nor any knowledge that does not presuppose and constitute ... power relations' (1980, 27). The intricate interrelationality of power and knowledge proffers a method for determining the precise historical conditions in which the discursive field of the 'Troubles' thriller naturalizes itself as representing the 'truth' about Northern Ireland. Indeed, in many of these texts one of the major mysteries to be explained and systematized is the riddle of a recondite Irish otherness. For example, Christopher Hawke's *For Campaign Service* claims that 'the answers were always more difficult to set right in this theatre of operations because of one highly unpredictable factor – the Irish mind' (57).[4] The British 'Troubles' thriller grounds its self-empowerment on charting a cartography of knowledge around this inscrutable enigma.[5] The representational mystification of Northern Irish society by these thrillers parallels the hegemonic framework theorized by Said's account of the 'radical realism' of the Orientalist text: 'such texts can *create* not only knowledge but also the very reality they appear to describe' (1995, 94). The deep attachments of power and knowledge accrued by such a discursive structure help explicate the viability of the trend, noted by Joseph McMinn, for thrillers produced by English journalists after their tours of duty in the North:[6]

> their strength and limitations as novels come directly from the ambiguous social position of 'on-the-spot' journalism. This position ensures access to privileged forms of knowledge but rarely to a community. In other words, the journalists/ novelists may divulge 'authentic' images of the much publicized protagonists because of the special kind of social intimacy developed over years of observation and contacts, but this is not a social intimacy (114).

Northern Ireland, then, in such a system of knowledge about Northern Ireland, becomes, to appropriate Said's terms, 'less a place than a *topos*, a set of references, a congeries of characteristics' (1995, 177). Whilst Ireland and Irish people

---

[4] Correspondingly, Private Nelson, the British soldier in Dowling's *Interface: Ireland*, 'was frightened of the dark, unpredictable Irish who nursed their hatred as a mother will nurse a child. He thought the only cure for them was death' (41), whilst John de St. Jorre and Brian Shakespeare attempt a survey of 'the Irishmen's baffling religious war' (82) in *The Patriot Game*.

[5] The coalescence of such representations with wider patterns of cultural and political hegemony is intimated by Margaret Thatcher's musing in *The Downing Street Years* on 'the overheated political world of Ulster' – 'what British politician will ever fully understand Northern Ireland?' (385) – which she blames for any errors in policy during her reign.

[6] Texts written by journalists include those by Tom Bradby, Peter Dickinson, Kevin Dowling, Gavin Esler, Stephen Leather, G.F Newman, William Paul, Donald Seaman, Gerald Seymour, John de St Jorre and Brian Shakespeare.

historically have figured in British spy and crime fiction,[7] it is interesting that the current deluge of thrillers concerned with explaining Northern Ireland has occurred under a period of Direct Rule from Westminster.[8] This representational convergence within a specific power relationship foregrounds the play and interaction, which Gayatri Spivak notes, in Karl Marx's *The Eighteenth Brumaire of Louis Bonaparte* between two verbs: *vertreten* (to represent as in speaking for or standing in for) and *darstellen* (to represent as in to re-present in art) (1988a, 276). In assessing the 'positional superiority' (Said 1995, 7) by which this representational framework is actuated, there is an interesting correspondence between the static yet unresolved system of the thriller form and Homi K. Bhabha's account of the insecure vacillation between 'fixation' and 'reactivation' (1994, 74) in the construction of the stereotype by a dominant gaze.

Under this gaze Northern Ireland as fetishized object is sought in order to restore to the dominant subject an original presence by masking its division and fracture: 'The fetish or stereotype gives access to an "identity" which is predicated on mastery and pleasure as it is on anxiety and defence, for it is a form of multiple and contradictory belief in its recognition of difference and disavowal' (1994, 75). By suggesting that the English subjectivities produced across the historical co-ordinates of the 'Troubles' thriller are not homogeneous or stable, I am not denying thereby the representational dominance of those subjectivities. Rather, I am seeking to situate that dominance in historical process, in an ongoing hegemonic struggle implicating not only relations between Ireland and England, but also a fractious assemblage of forces concerning class, gender, state formation, changing modes of production, crises of patriarchy, of the social ideologeme of the family, etc.

Therefore, despite the consistent effort to transpose historical problematics onto the Irish as 'a haunted race' (Shaun Clarke 1998, 127), tormented by their troubled history and barbarity, it is the task of this chapter to restructure the political unconscious of England's own historical nightmare, to textualize the materials and problematics which the British 'Troubles' thriller is produced both to repress and resolve. In short, to overturn this putatively stable, superintending presence and, in the words of Pierre Macherey, to 'trace the path which leads from the haunted work to that which haunts it' (94).[9] The precise determination of the historical conditions necessitating the discourse of power-knowledge, which is constituted by the 'Troubles' thriller, entails the redress of a twofold distortion. Firstly, it is

---

[7] For an excellent general survey see Keith Jeffery and Eunan O'Halpin's 'Ireland in Spy Fiction' in K. Wark, ed. *Intelligence and National Security* 5; 4 Oct 1990. A Special Issue on Spy Fiction, Spy Films and Real Intelligence. 92-116.

[8] Introduced on 30 March 1972.

[9] For the thriller offers a focalization of the more general mystifications of the national imagination of the English New Right: 'The problem of English racism – whether against the Irish or against black people – is not just a question of many English people having mistaken ideas about other people. It is also a question of the mistaken view that many English people hold of themselves, of Britain's history and of Britain's role in the world' (Liz Curtis, 1984a, 95).

imperative to dispute the 'truth' of this discourse as a direct representation and reflection of Irish reality; and secondly, it is equally incumbent to refute the suggestion that the identities producing and produced by such representations are the expression of an organic, popular, and above all, unproblematic Britishness.

In illustrating the dominance of the power-knowledge cartography through which the gaze of the international thriller market represents Northern Ireland, and moreover, in beginning to unveil the precise historical forces seeking to perpetuate this immemorial displacement, the reception granted to Tom Clancy's contemptible *Patriot Games* – a parallel American New Right text – is instructive. Despite the fact that, as Eamonn Hughes notes, this novel 'uses events in the North to drive its plot, but not one scene is set in Northern Ireland' ('Introduction', 6), Marc A. Cerasini contends that from a reading of the text 'we learn much about Irish politics and the history of the 'Troubles' in Northern Ireland' (26). There is a telling moment in *Patriot Games* wherein the CIA hero, Jack Ryan, stares into the eyes of the improbably Maoist Irish renegade, Sean Miller, and sees '*nothing. Nothing at all*' (122). The scene neatly symbolizes how this dominant gaze attempts to use Northern Ireland as an empty or open signifier, a historically voided space upon which to rehearse and inscribe its hopes and anxieties. Such a representational mechanism reaffirms the value of the concept of the political unconscious, the sense that the thriller does not disclose a direct reflection of Irish history, but rather that History itself induces an ideology of formal ruptures to be negotiated by the troubled workings of the text's *redemptive* and *repressive* modalities. The utilization of Northern Ireland as an empty signifier can be reclaimed from its displacement by the recognition of History as exhorting subtext. Jameson's formulation of Freud's 'The Uncanny' serves as an allegory of the political unconscious of the British thriller's formal solutions, the manner by which Northern Ireland as historically-voided receptacle displaces the unrepresented yet symptomatically inherent historical trauma of English social fracture: 'the formal articulation of uncanny or repressed materials may be organized as a kind of shell game ... in which the reader's attention is diverted to the empty receptacle in such a way as to replace the psychic effect the filled one would inevitably have determined' (1988b, Vol.1, 49).

Accordingly, we must rewrite the positional mechanism of the dominant discourse whereby Northern Ireland is projected as the intractable Id upon which a stable, civilized, Ego-located English subject and History are assembled. For example, in Gerald Seymour's *The Journeyman Tailor*, the British Intelligence operatives refer to 'Ireland, the abscess that governed their lives' (23).[10] This binary is analogous to the dominant-subordinate positionings of Said's account of Orientalism, wherein 'European culture gained in strength and identity by setting

---

[10] Additionally, in Hawke's *For Campaign Service*, an Army Officer suggests that 'the authorities would be justified in changing the name of the place from Ulster to "Ulcer" because that's what it is ... a festering sore on the backside of the United Kingdom' (222), whilst the author's note to *The Extremists* proclaims: 'Ireland has always been a thorn in the British Crown, and for nearly three hundred years the north-east corner of it has furnished an exceptionally trying barb' (Leslie, 1970).

itself off against the Orient as a sort of surrogate and even underground self' (1995, 3). Such a placement is an example of Declan Kiberd's account of the figuration of Ireland as 'a secret England called Ireland' (1995, 15). It is a hierarchization of subjective placings which recapitulates the dominant narrative paradigms of British history outlined by Cairns Craig, wherein a normative, seemingly self-contained English monad simultaneously situates and marginalizes obtrusive provincial forms: 'in the history of England, Scottish or Irish issues will be relevant only when they destructively intrude into the otherwise continuous domain of English narrative ... England has a history; Ireland will only acquire a history once it comes into the orderly and progressive world imposed upon it by England' (101).

There is an extraordinary ideological manoeuvre instigated by the production of a civilized English historical Ego upon an interruptive Irish otherness. For in the very moment of habituating itself as the linear and progressive model of History, this immemorial English paradigm is founded on the removal of itself from the dynamics of History, which are then projected onto the ideologeme of the 'Troubles'. In other words, Northern Ireland as a voided, open signifier opens up a *desiring space* for this dominant subject to foist and engage its own historical problematics even in the very act of avowedly disaffiliating and absolving itself from them. Hence, Chris Petit's *The Psalm Killer*[11] offers its readership a portrait of the deranged serial killer, Candlestick, who, although actually a former British soldier who grew up in England, only has his murderous urges eventually triggered by the gothicized terrain of Northern Ireland, which offers itself as the completion of this Ego-Id historical identity:

> When he arrived in Belfast he knew there was still something missing about himself and waited to discover what it was. He wondered if it mightn't connect with the sense of secrecy that pervaded his childhood, the time spent watching, waiting, hidden. He found what he was looking for in the clouded eye of a tortured man. The dumb, uncomprehending pain of the animals he killed was replaced by a terrible sense of recognition in the eye of his beholder that he was facing his nemesis. *Now and at the hour of our death.* He knew then that his destiny was destruction, killing people. Had he stayed in England he might have avoided this awful calling, but let loose in the grand labyrinth of Belfast, with its tortuous history, he became magnificent (66).

If we return to Bhabha's conceptualization of the stereotype, this passage assumes further significance in the dialectic of reinforcement contained by its gaze. A stereotyped image of Northern Ireland is authenticated for the dominant gaze by its reflection in the eyes of a corpse, producing a mutual identification or recognition

---

[11] Petit's text is interesting in the context of the New Right hegemony that I am tracing, in that Petit himself is a leftist film-maker and journalist. Although his use of the conspiracy text is designed to instantiate the corruption of the British state, the degree of Irish exoticism in his text suggests a comparable utilization of the North as an imaginary receptacle voided of its own inherent historical specifics by the British Left. An interesting oppositional thriller, which combines the Northern conflict with Yardie gangs and institutionalized racism in England, is Sylvester Young's *What Goes Around* (London: Blackamber, 1999).

through which the 'missing' component of Candlestick's identity is compensated. The dominant subject is accordingly restored to the narcissism of the Imaginary and a whole, ideal Ego by its petrifaction of Northern Ireland, in a confirmation of Bhabha's account of the fetishism of the stereotyped gaze: 'The stereotype is not a simplification because it is a false representation of a given reality. It is a simplification because it is an arrested, fixated form of representation that, in denying the play of difference (which the negation through the Other permits), constitutes a problem for the *representation* of the subject in its signification of psychic and social relations' (1994, 75). In other words, the essentialist, synchronic discourse of knowledge produced by the 'Troubles' thriller undertakes to efface the diachronic disruption of its own narrative by the very social materials which it seeks to represent. Put most simply, Homi Bhabha's work is prescient here as it demonstrates that stereotypes do not emerge out of situations of representational surety or truth (i.e. 'we can say these things about the Irish because they are self-evidently and common sensibly true'); but rather emerge out of a crisis in representation where a different reality is too complex to understand (i.e. 'we will have to resort to these stereotypes because we do not have the imaginative capacity to deal with this otherness').

An elaboration of the profound historical simplification of this England-Ireland, Ego-Id relationship, but also an opportunity to begin to relay precisely what historical problematics this mystification endeavours to both address and repress, is provided by *The Green Gene*, written by the former *Punch* journalist, Peter Dickinson. This novel concerns the white, middle-class Glister family and is set in a future England that is divided into racial zones, such as Saxon and Celt. The text centres on the quest to identify the behaviour of a hereditary gene, which gives Celts their green skin, an exploration made imperative because an increasing number of green children are being born to 'white' parents of mixed racial origin.[12] The book's dust jacket reliably informs its projected, optimal readership: 'We English are a decent race, balanced, rational and kindly. But is this virtue on our part, or is it simply luck? Suppose, for instance, that we had always had a subject race, a visibly different subject race, living among us'. The cover of this cautionary tale, which was published in 1973, also promises the text will uncover 'the green

---

[12] In many ways, this attribution of green skin to the Celt panders idly to the *reductio ad absurdum* of racism's representational delimitation: 'in pursuit of natural symbolisms of inferiority, racist discourses have never confined themselves just to body images. Names and modes of address, states of mind and living conditions, clothes and customs, every kind of social behaviour and cultural practice have been pressed into service to signify this or that racial essence. In selecting these materials, racist codes behave opportunistically according to an economy of means, they choose those signs which do the most ideological work in linking – and naturalizing – difference and domination within a certain set of historical conditions of representation. To make issues of in/visibility depend on physical appearance is to bracket out precisely these historical realities' (Cohen, 9). Perhaps the most insipid representation of Irish immigrants in Britain occurs in James Carrick's *With O'Leary in the Grave*: 'they are a raucous beefy race; unfashionably dressed and temporarily affluent, they are eager to get their money spent so that they may exchange the awful responsibility of having money for the uncomplicated pleasures of being poor' (2).

unpleasant land on the other side of the suburban curfew barriers', a pun which foregrounds the use of Ireland as a secret self upon which to rehearse English social fears. The threat posed to the stable bourgeois England represented by the Glister family home, and which is encoded in this arena of Irish otherness, is multifarious. The text dwells not only on determinate fears about Northern Ireland, and indeed, on historical patterns such as Irish immigration, but also anxieties, which would come to dominate the New Right hegemonic project: class antagonism, urban dislocation, a virulent racial, post-imperial trauma, plans for Welsh and Scottish devolution or separation, a crisis in patriarchy. Notably, it is the Glisters' daughters who bring the threat closer to home through their associations with various forms of this racial and class otherness.

Northern Ireland, therefore, as represented in this manner, is to be comprehended as a desiring space for this subject in crisis in which both to mystify and enact these anxieties. In reply to a journalist, who claims apocalyptically that 'we are living in the last days of the world', P.P. Humayan (not quite human?), the Indian computer genius hired to investigate the spread of the 'green gene', replies: 'I think the world has seen many last days ... You are lucky on this island, a rich, easy people. Your nightmares are things which other races take for granted. When they begin to become a little real, you think it is the end of the world' (80). Here, in the historical nightmare of the other, the broader stratagem behind the British thriller's investment in the Northern Ireland conflict is intimated: paradoxically, it produces through the discursive formation of power and knowledge a distanced yet comprehensible nightmare (i.e. the 'Troubles') in place of a nightmare which it cannot consciously begin to imagine (English history), but which, of course, it has been impelled into the process of imagining and resolving in the very form of these texts.

Consequently, in James Lund's 1976 text, *The Ultimate*, which describes Britain as 'a country in crisis' (15) under the Wilson government, the North is used as the focal backdrop:

> It was indeed a supreme achievement to have ridden so many storms in recent British history. But one crisis, Ireland, had proven to be the most intractable. It received only a cursory mention in the Queen's Speech and yet for four years it had given rise to a mounting horror both in Ulster and increasingly here in Great Britain itself. The horror, unbeknown to the participants in the deceptively soothing rituals of democratic pageantry, was set to get unbelievably worse (18-19).

However, baleful national portents preside over a depiction of Wilson's cabinet and bespeak a series of troubled English historical allegories:

> the walls were pregnant with meaning. Huge paintings dominated the room: The Flight of the Five Members in 1642 who took the course which prudence dictated, The Last Day of Parliament in 1629, which was followed, said the caption, by eleven years without a Parliament and then civil war and, most ominously and dramatically of all, a massive painting of five figures from antiquity entitled boldly The Burial of Harold (21-22).

The novel relates a plot to eliminate the entire British cabinet by an Irish-American republican and renegade CIA agent, Rick Collins. The IRA order Collins to halt his plan after the American government find out, but Collins resolves to execute his plan regardless and is eventually killed by the CIA on his way to England. However, his two German terrorist associates do eventually succeed in a final chapter entitled 'The Holocaust'. The epilogue relates how the Queen assumes all constitutional authority and martial law is declared as the Commissioner for the Metropolitan Police is granted unprecedented powers – moves, we are told, opposed only by left-wingers. Moreover, Prince Charles is appointed as Regent for the period of the emergency as an immemorial English continuity fantastically avers itself from historical fracture: 'In the event he ruled the country for eleven years without Parliament, thus repeating the history of 1629' (253). We can introduce a note of ominous irony into the mythic recurrence of a King Charles, who sutures historical disjuncture, by suggesting that the fragmentation of the post-war social settlement in 1970s England with which *The Ultimate* is forced to grapple, belies a period of historical flux theorized by Gramsci as an 'interregnum': 'If the ruling class has lost its consensus, i.e. is no longer "leading" but only "dominant", exercising coercive force alone, this means precisely that the great masses have become detached from their traditional ideologies, and no longer believe what they used to believe previously, etc. The crisis consists precisely in the fact that the old is dying and the new cannot be born; and in this interregnum a great variety of morbid symptoms appear' (Gramsci, 275-276).[13]

Therefore, whilst the underlying dominance of representations of Northern Ireland produced by the British 'Troubles' thriller has been established by the Foucauldian discursive methodology of Said's *Orientalism*, a sense of this struggle for hegemony and reordering in British society from the 1970s to the present necessitates an increasing verification of the Gramscian thrust of Said's text if these representations, their import and engagements, are to be situated in historical process. A Gramscian model ultimately resists the misleadingly consummate and inevitable coherence which Foucauldian power often attains.[14]

An analysis of the English interregnum circumvents the establishment of a stable British subject producing the discursive formation of the 'Troubles' thriller

---

[13] For a convincing application of the Gramscian interregnum to the North see Richard Kirkland's *Literature and Culture in Northern Ireland since 1965: Moments of Danger* (London: Longmann, 1996). Part of the reasoning for my placement of this study of the international thriller before a contextualization of Irish texts is to inculcate the sense that the North is by no means unique or anomalous. That is, dominant ideologies of organic attachment globally exhibit crisis from the 1960s to the present, so that the fracture of Irish Nationalism and Unionism which I shall uncover is by no means peculiar. In this chapter I shall draw upon Stuart Hall's illuminating Gramscian analysis of British society.

[14] As Raymond Williams contends, the concept of hegemony insists upon contestatory process, upon the dynamic of history: 'In practice hegemony can never be singular ... it does not just passively exist as a form of dominance. It has continually to be renewed, recreated, defended, and modified. It is also continually resisted, limited, altered, challenged by pressures not at all its own' (1977b, 112).

that is encouraged by a Foucauldian concept of power, which, as Aijaz Ahmad posits, dehistoricizes sections of *Orientalism*:

> in one range of formations, Said's denunciations of the *whole* of Western civilization is as extreme and uncompromising as Foucault's denunciations of the Western episteme or Derrida's denunciations of the transcendental Logos; nothing, nothing at all exists outside epistemic Power, logocentric Thought, Orientalist discourse – no classes, no gender, not even history; no site of resistance, no accumulated projects of human liberation ... and Orientalism is always the same, only more so with the linear accumulations of time (195).

Indeed, just as Ahmad castigates the suggestion that 'there *is* a unified European/ Western identity which is at the *origin* of history and has *shaped* this history through its *thought* and its *texts*' (167), we must interrogate the prevailing construction of England as a self-identical and continuous monad in Irish colonial and cultural theory, such as Declan Kiberd's homogeneous subject – 'If Ireland had never existed, *the* English would have invented it' (1995, 9) [my emphasis]. Seamus Deane similarly inculcates a reductive notion of what constitutes political unity, by normalizing Britain whilst concurrently peculiarizing Irish society: 'When a culture is politically homogeneous, like that of Britain, the sectarianism is externally rather than internally directed and is usually xenophobic in character. When, as in Ireland's case, the culture is politically divided, the sectarianism is largely internally directed' ("Political Writings and Speeches", 682). It is evident that Deane's dubious concept of political homogeneity provides a model of the British subject as a stable, originary presence which governs his own sense of national unity, which flouts the historical co-ordinates of class, gender, race and so on. It is through the mobilization of precisely these co-ordinates that the struggle for hegemony is waged, and for which popular fiction offers a vantage point.

There is a parallel between the popular text's attempt to equip its audience with a series of reading selves, whilst also seeking to produce across these axes an optimal or dominant subject or receiver, and the Thatcherite hegemonic project's attempt to organize the multifarious historical materials of the British interregnum. The dialectic of ideology and utopia in the 'Troubles' thriller offers one means of explicating the mobilizing efficacy of Thatcherism outlined by Stuart Hall: 'Thatcherism's "populism" signals its unexpected ability to harness to its project certain popular discontents, to cut across and between the different divisions in society and to connect with certain aspects of popular experience' (1988, 6). Thus, whilst Bruce Merry considers the thriller a 'plebian art form' (235) and Alan Titley likens it to 'modern folklore' (18), it is mystificatory to view the identities produced by these tests as an organic or direct reflection of 'the people'. To this end, Jameson asserts that 'The survival of genre in mass culture can ... in no way be taken as a return to the stability of the publics of pre-capitalist societies: on the contrary, the generic forms and signals of mass culture are very specifically to be understood as the historical reappropriation and displacement of older structures' (1992b, 19).

Accordingly, the construction of 'the people' by the New Right project, which crystallized in Thatcherism, entails a system of what my introductory chapter termed a Gramscian 'transformist hegemony', in which popular interests and anxieties in a period of crisis are assimilated to, and neutralized by, an emergent political subject.[15] The problematics, and indeed exigency, of producing such a populist political subject are disclosed by Douglas Hurd's *Vote to Kill*, a text which reveals the struggle between Old Toryism and the New Right. The text was published in 1975, the year in which Edward Heath (to whom the book is dedicated) was deposed as Conservative Party Leader by Thatcher,[16] and also the year of the Oil Hike, the discernible onset of international capitalist crisis, and profound industrial unrest in Britain. *Vote to Kill* provides an elegy for an Old England, as the aging, incumbent Prime Minister is usurped by the young demagogue, Jeremy Cornwall. The text exhibits a profound pessimism as to the capacity of either the Old or New Right to configure a unitary British political subject across the flux of late capitalist fracture and imperial and national decline, as the Prime Minister ruminates on the hegemonic collapse facing himself and Cornwall: 'No one can lead the British people. Not any longer. A mob or two here and there, yes, but not the whole people' (152).

This specific historical crisis is once again played out on the immemorial, and risibly racist, fabric of 'the essential bloodiness of Ireland and the Irish' (73), as the ahistorical 'Troubles' ideologeme provides a representational deep structure upon which to construct a transcendent national identity that overrides its material production. The old Prime Minister takes to the streets and tells a nationally-symbolic crowd:

> It is not my purpose to preside over the disintegration of the United Kingdom. If that is the will of the British people, so be it. But the Conservative Party cannot sail with that wind, cannot be swept along with that current. We are not time-servers, we are the anchor. We must hold the ship steady till the storm has blown itself out. And so this evening we call to our aid against those who march and shout, the stubbornness, the good sense, the steadiness of the British people (208).

Intriguingly, in constructing a transformist hegemony out of this 'Great Britishness', the Prime Minister recites Philip Larkin's 'Homage to a Government' – a poem which also serves as the text's preface – in his speech: 'He was ill, they knew that, despite the denials. He was courageous, that was clear enough. Above all he was there with them, not just a head on a poster, not an image on a screen, but a human body and a real voice. He had quoted from a poem they had never

---

[15] Stuart Hall describes Thatcherism's intervention in the very disjuncture of the interregnum's dialectic between emergent, dominant and residual forces as an 'authoritarian populism' (1988, 141) that sought to articulate the people/power bloc contradiction and alignment to a New Right hegemony.

[16] For an account of how Thatcher's election marked a decisive shift to the Right, and was not merely some historical accident, see Mark Wickham-Jones, 'Right Turn: A Revisionist Account of the 1975 Conservative Party Leadership Election'. *20 Century British History* Vol.8 No.1, 1997. 74-89.

heard before. He had touched a theme in which they desperately wanted to believe' (208). Ironically enough, as Larkin would become a Thatcherite apologist,[17] Hurd attempts to utilize the poem's post-imperial disenchantment at the withdrawal of British troops from Aden in the late sixties for economic reasons to satirize the perceived naked monetarism of the Thatcherism which overthrew Heath. For the primary means, by which the demagogic usurper in *Vote to Kill* seeks to mobilize the people and restore national greatness, is to demand the return of British soldiers from Ireland – a call which he claims Churchill would have made: 'It is time for the lion to roar again. It is time, my friends, for us, the people of England, to find our voice' (127).

Hindsight, of course, has taught that the Thatcherite hegemonic project could not base itself purely on neo-liberal economics. As with the return to 'Victorian Values', it engaged a complex national and historical imagination, which shall become increasingly apparent in the analysis of the dominant *redemptive* and *repressive* dialectics of the 'Troubles' thriller, and which Stuart Hall comprehends as a 'regressive modernization' (1988, 164) that sought to suture and mobilize the schisms of late capitalism. In short, the New Right project culminates in what John Newsinger deems 'a revived popular militarism that does not sustain empire but compensates for its loss' (1997, 143). Hence, in Hurd's text the English interregnum is mystified by the defeat of a Republican plot to kill the Prime Minister. The text's surface content, then, offers this as the most dangerous threat as a civilized, constitutional English subject is sustained through its positional superiority to 'the Irish fever, the worst variety known to man. It destroys all gentleness, truth, sensible calculation' (215).

However, what threatens ultimately the immemorial One Nation Heathism of Hurd's text is the knowledge that England has altered and ruptured, as conceded, in fact, by the filiative breakdown of the Larkin poem it cites wherein England becomes a different country. A comparable sentiment of historical disjunction is lamented by Walter Nelson's *The Minstrel Code*, wherein the Queen is held hostage in Buckingham Palace by a group of international terrorists that includes two 'Irish thugs' (144) from the IRA. Although the Queen is eventually rescued, the text nervously secretes that a complete, organic recovery is unattainable. After the final shoot-out, the Palace is described '*almost* as though the regal dignity of those apartments had never been disturbed at all' (223) [my emphasis]. The sense of a home disturbed or an immemorial recurrence dissolved is confirmed by the concluding passages wherein Jack Lash, a police commander involved in the security operation, resolves to return to his wife and family:

> home not just to Doris and the old house off the Lower Richmond Road, but home to a saner England than the one from which he'd come, an England in which life went on peacefully, where schoolboys rowed their eights upon the Thames, until they went off to seek their fortunes in different lands, as men always had done.

---

[17] Larkin's poetry, pervaded by the sense that 'England lurches on towards disaster' (Thwaite, ed. 584), provides a further cultural resonance of the New Right's assault on the post-war British State.

> Lash realized then he'd changed ... Where he had been and what had happened in
> the very heart of London seemed to Lash to have nothing to do with the England
> he loved; it seemed like some nightmare foreign land in which he'd been trapped
> for days, and then he wondered whether he wasn't merely getting sentimental. All
> that had happened – all the killings that were past, and all the murders yet to come
> – weren't happening some place far away, but here! That old England which those
> who were his age always remembered had disappeared, like figures vanishing into
> a London fog (231).

The structural incongruity between this knowable Old England and the vast,
shadowy reaches of the thriller form is reinforced by a nostalgic essay by P.D.
James in the Tory *Salisbury Review*. It harks back to 'the moral responsibility of
the individual' (1990, 12) in what James perceives as the Golden Age of detective
fiction between the wars – a fiction of the organic community which is historically
inaccessible to James's own historical moment and fiction. She mourns the loss of
moral assurance and social order putatively conferred by earlier forms of crime
fiction:[18]

> At the heart of the story we have a mystery and we know that by the end of the
> book this will be solved. This assurance that we live in a rational universe in
> which there is always a solution is deeply reassuring particularly in an age when
> we are beginning to feel that no matter how much goodwill we pour into some of
> our problems, whether they are economic, international, social, racial, the solution
> is literally beyond our capacity. We are living through an age of pessimism not of
> optimism (1990, 13).

As noted in my introduction, the cultural hegemony of the thriller denotes the
complexity and dislocation of the late capitalist state, in which James's
romanticized account of the single, resolvable crime is radically subsumed by a
confrontation with the social as itself mysterious.[19] Under such conditions Jameson
contends that attempts to map and redefine a society are pervaded by a

---

[18] This moral order is of course itself a fantasy, an imaginative resolution to irresolvable
social contradictions. The fact that a sufficient body of readers and writers could embrace
the social symbolism of this narrative points not to social cohesion but rather the viability of
this filiative ideology – a cultural tenability now irretrievable to James's late capitalist
moment.

[19] Therefore, whilst Jayne Steel observes that in F.L. Green's *Odd Man Out* Johnny's
terrorist activity thwarts his relationship with Kathleen and destroys 'a conventional family
life', it is noteworthy that in the era of late capitalism it is often the state forces who must
dislocate themselves from filiative or organic belonging. In Terence Strong's *Stalking Horse*
the SAS agent Max Avery assumes the alias of Patrick O'Reilly, a working-class Irish
immigrant from Liverpool, and it is the IRA detectives who must investigate this false
organic identity – suggesting a subversive formal logic which incriminates the mystery of
the late capitalist state. That state forces must utilize the filiative and communitarian
belonging of the figure of the terrorist, implies a mimicry which helps explain the
performative instrumentality of the Terrorist that this chapter will later trace in the utopian
allegories of the 'Troubles' thriller.

'conspiratorial ideologeme' (1992a, 22), as traditional social co-ordinates diffuse into increasingly untraceable institutional imbrications. This conspiratorial or paranoid ideologeme in the 'Troubles' thriller offers a framework for both Left (such as G.F. Newman's pessimistic, anti-establishment *The Testing Ground*, which is based on the Stalker Affair) and Right (exemplified by the work of Terence Strong) perspectives to engage in a hegemonic struggle to chart and redirect the crisis in the British State. The New Right hegemonic project has tended to predominate in the thriller form, as with Chapman Pincher's effort to redefine and mobilize state and society after 'many years of Socialist softness and indecision' (124) in *The Eye of the Tornado*, wherein the IRA threaten to detonate a nuclear bomb under Soviet supervision. As intimated by Pincher's fantastically paranoid plot, and initiated by a perceived crisis of the social democratic state in the 1970s, the conspiratorial ideologeme serves as a locus for the conflictive process of producing a hegemonic Englishness. This in turn reaffirms the need to resist the idea that there is a single, unitary dominant subject configuring the 'Troubles' discourse. Moreover, a sense of historical process and contestation in England facilitates the explication of the representational decontextualization of the Northern Irish conflict through its projection as a desiring space.[20]

The New Right assault on the post-war Keynesian state of macro-economic management[21] conveys that it is imperative to interrogate the mystification that the state is somehow homogenous or neutral. It is not a passive status quo but rather is the product and perpetuation of the political antagonisms of a specific set of social relationalities. An analysis of the New Right hegemonic project in the 'Troubles' thriller permits the rewriting of the putative anti-statism of Thatcherism, which can then be comprehended as a mode of state reformation in a period of interregnum. In many ways, the rogue, maverick voices of many of the 1970s thrillers articulate the class reconstitution and assertiveness which Thatcher desires to personify in her own rise to power: 'in the eyes of the "wet" Tory establishment I was not only a woman, but "that woman", someone not just of a different sex, but of a different class, a person with an alarming conviction that the values and virtues of middle England should be brought to bear on the problems which the establishment consensus had created. I offended on many counts' (129-130).

The figure of the disenchanted outsider is of course a standard and even overdetermined figure in crime writing, as in other forms such as the Western. However, what specific inflection inscribes the figure in the late capitalist context that Thatcherism sought to map? This newly-detached outsider shunning the post-war consensus reverberates in 'the cold, feral rage of the outcast who has every

---

[20] Such decontextualization is evidenced by Strong's *Whisper Who Dares*, which describes Gerry Adams as 'a fiery communist' (308) and delineates how 'the Provisional Republican Army was slipping into the hands of Communists from its bruised young roots up to the very top branches' (320). For an excellent historical account of the actual tensions between Irish Republicanism and the Left, see Henry Patterson's *The Politics of Illusion*.

[21] For general background Andrew Gamble's *The Free Economy and the Strong State* is illuminating. For accounts from the Left and the Right, see Will Hutton and Shirley Robin Letwin respectively.

man's hand against his' (217) displayed by the self-righteous protagonist in Andrew Lane's *Forgive the Executioner*. Comparably, the Special Branch officer, Cuthbertson, in Ritchie Perry's *Dead End*, is described thus: 'Cuthbertson was a maverick, somebody who didn't conform to any of the popular conceptions of law and order. He liked to do things his own way, paying scant attention either to the wishes of his superiors or the letter of the law if these interfered with what he wanted to do' (169).[22] Here, if further validation were required, are examples of popular fiction not simply reflecting some given and dominant order but rather actively intervening in the production of cultural process.

In many of the 1970s thrillers, the emergent New Right mavericks must still negotiate their social success on the grounds of the residual Old Toryism, as literally demonstrated by the miraculous imaginary solution to the problematics of the English interregnum detailed by Lane's *The Ulsterman*. Here the tough-guy loner Chris Boggs (whose real name is actually Christian Skipton Boggs, descended from an aristocratic family who lost their estate to taxes) eventually marries a young Irish girl who he has rescued from the clutches of the terrorists. She is herself revealed to be the adopted daughter of a Dutch millionare, whose millions then allow Boggs to buy back Skipton Hall, the family home. However, the tide of military populism noticeably produced during and beyond Thatcher's period in office, particularly after the focal point of the Falklands War, came to imbue these maverick voices with a collective resonance – a resonance which achieves its apotheosis in the development of SAS-related fiction.[23] For example, in Terence Strong's *Whisper Who Dares*[24] the SAS as 'unknown collective agent' (Paterson and Schlesinger, 58) unfolds a utopian space of belonging and redefined legality for the rogue individual:

> Turnbull was a loner, introverted, and his degree of independence and self-containment was his own personal measure of success. He never allowed this private driving force to form a barrier between his colleagues. If he had, it would have been impossible to work with the Special Air Services, where total trust, reliance and compatibility within a Sabre team is of paramount importance. He

---

[22] An American variant of these rabidly New Right English texts is offered by Jim Case's *Belfast Blitz* (New York: Warner Books, 1987).

[23] Interestingly, under the populist militarism of the Thatcher period the figure of the journalist mediating an Irish otherness to the 'Troubles' thriller's designated audience was in many ways usurped by the figure of the soldier – perhaps hinting at a growing political and cultural drift towards more military solutions to the conflict. An interesting interleaving of both trajectories is provided by *Cause of Death*, written by Falklands veteran, Simon Weston, and Patrick Hill, a journalist with both the *Daily Mail* and *The News of the World*. Texts by SAS veterans include those by Shaun Clarke, Andy McNab and Chris Ryan. The imbrication of such texts within wider populist New Right currents is conveyed by Eddy Shah's *Fallen Angels* – Shah being a Thatcherite entrepreneur who famously took on the print unions with his *Today* newspaper, which is now, ironically enough, yesterday's news, having been taken over and closed by the Murdoch media empire.

[24] The text gleans a distinctly Thatcherite message from the SAS's 'Who Dares Wins' motto: 'if you try hard enough, anything is possible' (183).

knew that he would never find the action he craved nor the independence he enjoyed outside the regiment, or at least not on the right side of the law (56).

In terms of the New Right transformist hegemonic project, it is conspicuous that the SAS is depicted as a cross-class, or indeed classless, mobilizational subject, as conveyed by Shaun Clarke: 'Apart from its recognition that the ordinary soldier can have as much to contribute as the officers, the Chinese parliament is a regular, healthy reminder that the SAS scorns the notion of class' (1993, 222).[25] In their contempt for officer rank 'Ruperts' (1993, 222) and 'Ponces' (1993, 258), Clarke's characters evince that this cross-class commonality is constructed primarily around an assertive masculinity, a newly-conscripted mutuality which also permits Andy McNab's protagonist in *Immediate Action* an alternative belonging to the degradations of his Welfare State childhood: 'I was on a free bus pass, free school dinners. I even had to stand in a special "free dinners" queue in the school canteen. It wasn't just me: the main catchment areas were Brixton and Peckham, so a lot of kids were in the same boat. But all the same, it was one particular gang I wanted out of' (12). This cult of masculinity surrounding the SAS, as with Mark Urban's contention that the regiment provides 'the opportunity to play big boys' games by big boys' rules' (247), attempts to override a specific historical crisis; it is, in John Newsinger's terms, 'a massive assertion of British masculinity in a troubled and dangerous world':

> The fascination with the SAS, with 'men behaving militarily', can be usefully seen as part of the male backlash against feminism and the women's movement. At a time when changing patterns of employment are contributing to the undermining of the certainties of traditional masculinity, of male self-confidence, the reassertion of a warrior masculinity restores men to their proper place in the order of things (139; 141-142).

I would add that there is a further subtlety and import in the SAS's profound cultural resonance that helps explicate its populist significance. For the era of late capitalism that has eroded conventional forms of masculinity is characterized by the shift to post-Fordism, by the decline of traditional industry and its replacement by a service-based economy of flexible specialization. The latter is particularly geared towards the employment and exploitation of increasing numbers of female workers, who are more poorly paid and more easily hired and laid off. The SAS, as their name itself implies, are paradigms of flexible specialization, and as such, proffer an idealized means of aggrandizing, and most importantly, masculinizing these economic relations, of paradoxically creating a mythic national virtue from the logic of conditions which attest to Britain's relative economic decline and the loss of much of its industrial means of producing wealth to the power of

---

[25] Similarly, Paul Bruce's *The Nemesis File* asserts that 'occasionally the SAS does attract Hooray Henrys, but not for long. They are soon sussed and RTU'd like everyone else who doesn't absolutely make the grade' (63), whilst *Day One* by Hugo Barnacle maintains: 'the SAS weren't given much to sirring. Their own officers they barely rated, paper-rank civilians from MI5 they'd rather take no notice of at all' (78).

multinational capital.[26] Thus, in Eddy Shah's *Fallen Angels*, a group of SAS renegades actuate a plan to eliminate the IRA militarily that was discussed but discounted by the government as being too politically risky. This action is shrouded in an aura of populist militarism by the head of MI6: 'nobody's against it. The public, even the Press. There is a grudging sort of respect and acquiescence there. Gives a whole new meaning to the word *privatization*. These boys are sorting out what the Government and the security forces should have dealt with a long time ago' (299).[27]

There is, nevertheless, a more utopian or collective framework within which the rogue individual may be re-articulated. Whilst the *repressive* modality of the text constitutes the SAS as the communal site of the vigilante individual, it is striking that in the thriller form another collective repository is afforded the lone agent. Even the most rabidly reactionary figures of the 1970s seem to share more with the criminals they pursue than with those for whom they pursue their torturous missions of social alienation. Notably in Gerald Seymour's *Harry's Game*, for instance, Harry Brown feels more affinity with his prey, Billy Downs, than with his political quartermasters in the British state. Indeed, such a bond persists into the era of the SAS text, where increasingly lone figures reject their official orders in following evermore solitary assignments in zones of engagement populated by figures similar to themselves. So where is the subversion or collective resonance in this seemingly increased social withdrawal of the loner? I shall briefly discuss Murray Davies's *The Drumbeat of Jimmy Sands* by way of exemplification. The text concerns Duggie Fife and Paddy O'Keefe, born in working-class Glasgow and Belfast respectively, who fought together in the Falklands War with the SAS but then eventually joined different sides in Northern Ireland. I want to suggest that the figure of the ex-SAS or special services figure, who continues to fight and operate after their official sanction has been removed is the site of a coded, collective yearning. For if, as I have suggested, the SAS are paradigms of flexible specialization, then, a refusal to be conditioned purely as dispensable labour to short-term work instigates something subversive. To be concise, it enacts a utopian revolt of labour in an era of flexible accumulation. In other words, the

---

[26] A celebratory analysis is granted by Tony Geraghty: 'the SAS, through its readiness to experiment and adapt, and its reliance on the judgement of the individual, has a better chance than most of coming to terms with high technology. In that sense, it is the shape of things to come' (19).

[27] Thus, we are given a dubious account of the Northern Ireland Peace Process and the role of the Republican movement within it: 'the IRA had refused to support peace talks and had continued their war of attrition with bombs and innocent deaths. Because of the Angels, terrorist action ceased on the mainland and in Ulster. For that, the British and Irish populace were extremely grateful. The public knew it might not last, but at least it could open the doors for the Provos and the IRA finally to come and join the peace talks' (393). In Andrew Melville-Ross's *Shaw's War*, the SAS renegade, Major Harry Shaw, 'caught the imagination of the British people' (267), and the Foreign Secretary tells the US Ambassador: 'Shaw has become something of a folk-hero, a national institution almost, and the pundits tell us that if the Government is not seen to have done everything possible to ensure his welfare the Conservative vote will be adversely affected' (271).

reapplication of specialized skill, even in the furtherance of some New Right vigilantism, does at another level proffer a rejection of the strictures of contemporary labour conditions.[28]

Additionally, the effort to hegemonize a Thatcherite political subject through this populist militarism actually belies its lack of acceptance, for, as Paterson and Schlesinger note, the SAS's 'secret identity bespeaks its unsettled legitimacy' (71). The resort to such authoritarian posturing impugns the hegemonic achievement of such a project, as to whether in Gramsci's formulation of the interregnum it attains a *dirigente* or 'leading' role, or stands only as *dominante* or a 'dominative' (55) force whose coercive non-consensuality discloses itself.[29] An important performative function of the 'Troubles' thriller's representation of Northern Ireland, therefore, must be not only to meditate upon the British engagement in the conflict, but also to offer an imperial trajectory concordant with, and justifying, 'an authoritarian drift towards simple militaristic solutions to increasingly ramified political and economic problems' (Paterson and Schlesinger, 72) within the British State in crisis, as evidenced by the handling of inner city communities or the Miners' Strike. Hence, if the full historical context of the English thriller's deployment of the 'Troubles', and indeed its anti-Irish racism, is to be comprehended, then it must be interleaved with related ruminations on producing a national and political subjectivity against 'the enemy within' (Thatcher, 370), with legitimization strategies for handling a range of historical dilemmas such as class antagonism, the reworking of patriarchy, and racial fears.[30]

What, then, are the precise consequences of utilizing Northern Ireland as a representational deep structure in this hegemonic struggle? I shall now seek to

---

[28] An interesting parallel here is David Harvey's reading of Ridley Scott's film, *Blade Runner*. Though more self-consciously post-modernist, the film shares with the special agent in the thriller the historical referent of late capitalism. As with the collective attachment between opposing operatives in the thriller, Harvey notes the similar plight of Deckard and the replicants: 'both Deckard and the replicants ... exist in a similar relation to the dominant social power in society. This relation defines a hidden bond of sympathy and understanding between the hunted and hunter' (1990, 310).

[29] Much SAS fiction is infused with an elegiac tone, given that it was produced after Thatcher's period in office. There are specific material reasons for this, given that many authors served up until the Gulf War. The impact of Peter Wright's *Spycatcher* case, and the consequent relaxing of the Official Secrets Act also provided a conducive cultural climate for would-be military authors.

[30] The transposition of militaristic discourse onto legitimization strategies for handling civil problematics is illustrated by Leon Britten's comment: 'Mass picketing – if I can use that popular misnomer – and violent street demonstrations, are acts of terrorism without the bullet and the bomb ... I sometimes get a dreadful feeling that democracy, like the setting sun, is beginning to sink in the west. It is time we did something about it'. Speech to Conservative Party Conference 10 Oct 1984. Cited by Okoje, 55-56. Thus, in *Trouble* by Michael Gilbert, an MI5 agent contends: 'If we were at war, it would be different. We could put a fence round this island that I'd defy anyone to break through. But we're not at war. Or not in the old-fashioned sense of the word. And we have to spend half our time worrying about whether we're standing on someone else's toes, or upsetting the public or giving a field day to the opposition press' (225-226).

demonstrate that the 'Troubles' function as the site of a series of compensatory allegories gesturing towards national and historical unity and resolution: allegories of family and filiative continuity, of home and community, of empire. The mythic historical longing which seeps through Thatcher's reading of the Falklands conflict helps intimate the imaginative mechanisms operative in such allegory:

> We have ceased to be a nation in retreat. We have instead a newfound confidence – born in the economic battles at home and tested and found true 8,000 miles away ... and so today we can rejoice at our success in the Falklands and take pride in the achievement of the men and women of our task force. But we do so, not as some flickering of a flame which must soon be dead. No – we rejoice that Britain has rekindled that spirit which has fired her generations past and which today has begun to burn as brightly as before. Britain has found herself again in the South Atlantic and will not look back from the victory she has won (235).

Similarly:

> When we started out there were the waverers and the faint-hearts, the people who thought we could no longer do the great things we once did, those who believed our decline was irreversible, that we could never again be what we were, that Britain was no longer the nation that had built an empire and ruled a quarter of the world. Well they were wrong (Cited by Hobsbawm, 'Falklands Fallout', 260).

Such historical elision attests to Patrick Wright's point that 'The national past is above all a modern past' (1985, 20). The ideological resonance of the 'Troubles' thriller for a fractured English imagination, the lost inheritance which its allegories reinstate, is suggested by Wright's account of the significance of the raising of the *Mary Rose*, Henry VIII's flagship, during the Falklands war and its blurring of moments of national greatness into a seamless temporal union: 'For "us" the contemporary "historical" event appears increasingly to be the one which marks the *recovery* and reaffirmation of the old ways. In this respect it is intrinsically archeological' (1985, 164). Wright continues that '"History" in this contemporary sense is evidently not about the *making* of a future, unless we understand that process to be a re-enactment of the imagined past – "our" moment of vindication and perpetuation' (1985, 165). In light of this seafaring metaphor of national grandeur, there is a curious scene in the closure of Shaun Clarke's *Underworld*, a text depicting a successful SAS mission to assassinate a group of IRA leaders supposedly threatening the establishment of a permanent peace through their extensive criminal empire, in which the SAS hero, Michael Burton, just prior to his final elimination of the remaining IRA leaders, is observed gazing at a 'transport ship out on the horizon, hazed in mist, looking ghostlike. The ship was clearly heading for England and Burton was following it. He was looking towards home' (433). This spectral voyager, which then disappears as a 'ghost ship' (445), offers an allegory of the imaginative trajectory of the British 'Troubles' thriller itself; of how its representations of Northern Ireland function as the terminal outposts of an imperial imagination ferrying its dream cargoes in a restive mythical transit. It belies the precarious circumnavigation of the present of a society that has increasingly lost sight of itself: a society set upon the obliteration of the working-class communities of its mining and industrial heartlands, upon the disenfranchisement and ghettoization of its inner-cities, upon the criminalization and feminization of poverty, upon the institutionalization of racism. The task, therefore, of the *redemptive* and *repressive* modalities encoded in the imaginary resolutions of popular fiction is to manage and override such fracture and contradiction in producing a mobilizational reading subject in the series of allegories which I will now examine.

The recourse to this imperial allegory in the 'Troubles' thriller consequently demands a circumspection with regard to Martin Green's postulation, in his study of the interrelation between popular adventure texts and the High Imperial Period, that such a trajectory may now be interpreted with a critical but also historical distance which reifies and absolves any contemporary national culpability or implication – and which, incidentally, the glorified nostalgia of his tone betrays:

> There is no longer need to turn away from the Empire, in that purposive way. It no longer has that power to seduce the young, the glamour of that enormous animal vitality. We can look at it directly, because it's only a moon now, not a sun. We can look up into the heavens, and study it, as a burned-out star, or rather a splendid constellation of stars (344).

Nevertheless, it is important to bear in mind that we are dealing not with the reconstitution of empire but with imperial allegory, with a historical imaginary – which is not to deny the oppressive form and effects of contemporary anti-Irish racism, but rather to imply that it must be comprehended in its historical context, in this case the interregnum of de-industrializing Britain.[31] Dismissing such racism as an immemorial oppression is actually to buy into the historical slippage of this imperial trajectory and its diagnosis of Irish history as 'one bloody mess after another ... It's the same old story, the same old sickness' (Carrick, 30).[32] However, this dominant representation of Irish history as peculiarly cyclical or iterative can be interrogated by our sense of the allegorical fabric of the English national

---

[31] In relation to racism, Stuart Hall has observed: 'Though it may draw on the cultural and ideological traces which are deposited in a society by previous phases, it always assumes specific forms which arise out of the present – not the past – conditions and organization of society. The indigenous racism of the 60s and 70s is significantly different, in form and effect, from the racism of the "high" colonial period. It is a racism "at home" not abroad. It is the racism not of a dominant but of a declining social formation'. Cited by Krieger, 101. Thus the title of Curtis's *Nothing But the Same Old Story* is slightly misleading, and reaffirms the dangers of the Foucauldian and High Humanist strands of Said's *Orientalism*.

[32] To this end, Seymour's *The Journeyman Tailor* grounds its enlightened English civility on the projection of Northern Ireland as an anachronistic backwater – 'he was headed for a war in which dinosaur traditions governed and destroyed a gentler and more reasoning age' (59) – and contrasts a progressive English history with the recurrent narrative displacement putatively characterizing and retarding Ireland: 'History doesn't go away here. Stories lose nothing by the telling. Stories handed down, father to son, family to family, close as frogs in a drain here' (242).

imagination in the 'Troubles' thriller and its historical fantasies. Indeed, the thriller's dominant representation of Northern Ireland as anachronistic stagnation concords with Joep Leerssen's formulation of the English imaginary's tendency to depict cultural otherness as reflecting older periods in History, in terms of *peripherality*, *liminality* and *allochrony*, which subsequently reduce 'the notion of Irish history to a stasis, an undifferentiated pool of diverse mementos and memories' (1996b, 50). In relation to the Northern Ireland conflict, of course, one of the primary functions of such allochronic displacement, and indeed the reification of History into some distant object, is to absolve Britain from any culpability, so that the situation is reducible to the problematic of an anomalous racial recidivism.[33] Rather than reflecting the aberrant cycle of Irish history, then, historical elisions such as Chris Boggs' attack on a Catholic hotel in Lane's *The Ulsterman* – 'He was an eighteenth-century Protestant Peep-o-Day Boy again, burning Catholic property' (151) – are more instructive of the processes of an English national imagination's investment in the 'Troubles'. Gramsci insists that 'it is certain that in the movement of History there is never any turning back, and that restorations *in toto* do not exist' (219-220). The hegemonic project of the New Right's revolution-restoration, which sought contradictorily to mobilize a popular subject 'not forwards into the unknown, but backwards into the familiar' (Scruton, 1990, vii) by inserting itself in the very rupture of the old, filiative England, necessitated an allegorical shoring of historical fragments to gesture beyond its own historical problematics. The *redemptive* and *repressive* imaginaries of the 'Troubles' thriller attest to the Right's populist, and ultimately mystificatory, appropriation of Walter Benjamin's conception of the methods of the historical materialist: 'The task of the historical materialism is to set to work an engagement with history original to every present. It has recourse to a consciousness that shatters the continuum of history' (1992b, 352). Ironically, of course, for a Benjaminian analysis, the allegorical imperative of Thatcherism's seizure of precise historical moments was the production of a national 'empty, homogeneous time' to conceal the fracture of its own historical predicament. It provides an instance of Patrick Wright's detailing of English culture's

> contemporary *orientation* towards the past rather than just the survival of old things. As so few guide-books ever recognise, this is not merely a matter of noticing old objects situated in a self-evident reality: the present meaning of historical traces such as these is only to be grasped if one takes account of the doubletake or second glance in which they are recognized. The ordinary or

---

[33] Ritchie Perry's *Dead End* – a text saturated by insipid, casual racism and sexism – illustrates this stratagem in its commentaries on Ireland: 'there's been trouble over there since the Irish Adam belted Eve over the head with a club and started inventing Guinness' (72); 'the Irish had been fighting one another ever since some caveman had invented the club and no amount of conferences or church services would persuade them to abandon a national pastime' (167).

habitual perspectives are jarred as the old declares itself in the midst of all this dross (1985, 229-230).[34]

For Benjamin the ruin is the paradigm of this allegorical imagination: 'In the ruin history has physically merged into setting. And in this guise history does not assume the form of the process of an eternal life so much as that of irresistible decay. Allegory thereby declares itself to be beyond beauty. Allegories are, in the realm of thoughts, what ruins are in the realm of things' (1977, 177-178). Whilst allegory acknowledges disintegration, it is nonetheless also a code of meaning which relies upon existing conventions of interpretation, its talismanic fragments gesturing to other signs and times. It thus opens up a dialectic between restoration and destruction, instigating an imaginative quest that attempts to equilibrate a sense of historical irretrievability with the reconstitution of complexes of collective meaning and value. Benjamin deems these contradictory temporal pressures 'the antinomies of the allegorical':

> Any person, any object, any relationship can mean absolutely anything else. With this possibility a destructive, but just verdict is passed on the profane world: it is characterized as a world in which the detail is of no great importance. But it will be unmistakably apparent to anyone who is familiar with allegorical textual exegesis, that all of the things which are used to signify derive, from the very fact of their pointing to something else, a power which makes them appear no longer commensurable with profane things, which raises them onto a higher plane, and which can, indeed, sanctify them. Considered in allegorical terms, then, the profane world is both elevated and devalued (1977, 174).

Hence, the Thatcherite return to 'Victorian Values' sought both to indict and redeem the present, simultaneously bewailing the demise of an imaginatively ordered, filiative England whilst producing and convoking repositories of collective meaning. An analysis of the function of the *repressive* and *redemptive* modalities of popular fiction must necessarily recognize that, even as they seek to mystify the material conditions of their production, they also elicit utopian longings and fulfilments. For strewn across the imaginary of the 'Troubles' thriller are precisely such ruins and fragments, emblems of empire and social cohesion, filiative runes of family belonging and hierarchy. For example, in Dickinson's *The Green Gene*, a Victorian ruin, discovered during a walk through the Irish racial Green Zone of London, registers a reactionary comment on the text's depiction of the future city troubled by class conflict, racial invasion and patriarchal

---

[34] Thus, Thatcherite apologists, such as Shirley Robin Letwin, maintain that Thatcher herself offered such a gateway beyond a debased present: 'The old morality did not ... completely lose its hold on the people of Britain. Like a faint melody, more nearly felt than heard, it remained an important strain in the atmosphere of the country and continued to impart a distinctive quality to life in Britain. Many yearned to hear the melody more distinctly. But being unaware of having heard it at all, they could hardly give voice to their yearning' (337). Thatcher, then, in Letwin's analysis provides such a jarring of perspective.

breakdown, but also points longingly towards a former splendour, and indeed, an imperial cartography:

> Once there had been here, too, neat plaster mouldings along cornices and over pillared porticos, but these had long fallen away. Whole facades were black with the smoke of sea-coal; most windows were broken, and woodwork paintless; occasional houses were better preserved, but painted such curious colours that Humayan guessed the paint must have been a cheap job-lot, or stolen by workmen at some building site. But the weighty architecture, the decay, gave most of the houses the look of those crumbling mausoleums in the British cemetery in Bombay (77).

Comparably, in Seymour's *The Glory Boys* a Victorian terrace used as a London safehouse by an IRA man gathers against its collective fantasy historical anxieties over Irish immigration, familial dislocation, class and social fragmentation:

> The street was made up of four-storey Victorian terraced houses. Up to fifty years ago these were middle-class homes, complete with maid and cook to work in the basement kitchens and to sleep in the attic bedrooms; expensive and sought after. But those families had long since abandoned the houses as ghostly, costly white elephants, and fled to the cheaper more territorially secure suburbs. The houses had disintegrated into flatlets owned by landlords who lived far from the premises (66).

Ironically, Belfast – given the contempt and gothicization its representation generally contains in 'Troubles' fiction and upon which I shall focus in a later chapter – also offers a utopian space for such allochronic investment, facilitated by its Victorian and industrial heritage. Frederick Nolan idealizes the university area as 'like a set of *The Forsyte Saga*, full of Victorian schools, churches and terraced houses' (130), whilst Shaun Clarke refers to Belfast's 'stately Victorian architecture ... If Belfast was not a pretty sight, it had been scarred by the very people laying claim to it' (1993, 195). A review of A.F.N. Clarke's *Contact* in the *Times Literary Supplement* demonstrates the interplay of *redemptive* and *repressive* modalities in the English national imagination, as although the Irish are again dismissed as inveterately violent, there is also a contradictory and emulous utopian gesture to the forms of community offered by Belfast and dissipated in Britain: 'The Belfast slums are violent just as the slums of Glasgow and Liverpool used to be violent – and also split along sectarian lines. But in Britain, the old slums were destroyed and the occupants sent to high-rise slums in the suburbs, where they are now even more miserable, but no longer tightly knot in their fierce, defensive communities' (Richard West, 455).

Therefore, on one structural level of the 'Troubles' thriller's political unconscious the Irishness which it seeks to destroy is also the desiring space of an evocative allegory of community, as conveyed by the national alliance regulated by the Tyrone Priest in Seymour's *The Journeyman Tailor* (which contrasts markedly with the uncertain popular subject addressed by Hurd's Prime Minister in *Vote to Kill*): 'He married the hard men, he baptised their children, and if they were ambushed he buried them in the Republican plot in the cemetery field ... They were the businessmen, the wealthy; the unemployed, the poor; they were the farmers and the tradesmen and the skilled workers; they were the volunteers of the Provisional wing of the Irish Republican Army' (62-63). This formal antinomy is illustrated by the recurrent 'terrorizing the terrorists' strategy employed by many of these texts, such as de St. Jorre and Shakespeare's *The Patriot Game*: 'It's the jungle – a green Irish jungle. You've got to descend to their bog level and treat them in the only way they'll ever understand' (83). Whilst the *repressive* modality vents an often rampant racism demanding the structural elimination of Irishness and Irish characters, the whole premise of 'terrorizing the terrorists' divulges an effort to adopt the values and wish-fulfilments encoded in the ideologeme of the Terrorist – an ideologeme invoking allegories of community, of assured masculinity, of national commitment. It is indeed precisely this yearning, utopian engagement that necessitates its formal eradication – it must remain an allochronic rune, if its allegorical efficacy and allure is to operate for a troubled national imaginary. In this manner, the *redemptive* and *repressive* dialectical investment is a paradigm of the formal logic of Orientalist discourse, which, Eamonn Hughes posits, is based not on assimilation or appropriation but on 'annexation' (1987, 100), so that the dominant subject of the 'Troubles' thriller seeks to restore to itself the collective value systems ascribed to the other and reworked in the political unconscious. Thus, in Gordon Stevens' *Provo*, the cynical journalist Patrick Saunders is embroiled in a 'Troubles' plot, with the security of the Royal family at stake, and finds the stirring of 'some misbegotten sense of duty, he laughed at himself, some misguided loyalty, even patriotism' (160).

The implications of the dialectic between annexation and *repressive* elimination are demonstrated by the closure of *Harry's Game*. Harry Brown successfully kills the IRA hitman, Billy Downs, but is then mistakenly mortally wounded by nearby British soldiers and shot whilst dying by Downs' wife. On the surface level, as J. Bowyer Bell relates, a tragic, ironic end to this British state hero's mission: 'Harry gets "The Man" and is killed by his own' (1978, 22). However, if it is recalled that Brown was originally an Ulster Protestant, then a much more profound structural resolution is sought. Under the attentive gaze of a British military presence, and indeed through its direct intervention, both the major Irish characters and ideological ciphers of the text, representing both Nationalism and Unionism, are deleted. There are, therefore, sweeping sociopolitical ramifications concerning the treatment of Irish people and the handling of the Northern conflict contained in the attempt to explain the 'Troubles' as an intractable racial peculiarity of the sequestered causality that Strong terms 'the cruelty of Irish history' (1995, 278). A superintending Britishness strives concurrently to disengage its responsibility and robustly assert its power, and, in *Harry's Game*, produces the formal exigency of Irish erasure: 'Each was determined to destroy the other' (242).

However, whilst the anti-Irish racism contained in the depictions of the 'zoo smell' (16) of the IRA characters in Lane's *Forgive the Executioner* is contextualized by studies of English racism such as the work of Liz Curtis, I would contend that there is an additional, or perhaps under-emphasized, intricacy in the racism directed against Loyalists in these texts and which unfolds further schisms in the thriller's production of a British identity. In *The Psalm Killer*, for example, the leading protagonist, Inspector Cross, imparts how 'the problem with the Ulster Protestants was they'd become Irishized, by which he took to mean a grand inability to sort one's own problems' (Petit, 524-525). In addition, a British Army Major in *The Bomb That Could Lip-Read* proclaims that 'The bigotry of the extremists made him ashamed of his fellow countrymen' (Seaman, 60).[35]

Such acts of seemingly mature, civilized British disavowal of Unionist and Loyalist beckonings of allegiance may be contextualized by the framework of Bhabha's theory of 'colonial mimicry' (1994, 86), which is useful not so much in its ascription of coloniality but because it proffers a mechanism for comprehending the contradictions produced by dominant and subjugated articulations of Britishness. The Loyalist entry into the signifying fields of this Britishness challenges the universality and authority of the dominant subject, which regards the former as the contestatory eruptions of, in Bhabha's terms, 'a subject of a difference that is almost the same, but not quite' (1994, 86). Liam O'Dowd posits that

> Ulster Unionists' frequent over-identification with British nationalist symbols has led to them being characterized as outside the realms of normal British politics. For many nationalists in Britain, unionism is an unwelcome reminder of the past – of the coercive nature of British State formation, of the role of militant Protestantism and of a fixation with Irish nationalism which seems irrelevant in contemporary Europe (108-109).

Where I would disagree with O'Dowd, then, is in his suggestion that Unionism embarrasses the dominant English nationalism by reviving an anachronistic past. Given the rampant patriotism of the populist militarism produced in these texts as imaginary solutions to the historical antinomies of the present, it is rather that this re-articulation of British symbolism serves to undercut the impartiality and omnipresence of contemporary English nationalist interventions in Ireland:

> the excess or slippage produced by the *ambivalence* of mimicry (almost the same, *but not quite*) does not merely 'rupture' the discourse, but becomes transformed into an uncertainty which fixes the colonial subject as a 'partial presence' ... It is as if the very emergence of the 'colonial' is dependent for its representation upon some strategic limitation or prohibition *within* the authoritative discourse itself. The success of colonial appropriation depends upon on a proliferation of inappropriate objects that ensure its strategic failure, so that mimicry is at once resemblance and menace (Bhabha, 1994, 86).

The representation of a neutral, civilized English subject regulating an obscure tribal war is threatened and destabilized by the subordinate, displaced, yet itself eventually displacing, gaze of Loyalism: 'What emerges between mimesis and

---

[35] Peter Leslie's *The Extremists* – published by the New English Library, the source of a number of unashamedly English right-wing thrillers – decries: 'The patriotism of the Orangemen is perverted by narrowmindedness – by bloody ignorance' (64).

mimicry is a *writing*, a mode of representation, that marginalizes the monumentality of history, quite simply mocks its power to be a model, that power which supposedly makes it imitable' (Bhabha, 1994, 87). Put succinctly, Loyalism as mimicry undermines the transmission of Britishness as universal value and democratic reformation, returning the British thriller to its implication in an English nationalist hegemonic struggle for meaning and empowerment.[36]

The seemingly tragic end to another thriller evidences another allegorical template in the British thriller. In Lane's *Forgive the Executioner*, the IRA terrorist, Siobahn (sic), with whom the hero, Alan Paine, had an affair, dies saving the maverick's life and eliminating her Irish compatriots. The text here points to another of this English imaginary's national allegories: a filiative shard, the reworking of the evocative fragment of the family as social signifier. For, as the final Irish character lies dying, a reconstituted family fantastically reveals itself to Paine and sanctions his actions:

> He heard children's voices in the passage, but did not see the shocked people crowding in to the doorway of the hotel chalet, nor hear Siobahn [sic] Mahoney ask chokingly for a doctor. Instead he saw his own children, Stephanie and Timothy, in his delirium ... Then he saw his wife, Ellen, and she was looking at him with a new understanding which she had not shown before. 'It's all right, Alan, I forgive you, God forgives you' (219).

The text actually opens with Paine's dissatisfaction at his dull family life and job as a desk clerk in the Ministry of Defence, and when his wife suggests that he rejoin the army he derides her 'pathetic illusions of grandeur': 'Britain is all washed up. There's no need for anyone anymore – just a few boys to be spat on and killed over in Ireland' (7). The ideologeme of the terrorist's formal function, then, is to furnish this symbiotic familial and national disenchantment, paradoxically through the latter's extirpation, with the means of reconstructing itself as an ideal allegory of filiative cohesion through which a revivified imperial and masculine self is secured. The imaginary resolution of an organic family spectrally ratifying the production of new British identities also permeates Andy McNab's *Remote Control*. In this text SAS soldier, Nick Stone, who has not seen his own family in over twenty years – suggesting a filiative crisis – decides to visit the idealized home of an SAS colleague in Washington after an assignment: 'I'd grown up with this fantasy of the perfect family and as far as I was concerned Kev had it' (53). However, Stone arrives to find that the whole family, with the exception of the youngest daughter have been murdered. It is the protection of this filiative rune which sustains Stone through his journey back to England, through a global conspiracy involving American State officials, British Intelligence and the IRA, and through the following admission as he brings the child with him from Washington: 'This wasn't her home anymore. Now she was the same as me. Neither of us had one' (406).

---

[36] A welcome study of precisely these tensions between British nationalism and Unionism and Loyalism is provided by the work of Alan Parkinson.

In the effort to construct a new hegemonic subject, the ideological unit of the family is hence a paradigmatic but contestatory site offering recourse to filiative intimations of a Britain of traditional continuity and organic wholeness. It is a core signifier for both Left and Right. New Labour voices such as Will Hutton bemoan 'the crisis of parenting and general communal decay which are at the root of so many of Britain's social problems' (15), while Thatcher contends that 'the breakdown of families is the starting point for a range of social ills' (629). Thatcher notably asserts that 'the nation is but an enlarged family' (Harris, ed. 1997, 123). This refraction of filiative codes onto the naturalization of social authority is mirrored in Gordon Stevens's *Provo*, wherein a crisis phone call between the Prime Minister and the Queen 'was no longer a discussion between head of government and monarch, was a conversation between a father and a mother' (465). Nevertheless, the problematics of a settled home, evidenced above in the conclusion of Nelson's *The Minstrel Code* and exacerbated by the interregnum, were in many respects compounded by the dialectics of home produced by Thatcherism. For the seeming delivery of 'home' to 'the people', to 'the family', through policies of private ownership and the sale of council housing, demanded as its requisite the problematization and disruption of existing patterns of community and relationality upon which 'home' was negotiated. As Thatcher's infamous assertion that 'there is no such thing as society, there are only individuals and their families'[37] conveys, the filiative allegory in the 'Troubles' thriller is necessitated by the irresolvable historical antinomy between the increasingly meritocratic, middle-class character of the modern state and idealized forms of residual commonality through which the former must seek to habituate and legitimate itself. The New Right hegemonic project in particular, then, was impelled to produce an imaginary solution to its contradictory attempt to insert itself in the rupture of the very filiative ideologeme of Victorian and imperial continuity to which it laid claim.

In the 'Troubles' thriller, the imaginary resolution again entails an allochronic utopian investment in a desiring space through which contradictory filiative allegories are reworked in the political unconscious. In Stephen Leather's *The Chinaman*, to give one example, a Vietnam veteran whose family is murdered by an IRA bomb relentlessly and personally hunts down their killers after losing faith in the state authorities' ability to bring them to justice. In the text's denouement 'the Chinaman' is mistakenly shot dead along with the IRA unit by the SAS. Rather than accepting this, however, as a tragic end to one man's quest to avenge the killing of his family, a grasp of the historical compromise and mobilization, which the *redemptive* and *repressive* structural modalities seek, enables the assessment of a more profound resolution to the contradictions of the British nation state. Both 'the Chinaman' and the terrorists serve as utopian repositories of codes of honour and filiative belonging which the text must rehearse and laud but then anxiously have eliminated, even as it presents them for recuperation by the emissaries of the state as residual traces of social formations which capitalism has sought contradictorily to harness and destroy.

---

[37] Cited by Jim MacLaughlin, 'The New Vanishing Irish' in MacLaughlin, ed. 136.

A comparable formal imperative is elicited by Clancy's *Patriot Games*, which Clancy himself considers a verification of his belief that 'the family is the basic building block of society, period. From my perspective, family is the beginning and end of everything that we're supposed to be working for' (Greenberg, 65). Moreover, in his review of this text wherein the CIA hero, Jack Ryan saves both his own family and that of the British Royalty from Republican attack, Marc A. Cerasini postulates that 'Clancy utilizes the royal family, and the family of Jack Ryan, for a thematic purpose. The importance – or, rather, the necessity – of the family unit to the continued health of human society is central to the theme of this novel' (27). By contrast, Cerasini persists, the terrorists 'are universal misfits, men without hope – they have no lovers, no families, and, by extension, no future. They possess neither comprehensible human emotions nor the normal societal bonds that make men truly civilized' (28). However, such interpretations elide the fact that the plot is actually driven by Ryan's killing of Sean Miller's brother, which then drives Miller on a quest for revenge. One reason for this erasure is the typically imperialist desire to obliterate other forms of family, of community, of belonging, that are perceived as oppositional or alternative, but my analysis is also proposing that this eradication is further necessitated by the utopian investment which an American capitalist society makes in Miller's filiative commitment, by the desire to disguise its annexation. A defence of the family that is premised on the destruction of the family: this formal antinomy exemplifies the contradictions of the purportedly civilized and stable social identities constructed by the international thriller's representation of the 'Troubles'.

Analogous textual mechanics are evidenced by Shaun Clarke's *Underworld* in which the SAS Sergeant, Michael Burton, mistakenly kills a child in a raid on a Republican home but, his Brigadier relates, 'Burton's accidental shooting of that unfortunate child in Belfast has, if anything, strengthened his bond to his own children. He will certainly have been making amends through his own children for what happened in Belfast' (71). Burton is, however, still racked with guilt by the episode and is presented with a means 'to find redemption or compensate for his past' (258) through a new mission to eliminate the IRA leadership and supposedly cement the Peace Process. On his way to completing his assignment, Burton's means of redemption is through an affair with a prostitute, Teresa, whom he rescues from the clutches of the paramilitaries, providing an obvious means by which Desire attempts to override History, and in particular a problematical sense of historical culpability: 'as he made love to her, Burton knew what true desire was, his need for her transcending his whole life's history and melting guilt in its heat' (425). When Burton confesses his story to her, we are informed that 'he felt redeemed, as if the love that had been given and received had healed the scars on his broken heart' (432). Ironically, it then transpires that Teresa was in fact the murdered girl's sister, and she kills Burton in the apocalyptic final scene – in which, incidentally, Burton does successfully exterminate all the terrorists – but is then driven to distracted suicide herself. Therefore, whilst the *redemptive* modality on some level attempts to atone for a disruption of the Irish family, another formal modality actually ensures that Burton's initial intervention achieves its historical completion as the last surviving member of the family dies, in an eradication parallel to that of the terrorists, intimating this English imaginary's correlation of the terrorist and the family as ideologemes for Irish people and society more generally.

Burton's relationship with Teresa also foregrounds a further allegory by which the British 'Troubles' thriller strives to produce a secure and mobilizatory identity through the use of Northern Ireland as a desiring space: namely, the recapitulation of an imperial masculinity; the simplification of the contradictions and complexities of the historical relationship between Ireland and England to a protracted colonial romance.[38] In Clarke's *Underworld*, the gendered terms of colonial discourse provide a primary relationality for naturalizing and replenishing the Orientalist positional hierarchy of Ego-Id historical representations, and the entrapment of Teresa and Burton in the same, reciprocal historical identity underlines the utilization of the 'Troubles' as a secret self: 'Ya still have nightmares about the other one, that poor wee child who ran screamin' out of there. Yeah, that was me, Burton. That was me at nine years old. Ya shot my Dad an' my sister and that drove m' Mum mad an' then you an' I shared our separate nightmares, though we both had the same dreams' (458). Intertwining Irish and English national identities on one level, this stratified British historical binary seeks (contradictorily on the very mechanics of its positionings) to exculpate and disaffiliate a civilized English self. Thus when the text engages the reader in its many sordid sex and violence scenes, Burton, it is affirmed, is 'divorced from his decent self' (325). The North is once more voided as the desiring space for the imaginary resolution and indulgence of the contradictions of that 'decent self': 'Burton's interest in the Regiment was as deep and abiding as his love for [his wife]. He was, in fact, interested in military history in general and in the peculiar psychology of professional soldiers. Though a civilized man, he felt happiest when fighting a war and had never worked out why this was so. He was not a violent man by nature, but he certainly thrived on risk and took pride in doing his duty well' (107). The performative instrumentality of Ireland as empty receptacle, as the nightmare of the other, helps explicate the discursive complexes producing the paradox noted by Liz Curtis: 'Britain has one of the most violent and uncivilised histories of any European country, yet the orthodox view is that the English are both non-violent and civilised, and that it is the people whom Britain has oppressed who are violent and uncivilised' (1984a, 96).

The historical problematics of the North, under the codification of this allegory of imperial masculinity, become reducible to the perilous allure of the *femme fatale*, as with the North-as-prostitute in *Underworld*: 'those eyes were unavoidable, that face was flame and heat, and like a moth, he was being drawn to his own destruction' (324). The text then completes the transposition of these deadly traits onto the nation itself: 'Ireland, even the North, was a wild country and its passions ran deep. Beneath the charm of this place were murderous feelings that

---

[38] To an extent, the 'Troubles' wishes the resumption of a traditional frontier, imperial masculinity capable of finding new forms of manliness for metropolitan acceptance and consumption. For salient work on this tradition of English masculinity see work by John M. MacKenzie (1987); David B. Espey (1978); Richard Phillips (1997).

blew in on the wind' (441-442). In constructing a potential and optimal readership for the 'Troubles' thriller, this colonial romance obviously privileges male subjective experience and seeks recourse to an immemorialized collective masculinity upon which a national identity may be established and reconfigured.[39] Notably, *Underworld* relates that its SAS hero 'had seen enough to last him a lifetime, enough to break many men, but he stood there unbroken' (Clarke, 442), and this seamless masculinity brokered from the imperial liaison offers a respecification not only of the discourse of colonialism but also a homogenizing point of suture to circumvent social and historical flux and contestation.

The allegory of an imperial masculinity is engaged by the *redemptive* and *repressive* modalities of popular fiction to enact the potential scenarios of this desire and its resolutions to historical dilemmas. Vindications of military intervention, for example, are performed through the utilization of a perverse Irish sexuality to imply that such violence on some level actually satiates an Irish craving, as in the relationship between the SAS major and his Celtic Lance-Corporal in Nelson's *The Minstrel Code*:

> The rage which rose in him whenever he thought of those terrorists was in him still, and the energy in that rage throbbed into his groin and impaled the girl upon a shaft of iron ... He had made love to her only twice before, and each time it had been as fierce and frantic as it now had been, and each time also Major Shaw had afterwards left to fly off on a mission, and to return later with the cold-eyed look of death upon his face. Sheila Row, the Scotch-Irish blood streaming through her hungry body, found making love to such killers the most fantastically fulfilling and erotic thing she'd ever imagined (172).

Alternatively, the recapitulation of this colonial romance also authorizes the concession and expurgation of a sense of historical guilt, as illustrated by Newman's *The Testing Ground*. The text, which centres its plot on the Stalker Inquiry, begins with the pederast Head of British Intelligence, Sir Michael Newfield, making his way to an East Belfast boys' home, determined to pass on his AIDS virus as a kind of punitive retribution. When MI5 later inform the Stalker-figure, Jack Bentham, of Newfield's pederasty and illness, they laughingly refer to the North as 'a veritable mud-pit we're all wading around in' (327). This figuration of Northern Ireland as a violated boy's anus signifies an awareness of the corruption and denigration of the sexualized terms of the imperial attachment. The text offers a redemptive romance in the affair between Bentham and Maureen McFadden, the mother of a child murdered by the Shoot to Kill policy which Bentham has been sent to investigate. However, whilst on one structural plane Bentham's love for McFadden spurs his inquiry on to uncover the truth, the

---

[39] Lane's *The Ulsterman* exemplifies how the most rudimentary gender formulations of colonial discourse are recapitulated, as the empowerment conferred upon Chris Boggs is produced through not only his subjugation of a willing femininity but also the debilitation of Irish masculinity: 'he was a Protestant policeman, and she was a Catholic patriot. But he was a *man*; she knew that instinctively. He was not like her husband – an aging repressed queer' (23).

imaginary resolution to a British articulation of culpability proffered by this romance is evinced by the Irishwoman's reaction to Bentham's admission that he is conducting the investigation for her: 'Don't do it for me, Jack, I told you, I would rather forget' (295). This sanction of historical amnesia and McFadden's subsequent murder confirm how the fantasy of this figuration of the Irish female functions as the site of an expression of a historical guilt and its erasure.

Hence, the formal elimination of Irish figures in the British 'Troubles' thriller demonstrates that the representation of Northern Ireland as a desiring space in which to construct a stable English identity, to seek to circumvent the historical rupture of class, community and masculinity, entails the writing of the people of Northern Ireland out of their own historical moment. In Clarke's *Underworld*, the SAS hero Burton claims as he nears the completion of his covert operation that in eliminating the final two IRA leaders at their home and secretly disposing of them that 'There'll just be an empty house' (445) – a phrase which succinctly intimates the problematics presented to Irish thriller writers when engaging in a discursive field which has instigated a dominant configuration of representations of the North as historically voided, as exoticized empty receptacle. In contextualizing the problematics of home, of representing Irish history and Irish communities produced by such hegemonic inflections in my next chapter (on Unionist and Nationalist representations) I shall utilize Joep Leerssen's formulation of 'auto-exoticism' (1996b, 37).

Nevertheless, given that I have attempted to illustrate hegemonic process and contestation within the British subjectivities produced across these texts, it is worth considering not only the disservice the 'Troubles' thriller perpetrates on the Irish, but also what justice it affords the millions of people unemployed during this era of putative national greatness, the dissipated communities of the mining villages, the disenfranchised people of the inner city or the scapegoats for the destruction of the Welfare state. There is a certain vacuous pathos in many of the historical allegories insinuating themselves in the English national imaginary of these texts, huge discarded hulks retrieved and raised as paradoxical bearers of a collective historical amnesia in the very act of their being remembered. However, the analysis of the interplay of the *redemptive* and *repressive* modalities of popular fiction in this chapter has indicated that the 'Troubles' thriller is not mere mass manipulation or propaganda. The dialectic between ideological framing and utopian longing must be kept in sight if the attempt to comprehend the mobilization of a popular subject within and across these texts is to be achieved. To this end, the closure of Hugo Barnacle's *Day One*, a text set against the backdrop of the Falklands war in which an IRA plot is resisted, is revealing. As the Task Force embark to do battle, a resonant seafaring allegory seeks to withstand its hiemal pessimism by convoking a litanous lost geography of provincial and working-class sites of tradition and community within an insistent imperial trajectory: 'A thousand miles away to sea already, exercises over, the first ships, the tanker *Tidespring*, the frigates *Brilliant*, *Arrow* and *Plymouth*, and the destroyers *Antrim*, *Glamorgan*, *Glasgow*, *Coventry* and *Sheffield*, head on south, towards the winter' (272).

Chapter 2

'And What Do You Call It?': The Thriller and the Problematics of Home in Northern Irish Writing

'The North is a cultural corridor'.
Edna Longley

Home is supposed to be familiar, particularly for filiative ideologies. Can one therefore be at home in a contested territory such as the North, where one is nationally two places at once? Rather than viewing the problematics of home in the North, however, as induced by the impacting of two narrative coherencies (i.e. British and Irish Nationalism), this chapter intends to investigate how the Northern state evidences the contradictions of both.[1] The preceding chapter suggested that the problematization of home is by no means peculiar to Irish culture and also forms the basis of the wistful, imperial allegories of an English imaginary and the range of filiative belonging in American culture. Undoubtedly though, the concept of home within Irish culture is tainted by a specific colonial inflection, which obviously makes the place one inhabits become strange. Yet the problematization of home and belonging in Northern writing is not reducible to a colonial affliction or binarized national collision, but also invokes a complex totality of displacements such as class and gender. I shall initially examine both the problematics and the strategic affinities operative in the engagement by Irish writers with overarching international representations of the North as historically voided.[2] A constructive theoretical framework for quantifying such a representational hegemony, through which Irish historical agents are written out

---

[1] Feargal Cochrane declares that, in relation to the North, British and Irish Nationalism 'resemble the benevolent visitors to their schizophrenic relations in a mental home' (1994, 378-379). Cochrane's metaphor neatly suggests a regulated 'home' that constructs a false intimacy and privacy – a theme which will inform this chapter. A consummate account of the incapacity of both Irish and British Nationalism to deal concretely with the Northern state is offered by Joe Cleary's '"Fork-Tongued on the Border Bit": Partition and the Politics of Form in Contemporary Narratives of the Northern Irish Conflict' *South Atlantic Quarterly* 95;1. 1996. 227-276.

[2] In a sense, such a sedimentation goes to the heart of how hegemony functions, by producing a pleasure for Irish readers and authors alike, which internalizes the political estrangement of the discourse and makes the experienced historical moment less and less familiar.

of their historical moment, is provided by Joep Leerssen's formulation of 'auto-exoticism'. Therein 'Ireland is made exotic by the self-same descriptions which purport to represent or explain Ireland' (1996b, 37).[3] The international thriller's *repressive* desire to explicate the recalcitrant mystery of Northern Irish society provides a specific historical representational bloc, which attests to Leerssen's postulation that the post-Union articulative skew of Irish identity bequeathed a profound and persistent historical legacy that continues to view Ireland as 'an anomaly, a riddle, a question, a mystery: something to be explained, an explicandum' (1996b, 38). Nevertheless, in a late capitalist and popular cultural context, it is important to bear in mind that we are not dealing only with the imperatives of colonial cartography or the mechanics of exoticism but also with processes of commodification in the thriller. Furthermore, the binary oppositions of colonizer/colonized, metropole/periphery, England/Ireland, tend to homogenize and position their constituent parts into self-contained integrity. The national formation is a contestatory terrain, which seeks to order a specific constellation of class and social forces as part of a wider world system. Thus, in utilizing the auto-exoticism framework as a means of contextualizing the negotiations between a range of dominant and subordinate subject positions, due attention must be given to the concrete historical displacements of class and gender if the mystification of a unitary national subjectivity is to be circumvented.[4]

In examining auto-exoticism in the 'Troubles' thriller, I do not want to suggest that the thriller form itself, and by extension, the global market are themselves external to or outside of Irish fiction. For this would itself be a preposterous piece of auto-exoticization. I am therefore not implying that the thriller is in itself an imposed representational estrangement upon disempowered Northern writing but rather that it often seeks to reactivate and maintain lingering sedimentations of exoticized discourse on Ireland more generally. It is important to grant Northern writers agency within specific historical conditions with regard to the state. The delineation of all Irish writers as passively afflicted by auto-exoticism and the alienating gravitational pull of the metropolitan market actually serve to exculpate Irish Nationalism and Unionism as systems which have effected their own class

---

[3] Whilst Leerssen's model specifically addresses the nineteenth-century Irish novel after the Act of Union, its account of the post-Union shift in the articulation of Irish identity within a metropolitan frame of reference and the concomitant need for Irish novelists primarily and exigently to address a *destinataire*, an intended or target, and most importantly, empowered, audience beyond Ireland does proffer a valuable historical apparatus, to be utilized critically and with care, for investigating the relation of Irish novelists to the international thriller market.

[4] Moreover, by utilizing Leerssen's model, I am discussing the North through a framework focused upon 'Ireland' more generally. My justification for this apparent slippage is twofold. Firstly, that the international thriller seeks to resuscitate stereotypes of 'Ireland' as putatively distilled in the Northern 'Troubles' and its apparent perpetuation of the traumatic historical paradigm. Secondly, both Irish Nationalism and Unionism/British Nationalism lack the cognitive capacity to map the Northern State as a national conjuncture and consequently engage in a stereotyping for which the exotic 'Ireland' provides a ready discursive arsenal.

and social displacements. In short, it fails to acknowledge that the portrayal of Northern Ireland as unresolved stasis by Irish writers is often an active and indeed necessary formal response to historical antagonism and change by indigenous dominant ideologies in crisis. So stereotyping is not circumscribable to the representational zero degree of some unitary colonial formation.[5] With regard to post-colonial theory, Colin Graham astutely deems Ireland to be a *fractured* or *impacted* (1994, 42) entity as a European colony, both metropolitan and peripheral. But it is also necessary to reflect upon all national formations under capitalism as impacted in another much more terminal sense: as configurations of antagonistic class and social forces.

With these qualifications, I shall attempt to utilize Leerssen's theoretical model. Certainly the thriller's concentration on the 'Troubles', as an overloaded ideological complex of stereotyped national traits and determinations at their most elemental, affirms the continued and underlying prevalence of Leerssen's framework.[6] Leerssen maintains that the perspective is always '*on* Ireland *from outside*; no matter how sympathetic that perspective may be, no matter how much the propagandistic intent of the novel may be to create a positive understanding for Ireland, Ireland is always a passive object of representation' (1996b, 36). An emphasis on the political unconscious, however, defeats any attempt to regard History, and in this case, the North, as a reified object of representation. Even as many of these thrillers attempt to perpetuate representations of Ireland as immemorial trauma, the political unconscious provides a timely censure. It is a reminder of the prior, ineluctable subtext of historical problematics and class anxieties, which exact such ideological fantasies. The dehistoricized stasis of the thriller's representations of Northern Ireland produces a wilful historical amnesia and attenuation that is compounded in a double-bind by a wider historical attachment to the myopia of late capitalism and postmodernism. As a result, Jameson's eloquent portent becomes particularly appropriate:

> History can be apprehended only through its effects, and never directly as some reified force. This is indeed the ultimate sense in which History as ground and

---

[5] I suggested in my previous chapter that the imperial allegories of the British 'Troubles' thriller sought not only to grapple with Anglo-Irish relationships but also to constellate and disguise a series of historical materials concerning class, gender, race and sexuality around a dominant subject. In an ironic but nonetheless historically-vindicated way, therefore, post-imperial England is itself the last colony, whose demystified social inequalities are now unraveling. Stereotyping and exoticism, that is, do not have an originary (colonial) subject but are more concretely devices deployed within a range of historical conditions by dominant representational frameworks.

[6] Leerssen contends that *auto-exoticism* induces the desire 'to look for one's own identity in the unusual, the extraordinary, the exotic aspects of experience, to conflate the notions of one's distinctness and one's distinctiveness. Irish history, as a result, tends to be traced back to mythical, fictional but colonial roots; Irish life tends to be reduced to its un-English roots' (1996b, 225). However, as I have suggested, Leerssen's model, under a binarized colonial model, presents auto-exoticism as only an unwilled self-estrangement, a colonial displacement.

untranscendable horizon needs no particular theoretical justification: we may be
sure that its alienating necessities will not forget us, however much we might
prefer to ignore them (1996, 102).

The task, therefore, is to trace the unswerving lessons etched by History as an
ideology of form, which sunders the strategies of representational delimitation
produced by the conventional 'Troubles' thriller.

I shall begin by analysing how Irish authors attempt to position themselves,
within an economy of auto-exoticism, as mediators of a strange Irish otherness to
the international thriller market. This interpretative stance of knowledgeable
mediator is particularly evident in writers who have either emigrated or writers
with Irish links who have established successful careers as thriller writers in the
fiction industry, such as Jack Higgins, Daniel Easterman and Victor O'Reilly. For
these 'name' thriller writers, Ireland becomes, through the authenticity granted by
their Irish attachments, a terrain to be explained to a world audience. In O'Reilly's
paranoid, reiterative realm of counter-terrorism – 'a world with no exit' (1994,
16) – Ireland, in the guise of his aristocratic hero, Hugo Fitzduane, becomes one
port of call in an interminable worldwide network of corruption and counter-
measure. Easterman's *Day of Wrath* utilizes its representation of 'the Northern
Irish jungle' (1995) as the static backdrop for a bizarre international conspiracy.[7]
The value of Northern Ireland to the thriller form after the end of the Cold War
draws directly upon exoticized sedimentations produced by the first two decades
of the conflict, which established its displaced and atavistic functionality. Shaun
Herron, who was born in Carrickfergus and emigrated to Canada from where he
published a series of thrillers starring his CIA hero, John Miro, subsequently used
the 'Troubles' as the setting for two books. One, *Through the Dark and Hairy
Wood*, dealing with Loyalist paramilitaries, and the other, *The Whore Mother*,
with Irish Nationalism and Republicanism. The auto-exoticization of Ireland as a
strange, mysterious land provides much of the thrill or suspense in these texts:
'Nowhere in the world ... could paranoid men find a more deeply paranoid setting
than this one to work in' (Herron, 1973a, 148).[8] The two fundamental components
of auto-exoticism outlined by Leerssen are capitulated in Herron's texts. Firstly,
Leerssen notes 'the constant automatism of explaining Ireland in terms of its past,
as if the Real Ireland is somehow unfinished business from bygone ages, or has a
privileged relation to the past that here is more immediate than elsewhere' (1996b,

---

[7] In the text, Muslim leaders at a conference in Dublin are kidnapped, in retaliation for the
taking hostage of SAS agents during the Gulf War, by CIA operatives improbably led by
David Koresh, who, the text relates, was rescued from Waco by the FBI in a secret deal.
Here, the terrain of the Northern conflict functions as an exoticized anyplace, readily
transposable with other stock trouble spots in the international thriller's reiterative,
interchangeable locale. Hence, Easterman describes 'the war zone of West Belfast' in the
following terms: '[i]t is the West Bank in another place. No-one really wants to be here,
no-one dares live anywhere else' (169).

[8] Herron's work thus affords a reactionary thrill through an immersion in the insecurities of
sheer, displaced otherness in the guise of 'the native Irish genius for conspiracy and
intrigue' (1973b, 241).

38). Accordingly, we are informed in an extraordinary piece of pithy historical elision in *Through the Dark and Hairy Wood* that 'in 1645 the Johnstones came from Scotland. One of them, in the long passage of time, founded the Loyal Orange Order. In time – in the 1960s, which is only a day or two from 1645 – an O'Neill again governed Ulster and Johnstone's Orangemen dragged him down' (1973a, 164).[9]

The second mainstay of auto-exoticism is, Leerssen contends, 'the tacit but by no means self-evident presupposition that Ireland is most itself in those aspects wherein it is most un-cosmopolitan, most unlike other nations' (1996b, 38). Thus, in *The Whore Mother* Ireland readily removes itself, for a disillusioned Irish Republican, McManus, both spatially and temporally from world progress: 'He felt disassociated. That was what the look and the feel of Ireland did to Irishmen. It made you feel disassociated – from any kind of responsibility, from anything tangible, from the rest of the world. The world was so very far away from Ireland – at a great distance over the hills and through the mists and far far away. It was far off in the present' (1973b, 120). The text endorses an auto-exoticization process, which Leerssen describes as 'almost obsessively peripheral' (1994, 1). It reactivates what Leerssen saliently formulates, following Bakhtin, as the Celtic *chronotope*, a representational mechanism withdrawing Ireland into the timeless, or more correctly, allochronic seam of the metropolitan/periphery binary: 'History as a process is of the centre. The periphery is lost in a cyclical, natural or static time-warp, forgotten by history, bypassed by history' (1994, 4).

Interestingly, the most glaring displacement in *The Whore Mother* facing the runaway, disillusioned Republican idealist is that of class – the failure to construct a form of home or belonging with the working-class:

> These mean Belfast streets depressed him. They had been his home for nine months, though when he let the word home into his mind the idea that this place could in any sense have become his home repelled him. It had become his prison. The Antrim Road was his home, among Belfast's Protestant middle classes. The first thing he learned when he came here to the Falls – a young Ulster Catholic trying, as Conor Cruise O'Brien had put it, forever romantically to create the heroic past – was that he was an Ulster middle-class Catholic who was as distant from Ulster working-class Catholics as were the Ulster middle-class Protestants. The first undermining blow to his illusions of Irish Catholic comradeship was in his distaste for the coarseness and vulgarity of his comrades. They were urbanized peasants, without the earthy originality of the peasant, or the concrete poetry of his vocabulary (1973b, 13-14).

In the text a deranged Mother Ireland figure shelters and indeed seduces McManus. McManus ultimately considers her and by extension Ireland 'the

---

[9] Despite the text's frequent intertextual references to Louis MacNeice – as in '[t]heir ignorant dead hung over the ignorant living like a plague. They were tribesmen. Their conflict was tribal. Both sides attacked British soldiers for trying to keep them apart' (1973a, 161) – it is evident that the text has no political vision to offer other than its somewhat wearied depictions of tribalized anachronism.

whore we never leave ... No matter where we go we're always here' (1973b, 266), and he declares when they are both caught that 'we were born to self-destruction, child' (1973b, 251). She then burns her house down in a self-dispossession heavily symbolic of auto-exoticism. But it is notable that the text's desire to dehistoricize and disaffiliate Ireland, which culminates in this self-sequestration, designedly intends to retreat into an overarching, immemorialized displacement through which to subsume and mystify the text's class disjuncture. Indeed, the dismissal of the working class as 'urbanized peasants' in the passage above intimates the dislocation of an ideology of a lost, romanticized social order.

The displacements of class or gender, as structurally constitutive of the production of a dominant national subject, must therefore be fundamental components of a study of the problematics of home in Northern Irish writing, if such an undertaking is to be wrestled from collapse into a homogeneous, undifferentiated national-colonial affliction.[10] How does the thriller contribute to this negotiation with home in Northern writing? In an essay on internal émigrés in the Irish novel, Terry Eagleton asserts that 'it is possible to see Ireland as populated by nothing but outsiders' (1998, 216). In an otherwise excellent essay, Eagleton tends to homogenize Irish novelists into a unitary national subject of outsiders without due attention to the additional and concrete dispossessions of class or gender. Consequently, in Eagleton's analysis, the cogent class dynamics in a text such as Patrick MacGill's *Children of the Dead End* become reducible to the same national subjective condition as the privileged posturing of Francis Stuart's outcasts. It is disappointing, but nevertheless symptomatic of the utopian figuration of Ireland as homogeneous, oppositional subject by sections of the British Left, that an accomplished Marxist critic such as Eagleton, with his commanding Althusserian grasp of the ideology of the text and its unsaid, should draw such uncritically direct and unitary correlations in Irish fiction between text and nation, text and History. Thus, whilst Eagleton correctly posits that 'throughout Irish writing, a lonely outcast hungering for freedom revolts, usually unavailingly, against a censorious social order' (1998, 243), it is vital to specify the conditions of such displacement. Often in the 'Troubles' thriller we are confronted, in a reworking of this trend in Irish fiction, with isolated individuals displaced from the traditional social co-ordinates and ideological bearings of the organic communities of filiation. The thriller's own historical emergence amidst the fracture of *idées reçues* in modernity – its attempt to decipher the increasing illegibilities of the social and construct a cartography and belonging from the disruption of former attachments – does provide a formally symbolic means of engaging with the negotiation of home in Northern Irish writing. The thriller's encounter with the dislocations of modernity intimates that its deployment in the

---

[10] For, in a very real sense, those dispossessed from dominant national and historical narratives have never really been home, so that, according to Ernst Bloch, for such collectivities, home becomes a projective, utopian condition: 'If human beings have grasped themselves and what is theirs, without depersonalization and alienation, founded in real democracy, then something comes into being in the world that shines into everyone's childhood and where no one has yet been at home' (quoted by Moylan, 21).

representation of Northern Ireland frustrates the reduction of the plight of the fictive outsider either to a unitary colonial or subversive condition. In many ways, the thriller's attempt to map and uncover social disruption is a thoroughly, even paradigmatic, modern cognitive mode:

> The process of modernization, even as it exploits and torments us, brings our energies and imaginations to life, drives us to grasp and confront the world that modernization makes, and to strive to make it our own. I believe that we and those who come after us will go on fighting to make ourselves at home in this world, even as the homes we have made, the modern street, the modern spirit, go on melting into air (Berman, 348).

Thus, auto-exoticism, whether enforced or willed, serves to overwrite the utopian grappling with displacement in the thriller. Such formal tension is neatly disclosed by Moore's *Lies of Silence*. In Moore's hands, the thriller re-functions his recurrent theme of isolated dissatisfaction with the North, as Michael Dillon's exile provides a privileged vantage point for such a position: 'The minute we got out of Northern Ireland I saw this thing for what it was. A moronic bloody mess. To hell with it' (230). This estrangement confirms Eagleton's broad thesis that 'the Irish novel returns recurrently to those who are both home and away, present and absent simultaneously' (1998, 215). Nonetheless, a complex politics of form is operative in the text that enables a more precise consideration of this dislodgment.

Terence Brown was perhaps the first critic to comment upon the nature of realism in Moore's work, upon how seemingly straightforward realist texts reveal under closer scrutiny 'something unsettling' and off-kilter (1988, 175). Brown perceives that Moore's work explores the possibility that within 'the world in which realism seems an appropriate literary tool there may be things of which it cannot take account' (1988, 183-184). Although Brown focuses primarily on religious faith and fictive artistry, his insight lends itself to a more political reading of form in *Lies of Silence*. The domestic realist plot, concerning Michael Dillon's relationship with his wife and his affair, is subsumed by the thriller when his home is taken over by terrorists. As noted in my discussion of *Victims* and *Proxopera*, a great deal of the terror of the 'Troubles' thriller is unconsciously textualized in this return of the repressed overrunning the putatively stable, propertied interior, which must confront its uncanny doubles. Here, the emphasis is much more urban and bourgeois however. When Michael Dillon emigrates to England he obscures Ireland's historicity in a penumbral inconsequentiality: 'already Ireland seemed a small empty island, lost in the shadow of this land with its millions of people and its history linked to a larger world' (214-215). Here is a paradigmatic moment of the auto-exotic displacement of representing oneself in one's otherness, in one's non-Englishness. However, this deployment of the thriller, as a signifier of the immemorial trauma of an anachronism bypassed by History, is a complicit engagement of form, which seeks to conceal the historical anxieties etched into the text's very form. The usurpation of this bourgeois interior by the figure of the terrorist again actuates a determinate class anxiety, which the generic signal of thriller as exoticism seeks to overarch. This is encapsulated by the confession of Dillon's wife when she is taken hostage: 'I was no different from the poor bloody people who're so scared of them [the terrorists] they keep their mouths shut when the police come around' (133). The text rehearses the inability of filiation to house class antagonism.

Interestingly, of course, the stable bourgeois interior of Dillon's home was already destabilized by his infidelity and his desire to leave his wife. In terms of the interplay of *repressive* and *redemptive* modalities, the figure of the terrorist, so vilified at one textual level, also serves a utopian function. By taking Dillon and his wife hostage in their own home the core filiative ideological signifier of the family is temporarily re-united. Typically in Moore's work, it is the constraint of the filiative which leads his characters into feeling 'trapped' (114) in Belfast, and the guilt at seeking to escape the gravitational pull of this representation of community necessitates Dillon's formal erasure with his killing in the final scene. This specific historical crisis of filiation, and indeed the bourgeois interior, is rewritten through the mediation of the generic code of the thriller, which, in this range of formulations, attempts to collapse such historical anxieties into the terror of the North as anachronistic, perennial trauma.

With specific reference to Irish Nationalism and Unionism, the thriller form does offer a modality for uncovering the tension between state and nation in both ideologies, which, though formulated and rehearsed in different manners, indicates a crisis in the social mappings and co-ordinates of filiation. The problematics of home for Irish Nationalism is succinctly encapsulated by the title of Fionnuala O'Connor's study of Northern Catholics, *In Search of a State*. The dislocation of Northern Nationalism and the problematization of the filiative teleology of a united Ireland are conveyed by Bernard McLaverty's *Cal*. The displacement of Cal McCluskey and his father, Shamie, as the remaining members of a diminishing family which has lost Cal's mother and brother, foregrounds the disintegration of filiation. Cal and his father are the only Catholics living in their estate, which is presided over by a Protestant-owned factory, the abattoir.[11] Notably, Cal and his father find themselves 'whispering in our own house' (28) under the threat of Loyalist attack. The final dispossession occurs after their house is torched and Cal's father is committed to Gransha Mental Hospital whilst Cal himself significantly lives in an abandoned dwelling on the Protestant Morton's property. When the McCluskeys are first subjected to threats by Loyalists, Cal's father declares that 'no Loyalist bastard is going to force me out of my home'. This prompts the following reflection from Cal: 'it wasn't a single bastard, it was an accumulation of them. The feeling of community that they managed to create annoyed him and the stronger their sense of community grew the more excluded and isolated the McCluskeys felt' (9). As with Unionist fears of the pan-Nationalist front, this begrudging anxiety about the

---

[11] This is broadly in keeping with Nationalist figurations of dislocation, for as early as F.L. Green's *Odd Man Out*, wherein Johnny's flight from the robbery of the Protestant factory and fugitive position in the city offer a Nationalist allegory of displacement within the Northern State.

homogenous Other in the equally filiative mechanics of Nationalist ideology is echoed in Fionnuala O'Connor's postulation that 'in the face of a united Unionism that controlled the Northern Ireland State, nationalism before the Troubles was above all disorganised, and Northern Catholics were by and large politically helpless, hopeless and cynical' (44).

The need to reintegrate an organic community in the place of a united Unionist identity of interest informs the text's most desirous formal unconscious. For the text's plot effects a second order Oedipal framework, which indicts the limitations of Irish Nationalism's ability to map the North. As a Catholic, Marcella Morton's marriage to an RUC officer violates the filiative belonging of Irish Nationalism. Cal's involvement with the murder of her husband and eventual Oedipal relation to her as provisional son-lover signify the replacement of one filiative model with another in an imitative, vicarious reconstitution. The Mortons effectively offer an idealized yet reductive family romance for the filiative breakdown of the McCluskeys within this emulative schema. The challenge to Irish Nationalism presented by the Northern state thus produces only a sense of fatalism, an Oedipus-type figure bound by natural and generational imperatives. The text's closure inculcates this resigned passivity, as Cal awaits his crime to be uncovered by the RUC as bearers of justice and order: 'The next morning, Christmas Eve, almost as if he expected it, the police arrived to arrest him and he stood in a dead man's Y-fronts listening to the charge, grateful that at last someone was going to beat him to within an inch of his life' (153). The text thereby rescinds its qualified transgression, the temporary removal of the Law of the Father, figured as the Northern state apparatus, which facilitates a space in which a Northern Irish subject dissolves not only Northern Ireland but also its own placement in that state. The conspiratorial mechanics of the thriller stand redundant as the state formation ultimately remains unchallenged by the text's desire to mystify its own situatedness.

The *leitmotif* of the abattoir as a metaphor of the conflict further removes the North from the grasp of human agency as a production line of brutality and slaughter. Therefore, although the text does attempt to debunk the mythic motivations of modern Nationalism, the heroism which it tries to attribute to the people of the North becomes reducible, through this doomed filiative perspective, to a stoic ineffectuality: 'People were dying every day, men and women were being crippled and turned into vegetables in the name of Ireland. An Ireland which never was and never would be. It was the people of Ulster who were heroic, caught between the jaws of two opposing ideals trying to grind each other out of existence' (83). All the text's filiative mechanics can shore against the conflict and the discourse of the 'Two Communities' is a violated private life. An ideology of formal materials is therefore once more pertinent to this text, as the thriller genre interferes with the bourgeois notion of domesticity and of essential humanity contained in the love plot. Margaret Scanlan posits that 'The novel itself is threatened when the contest between private and social life, one of its oldest themes, is so manifestly unequal. The present is indeed unbearable, and the realistic novelist does not imagine solutions' (1985, 151). Thus, in terms of the politics of literary register, the very act of writing a thriller becomes an indictment of not only the conflict but also Northern Ireland itself and its human agents. As suggested above, the text does seek to imagine a solution to the historical conditions of its production in the form of the reductive Oedipal framework through which a filiative ideal is mimicked if not recapitulated.

Two thrillers written from an Irish Republican perspective utilize the genre to shore an organic community against a criminalized state. *Defenders* is written by a former Republican prisoner, Gerry McGeough, whilst Sean Murphy from the West Belfast Writer's Group produced *Foreign Chains*. I have sought to exercise a theoretical discrimination regarding the representational disposition of the 'Troubles' thriller's international *destinataire* as, by turns, hegemonic imperative and strategic attachment for the dominant ideologies in Ireland. Consequently, it is striking that both texts invest in the depiction of Irish History as recrudescent 'Troubles' in the form of a kind of family saga popularized most notably for an American market by Leon Uris.[12] The family saga mode is deployed to trace the organic continuity informing the current 'Troubles'. Home is seemingly secured by this filiative bond, which resists an alien British State. In *Defenders*, a familiar Nationalist conjuncture of place and identity, mythicizing the historical as natural bequest, is produced in the following scene in which Gallagher beholds the Tyrone landscape: 'Gazing out over that magical landscape, he now saw it in its historical context. That's where it was fought, he noted, referring to a battle that had taken place in the glen below nearly four centuries earlier in which Gaelic clansmen had triumphed over a larger English army' (McGeough, 4).[13] *Defenders* deploys the negotiations of legitimacy encoded in crime fiction to oppose Ireland (as organic legacy of custom and community) against Britain (as social conspiracy of law and state). However, as posited earlier, the thriller form signifies precisely the historical overwhelming of this filiative fantasy. In fact, the verbs employed in the depiction of the landscape signal a crisis in such a representational economy:

> He was *captivated* by the scene laid out before him, in which a near-mystical glow seemed to emanate from the very landscape itself as the wide valley basked itself in silver moonlight ... He imagined the roar and clash of the battle for a moment before *occupying* himself with more philosophical thoughts. Could one of my own ancestors be lying amongst that pile of bone dust, he wondered, making out the silhouette of the dark thorns. The idea of such a thing being possible evoked a deep emotion within him, a strong sense of attachment to the

---

[12] McGeough's *Defenders* most obviously solicits through the thriller form an Americanized international *destinataire*, as divulged by the careful plotting of scenes which gesture to an intended audience. In the text, the IRA hero, Turlough Gallagher, explains Irish History during an airplane flight to an American he meets in Paris, and this romanticized Nationalist rendering is interspersed with an RUC interrogation and beating of IRA suspects. Notably, in terms of presentation of violence, the text never depicts the victims of Republican violence, dealing only with the British killing of Republicans.

[13] For an excellent discussion of place and ideology in Ireland see Eamonn Hughes, ''Could Anyone Write It?': Place in Tom Paulin's Poetry' in Graham and Kirkland, eds. 1999. 162-192.

land and its people. It was this awareness of belonging and tradition that motivated him (1; 5) [my emphasis].

Here a self-captivated, self-occupied ideology of organic belonging is accosted by the seclusion of its own imaginative incarceration. The text attempts to reduce the problematics of its production of home to a purely colonial displacement, as evinced by the description of the motivations of a Derry volunteer: 'he wasn't just fighting for his homeland, he was fighting to go home. As long as the British were in occupation he couldn't do that. Let them go home to their own country and take their damn Loyalists with them. If they're so frigging British, let them be British in Britain and leave Ireland to the Irish' (130). This colonial disruption of home echoes the Irish-American crime fiction of Bartholomew Gill and his McGarr series. In *McGarr and the Method of Descartes*, Paddy Greer, a journalist originally from the Short Strand, similarly reflects on a house search as a paradigmatic affirmation of the colonial displacement of History as a site of familial attachment:

> If in Ireland, Greer had some years later realized, history is genealogy, then those troops, in gratuitously defiling what little material history his people possessed, had taken a first but irrevocable step toward their eventual withdrawal from Ulster. Everything that had been ruined in those rooms had been laden with the history of his family, the paltriness of which made it all the more precious (1985, 6).

During the only foray into the city in *Defenders*, Gallagher travels to Dublin, where he meets a 'weirdo' (McGeough, 3) student with a nose ring and his girlfriend, whom Gallagher tells should leave him. Gallagher eventually woos and marries her, taking her to live in Tyrone, in an attempt to incorporate divergent strands of Irish identity and subjectivity – with the female character as cultural signifier – into the organic belonging rooted in Gallagher's homeland. However, it is exactly this filiative overdetermination which ultimately dispossesses Gallagher's concept of home, as conveyed by his attitude to his brother's joining the extended family at their farm:

> He was nearing home. Home. Though he'd grown up there and even been born there, the house was becoming less and less like the home he'd once known, especially since Michael and his family moved in after their father's death a couple of years ago ... Turlough was familiar with all the rational reasons and explanations, but he still felt a sense of loss and disliked the uneasiness he now experienced in the only home he'd ever known (35).

Although the murder of Gallagher's wife by the British and their pursuit of him are offered as the reasons for his emigration to America, it is the implosion and imprisonment of filiation, which ultimately impels his departure to New York where he finds 'there was an energy, a vibrancy about the place that dispelled his sorrow and somehow offered hope. He felt he was taking a new direction in life. Where to, he had no idea. But things were going to be better, of that he was certain' (233). Here filiation disintegrates in its own representational delimitation of the North. The text thus foregrounds the tension in Irish Nationalism between exile and emigration, a conceptual and ethical distinction, which necessitates the negotiation of dislocation as resulting from a directly colonial experience and from participation within the global economy. As Kerby Miller observes: 'One cannot study modern Ireland without realising the central importance of massive, sustained emigration' (1985, 3). Such a displacement is an obvious problematization of home and contributes extensively to the justified attribution of a colonial framework to Ireland: not only by assessing historical emigration but also by explicating the contemporary economic upturn in the indigenous Irish society, which would have been impossible without such a massive removal of people.[14]

Nonetheless, this colonial legacy, though irreparable, is not exhaustive and serves to solidify an Irish Nationalist discourse on emigration that obscures more contemporary determinants informed by class relations and social structure within Ireland and its attachment to the global market. In short, the reductive Anglicization of Irish emigration and loss of home as familial locus in McGeough's *Defenders* obscures the contemporary historical practice of emigration within a late capitalist world order. Jim McLaughlin formulates Irish emigration as

> a social process linking core-formation within Ireland and the international economy while simultaneously contributing to the peripheralisation of the Irish state ... far from being untouched by the forces of industrialisation, irish labour occupied a central position in the international division of labour and workers from Ireland have been crucial in the formation and maintenance of core areas of global capitalism ('The New Vanishing Irish', 155).

In *Defenders* the British disruption of organic community seeks to disguise the over-laden filiative model foundering in the constriction of its social mapping of Ireland. Gallagher's emigration to the United States as a source of hope simultaneously attempts to escape yet renew this disintegrating identity in a manner symptomatic of Irish Nationalism's rewriting of emigration. Eamonn Hughes uncovers

> the way in which migration is seen not as a modification of cultural identity, a taking on of a new, composite identity, but actually a reinforcement of one's original identity. This can be linked to the idea of a migrant mentality, arising from the long-standing tradition of migration from Ireland, in which migration reinforces, rather than weakens or modifies, one's originary identity since migration has become such a central factor in that identity. In other words, despite migration writers spend their time examining their original identity rather

---

[14] For two nuanced accounts of Ireland's coloniality challenging absolute refutations, such as Liam Kennedy's (1993), see Eamonn Hughes 'Forgetting the Future', *Irish Review* No.25 (Winter/Spring 1999-2000). 1-15. and Colin Graham, 1994.

than constructing in a new composite identity. It is on this basis that they can be reclaimed by Irish culture (1995, 149).

How does the thriller function for Irish Nationalism in negotiating the spatial consequences of emigration to America and Britain? Hughes notes that there is no comparable text written from an Irish migrant perspective in Britain for an Irish-American thriller such as George V. Higgins's *The Patriot Game*. Therein the FBI hero is able to defend the Amercian values upheld by mainstream Irish-America against Irish Republican attack, so that 'a new composite identity overrides the originary identity' (Hughes 1995, 143). The positionality of this Irish-American identity, allied to the state and opposed to the community in this thriller, allows us to refine our account of the problematics of home within Irish Nationalism's mythicization of its homogeneous displaced subject as universal oppressed. It facilitates a deliberation upon the insinuation of this mythic identity within global networks of power and projected sets of social relations within Ireland.

Clancy's *Patriot Games* discloses the Irish-American contribution to a reconstituted, New Right white racial hegemony in the United States. Cemented by the 1990 Immigration Act, Eithne Luibheid traces a New Right transformist hegemony, which reformulated its ethnically buttressed dominance against the racial equality campaigns of much more materially oppressed minorities. Luibheid observes 'how white race has shaped new Irish immigrant access to jobs, housing and education, as well as it re-shapes immigrant Irish identity in a direction toward white "American-ness" ' (Luibheid, 267).[15] In Clancy's text, the FBI hero, Jack Ryan reclaims Irish-American identity as a component of a civilized late capitalist world order of 'international co-operation' (462) against the encroachment of terrorism. His defence of the British Royal Family foregrounds the New Right hegemonic alliance informing the text, which seeks to rewrite in its own hegemonic terms the historical trend, noted by George O'Brien (1995), for Irish characters to appear in hard-boiled thrillers often as links in chains of criminality uncovered by these texts:[16]

> Where I come from we – that is, Irish Americans – have made out pretty well. We're all in the professions, business, and politics, but your prototypical Irish-American is still a basic police officer or firefighter. The cavalry that won the West was a third Irish, and there are still plenty of us in uniform – especially the Marine Corps, as a matter of fact. Half the local FBI office lived in my neighbourhood ... In America we are the forces of order, the glue that holds society together (Clancy, 48).

---

[15] The most obvious linkage between the American establishment and the 'Troubles' thriller is *Terrible Beauty* by Peter T. King, a member of the US Congress and the Chairperson of the Congressional Ad Hoc Committee for Irish Affairs.

[16] One of the most notable examples of the trend identified by George O'Brien would be the character of Dusty Regan in Raymond Chandler's *The Big Sleep*. The character is regalvanized for the New Right by Michael Winner's woeful film remake.

Such a conjuncture imparts not only the assimilation of sections of propertied Irish-America into a newly recomposed white hegemonic bloc but also the willingness of Irish Nationalism and Republicanism to align themselves with the dominant social configurations of the capitalist world order.[17] My point here is that 'home' as an ideological and ethical centre within Irish Nationalism is not reducible merely to a colonial displacement. Rather its import functions as a filiative mechanism, which not only intends the maintenance of specific social relations and representations within Ireland but also inserts itself within global sets of relationships and hegemonic attachments. The thriller offers a modality, through which mediations between custom and community and state and society redefine and transpose their legitimacy, sending ultimately contradictory ideological signals in addressing different sets of social relationships and state formations. Despite this aura of legitimacy afforded by the rapprochement with New Right hegemony in the United States, I have attempted to unveil the antinomic disintegration of filiation in Irish Nationalist discourse in the very process of confronting the national configuration that it is designed to uphold. The deficiencies of this filiative model are more evident in thrillers addressing home and the nation in Britain, where this American hegemonic attachment is largely unavailable and thus cannot proffer a superficial resolution to such disjuncture.

Eamonn Hughes registers 'the comparative absence of a fiction about Irish-Britain in the sense of a located and, at some level, stable and secure, community which sees itself as Irish-British and which requires cultural articulation' (1995, 143). In this context, Ronan Bennett's *The Second Prison* is elucidatory through its use of crime fiction modes to surmount the problematics and establishment of home for Irish Nationalist discourse. The text combines two formal mechanisms emitting conflictive constitutions of the social. On one level, the ideology of organic community encoded in early forms of detective fiction is employed to structure the plot concerning Kane's Republican past and his wish to ascertain the informer in his ranks. Another generic stratum, however, evoking the conspiratorial ideologeme, effects Kane's contact with the British state and criminal justice system. In attempting to detect which member of his old active service unit violated the communal code, the organic resolution imagined by earlier crime fiction forms serves structurally to bolster Kane's belief that 'this thing has to be resolved' (125). Otherwise, the text informs us, when Kane resolves to track down his former colleague, Dec: 'I can't walk away from Dec. If I do that then I repudiate everything I was part of ... If I walk away from Dec I'm turning my back on the rules I have lived my life by' (125). So the formal

---

[17] The fundamental contradiction for the New Right 'Family Values' of Clancy's text, therefore, is that the family (as filiative ideologeme) is not absolute, so the specific Western structure of the nuclear family is valorized as the Irish model of the clan and of kinship is extirpated. Interestingly, the British Royal family, whom Ryan saves, are one level sacral transmitters of filiative tradition, but on another their real relevance to the text is as postmodern and transnational celebrities – an antinomy which the Ryans attempt to embody.

exigency of resolved crime reconvenes the organic community and its moral and societal codes.

However, this filiative whole is unable to aggregate into a totality Kane's desire for 'a thread, some link, some connection, something to explain the past and to show me how things would turn out' (92). It is exactly this foreclosure which is subsumed by the conspiratorial ideologeme as Kane increasingly becomes aware that he is himself being used in a bigger picture by the Anti-Terrorist Squad officer, Tempest.[18] The text ends with Tempest's killing of Kane's last two associates from his unit, after which he lets Kane go free. Kane hears a final shot when leaving and assumes that Tempest has committed suicide having completed his mission, in a seeming collapse of the text back into the resolvable crime, but it transpires later in press reports that his body was not found at the scene. This inconclusiveness defeats the rounded closure and bespeaks the incapacity of filiation to map both the conspiracy and the social relations to which it points. The text must acknowledge the breakdown of the co-ordinates provided by the Irish Nationalist organic community, as neatly suggested when Kane becomes ever more aware of a larger conspiracy and feels 'as if a reference point on a map I was depending on to bring me to safety had turned out to lead to an infested swamp' (181). Whilst Kane asserts that 'you can't be free in a place you don't belong' (41), the organic, originary home purported by Irish Nationalism is not merely prevented by colonial displacement in Britain but also by the very historical subsumption of that ideology. This ideological occlusion functions as a kind of third subjective prison to which the conspiratorial mechanism provides a re-coordination of cognitive orientations in seeking to map place.

The thriller equally proffers a representational mode for tracing the breakdown in Unionist filiation, which had not only organicized community within the Northern State but also nurtured the naturalized bond with Great Britain.[19] Particularly after the focal point of the Anglo-Irish Agreement, the self-identical mythic community of Unionist discourse increasingly had to find new articulative, narrative apparatuses for renegotiating a hegemony in crisis. After the Anglo-Irish Agreement, then, many key Unionist figures sought systematically to resuscitate its residual-dominant formation.[20] The Ulster Society, which was formed in 1985, published Blair McMahon's *Nights in Armour*, a thriller written from an RUC

---

[18] Tempest is a propitiously named character: to the bafflement of the reductive, filiative ideologeme and its desire for resolved closure, he functions as a kind of Prospero figure conjuring a web of intrigue and conspiracy around the actions of Kane's unit of latter day Calibans, all of whom are methodically eliminated by his plans.

[19] The dissolution of Unionist state hegemony, or perhaps more correctly, the necessary incapacity of Unionist filiation to map its own state, are suggested by the title of Susan McKay's recent study *Northern Protestants: An Unsettled People* (Belfast: Blackstaff, 2000).

[20] See, for example, texts by Aughey, English, and Walker eds., McCartney, Roche, and Bardon, eds.

perspective.[21] It offers a direct link between this urge for articulation within
Unionism and the thriller as an international popular platform through which to
debate representations of Northern Ireland and to relocate the position of
Unionism. I do not want to attribute too much significance to this specific
instance. Rather, in terms of the politics of form, I will analyse how thrillers
written from broadly Unionist perspectives share their historical referent with
Unionist discourse's search for a renewed sense of home, amidst the term's
dissolution as hegemonic and filiative surety. (Though I shall also discuss
Resurrection Man, written very much interrogatively on Unionism).

Roy Bradford's 1981 text, *The Last Ditch*, utilizes generic components of the
thriller at a moment of hegemonic disintegration to signify the degradation of not
only the Unionist cause but also Northern Irish society itself.[22] The italicized
preface, wherein 'feral' (3) Loyalist terrorists mutilate a colleague, adumbrates
the text's attempt to detach such violence from an idealized former tribal unity.
The text offers a somewhat pessimistic, elitist allegory of the Ulster Worker's
Strike through the eyes of the Unionist Cabinet Minister, Desmond Carson:

> The standard bearers were not the ones he would have chosen. These were not
> the men of 1912 who had come from farm and foundry and signed a Covenant to
> keep Ulster for ever British. In the Battle of the Somme, that compact had been
> sealed with their blood. Then, everyone had been in, the Movement-peers, mill-
> owners, shipwrights, linen workers, clergy, rich and poor, men and masters
> bound together and fired by the same high purpose ... As Carson saw it, today's
> defenders of the faith were hard, venal men, some with a record of crime. True,
> there were those who acted from a sense of tribal duty, imbued with the fervour
> we call patriotism. But bad money tends to drive out the good (101).

Bradford deploys the thriller to produce a paranoid assemblage of conniving
British Government officials, fellow Unionist politicians, the media, innately
recalcitrant Republicans and, most significantly, a Loyalist working class
detached from its putatively tribal and traditional hegemonic attachments. But the
text's most insidious crime, which ultimately symbolically bespeaks the
untenability of the filiative unity idealized in 1912, is Carson's affair with a young
Catholic. This betrayal of his wife and daughter in reductively filiative terms
intimates the limited scope of the text's social mappings. How does the thriller
confront precisely this filiative dissolution, and more importantly, in terms of the
state, de-legitimize its idealization of the past as organic unity?

Arthur Aughey, still reeling from the signing of the 1985 Agreement, issued
the following dismissal: 'the way in which Unionists have presented their own

---

[21] The Ulster Society also published Sam Brian's pessimistic 1996 text *Winter's Return* in
the wake of the ceasefires. The text invokes fears of a dissident Republican winter of
violence and also suggests that victims of violence should exact collective revenge if
amnesty is granted to terrorist prisoners.

[22] The text's resignation anticipates the Unionist fracture after the Anglo-Irish Agreement
but also bespeaks something of its immediate context, such as the emergence of Ian
Paisley's Third Force, the Hunger Strikes and the political development of Republicanism.

case, or failed to do so, has in no small measure contributed to their sense of isolation and effectiveness' (Aughey, 1989, 1).[23] Moreover, Francis Mulhern comments upon 'the stilted style of Unionist discourse, which, at its most pained, could seem to mark a radical alienation from speech itself – a kind of symbolic death' (1998, 21). This terminal rendering of Unionism is darkly explored by Eoin McNamee's *Resurrection Man*, which unveils the literally torturous expiration of filiative identity. In many ways the inarticulacy so bemoaned by Aughey is personified by the figure of Victor Kelly's father, who, we are informed, slips 'from one region of silence to another' (10). The text provides a stark allegory of the crisis in the maintenance of the authority of Unionist hegemony, through its utilization of an Oedipal contest between father and son. Victor's mother, Dorcas, witnesses the following scene: 'There was never an expression the equal of the one on Victor's face as he looked at his father. It was a stare of exact hatred for the wrongs that man done his family. She could see her son's torment with deep lines on the forehead and darkness under the eyes. James faced him with a like expression' (56).

The Oedipal framework serves somewhat regressively as a strategy of representational containment, which seeks to rationalize the symbolic death purported by Mulhern's analysis. It is a filiative code designedly conceived to encompass this hegemonic antagonism within its own organic, familial and ultimately dehistoricized terms as a reiterative conflict, a regenerative death in its archetypal symbolic order. Nonetheless, it also functions allegorically to denaturalize the constitutive and formative violence of the Unionist hegemony, laying bare its coercive *dominante* force under the conditions of class fragmentation in the Northern conflict.[24] Even under this rudimentary Freudian schema, the text insinuates a return of the repressed, which demystifies idealized filiation and reconvenes its violence and antagonism. The text has been criticized for its reductive portrayal of Protestant culture as a dreary scripture, a stoic rote of Saturday afternoons at Windsor Park, drinking dens and fanatical preachers. Yet the astuteness of its troubled familial allegory with regard to Unionist hegemony intimates that force and violence are not interruptive of the organic order of Unionism's filiative model of society but are rather deeply ingrained within it.

Thus, the Freudian model on one level dangerously suggests, in accordance with the paternalism of Unionist hegemony, that the class fragmentation, and more importantly the Loyalist violence that has occurred since the 1960s, are reducible to a patriarchal abnegation of authority and the unleashing of its unruly son. Nevertheless, the father functions largely as an absent centre in the text, just as the state and History so loom in Unionist accounts of the North, a determinate

---

[23] The work of Fergal Cochrane is particularly instructive as a contextualization of the period.

[24] Although it takes as its subject the Shankill Butchers of the 1970s, the most immediate context for McNamee's text, which was first published in 1994, was the massive upsurge in Loyalist violence preceding the first ceasefires. For an account of the original context of the 1970s, see Martin Dillon *The Shankill Butchers: A Case Study of Mass Murder*. London: Arrow, 1990.

historical aporia attesting to the problematics of a hegemony to which the text returns its repressed violence. Dorcas's comment upon her husband draws a direct parallel between father and son, drawing the text's broader violence within the realm of this silence: 'A husband is a thing like a knife. He is a cause of pain. If he was not so quiet and strange she would have said to him straight out' (144). Despite this Oedipal structure, the gothicized conspiracies and corruption imbuing the text establish attachments beyond the silent, organic patriarchy, establishing a shadowy yet social substance to its reposed quietude and the limits of its authority.

The Oedipal ritual in which Victor shaves his father – whose stroke confirms his silence and paralysis – is notably not the final scene, despite its filiative import as a final ceremonial calling to account and return of repressed violence signaling the dissolution of patriarchal authority: 'That's you done, da . . . I finished him and now I got to go' (227). It actually immediately precedes Victor's assassination by unknown agents, involving his own paramilitary handlers. It is these shadowy conspiratorial figures and their promptings, which serve to project the text's trajectory beyond the filiative crisis into the social itself. The conspiratorial figures thus serve as the ghost writers, the ultimate historical authors and spiritual signatories, of the guilty scrapbook which James keeps of his son's crimes, and which symbolizes the much more historical guilt finally bespoken by exactly this silence and absence.

It is the clandestine conspiracy of paramilitary leaders and state agents, which incriminates a wider network of social forces and suggests a historical context that reaches beyond the family unit and its ideological scope to inculpate the social totality itself. This textual level of the novel which prevents its portrayal of violence as a deranged anomaly that would ultimately serve to absolve the hegemony of the state, and which would collapse the text into conventional, dehistoricizing accounts of violence strategically necessitated by the Unionist ideology of the organic society: 'Violence must be portrayed as an aberration, or, particularly in the case of violence against the security forces, as justifiable response to republican violence and British government policy; otherwise the continued existence of Northern Ireland requires even more strenuous exercises in legitimation' (Clayton, 1996, 159).

For the danger in portraying the violence in Northern Ireland from the 1960s onwards as purely a crisis in familial authority resides in its suggestion that its resolution requires the authoritarian and natural censure of the unruly working class by the propertied and dominant parent-figures of society. Such profound organic and hierarchical import cements the 'Two Communities' model, which has structured even some of the better post-war historical accounts of the North, as in the work of Sabine Wichert:

> The subsequent ossification of the vertical sectarian divide ... was now combined with a horizontal social and economic division within each community, with the working classes of each side as the main carriers of the more conservative, irrational and extreme political philosophy, to be realised, if necessary, by violent means. The middle classes of each side would by and large have been willing to

support a compromise. This new development meant that the traditional parties effectively lost control of working-class support and split. Out of this division new and more extreme parties, with predominantly working-class and lower-middle-class support, emerged on both sides (2-3).

Such analyses, and their suggestions of traditional, self-evident hierarchies and empowerments, contain two convenient elisions. Firstly, the fact that the conflict has actually served to solidify and resurrect precisely such hegemonic configurations in crisis. Secondly, that the emergence of political parties with genuinely working-class constituencies, such as the PUP and the UDP, though still seamed by Unionist discourse but who share their historical referent with other community-based initiatives that have dissolved sectarianism, has disrupted the mythic coherence of the organic community. Such affirmative class initiatives have not accidentally coincided with the fracture of the myth of an organic identity of interest in Unionist discourse, but have actively assisted the precipitation of a hegemonic crisis typified by the filiative breakdown of Norman Porter's lamentation: 'traditional Unionist solaces of unity, nationalist resignation and British support are no longer available: the so-called Unionist family is internally divided' (Porter, 1). *Resurrection Man* successfully indicates not only the constitutive violence and hegemonic crisis of this filiative model – even as it recapitulates it on one level of its formulations – but also more importantly signifies its inability to map the social totality, to confront its own exercise of power.

So what Unionism must confront (often in spite of the intentional politics of its authors) in the thriller is not only the collapse of itself as an organic community but also the range of social relationships disclosed by uncovering the state formation, as demonstrated by the work of Richard Crawford and Sarah Michaels. In Crawford's *The Minstrel Boy*, Northern Ireland is presented in prelapsarian terms before the 'Troubles' disruption of this ordered harmony: 'The one thing that I can remember is that nobody gave a fiddler's frig what religion you were, and you could go anywhere, anywhere at all, and no one would touch you' (98). In the novel Colin Rea attempts to join the RUC but is rejected, indicating an alienation from the state. His father, Stevie, who was crippled by an IRA bomb, functions as a hardman nostalgically gesturing to the ordered, knowable community: 'For nearly ten years Stevie Rea had ruled his little patch of the Shankill Road like a minor and absolute king' (1). Here it is propitious to invoke Allen Feldman's distinction between *the hardman* and *the gunman*, wherein, through antithetical relation to the anonymous collectivization of violence in the modern state, 'the hardman's violence represents the extreme individuation of performance. This is based on narratives of the body that construct the hardman's singularity in the community. Through the self-construction of the self in violence, the hardman came to signify the self-contained and autonomous singularity of his community' (52-53).

What the text must confront, however, is the breakdown of this organic order, as Colin's inability to attach himself to the state apparatus in the form of the RUC leads him to join Loyalist paramilitaries and become involved in a murder. The thriller as a form produced through the fracture of established social codes and co-ordinates provides a modality for negotiating the dissolution of these seemingly natural attachments and moral relativity, as the book's cover informs: 'In a war where nothing is simple anymore, Colin is about to find that the line between enemy and friend, crime and punishment, is very thin indeed'. Although Colin's father is embittered, he had warned his son about involvement with paramilitaries, so that when he discovers his son's activities, their disagreement which allegorizes the broader questions of social and moral legitimacy is described as 'family trouble' (99) in standard filiative terms. Nonetheless, Colin's disagreements with his father and mother ultimately signal filiative crisis: 'Colin felt suddenly that he had no place there, that this was no longer his home, that these two injured people would be better off without him' (180).

Whilst the text concludes with Colin's capture and his sense of the justice of his impending imprisonment in the seemingly ordered conclusion of the resolved crime, it is this radical dispossession that remains. This theme is pursued more deeply by Crawford's use of the conspiratorial text in *Fall When Hit*. The text scrutinizes not only the filiative crisis of Unionism and its social legitimacy but also the organic ideological bond with the British State. When his car is rammed off the road, UDR soldier, Garret Cairns, shoots his way out of the incident and kills someone who turns out to be a covert British agent. He escapes from the scene with a woman whom the British had been tracking due to her possession of a tape containing evidence of the British negotiations with the IRA. Following his arrest and an attempted cover-up, alienated from the British state by these events and the Secret Service pursuit of himself and the woman, the thriller's conspiratorial ideologeme provides a mode for the critical regard of these social forces as a totality: 'The enormity of it staggered me. I couldn't envisage such massive deceit' (239). This totality of social forces presents Kearns with a crisis in the authenticity and legitimacy of his own narrative which the thriller form is itself an effort to renegotiate: 'What gets me is the fact that no one seems to believe my story. No one trusts a word I say. No one listens' (57). Although he eventually clears his name and that of Alison – with the unofficial assistance of some RUC officers – 'hard, proud, loyal people' (199) – the conspiracy's charting of endemic corruption cannot facilitate a resolved closure compatible with filiation.

Sarah Michaels' *Summary Justice*, the cover of which proclaims it as the tale of 'one man's war against the IRA', relates the killing of the family of RUC officer, Barney Somerville, and his subsequent quest for revenge. The reactionary, militaristic politics of this adventure or revenge generic component of this thriller is nonetheless structurally forestalled and subsumed by its conspiratorial underpinning. Despite its intentional textual politics, *Summary Justice* exemplifies the class allegory produced in however sublimated a formal level out of the dissolution of the organic community. The conspiracy provides a cognitive chart of the social forces which confront Somerville at the site of this filiative breakdown and his resultant detached position of contemplation, as the book's dust cover affirms: 'Disowned by the intelligence services, spurned by the army, rejected by his masters and ignored by the government, Somerville becomes the uncontrollable force that cannot be predicted, cannot be stopped as he enacts the deadly chilling code of summary justice'.

In many ways, the text revels in the symbolic death suggested by Mulhern. For in its radicalized confrontation of the social totality the family now functions not as a current and natural touchstone but rather as a filiative fragment, a purely allegorical bearing: 'I decided to die the day the remaining pieces of my family were buried. You can't kill me' (259). It transpires that the bomb which killed his family was intended for Somerville because his investigations into racketeering were on the verge of uncovering a criminal network involving not only terrorists but also businessmen, Unionist figures and police officers. A single ordered restoration is impossible in the face of this web of corruption. Indeed, we learn that Somerville was himself utilized and encouraged by a senior figure in British intelligence, who viewed Somerville's rogue revenge on the Republican movement as an excellent way of damaging the IRA. This senior figure rationalizes his use of Somerville and his final eradication: 'national security is a very dirty game sometimes requiring dirty decisions' (299). The preface of the text, in which Michaels asserts that the novel is based on an actual event, serves to confirm how the conspiratorial ideologeme traces a social network of criminality out of the single crime which is now deemed untenable:

> Sometimes things happen in Northern Ireland which never make the headlines; in fact, they may never make the news at all. This story may be one such story. It is the story of a man who disappeared; his body was never found. Some said that he was driven by tragic circumstances, which had engulfed him, others that the complete affair had more sinister undertones (i).

Thus, particularly after the Anglo-Irish Agreement, crime as a conceptual template through which to map the social assumes a prescience for Unionism. It procures a modality with which to articulate the extirpation of the organic community in its discourse, and amidst this fracture and hegemonic crisis, to encounter the demystified relations concussed in the social as state formation. Notably, however, Michaels' text attempts to seam this utopian social geography of the text within Unionist discourse, to reinscribe it within the *repressive* modality. This delimitation is achieved through Somerville's singled-handed assault on the IRA and the vilification of the crime of collaborating with Republican terrorists by Unionist figures whose corruption is rather regressively symbolized by the aristocratic decadence and homosexuality of one of the conspirators. The text thus attempts to retreat from the more radical illegitimacy of the state formation as patterned criminality.

Keith Baker's *Inheritance* is the text written from a broadly Unionist perspective which most successfully utilizes the conspiratorial ideologeme to infuse a pathogenic Unionist body politic with arterial criminality and uncover the terminal rending of the filiative order. In the text, Jack McCallan returns to the North after the death of his father and effectively acts as the final, unwilling executor of the ideology of the North as organic order and of the 'Troubles' as interruptive yet extricable aberration. At a time when many strands of Unionism, after the fracture of the Anglo-Irish Agreement, were seeking to withdraw into an organic self-identical community supposedly traversing hegemonic crisis, *Inheritance* rejoins that there is no mythic return to the filiative home but rather a historical return of the repressed beholding the Northern State as the text's constitutive mystery. *Inheritance* demonstrates that the call for greater Unionist articulacy must not merely encounter a former inarticulacy but also a determinate historical aporia – the 'eloquent silences' (1976, 89), to employ Eagleton's term, of ideology so neatly symbolized by Victor Kelly's father in *Resurrection Man*. This is the text's most lingering and insistent inheritance bequeathed in the filiative extinction: a critical appraisal of the power and illegitimacy of the state:

> Under the old Stormont regime, unionists relied on the fact of power to do their talking for them. Political argument of the abstract kind was left up to those – nationalists – who were excluded from power in Northern Ireland. That inheritance of political inarticulateness, an inheritance which almost constitutes a form of apoliticism, has frustrated attempts to address adequately the current nationalist challenge to the Union (Aughey, 1989, vii).

The text's most determining inheritance, then, is paradoxically a disinheritance: a dis-filiation coterminously re-affiliating of Unionism's organic ideology to its dedifferentiated historical context. *Inheritance* is set in 2016, twenty years after the end of the 'Troubles' that have seemingly been confined to the Ulster Folk Museum, which now contains such reified artifacts as Free Derry corner and Carson's statue. It is also related that Irish Republican prisoners have been sent to the United States with Green Cards because 'when you were trying to rebuild a country you did not need platoons of bomb-makers and snipers sitting around with nothing to do' (50). Thus, in one register of the text's mechanics, the 'Troubles' are again reducible to an extractable blight on an otherwise ordered Northern Irish society. Accordingly, History as binary – rather than dialectical – stasis is commodified and nostalgically recuperated in the form of the Folk Museum, which displays the historical as archival curio, removed if not resolved criminal object. The conspiratorial ideologeme, however, subtends this account of the 'Troubles' through the social fabric of its clues and faithfully reinscribes the historical significations etched in the silences of the blank narratives preceding and supplanting the 'Troubles'. Jack McCallan unearths a tangle of covert, state-sponsored killings in the run up to the Peace Process which involve not only his late father and his RUC colleagues, but also prominent businessmen and the Chief Constable of the new Police Service of Northern Ireland. Thus the 'Troubles' actually infect the social totality and the shadowy reaches of the state.

The sheer complexity of the social forces confronting the individual consciousness in the form of seemingly incommensurable clandestine clues and intrigues threaten to overwhelm McCallan: 'Each question in his mind led to another, all of them impossible to resolve ... There were too many things that were not quite right. Each one on its own – no problem. But coming together – that was another matter' (172). Nonetheless, under the workings of the *redemptive* modality, and out of this co-ordinative loss, McCallan provides a 'link' (267) between the disparate social levels, which functions as a utopian class allegory grasping the totality in the form of conspiracy. The relativized moral and legal terrain of the conspiracy is shown to be beyond the scope of the ideology of earlier crime fiction and the detective's role as ethical agent. It transpires that McCallan's father was murdered by Laura Miller for his role in the initial conspiracy which killed her father. So McCallan's father and Laura Miller function as both victims and criminals, their roles doubled up in a more consummate pattern. The official cover-up of the conclusion indicates not only that the State seeks to restore order by a criminal act, but also that this supposed order was itself criminally based to begin with.

This cyclical criminal pattern, as a *repressive* textual mechanism, is readily rewritten and arrogated by the hegemonic metacode of the 'Troubles' thriller's implication in the discursive continuance of the traumatic paradigm of Irish History. It does, nonetheless, in terms of Unionism and its hegemonic crisis, articulate a utopian historical affiliation of the social totality in its adjudicatory meditation of the Northern State's legitimacy. In short, through the filiative crisis symbolized by the death of McCallan's father, the organic order of Unionist community is exposed not merely as ideologically degenerative but as morally degenerate.[25] Upon learning of the involvement of his father's associate, the businessman, his 'Uncle' Henry Lomax, and the use of Miller as a scapegoat for the original conspiracy, McCallan's filiative displacement facilitates a cognitive transposition, which grasps the social with reconstituted significance: 'He saw everything with different eyes. Words echoed in his ears with a different sound, a different meaning. There was Lomax's defence over dinner of what he assumed was Miller's handiwork. But it had not been Miller he had been defending at all: it had been his own actions and those of his fellow murderers that he had been attempting to justify' (322-323).

In Colin Bateman's thrillers, satire and an ironic regard of exoticism become the means of effecting an elevated social contemplation, as personified in his character of Dan Starkey – the 'Unionist with a sense of humour' (1995b, 9).[26] Bateman's texts, however, also indulge in such auto-exoticism even as they parody it, as perhaps indicated by the increasing leaning towards the United States in his work and the hegemonic and enticing gravitational pull of the international market. The gothicized figuration of Crossmaglen as Crossmaheart in *Cycle of Violence* would not seem out of place in some of the most rabid British texts discussed in my second chapter, and the text's contempt for the town's inhabitants – 'The planners had taken everything into account, except human nature. They transferred scum from slums into scum with immersion heaters' (1995a, 26).

---

[25] It thus refutes the idealization of both order and the North in McMahon's *Nights in Armour* of 'the good old days, a golden age that ended forever in August 1969. Northern Ireland had been one of the most peaceful, law-abiding societies in Europe' (192).

[26] One note of caution, which could be introduced at this point, is Terry Eagleton's account (1997) of how Unionism has increasingly sought the jargon not only of pluralism but also of a post-modern effacement which is actually intended to preserve its formations and mask its power.

Despite this indulgence, the positioning of Starkey in *Divorcing Jack* as official government guide for a group of foreign journalists does foreground the text's tacit awareness of what Bateman will later deem 'the terror tour' (1996, 218) of the exotic frameworks confronting the Northern writer in the thriller. In this respect, Starkey's subsequent account of how the North functions for the NORAID employees and Irish-Americans in *Of Wee Sweetie Mice and Men*, as 'a bit of a thrill for armchair terrorists' (1996, 218), provides a self-referential, basic summary of the thriller form itself. Bateman's gothicized North revels in parodic and anaclitic derangements that undoubtedly destabilizes the authority of the international 'Troubles' thriller's dominant representations. Nonetheless, Bateman's satire is on one level also an attempt to find an articulate Unionist voice in the popular cultural form of the thriller,[27] though in Starkey's ironic detachment the conspiratorial mapping necessitates an examination of the state formation so denied by the earlier ideological silence that I have traced. In *Divorcing Jack*, Starkey unearths a clandestine web of crime which eventually implicates in terrorist activity the newly-elected Northern Irish Prime Minister, Brinn (though this conspiracy entails his Republican connections – there is a limit to the ironic curb on Bateman's Unionism). Nonetheless, the class allegory in this detached regard of the social totality is constitutive of one of the text's many displacements. Starkey travels through a whole series of houses in the text but home as a permanent locus is obsessively central through its very omission.[28]

On one level, Bateman's texts serve as a reminder that Northern Ireland is always at least two places: a problematic, forestalling entity for both Irish and British Nationalist teleologies. As Starkey informs the heavyweight boxer, Bobby McMaster, in *Of Wee Sweetie Mice and Men*: 'I'm from Northern Ireland, Bobby, same as you, not England, not Ireland, it's home, I couldn't be much bothered fighting to make it one thing or the other, but if someone walked in and forced me into one thing or the other, then I might get more protective about it' (1996, 161). Similarly, in *Divorcing Jack*, Starkey initiates the following exchange with Charles Parker, the CIA agent masquerading as an inquisitive fellow journalist:

> '[S]tick to calling it Northern Ireland, although you'll hear variations. If you're a Loyalist you'll call it Ulster, if you're a Nationalist you'll call it the North of Ireland or the Six Counties, if you're the British Government you call it the Province.'
> 'And what do you call it, Mr. Starkey.'
> 'Home' (1995b, 46).

At a national level, then, Northern Ireland is lived, ambivalent contradiction, a confirmation of Eamonn Hughes' account of the 'richly ambiguous statement of

---

[27] Interestingly, the film version of *Divorcing Jack* largely represses Starkey's Unionism, in a confirmation of Brian McIlroy's thesis that British film generally eschews Unionist perspectives (1998).

[28] It is worth considering to what extent Bateman's work is aligned with an Irish quest narrative tradition, that home is only truly recognized by leaving it behind. Nevertheless, this study is committed to revealing the formal symbolism of the crime form itself.

the always-at-least-dual nature of the Northern Irish and their cultures' ('Introduction', 10). However, it is important to trace the additional displacements and fissures of home in Bateman's texts, which shall adumbrate my next two chapters. Otherwise the theme of dislocation becomes reducible to that of the anomalous duality of nationality, a collision of two homogenous identities purported by Seamus Heaney's schema of 'living in two places at the one time' (Kearney, ed. 1990, 23). The most crucial displacements are those of the city and of gender. Bateman utilizes the historical symbolism of the thriller to mediate not only the disruptions of urban space but also the provisional cartographic mode of a masculinity deprived of its traditional co-ordinates and securities. These concrete displacements rupture the supposedly homogeneous national formation, and, of course, also provide the very constitutive means by which a dominant national subject is produced. There is a notable representational withdrawal in the closure of *Divorcing Jack*, which bespeaks a specific gender politics, wherein Starkey recoils from contemplation of the state into a consideration of the recurrent mystery of his relationship with his wife: 'I did not think of politics or the state. Of Brinn and the lionization that was already roaring into place. I did not think of the book I was going to write that would make the propagators of his false martyrdom an endangered species. I did not think of the senseless deaths and the needless cruelties. I thought of Patricia' (1995b, 280).

Whilst one immensely determining factor in the deployment of the thriller by Irish writers is the representational dominance of the international thriller market and its discursive field of hegemonic representations, the form also proffers a means of navigating a crisis in traditional social co-ordinates and value systems for a range of ideological positions seeking to restore a hegemonic subject. However, it is exactly this hegemonic struggle, which alerts us to the deficiencies of the homogenized national allegory, the unitary national subjective condition. The dialectic of ideology and utopia in the 'Troubles' thriller endeavours to produce an optimal subject across the conflictual interstices not only of the national but also of class, gender and urbanity. Bateman's work evinces a subject attempting to reterritorialize itself, to instigate a dominant conjuncture of belonging, masculinity, Unionist identity and late capitalist bricolage, which intimates that such mappings must be addressed and unravelled. And this chapter has sought to fissure both Irish Nationalism's and Unionism's construction of organic identities of interest by examining how the thriller discloses the very social dynamics of class, gender and place which both ideologies seek to repress.

The incapacity of both Irish Nationalism and Unionism to map effectively their societies is foregrounded by the challenge of urban space, which forms the basis of my next chapter. In particular, I wish to highlight the deficiencies of the filiative place produced by both ideologies. Both formations saturate the national and the public space with a dangerously mystified familial intimacy. In so far as dominant Irish culture seeks to ingrain the filiative *topos*, an interesting point of reference is afforded by Richard Sennett's *The Fall of Public Man*, which grants an instructive methodology for calibrating the proper constitution of public space, for the establishment of what I have termed affiliation. Sennett posits that 'intimacy is an attempt to solve the public problem by denying that the public exists' (1977, 27). Moreover, Sennett continues that 'the belief in direct human relations on an intimate scale has seduced us from converting our understanding of the realities of power into guides for our own political behaviour. The result is that the forces of domination or inequality remain unchallenged' (1977, 339).

My next chapter intends both to expose and challenge the power relations of both Irish Nationalism and Unionism as filiative ideologies. Sennett argues that 'a city is a milieu in which strangers are likely to meet' (1977, 48). Here the stranger is not just an outsider or alien somehow intimately trespassing in a fully known, self-affirmative place, which is of course a recurrent theme in Irish writing, but rather a stranger as an unknown within a properly constituted public space, in which identities are renegotiated and re-affiliated according to historical change. As Sennett puts it: 'the behaviour is at a distance from everyone's personal circumstances, and so does not force people to attempt to define to each other who they are. When this occurs, a public geography is on the way to being born' (1977, 49). The State, the public space and the urban – all of which are central to the thriller form – are therefore diametrically at variance with the false intimacy of the national-filiative ideologeme informing Irish Nationalism and Unionism. The recurrent incompleteness of the family as ideologeme in the texts discussed in this chapter insinuates the inability of this form of social spatiality to comprehend fully the complexity of our historical moment. One of the subversions of the thriller is its capacity to textualize the covert, what should remain secret, and this obviously assumes a further potentiality in a social formation mapped as an intimate space. Despite the frequent critical reading of how the supposed crudity of the thriller form points to the impossibility of a stable, private life, the confrontation with the filiative *topos* intimates, in contradistinction, that it is a public life which is yet more difficult to constitute within the dominant parameters of place in the North. And whilst this may seem a minor point, it has enormous ramifications for Northern Irish society. For the new devolved assembly in the North, which should be the establishment of a properly constituted political and public space, is still conducted as a private, intimate space of tribal community – as demonstrated by the fact that for any legislation to be passed a majority is required from members who must identify themselves as either Nationalist or Unionist, as figures of community whose aim is designed to occlude the instigation of a fully civic and public space. Equally, just as the conflict has been conducted as a 'dirty war' of covert operations and countermoves, so too the Peace Process has occurred 'behind closed doors', in private, and in keeping with the intimate, tribal spaces of Irish Nationalism and Unionism and their eschewal of the properly representative politics of Sennett's public sphere. And despite all the rhetoric about the difficulty of bringing the 'two communities' together, it is evident the two dominant ideologies in Ireland actually have a most profound and exigent affinity. For Irish Nationalism and Unionism are precisely *shared* attempts to occlude the full historical and social complexity of Belfast and this island itself, which entails a consideration of class conflicts, popular radicalisms, struggles for women's rights, the dialectics of urbanity and so forth. The following chapters will discuss exactly how the thriller form re-politicizes the organic, tribal spaces of Unionism and Irish Nationalism.

Chapter 3

'New Languages Would Have to be Invented': Representations of Belfast and Urban Space

'I must have walked as many streets as I did in my dreams'.
Dashiell Hammet, *Red Harvest*

In examining the depiction of Belfast in the 'Troubles' thriller, this chapter shall also address the problematics of representing the city for the dominant ideologies in Ireland more generally. Urban space threatens the social cartographies and spatial visions of Irish Nationalism and Unionism, both of which I shall deem *rusticative* ideologies: which is to say, ideologies entrapped in a mythic orientation towards a rural idealism.[1] By this I mean that Irish Nationalism and Unionism literally ground themselves on a pastoral conservatism which has profound implications for the representation of place and social relations in Irish culture. Filiation bases its continuity on the organic and essentialist as a means of seamless naturalization. For instance, Seamus Heaney's parish is structured around the father, as a readily politicized terrain often standing metonymically for the nation, in which language, self and place mythically cohere beyond the requisitions of History.

In consonance with filiation, John Wilson Foster's contention that both Belfast and Dublin remain 'overgrown villages, being personal, neighbourly and communal' (1991, 37) foregrounds the effort to rework the ideal of what Raymond Williams terms the 'knowable community' of the countryside in pastoralism's production of social space. The sweeping ideological import of this construction of filiative locality is indicated when Foster transposes his denial of city experience – 'only with reservation, then, could we claim that in reality or in fiction Ireland has developed a particularly urban consciousness' (1991, 37) – onto an entire national episteme in order to habituate his postulation that Ireland as a whole 'exhibits paradoxically a nationwide provincialism' (1991, 38). What is at stake here, therefore, as my last chapter suggested, is the opposition of private and public spaces. Within such a binary, the country functions as the place of family, kin and

---

[1] One meaning of the verb to rusticate, or to send to the country, is to suspend a student from university as a punishment. It could be suggested a similar cognitive banishment is foisted upon city dwellers in Ireland by Irish Nationalism and Unionism for the crime of living in a city.

neighbours (that is, people, in Sennett's terms, who are known even when apparently other as in Heaney's 'The Other Side'). The city, contrastingly, is the place where strangers must be negotiated and lived with, even as they remain unknown.[2]

The denial of the urban is conventionally regarded as the preserve of Irish Nationalism, which is seen to eschew Belfast, its founding Protestantism, industrialism, and colonial and Victorian architectural detritus.[3] Heaney's 'Docker' is a paradigmatic poetic instance of this tendency, which is articulated in fiction by Michael McLaverty's symptomatically titled *Lost Fields* and the carceral city of his *Call My Brother Back*. It is perhaps usually unacknowledged that a similar filiative nostalgia imbues Unionism's experience of the city. It is worth considering that the annual Orange March on the 12th July is to The Field, its ritualized procession through the streets an attempt to construct from the social fracture of Belfast a unitary urban narrative adumbrating the reaching of a redemptive pastoralism.[4] Similarly, Hugh Shearman contends that:

> Perhaps the fairest general comments about the Ulsterman is that he is, for the most part a countryman at heart. Even those who live in the city of Belfast normally have relations in the countryside, and that rigid division between rural and urban habits and traditions, which is so marked in some of the larger conurbations in Great Britain, has not yet developed in Northern Ireland (1968, 70).

This *rusticative* imperative within Unionism undercuts the intimation in Terence Brown's essay on 'Normalcy in Belfast' that the denial of the city is purely nationalist: '[h]ad Belfast proved dangerous or in obvious disintegration, ordinary life clearly still impossible for the inhabitants, then the place would have been scary but comprehensible since, in nationalist ideology, it has no right to exist' (1985, 7). Brown continues that 'the conflict in Northern Ireland of the last seventeen years, grievous and desperate as it has been, has not fundamentally shaken the Unionist population out of its conviction that daily life is possible, and so they do all in their power to make it so' (1985, 7). Within such a formulation, Belfast is figured as a normative Protestant settlement to be defended against

---

[2] It is interesting to consider whether Wilson Foster's position is actually analysing a cultural form or merely replicating it ideologically. Does he assert that the city as public space is represented in Ireland as a series of private spaces or is his thesis itself hankering after the idea of private, familiar space through which to circumvent the consideration of a properly constituted public, political and urban space? A similar ambivalence, pinioned between a desire to confront the problematics of Irish urban space and a comforting withdrawal from it, is to be found in Fintan O'Toole's 'Going West: The Country Versus the City in Irish Writing'. *The Crane Bag* Vol.12, No.2, 1987. 111-116. Here the tenement functions as a preserve of filiative kinship.

[3] An engaging history of Catholic settlement in the city is provided by A.C. Hepburn *A Past Apart: Studies in the History of Catholic Belfast 1850-1950*. Belfast: Ulster Historical Foundation, 1996.

[4] Here the work of Neil Jarman is particularly instructive.

Catholic subversion, which helps explain the role of Unionist hegemony in ensuring that property and social relations are untouched or unchallenged.

Brown's filiative identity of interest and its eschewal of class conflict in mapping urban space demonstrate one of the primary functions of the tribalized space of pastoralism. Certainly the *rusticative* directions of Unionism and Irish Nationalism are not ideologically identical. There is perhaps a migratory tenor resonant within Irish Nationalism's social spatialization. Such a resonance relates to the experience of dispossession, to the Famine and the loss of the land or country in all of its meanings, and residually structures the urban visions of such an ideology. This historical dispossession should most definitely not be discounted, but nor should it impair a consideration of how the present *rusticative* function of Irish Nationalism in both nation states in Ireland maintains concrete forms of social inequality. It therefore shares this mystification with Unionism as its ultimately determining social role. Unionism notably frames its hegemony in terms of paternalism, a perceptual patterning of self, place and the social that designedly overrides the class basis of its own production through an exigent transit into pastoral myth. There is perhaps also a sense of guilt, exhibited by the distrust of many Protestant poets for the city, which acknowledges in some way the historical development of Belfast as a corporate town, a symbol of colonial settlement. This necessitates the envisioning of a nostalgically regenerative recourse to the rural that finally seeks not only to dissolve the class fractures within Unionism but also to provide a sacrosanct belonging beyond the indignities and corruption of settlement itself. In keeping with these nuances, Edna Longley contends that for Protestant and Catholic writers Belfast is respectively either 'your fault or your fate' (1994, 107).

Mutatis mutandis, the *rusticative* ideologeme central to Unionism and Irish Nationalism wills in its production of a rural-urban opposition the dissembling of class realities into tribal bonds. As Luke Gibbons observes, 'idealizations of rural existence, the longing for community and primitive simplicity, are the product of an urban sensibility, and are cultural fictions imposed on the lives of those they purport to represent' (1988, 208). Within the *rusticative* conveyance of Irish Nationalism and Unionism the country looms as the mythic point of suture, through which both ideologies seek to circumvent their own inability to map and articulate the very social and economic relations which they nonetheless seek to habituate and order.[5] The tribal place is thus the disorientation of class cartography.

---

[5] The term *rusticative* therefore hopefully indicates that the various subjectivities producing pastoral social visions are embedded in urban situations from which the perpetual mythic flight is sought. Indeed, in considering the application of the country and the city, to appropriate the title of one of Raymond Williams's finest works, it is worth recalling the Latinate origins of the word 'country', in *contra*: meaning variously 'in comparison with', 'in opposition to', 'contrary to', 'opposed to'. Constructions of the rural and the pastoral, it then follows, meet precise historical requirements for an urban subject. Rather than viewing the country and the city as forming an immemorial opposition, it is more telling to dialecticize the terms as comprising the complementary ideological investments of what are ultimately unitary dominant subjectivities attempting to maintain specific sets of encompassing social relationships under pressure of the same historical moment.

To this end, this chapter shall assert that the thriller form itself embodies such conflictual mappings. Its more reactionary mappings of criminalized otherness seek to disguise and maintain the class organization and political shape of the city, as the more utopian vision of the city as a traceable network of crime demands its interrogation. The city provides a focal point for the fundamental contradictions of capitalism and their impingement upon human consciousness. It becomes the site, according to Raymond Williams, of 'the coexistence of variation and apparent randomness with what had in the end to be seen as a determining system: the visible individual facts but beyond them, often hidden, the common condition and destiny' (1973, 154). The utopian function of crime fiction, therefore, attempts to map such complexity, even as its more regressive form seeks to dissolve social cartography into consummate riddles of otherness and dislocation. Given that 'the history of capitalism is simultaneously its geography' (Storper and Walker, 10), the thriller form thus embodies a fundamental contradiction. For the city is to be situated as the place where capitalist spatialization is at its most complex, convoluted and encrypted, but also dialectically at its most pronounced, discernable and decodable. Thus, Williams notes the double condition of the city, wherein lies its true meaning as a dominant social form, expressing 'the random and the systematic, the visible and the obscured' (1973, 54).

In assessing the social complexity of urban space, and also in quantifying how that complexity is either acknowledged or obscured in the thriller form, Roland Barthes tellingly observes that 'the city, essentially and semantically, is the place of our meeting with the *other*' (1986, 96). Such otherness is, however, profoundly estranged from the intimate intruder typified by Heaney's aforementioned 'The Other Side'. Otherness in crime fiction may be mapped, to employ Bakhtin's terms, dialogically as a complex network of social forces dialectically encompassing both possibility and limitation, or monologically as superintended constituents of a Panopticon purview. The mechanics of exoticism finds its ideological significance in the atemporal supplanting of Belfast into 'an unspecific battlefield' (Hughes 1996b, 141), a displacement that effects the mystification of Benjamin's historical consideration that all 'cities are battlefields' (1983, 61).[6] Ralph Willett affirms that 'to regard the city as unreadable, an impenetrable blur, is to ignore distinctions of gender, class, race and economic status' (2). There is accordingly a deep formal antinomy in the 'Troubles' thriller's urban mappings. It contrarily enacts, through the compass of crime, properly historical conflict in the city, but also immemorialized conflict in its desire to order and regulate. For Gerald Seymour, in whose *Harry's Game* Belfast is the infernal site of 'hatred, terror and bestiality' (49), Belfast is the 'world's worst urban guerilla battlefield' (1983, 136). It functions as the reusable locale in an elucidation of the investment of the international thriller market in this voided anyplace. In refuting this exoticized battlefield, the utopian class mappings of the thriller form ultimately operate as adjudicatory nodes through which to adapt the cognitive navigations of Benjamin's *flâneur*: 'No matter what trail the *flâneur* may follow, every one of

---

[6] To this end, Lewis Mumford posits that 'the city became a battleground for conflicting cultures, dissonant ways of life' (323).

them will lead him to a crime' (1973, 41). The contestatory structure of such navigations in the thriller is produced directly by the heterogeneity of urbanity itself and its political agents: 'meaning in the city is multi-coded. Each social group possesses its own conception of urban space just as the different interests in the city compete with one another over control of the social surplus' (Gottdiener 'Culture', 206).

The polysemous fabric of urban space, its implication in historical process, disrupts not only the seamlessly homogeneous linguistic and communal attachment of Irish Nationalism and Unionism, but also the hierarchical ordering of social space in the *repressive* mechanics of the thriller form. The city as contestatory, imaginative terrain is the opposite of the closed system of the nation.[7] The city is itself an alternative narrative, or producer and repository of transgressive narratives and histories, to the nation and to the fugitive pastoralism which myopically stalks the mean streets of the conventional 'Troubles' thriller. As Glenn Patterson says of Belfast: 'the city rewrites itself – and is rewritten – constantly, generating new realities and fictions' (1994, 43).[8] The fearful recoil from the urban and its disruptive potentialities by both Nationalism and Unionism perhaps helps explain the recurrent gothicization of Belfast in contemporary fiction. As Eamonn Hughes posits: 'the city is ... a form of hell for ideologies which promote a tribalistic knowing your place as the only way of knowing yourself' (1996b, 153-154). Thus, Belfast is ultimately an infernal symbolic death for precisely these increasingly untenable organic ideologies.

In consequence, it is unsurprising that, as Raymond Williams notes, the city in literature recurrently provides a landscape for various forms of social pessimism (1973, 241). This pessimism is to be understood therefore not merely as about society itself but rather self-referentially as about the tenability of the subject ideology configuring such a discourse. The city throws such ideological maps into disarray: 'Urban life muddles through the pace of history. When this pace accelerates, cities – and their people – become confused, spaces turn threatening, and meaning escapes from experience' (Castells, 1994, 20). In the thriller, which offers both utopian and ideological mechanics for reinscribing such meaning into the social, 'Belfast' often functions as the malevolent signifier for social pessimism, providing a name and a refuge for the most reactionary attitudes to the working class, to women, to race, and to social otherness. It is strictly this form of dominant infernalization with which I wish to take issue. For to undercut this representation of Belfast as Hell is not to deny that the city is the site and catalogue of social inequalities, oppressions and deprivations. As Benjamin observes: 'To

---

[7] I could somewhat mischievously suggest that the complexity with which the city defeats the national imaginary is intimated with regard to crime fiction by Raymond Chandler's assertion that the genre concerns 'a world in which gangsters can rule nations and almost rule cities'. 'The Simple Art of Murder'. *Pearls are a Nuisance* (Harmondsworth: Penguin, 1973). 197.

[8] A thorough account of urban literature is afforded by Richard Lehan's *The City in Literature: An Intellectual and Cultural History* (London: U of California P, 1998), and Burton Pike's *The Image of the City in Modern Literature* (Princeton: Princeton U P, 1981).

determine the totality of forces in which ... modernity imprints itself would mean to represent hell'.[9] The radical, utopian function of detailing city space as covert networks of crime in many ways seeks the drafting of just such a Benjaminian map of hell. Rather it is the hellish, lost bearings of a contemptuous social pessimism that I intend to destabilize. Under such representational conditions, Belfast is never itself as a historically complex place, it is perversely a home for its own dislocation. Belfast's streets, voided of human agents or socioeconomic relations and forces, become the arterial occlusions of a terminally afflicted heart of darkness, its architecture projects the sepulchral, neural landscape of its inhabitants' monumental psychopathologies.

Thus for the serial killer, Candlestick, in Chris Petit's *The Psalm Killer*, 'Belfast was a maze to get lost in, where the darkest deeds stayed secret' (65). Possibly, therefore, the character of McClure and his manipulative, clandestine roles in *Resurrection Man* yields a self-referential appraisal of the more reactionary thriller's provision of its terrible thrills in an urban cartography of social pessimism and exotically fearful allure:

> Fitting himself to the secret fear, the hidden desire. Victor had seen him change his character four or five times a day, moving through a series of cold and dextrous personalities. McClure realized that people needed to confide those dangerous thoughts. They had to have a companion to guide them through the strange architecture of their loathing, someone to share its lonely grace (McNamee 1994, 99).

In Shah's *Fallen Angels*, Belfast, which is 'not like the rest of the world' (139), is the 'city of Terror and Death' (146). In the novel, Belfast's inhabitants revel in the gothic as a way of life, as conveyed by the depiction of the people of the Short Strand: 'horror to them was just the normality of the day' (69).[10] The representational role of this gothic content in the 'Troubles' thriller not only seeks to override the terror etched formally in the political unconscious, but also strives to absolve the rest of society from its reactionary map of hell produced by gothically estranging the working-class:

> The whole Protestant-Catholic thing was a working-class war, just as the quality of their leaders was. Their leaders and generals were plumbers and shopkeepers, not professional soldiers or politicians brought up on university degrees ... Until they could bring themselves into the modern world, they would always continue in this struggle with no meaning and no end. It was a tribal reaction, no different from those seen in the genocidal wars of Africa or Asia (Shah, 176).

---

[9] 'Die Totalität der Züge zu stimmen, in denen ... Moderne sich ausprägt, heißt die Hölle darstellen'. *GS* V. 1011.

[10] Peter Preston and Paul Simpson read McLaverty's *Cal* in the following way: for them, Cal is 'both oppressed and victimized by the spirit of the city. That spirit of murderous violence is personified in its politically active inhabitants, driven by ideological arguments that are exposed as spurious and dehumanizing' (11).

The attempt to construct such exoticized images of Belfast presents a specific formal application of the more general cultural and cognitive apparatus, whereby dominant subjects dehistoricize urban space through the recourse to discursive metacodes of representational containment. As M. Gottdiener asserts:

> given the polysemous or multi-coded nature of urban life, the need of some groups for more stable, uniformly conceived representations requires a management of the clash of oppositional environmental typifications. It is important to ask, on the one hand, what the groups are which possess a need for overarching, historically invariant symbols and, on the other, what the mechanisms are that are utilized to achieve ideological hegemony ('Culture', 207).

Gottdiener continues that 'the study of the city image, then, compels us to investigate the struggles for control of space and the manner by which certain ideological representations succeed while alternatives fail to materialize their traces' ('Culture', 216). The theoretical purpose of this chapter's analysis of the representation of Belfast in the thriller, therefore, seeks to refine our sense of the political unconscious in rematerializing these forgotten traces of historical process and contestation. I shall strive to harness the re-etching of History onto urban space with what urban planning would term *lines of desire*: with the symbolic cartographies and conflictive topographies through which human agents map the city and, in doing so, redraw the imputedly empirical sectarian geography of Belfast.

There is thus a twofold historical evisceration enacted in the conventional representation of Belfast. The discursive exotics of the international thriller offer a metacode restructuring, and indeed restructured by, hegemonic canons within Irish fiction of writing Belfast. The 'Troubles' thriller often functions, therefore, as the focal point of established popular cultural sedimentations depicting Belfast as hostile otherness. Here, 'Belfast' and the 'Troubles' bring one another into focus, tautologically affirming one another's hellishness, in a radical dehistoricization of both. In F.L. Green's *Odd Man Out* Belfast becomes the terminus of 'dread anxieties and morbid ideas from centuries of fanatical extensions of the will into regions of darkness and insurrection' (68). Green's otherwise excellent text, which remains one of the most engaging representations of Belfast in the thriller genre, does disclose a complexity beyond this morbidity however. The attack by the IRA leader, Johnny, on a Protestant factory, and his subsequent trail through Belfast's streets, in many ways offers an allegory of the position of an Irish Nationalist consciousness in the perceived hostile territory of Belfast as a total culmination of Protestant industrialism and social settlement. Belfast, in Max Caulfield's sensationalist novel, *The Black City* (1952), is locked in 'a pattern, it seemed, that nothing could change' (97). Written from the perspective of a Belfast Catholic, this text again associates the city with a dreary founding Protestantism, and an enduringly oppositional history:

> It is the Black City because of what is between Protestant and Catholic, between mongrel Briton and Mongrel Irishman, that is, narrow hatred and bigotry. It is not

> much of a place as cities go, a nineteenth-century industrial profusion of shipyard gantries, linen mills, factory chimneys, flaking pubs, oily river basins and mile after mile of narrow mean streets (5).

The degraded city is notably framed by an idyllic pastoral vision, in which a specifically hackneyed male subject redeems itself territorially through the conventionally gendered terms of Irish Nationalism's national cartography: 'you can see the curious Irish mountains, round and beautiful as a woman's breasts, rising in melancholy loveliness to the right ... the exiled heart stretches out and lingers there' (6). Despite the Catholic-Nationalist perspective, the text and its 'exiled heart', in which the *rusticative* ideologeme is encoded, shy away from the 'labyrinthine depths' (46) of the Falls and its otherness (even as it utilizes this exoticized space for its adventures and voyeuristic thrills, in a disclosure of the class geography of its subject).

W.A. Ballinger's voyeuristic 1969 text, *The Green Grassy Slopes*, recounts the defeat of socialism in 1930s in the 'mean streets' (81) of Belfast, and is greatly prompted and informed by its contemporary context and the onset of the present conflict. Although there is a utopian dimension to the text's depiction of Belfast – 'the smoke blurred the city's shape, softened its colours, transmuted it into something a little less than real, muted its harshness' (11) – it more consistently reinstates the dominant gothicization of the city and its bleakness, symbolized by the shipyard:

> by the Lagan stood the gantries of the shipyard, rearing high and bleak among the rows of little houses that surrounded it, dominating the city they had created ... There were no completing hulls on the ways, no clatter of riveting hammers that would have reached even to the hilltop; there was only that tall, gaunt, structural assembly waiting like Frankenstein's monster to have life breathed into it (11).

This stage gothicism attests to the terror in the text's political unconscious induced not merely by the city but particularly by its working class. Although the text seeks often sympathetically to detail the defeat of socialism within the Protestant working class, its own class cartography undermines this sympathy through the formal terror of its monstrous *unheimlich* silences.

Given this urban displacement of the national narrative, which prompts such *rusticative* ideological mechanics, the thriller does seemingly offer a literary mode for such confounded ideologies to attempt cognitively to trace the labyrinthine complexity of the city.[11] For the thriller developed historically in its hard-boiled American form as a means of mapping and negotiating the modern, urban wilderness, wherein previous ideological co-ordinates and social bearings diffused and vanished. As Raymond Williams notes: 'the opaque complexity of modern city life is represented by crime' (227). In the capable hands of a writer such as Dashiell Hammett, the thriller becomes a radical form, wherein crime functions as

---

[11] For a definitive account of the crime form's negotiation with urbanity see Ralph Willett's *Naked City: Urban Crime Fiction in the USA* (Manchester: Manchester U P, 1996).

a connective fabric through which an otherwise increasingly meaningless and shadowy society may be not only mapped, but also investigated and judged. The genre is also, however, the preserve of writers such as Mickey Spillane, intimating that its form is a dialectical terrain whose social symbolism emits often contradictory ideological signals. For Spillane, crime is not a cognitive means of charting the city as a map of the corruption of capitalism and modernity, but rather structures a rather more reactionary, paranoid terrain in which the city houses an illegible Otherness (whether class, gender, or racial) which must be revealed and regulated. It is unfortunately this latter, more reactionary form which has tended to predominate in the 'Troubles' thriller. The degradation of Belfast as an inert void within the pastoral vision of Nationalism and Unionism readily collapses into discursive sedimentations established by the international thriller market, which largely bases thrills on its exoticization of the North as a dangerous anyplace. For example, Seymour's *Harry's Game* describes Belfast as 'the adventure playground par excellence for the urban terrorist' (50). Such representational annulment further impacts upon the displacement of the urban in Irish writing, and tends to ensure that many Northern Irish thrillers autoexotically exhibit an anxiety about the control and decipherment of Belfast as sheer otherness.

In many respects, the *repressive* modality of the thriller's criminalization of urban illegibility wills the reconstitution of Williams' 'knowable community' in a thoroughly depleted form. For the homogeneous otherness, through which urban space is portioned by the *repressive* mappings of the thriller, substitutes the community as either known or knowable for that which is controllable or regulatable. In short, a fixed relation of place and belonging here rests on the *detectable* or *decipherable* community. The most delimitative rendering of such community is perhaps provided by *Harry's Game* and its circumvention of the affiliative and dynamic social formations produced by the city:

> Strangers were the traditional enemies in the village-sized Catholic communities of Belfast. The Short Strand, the Markets, Ardoyne, Divis, Ballymurphy ... all were self-sufficient, integral units. Small, difficult to penetrate, because unless you belonged you had no business or reason to come. They boasted no wandering, shifting groups, no cuckoos to come and feed off them ... There were no strangers. You were either known or not admitted (Seymour 1975, 117).

The textualization in the political unconscious of what is 'not admitted' by these detectable, intimate communities, not only in terms of class but also gender (given the desire to 'penetrate' such otherness in the above passage), dismantles such dominant representational strategies and confronts them as mechanisms designed to disable an integrated grasp of the totality of social relationalities. The anxiety produced by such detectable communities, and the desire to control them, is certainly not peculiar to the representations of Belfast in the thriller. As Neil Jarman observes: 'Rather than being unique to the situation in Northern Ireland, the practices of containment, surveillance, resistance and redefinition are unique only in their intensity and concentration' (Bender, ed. 135). Benjamin posits: 'fear, revulsion, and horror were the emotions which the big-city crowd aroused in those who first observed it' (1973, 131). Crime fiction, for Benjamin, emerged historically as an attempt to rewrite, rename even, the horror of the anonymity of the city: 'the masses appear as the asylum that shields an asocial person from his persecutors. Of all the menacing aspects of the masses, this one became apparent first. It is at the origin of the detective story' (1973, 40).[12]

What distinguishes the crowd in the 'Troubles' thriller from the crowd in other thrillers, is the specific inflections written into the former by the varying forms of otherness encoded in the representation of Belfast. Dana Brand notes the fundamental association of crime with illegibility in detective fiction: 'One implication of this reiterated association is that illegibility is itself a form of crime. It is a transgression against the interpretive laws imposed by the flâneur upon the city' (224). Thus, 'the entire crowd, according to this formulation, threatens the physical and epistemological well-being of the narrator' (225). In the 'Troubles' thriller, the point of narratorial focalization is often, by turns, that of the gaze of the international thriller market on the recidivist otherness of Irishness, that of the *rusticative* cartography and its production of tribal otherness. In terms of the international thriller, Shaun Clarke's *Red Hand* typifies the representation of Belfast as a cartography of total criminality: 'This was Belfast, a city at war, and everyone in it was a victim, which meant that everyone was also potentially dangerous' (1998, 202). Thus, Belfast as sheer, hostile otherness revels in the exotic and what I shall deem a *weak* formulation of the uncanny (which will be given a stronger rendering later in this chapter): 'nothing in this city could be deemed to be unusual – the unusual was commonplace' (1998, 233). For Shaun Clarke, Belfast is Seymour's adventure playground, shorn of its play, as 'the worst killing ground in Europe' (1993, 65). It is telling that when his fiction attempts a more positive delineation of Belfast, the primary utopian and allegorical investment is in landscape and to the detriment of a degraded Belfast populace:

> To most of the English, Belfast was a dreadful place of slums and bricked-up houses, but these were actually in the minority and the city was actually very appealing with its stately Victorian architecture, the pastoral River Lagan, numerous parks and surrounding mountains, green hills and farmlands. If Belfast was sometimes not a pretty sight, it had been scarred by the very people laying claim to it (Clarke 1993, 195).

Equally, in the thrillers produced by Irish writing, it is notable that the *rusticative* ideologies of Irish Nationalism and Unionism, in attempting to incorporate an imaginary pastoral community into the city in an unfeasible manner, reinforce the deterioration of the community as known experience into estranged surveillance. The *rusticative* imperative contorts urban space as merely the corrupted

---

[12] Or, as Benjamin later wrote, the fear of the crowd comes to represent the horror of the complexity of the city itself for traditional social mappings: 'it erases ... all trace of the individual: it is the latest asylum of the outlaw. It is finally, the newest and most impenetrable maze in the labyrinth of the city'. 'Sie verswischt ... alle Spuren des Einzeln: sie ist das neueste Asyl des Geächteten. Sie ist, endlich, im Labyrinth der Stadt das neueste and unerforschlichste Labyrinth' (*GS* V, 559).

continuance of the intimate, tribal territories of the national imaginary. The specifics of the crowd in the mechanistic 'Troubles' thriller, then, its inexorable geometry of otherness, produces a topography of ghettoes and monologic enclaves which serve to naturalize social inequality. These spatial orderings of otherness also seek to stall the dialectics of urbanity; they produce instead a spatiality of what I shall term *oppositional enclosure* to be regulated and patrolled. What is notable about such oppositional enclosure and the stalling of dialectics is its consonance with the traumatic paradigm of Irish history and its sectioned oppositions.

In terms of urban space, then, the account of an iterative conflict between two tribal monoliths is literally made concrete in an immutable sectarian geography of Belfast ghettoes and one-way systems. By way of illustration, Moore's *Lies of Silence* depicts Belfast as comprising 'graffiti-fouled barricaded slums where the city's Protestant and Catholic poor confronted each other, year in year out, in a stasis of hatred, fear and mistrust' (21). The graffiti indelibly etched as demarcatory totem on the walls of these static enclaves offers itself as an attempt to recapitulate the conventional assemblage of language, place and identity in Irish culture. This fixed signification is thus structurally incompatible with, and fundamentally denaturalized by, the thriller form and its historical emergence as an attempt to chart and resolve the anonymous, disconnective signs and riddles of the city in a response to the breakdown of precisely such organicism.

What is most notable about Moore's attempt to concretize the traumatic paradigm of Irish history, is that it contravenes the symbolic spatial codes of Moore's other Belfast fiction in a confirmation of the representational delimitation produced by the *repressive* modality of the thriller. For example, in *The Lonely Passion of Judith Hearne*, the City Hall and its surrounds are depicted as 'the designated centre of the city' (102). However, as Eamonn Hughes notes (1996, 146), the text decentres this static order through an elaborate symbolic geography. Therein Miss Hearne descends from the Catholic middle-class heaven of the Antrim Road, through the purgatory of a Camden Street flat and into the hell, 'the dark place' (173), of working-class, Protestant Ballymacarret. Despite the encasement of an immutable sectarian geography in *Lies of Silence*, there are moments when this map breaks down formally in an unwitting gesture towards the spatial antinomies of the 'Troubles' thriller. The displacement of the Dillon home, its transmutation into somewhere 'no longer familiar' (157), signals not merely the auto-exotics informing the thriller in Irish writing but also a much more powerful estrangement, which is etched by the absent cause of urban space itself: namely, the Freudian *unheimlich*, which lacerates the mythic and the tribal consciousness. Here the *weak* articulation of the uncanny as exotic is disrupted by the eruption of the uncanny as social and historical force. For when carrying the bomb to the hotel where he is manager, Dillon's own mental cartography undergoes a self-reflexive re-evaluation, as an 'ironic procession' (79), by its very displacement:

> It was a route which on a normal day was far too familiar to evoke in him any thought of what he was passing but this morning, in a car that was a moving bomb, followed by terrorists who could radio in an order to kill his wife, he was

driving for what might be the last time through this ugly, troubled place which held for him implacable memories of his past life (79).

As Mike Davis asserts, 'mental geographies betray class prejudice' (375). In *Lies of Silence*, Dillon's own symbolic cartography of Belfast is tellingly middle class and produced in contradistinction to that of the homogenous 'poor' who inhabit the text's tribal ghettoes. Thus, the production of such filiative enclaves bound in ahistorical opposition ultimately belies the specific social subjects of that production. Moreover, although Dillon views the Antrim Road middle class 'as though they were residents of a city thousands of miles away from bombs and guns' (102), the thriller form also issues a historical return of the repressed that maps the city as a totality of social relationships. Therefore, in spite of the attempt to concretize an Irish historical paradigm of oppositional enclosure, the text belies its own subjective mapping that defeats such representational stasis and accords with Williams' assertion that the city is 'at once a social fact and a human landscape' (1973, 158).[13]

Daniel Mornin's *All Our Fault* grants perhaps the most succinct example of both the fracture of the filiation and the Marxist potentiality of the Freudian *unheimlich*. The text centres on the attempt of the Kelly family to find their lost father, Liam, after a night's rioting. If we return to the apparatus of organicism producing Heaney's patriarchal parish, the father's quest to 'get back to his family' (21) signals the final recantation of the topographic filiation of Heaney's model. Although the text, presided over by a stage gothic moon, depicts Belfast as 'dying' (77), it also heralds formally the extirpation of the tribal place. Kelly feels continually 'trapped' (78) in Belfast, as is Michael Dillon in *Lies of Silence* (114), in a recapitulation of the carceral city, which has pervaded Catholic and Nationalist accounts of Belfast. But there is also a liberation from the perceptual attenuation of the *rusticative* imagination. When Liam is abducted by a Loyalist gang, there is a moment of recognition between the former and the paramilitary, Kenny. The Loyalist experiences 'a niggling familiarity with the man that makes him think that he should be buying him a drink rather than beating the living daylights out of him' (156). When it transpires that the two were former childhood friends, this refamiliarization can be interpreted as a somewhat regressive attempt to reinstate the familiar stranger as knowable and organic, who has been displaced by the aberration of the 'Troubles' and indeed the city itself. But this encounter, in terms of the tribal self and place, with sheer otherness has a much more profound resolution if we consider the full dynamics of the Freudian *unheimlich*.

Upon remembering Liam, Kenny feels 'the thoughts start to turn his captive from a member of the enemy to a once intimately known, even loved, friend that

---

[13] Similarly, Dorothy Porter notes, with a relevance to the imaginative decentrings of Belfast across many of Moore's Belfast novels: '[a]ll cities have two aspects: abiding idea of the city as revered and deplored centre of religious, military and political power, and the physical presence of the city in identifiable space and time. But it is as hard to comprehend the city in space and time as it is to ignore it. The city in its second empirical aspect turns out to be as much a function of the imagination as in its first' (42).

he had liked more than he had always let on' (165). This movement from estrangement to recognition broadly parallels Liam's own effort to negotiate his way through the unfamiliar streets towards home: 'he will press on through the streets, hoping to recognize something in a once intimately known area' (77). To a large extent, the city itself as labyrinth functions as an exemplary social form of Freud's initial formulation of the *unheimlich* as 'something one does not know one's way about' (1990, 340). In Freud's dialectical methodology, however, the *heimlich* or homely comes to exhibit a meaning which is identical to its opposite, the uncanny. For one of the designations of the homely is, through an overdetermination of the familiar, the development of the homelike into something which is withdrawn from the eyes of strangers, something secret or concealed. Thus, 'the uncanny is that class of frightening which leads back to what is known of old and long familiar ... the name for everything that ought to have remained secret and hidden but has come to light' (1990, 340).

Despite the exotic displacement of Belfast in the thriller genre, therefore, there is a much more powerful form of estrangement and mapping in the uncanny, which takes the form of a class allegory in this dialectic of defamiliarization and belonging. In many ways, both class and class oppression are the ultimate estrangement from one's self, one's labour, one's place. But it then follows that out of this ultimate alienation, class consciousness and the remapping of one's society are the ultimate enlightenment for which the total map of the city metonymically stands. Freud firmly equates the *unheimlich* with repression: 'the uncanny is in reality nothing new or alien, but something which is familiar and old-established in the mind and which has become alienated from it only through the process of repression' (1990, 363-364). Thus, the attempted repressions of the various maps of Belfast in the thriller, whether postmodern, International New Right, Irish Nationalist or Unionist, are alienated territories offering imaginary resolutions to the class and social tensions of the city as totality that are redeemed by the utopian formal modalities of crime fiction.

The thriller, then, for writing from an Irish Catholic background, such as Moore's or Mornin's, provides a means not just of exoticization but also an issuing of the uncanny that dialectically produces socially symbolic geographies which, to return to Mike Davis, betray class prejudice and indeed class consciousness that ultimately confirm their urban belonging. This dialectic also produces formal antinomy in *Fall When Hit*, written by the Protestant novelist, Richard Crawford, in an elucidation of the contradictions of Unionism. The embroilment of UDR soldier, Garret Kearns, in a state conspiracy provides an alienation from his rural belonging: 'I was changed and different and my normal places were strange to me' (1993, 36). Pursued into the city, Belfast and its 'dark labyrinth of streets and alleys' (1993, 123) on one level again offers itself as the focal point of this estrangement and debasement. Kearns' bewailing his plight in the city neatly uncovers the ideological usage of the *rusticative* codes of Unionism in its juxtaposition of rural value with the degradations of the urban: 'years of obedience and service to the Crown and now come to this, hunted by its agents, forced to seek sanctuary among the scum of the gutters' (1993, 101). However, as a fugitive, Kearns is also impelled to concede a form of possibility in Belfast: 'at least in the city you can hide' (1993, 180). Indeed, it is precisely the city, which enables Kearns to surmount his tribal identity and its paternalist nostalgia as a prerequisite for his effort to chart the state structures and conspiracies that envelop him. On another textual level, therefore, even as it functions as the culmination of social decline for the nostalgic *rusticative* subject, Belfast is proposed at the same time as the aggregation of the possibility of a social and cognitive cartography.

Therefore, mental cartographies of the city are not merely content but also form in the thriller, which maps the city in a way which contravenes tribal place and the traumatic, oppositional historical paradigm. To this end, E.M. Forster's 1919 essay on Forrest Reid succinctly conjoins figurations of Belfast as exotic; the site of restive historical spectres; the corruption of the pastoral:

> Unreal yet squalid, its streets lack either picturesqueness or plan, and manage to exclude all prospect of the mountains that neighbour them ... she is haunted by a ghost, by some exile from the realms of the ideal who has slipped into her commonsense, much as the sea and the dispossessed fields, avenging nature, have re-emerged as dampness and as weeds in her streets (92).

What this peculiarization of Belfast therefore elides is the global urban experience of the city, its *unheimlich* juxtapositions and cognitive overlappings, as evidenced by the London of Ian Sinclair or Patrick Wright. Wright's own excavations of London insist: 'History is not just a matter of old relics: it also lies around as morbidly unfinished business, as ghosts and strange potencies that seep round the edges of every reforming design' (Wright, 1991, 165). There are varying class mappings and investments in the perceptual ordering of city space, which finally belie the various subjective positions formulating this kind of psycho-geography, so that even texts proposing the most immemorialized forms of urban representation betray themselves. In this respect, the refuge of Victor Kelly in the ruins of the public baths in Tomb Street in *Resurrection Man* allegorically gestures to configurations of decayed civics, social reformisms and industrial deprivation. Indeed, although the text deals with Loyalist paramilitaries it is notable that its urban imaginary often articulates the carceral fatalism of Irish Nationalist representations of Belfast, so that Victor Kelly is only truly at 'home' (70) in prison at the deeply symbolic Crumlin Road jail. McNamee, a young Catholic writer from Kilkeel, misspells both the Donegall Road and Shaftesbury Square, two hugely significant names in the history of Belfast[14] and its street names, in an almost wilful act of dispossession from this heritage.[15] In addition, the fatalism of the Resurrection Men's victims seems to confirm Edna Longley's thesis on Catholic writing and Belfast. These symbolic mappings in the text are distilled in

---

[14] The Donegall name is especially weighty, given that the family were in sole control of Belfast until 1844.

[15] Despite its representation of Loyalism, therefore, the text also bespeaks a Catholic nationalist perspective on the city, particularly in its carceral rendering: 'the placenames which McClure continued to enumerate seemed part of a strange other topography, surveyed and mapped and returned to silence' (222).

the consciousness of Jim Curren, one of the Resurrection Men's victims, just before he is murdered:

> It seemed that he could see the city clearly on nights like this and it was a place of age and memory. He thought about the *Titanic* built in the shipyard, the closed linen mills, the derelict shirt factories, the streets of houses built for workers and other edifices constructed by speculators who seemed to have this modern city in mind, their designs weathered down to create a setting for injured lives; this city like gaunt others they had created on shallow, muddy deltas or desolate coasts guided by infallible principles of abandonment (112-133).[16]

There is nonetheless a powerful class allegory in the text, which utilizes crime fiction to map the injuries and injustices of this industrial and class heritage. Furthermore, McNamee's controversial *Resurrection Man* is a vastly significant text in considering the representation of Belfast in the thriller, in that it performs both stylistically and formally the transgression of filiative, tribal cartographies within the urban context even as it indulges them. I want to devote sustained attention to McNamee's text, as, given the wealth of material here, it distils many issues concerning the thriller's representation of Belfast. The text not only supersaturates the gothic excesses of the form but also points self-referentially to both its limitations and the specific possibilities encoded in the urban cartography of genre. Furthermore, the tracing of the conflictive cognitive maps operative in *Resurrection Man* subverts the more passive sense of human subjectivity produced by the *repressive* modality of the novel: 'It seemed that the city had itself decided to devise personality for them, assign roles, a script to accompany a season of coming evil' (159). In fact, a utopian figuration of the conflictive mappings in the text rewrites the passively followed script, making the city, in Barthes' term, *scriptible* (1990, 3), a site/sight for oppositional interpretation. When the first victim is uncovered in the text, we are informed that 'the root of the tongue had been severed. New languages would have to be invented' (16). This sense of linguistic breakdown and the need for new meanings and co-ordinates are due not only to the text's attempt to comprehend a horrific violence but also its confrontation with the dialectic of urban fragmentation and possibility. In its own dark way, *Resurrection Man* heeds J.G. Ballard's call for a writing which 'offers a set of options and imaginative alternatives' (1990, 9).

Nevertheless, Glenn Patterson considers the novel a petrifaction of Belfast as 'an inert, knowable thing, yielding its truths to necroscopic investigation. More, it is a city whose mortification precludes all possibility of change' (1994, 43). By contrast, I would assert that it is exactly such change which ultimately defeats the text's immutable sectarian geography and insinuates itself in the text as formal antinomy. Even as the text performs the reduction of Belfast cartography to

---

[16] Whilst the *Titanic* is used here, as in so many texts, as a symbol of the doomed nature of Belfast and its urban inferiority, the building of the ship, along with others of its kind, actually attests to the prominent and advanced role that Belfast played in the industrial and ship-building world economy at the time.

detached postmortem, it also self-referentially uncovers the inadequacies of the conventional mortification of Belfast. The symbolic encounter with city as inquisitive autopsy reaches its apotheosis in Asher's *Shoot to Kill*:

> It was an evil, gloating presence. It was a vicious, dying carcass with its entrails slashed open, dripping pools of blood and filth and vomit and lashing out in its death throes. There was no excitement here. There was no adventure. This was an evil place, the embodiment of evil, like a disturbed ant-hill turned on itself. A stink hung over the city, a smell of death, of dying places, of the damp-sodden rags of civilization, of animal pens in a vast market, of an enormous concentration camp guarded with barbed wire, search-lights, towers, machine-guns, guards with batons and barred windows (126).

Of course the thriller precisely seeks to produce 'excitement' and 'adventure' from this social anxiety. In doing so, it divulges the historical position and social subjectivity of its mappings.. Indeed, yet another military memoir-inspired book, A.F.N. Clarke's *Contact*, intimates how 'Belfast', under such representational conditions, functions not as itself but as a historically-voided and pseudo-metaphysical landscape into which a voyeuristic subject foists and displaces its own guilts and turmoils: 'Belfast, I live and breathe you. Belfast, you are etched deep within my soul. Belfast I have become you and carry the stink of your corpse like a cause' (77).

To this end, the ideologeme of Kelly's character in *Resurrection Man* stylizes into overdetermination some of the most reactionary mappings of the thriller form itself. In demonstrating how *Resurrection Man* decentres the sectarian mortification of Belfast, it is significant that the putatively Catholic name of the character of Victor Kelly, based on the Shankill Butcher, Hugh Leonard Murphy, is itself a displacement; a hybrid, unsettled signification, which contradicts the sectarian and linguistic absolutes that he represents in the text. As a reaction against this liminality, Victor Kelly's imaginative attempt to make 'the city become a diagram of violence centred about him' (11) in many respects foregrounds the representational delimitation of both the conservative thriller and the conventional depiction of Belfast, which strives to fixate a map of the city through an ossified compass of barbarism that disavows historical complexity.

The spatial allegory in *Resurrection Man*, between the perfect ritualized murder and 'sectarian and geographic certainties' (17), admittedly concurs with Patterson's criticism of the text as dissecting 'the city as cadaver' (1994, 43). This representational economy, wherein location is secured and otherness excised through the mediations of the body and *topos* in terms of the knowable and the alterior, ultimately attests to the representational violence inflicted upon Belfast by the thriller form and its cartography of tribal paranoia. Stallybrass and White's dictum that 'thinking the body is thinking social topography and vice versa' (192) highlights the relationship between the violation of social space and the body, at the site of which profound anxieties and antinomies endure. Feldmann contends:

> The magnification of the violated body as a spatial unit and the transgressive aura of certain branded spaces are complementary signs of social deformation. Through

their violent cathexis, body and topos communicate fearful alterity. The silent horror that grows around deformed spaces subtracts these sites from assumed contexts and anchorages. The disappearance of bodies from specific spaces becomes the sympathetic expulsion of those spaces from their social surround (63).

Just as Victor Kelly is impelled to mutilate the bodies of a tribal otherness, so too his conception of a perfected and immunized urban totality requires the obliteration of opposing sanctuaries: 'He pointed out the different parts of the city to her. New Lodge. The Short Strand. He described how you could wipe them off the map from here. Artillery fire directed with precision. Repeated sorties' (45-46). Thus, Feldmann discloses that 'sectarian murder was not so much an expression of community consensus as it was a rhetoric by which social solidarity was formed by focusing social consciousness on politically charged objects, miniaturized referents of more expansive yet unrealizable geographies' (73). The strategies of urban representational containment encoded in the ideologeme of Victor Kelly's character therefore unfold as an attempt to mitigate a tribal 'corps morcelé' (Lacan 1977a, 20)[17] through a fetishized spatial utopianism of both seamless, topographic filiation and ideal body: 'The absence of a stable sectarian spatial order and the dispersal of symbolic totality furthered the investment in part objects as substitutes and supplements of the absent whole' (Feldmann, 81).

As Eamonn Hughes points out: 'to accept a restrictive stereotype of Belfast or any other city or community, is to visit a kind of violence on it and its inhabitants by refusing the particularity and variety of their stories' (1997, 157). The text discloses this representational violence and its discursive mechanics and political applications. The violation of the bodies of the human agents, who disrupt the geometries of Victor Kelly's ordnance map, or indeed whose victimhood produces such geometries, highlights the historical shift in mapping from the experiential, subjective cartography of the human agent towards the externalized and mediated geographies of urban planning. In a way, the Resurrection Men murders are an attempt to extirpate what Donatella Mazzoleni deems the 'total aesthetic' (297) of urban experience, through which the simulacra and sensory apparatus of human agents attempt to produce a sense of place. As they patrol the environs of west and north Belfast in their car, removing unwitting pedestrians from the streets, the Resurrection Men allegorize the urban planning strategies of the area, the role of the misnomic Westlink and the systematic ghettoization of working-class communities.[18]

Additionally, the ritualized nature of the killings, their spatialization of necropolitan stasis, uncover the territorial imperatives of Irish Nationalism and

---

[17] That is, 'the body-in-pieces', a retroactive fantasy effected by the imaginary unity of the mirror stage, which I am here formulating as the imagined ideological unity of filiative space.

[18] There is also a strong labour history to the streets of North and West Belfast, which are not reducible to the conventional 'killing zone' depiction. For a spirited account of the Trade Union activity in the area in the 1920s and 1930s, see Paddy Devlin *Yes We Have No Bananas: Outdoor Relief in Belfast 1920-39*. Belfast: Blackstaff P, 1981.

Unionism, the mortification of human agency within a mythic consonance of self, place and other. In the monumental survey, *The City in History*, Lewis Mumford asserts that the emergence of the city or early urban forms of settlement coalesces with a decisive shift in cultural forms, broadly schematized as a shift from ritual to drama, which marks a transformation from the stable and repetitive to the dynamic and narrative. The gang's use of ritual to mythically define place is thus a glaring denial of dialectical urban consciousness. The figuration of Belfast as necropolis also has a somewhat reactionary mythic resonance. Mumford speculates that the first germ of the city was the ceremonial meeting space, the collective barrow of the dead: 'the city of the dead antecedes the city of the living' (15). Thus the first streets were the rows of graves laid down by nomadic tribes, who periodically returned to such gravesites and eventually settled beside them. The use of the necropolitan locale to fixate place for the hybridity encoded in the character of Kelly ultimately castigates the mortification of urban space and human agency in both Irish Nationalism and Unionism.

So on one level *Resurrection Man* does recapitulate the immutable sectarian geography dissecting Belfast as carcass: 'the city in all its history devised as a study of death' (158). The text also, however, conveys how the city defeats the imposition of such a tribal cartography, setting it apart from the more reactionary thriller's criminalized zones of otherness. Despite the mortificatory imperatives encoded in the ideologeme of Kelly's character, the text ultimately attests to the fact that '[t]he landscape is never inert, people engage with it, rework it, appropriate and contest it. It is part of the way in which identities are created and disputed, whether as individual, group or nation-state ... landscapes are thus polysemic, and not so much artifact as in process of construction and reconstruction' (Bender 'Introduction', 3). For Victor Kelly's 'inventory of the city, a naming of parts' (27), ultimately breaks down under the strain of change and historical process:

> sometimes on one of these runs he would say, where are we? He sounded surprised as if he had suddenly discovered that the streets were not the simple things he had taken them for, a network to be easily memorized and navigated. They had become untrustworthy, concerned with unfamiliar destinations, no longer adaptable to your own purposes. He read the street names from signs. India Street, Palestine Street. When he spoke them they felt weighty and ponderous on his tongue, impervious syllables that yielded neither direction nor meaning. Sandy Row, Gresham Street ... he would attempt to sketch portions of the city, working fast and silent, streets discarded, corrected, gone over again and again until they yielded up names, faces. Each one seemed incomplete (163).

The incompleteness of his tribal mappings of place is important as it signals the inability of this sectarian cartography to articulate the city as a total aesthetic of psycho-geographical territories. It suggests, to quote the novel itself, 'something beyond the capacity of maps' (13), something beyond this static tribal cartography in the thriller. This static sectarian geography is typified by *Harry's Game*, wherein the British Intelligence services show the eponymous agent, Harry Brown, a 'tribal map' (50) that he must memorize in order to ensure his survival. Often thriller writers themselves seem to adopt this approach and their many errors and misspellings in depicting the various one-way systems and ghettoes, which they supposedly know so well, finally attest to Ciaran Carson's censure in *Belfast Confetti*: 'No, don't trust maps, for they avoid the moment' (43). Indeed, this kind of static or mimetic and supposedly empirical mapping of Belfast is neatly satirized by Bateman's *Divorcing Jack*, wherein a car chase makes a stop at 'a closed petrol station on the Stranmillis Road' (141). This garage does not actually exist in Belfast. Its inclusion in the ubiquitous retailing of streets and sights in the chase suggests a shrewd acknowledgement of a minority yet expert readership, a parodic and conniving play with the exoticism of Belfast, which signals the limits of this form of empirical staging.

In *Resurrection Man*, Kelly's gang themselves, by murdering and erasing human agents as they make their way across the city, attempt to impose the tribal mapping of place onto the complexity of the city in a manner, which again self-referentially provides an analogue of the conventional thriller's representation of Belfast. Its mortified necropolis seeks to repress *the lines of desire* of human agents subjectively and dialogically mapping the city. As this strategy of representational containment breaks down, the text anticipates, admittedly, rather than fully articulating, 'a dreamtime of voices' (61). The formal tensions of McNamee's text validate Burton Pike's postulation that 'the city always speaks, and with many voices' (ix).

The text's ritualized performance of violence and, indeed, stylized consideration of representational violence in the thriller, demonstrates that the highly-segregated space of Belfast and contemporary urban planning (in an obliteration of the actual experience of brutalization and suffering endured by its occupants) serves to satiate the cartographic imperatives of bourgeois ideologies of Irish Nationalism and Unionism: 'Within the ideological and topographic form of the sanctuary, experiential deterritorialization emerged as the dominant condition of social reality, as utopian territorial icons emerged as axial ideological projections of national redemption and ethnic integrity' (Feldmann, 42). Central to the delimitation of urban space by Irish Nationalism and Unionism, which is encoded in both the concretized stasis of many thrillers and in the defensive urban planning strategy adopted during the last thirty years of conflict, is the production of the 'sanctuary' as eulogized and inviolate space: 'the creation of the sanctuary automatically designated an ethnically opposed adjacent community as a targeting-targeted formation' (Feldmann, 37). Given that this book has traced the 'utterly resigned terror' or dread of ideologies in crisis, I wish to term this reductive mapping of urbanity a *terror*-torial mechanism. By addressing these cartographic exigencies as *terror*-torial imperatives I intend a dialectical phrasing which makes two points. Firstly, that I wish to designate Unionism and Irish Nationalism as ideologies whose spatial visions only function through strategies of both imaginative and material delimitation and terror that visit a prohibitive violence upon the complexity of people and their urban territories. Secondly, and more optimistically in the other aspect of this dialectic, the urban terrains of both ideologies become *terror*-tories because the city is the place where Irish Nationalism and Unionism finally rupture. The city is the place where the envisaged tribal communities of both are unmasked as failed and anxious attempts to disguise their own terror that urban and historical dynamics will always transgress and defeat the boundaries of their putatively naturalized and organic communities.

The importance of *Resurrection Man* is that it actuates the tensions of such *terror*-torial imperatives. The failure of this *terror*-torial mapping is enacted in the very form of *Resurrection Man* itself. Given that Mumford defines the city as a 'multi-form', urban writing itself is subject to this multiplicity. To this end, Gerry Smyth's account of the novel is interesting:

> novelistic discourse mixes with other genres such as documentary, *film noir*, philosophy and crime thriller, making it difficult to settle into one consistent reading position from which to make sense of the narrative ... the novel resists any straightforward reading, attempting to insinuate at a formal level the problem of alienation which would appear to be the text's major theme (1997, 120).

Surely this multidiscursivity is one of the novel's strengths, setting it apart from the more formulaic thriller. Its dialectical fabric overrides Victor's spatial vision and thereby verifies Ken Worpole's account of 'the endless myths, genealogies and stories' (1995, 187) produced by urban space and its human agents. It is also here within such *lines of desire* that the utopian, class allegory contained within urban cartography of the radical thriller form is to be uncovered. For Kelly's incomplete tribal map exists in formal tension in the text with a more conspiratorial mapping that ultimately subsumes the former. Many of the characters, not least Victor himself, find themselves working to 'a hidden imperative' (197), their lives imbued with 'unknown resonances' (150). Benjamin once commented that 'the original social content of the detective story was the obliteration of the individual's traces in the big-city crowd' (1973, 43). While this riddle of the self is still relevant to the individual's relation to the city and crime fiction, its co-ordinates have been subsumed by the conspiratorial mapping, which I have identified in the thriller. Conspiracy, therefore, functions in however degraded a form as a utopian mode, offering a class allegory that seeks to reconvene urban fragmentation as totality.

Indeed, the sense in *Resurrection Man* that events are structured by 'an unimaginable necessity' (77) returns us very succinctly to the terms of Jameson's political unconscious. The conspiracy centres on the figure of McClure and ultimately entails a network of paramilitary figures, police officers and state officials. Thus, on one level, when the text depicts Belfast as the 'scene of a great crime in the hearts of men' (92) it recapitulates a more regressive notion of Belfast as fallen city, as a malign architectural projection of the inner landscapes of loathing of its depraved inhabitants. At another level of the text's formulations, that of the conspiratorial mapping, it also functions in a utopian manner in gesturing by means of criminal pattern to the urban totality itself, its social relations, the dialectic of its inequalities and potentialities, its fragmentation and affiliation.

Consequently, the *lines of desire* encoded in the conspiratorial thriller's mapping of urban crime, which offer a guide to the urban totality, in many respects parallel Frederic Jameson's concept of 'cognitive mapping'. Therein the symbolic geography of the individual's attempt to reconcile his/her urban displacement with a sense of the city as total network is extrapolated to our contemplation of the social structure itself. Here Jameson rearticulates in thorough Marxist terms Kevin Lynch's formulation of 'the imageability of the city': 'You can provide the viewer with a symbolic diagram of how the world fits together: a map of how the world fits together: a map of written instructions. As long as he [sic] can fit reality to the diagram, he has a clue to the relatedness of things' (11). Lynch's model is entrapped by the limits of an arid phenomenology and lacks a conception of human agency and historical process. Thus, Jameson's emblematic usage of the mental map of the city space, as allegory for the mental map of social and global totality, negotiates 'a gap between phenomenological perception and a reality that transcends all individual thinking or experience. The concept of cognitive mapping ... therefore involves an extrapolation of Lynch's spatial analysis to the realm of social structure, that is to say, in our historical moment, to the totality of class relations' (1988a, 353). Otherwise, as Jameson observes, 'the incapacity to map spatially is as crippling to political experience as the analogous incapacity to map spatially is for urban experience' (1991, 416). The utopian function of the tracing of crime in the thriller thus coalesces political and urban cartographies, so that cognitive mapping acts not only as the code word but also the methodology of class consciousness:

> the dialectic between the here and now of immediate perception and the imaginative or imaginary sense of the city as an absent totality ... presents something like a spatial analogue of Althusser's great formulation of ideology itself ... this positive conception of ideology as a necessary function in any form of social life has the great merit of stressing the gap between the local positioning of the individual subject and the totality of class structures in which he or she is situated (1988a, 353).

The exigency of this imaginative negotiation of the displacement between the local agent and the totality is confirmed by Hana Wirth-Nesher's comment that 'cities promise plenitude, but deliver inaccessibility' (8). She contends that the city has more to do with absence than presence, with inventing rather than physically constructing the cityscape. The city is, ultimately, for Wirth-Nesher, an unending seriality of partial visions, which seemingly debilitate subjective experience. Moreover, Moretti posits that 'the city dweller's life is dominated by a nightmare – a trifling one, to be sure, – unknown to other human beings: the terror of "missing something"' (1988, 119). And this is exactly the terror of the *terror*-torial mapping, the dread of its own deficiency; whereas the cognitive desires emboldening the *redemptive* modality of the thriller's urban mappings use crime to reconnect the city as a totality. This dialectic of presence and absence in the psycho-geographics of the urban suggests that the city provides a fundamental focalization and justification of Jameson's theory of the political unconscious, its attempt to reconstruct the unfigurable force of the totality.

Notably Kelly's tribal map is unable to comprehend the city as a total system:

> In the morning he found a skylight on the roof and climbed through it to find
> himself on the roof on the side which faced away from the water towards the city.
> A different territory now that he was looking at it from this height, seemingly
> unreliable with slithery, grey rooftops and the dominating bulk of the city hospital
> looking prone to moodiness, as if it were at any minute liable to become detached
> from its surroundings and begin a surly flotation seawards (203).

Victor's tribal sense of the city notably produces in the above passage an image of
the city as 'a different territory', an alienated locale beyond his perceptual grasp.
So McNamee's deployment of the conspiratorial ideologeme to suggest something
beyond the capacity of the tribal map divulges the political and cultural
applications of the filiative *topos*. For the *lines of desire*, encoded in the mappings
of the thriller, reintegrate the historical *unheimlich* and dialecticize the image of the
city in the manner of Benjamin's assertion that 'the dialectical image is to be
defined as the *unheimlich* remembrance of a redeemed humanity'.[19] Such a
mapping thereby circumvents the frozen ache of Moore's graffiti-bound enclosures
which are 'the image of the city' (21) in *Lies of Silence*. In many ways, the
challenge in producing a formal analysis of *Resurrection Man* resides in the need
to rupture the mythic framework of the tribal map with the dialogic dynamic of
urban space. According to Williams: 'out of cities ... came these two great and
transforming modern ideas: myth, in its variable forms: revolution, in its variable
forms. Each, under pressure, offers to convert the other to its own terms. But they
are better seen as alternative responses, for in a thousand cities, if in confused
forms, they are in sharp, direct and necessary conflict' (1973, 247).

Resurrection Man is itself the textual enactment of such 'confused forms'. In
stressing the utopian cartography of urban crime, both the delimitative
representational function of the tribal map and its historical referent begin to
unfold. The tribalism secured by the filiative topography is conventionally
regarded as the embodiment of Belfast's anomaly within the normative global
experience of (post)modernity as developmental teleologies. For example:

> the history of Belfast during the past two hundred years is something of a paradox.
> On the one hand, in economic matters the city developed rapidly by being as
> modern and progressive as any other of the great industrial centres in the United
> Kingdom (and unlike anywhere else in Ireland). Belfast had much the same urban
> social problems too, and its municipal government expanded in a similar way to
> tackle them. On the other hand, it developed patterns of community division and
> conflict, based on religion, which in their severity and permanence have rendered
> it unique among the cities of the British Isles (Maguire, 1993, 9).

In this passage the tribal is devoid of social or historical context for it exists in
abeyance of the progressive narrative of normative urbanity as a confirmation of
the 'anachronistic passions' (Heaney, 1969, 757) sedimented in Belfast. Such a

---

[19] 'Das dialectische Bild ist zu definieren als die unwillkürliche Erinnerung der erlösten
Menschheit' (*GS* I. 1233).

formulation exonerates modernity and postmodernity, as almost exclusively progressive or manageable forces, from producing specific tribalisms.

Given the profound socioeconomic change occurring in Northern Ireland from the 1960s onwards, tribalisms are not so much to be calibrated as a reflection of the reality of the tribal place, but rather as a somewhat regressive and reactionary imaginary resolution and reordering of that change and upheaval. Indeed, sectarianism has historically functioned to try and absorb the dissolution of traditional social co-ordinates and identities under pressure of historical rupture. Victor Kelly's violent fascination with 'the possibilities of transformation' (63) indicates that the ideologeme of his character stands as an allegory for the attempt to build and territorialize violence into Belfast. This transformative imperative demonstrates sectarianism's effort to shape urban space into a tribal configuration in the furtherance of specific dominant subjectivities rather than its being a reflection of that tribal configuration as immemorially given. Hence, my definition of the *terror*-torial imperatives of Irish Nationalism and Unionism is intended to uncover both not as *reflective* ideologies of place (i.e. that they embody some preordained and organic communal identity) but also *productive* ideologies that seek to mystify complex historical and social dynamics.

Moreover, in the novel the sectarianism of Victor Kelly's key manipulator, McClure, appears performative, almost self-effacingly ironic, and gestures towards the historical conditions of late capitalism's reification of place, identity and belonging through which the ghettoization of working-class communities in postmodern cities is rationalized.[20] Indeed, in locating tribalism as a social formation within the currents of postmodern urbanity rather than the atavistic past, it is noteworthy that Manuel Castells considers the cosmopolitanism of the elite and the tribalism of the local community to be 'the fundamental division of our time':

> It opposes the cosmopolitanism of the elite, living on a daily connection to the whole world (functionally, socially, culturally), to the tribalism of local communities, retrenched in their spaces that they try control as their last stand against the macro-forces that shape their lives out of their reach. The fundamental dividing line in our cities is the inclusion of the cosmopolitans in the making of the new history while excluding the locals from the control of the global to city to which ultimately their neighbourhoods belong (1994, 30).

Resurrection Man evinces that such tribalisms in Belfast are not reducible to the intractable persistence of the atavistic. The text in fact testifies to the impossibility of the authentic, organic attachments of sectarian idcology's ordering of social place. In the text's highly stylized identities, the mechanics of sectarianism as performance are uncovered. The tribal map as the organic landscape of belonging of the working class is demystified as a representational hegemony, whose

---

[20] The journalist Ryan ultimately senses the performativity of McClure's sectarian rotes on God and Empire: 'It was a speech Ryan had heard often before. The same wintry tone ... But Ryan thought there was something fraudulent in McClure's delivery, a tone of mockery' (151).

delimitational function serves the maintenance of the state and its perceptual grasp of the totality of social relations encoded in the ideologeme of McClure. So taking on board Castells' theorization of the cosmopolitan access of the elite and the tribal enclosure of the working class in late capitalism, the radicalism of *Resurrection man* and the thriller's conspiratorial map more broadly become apparent: the utopian figuration of society as criminal totality affords access to a comprehensive map of the social which late capitalism would repress and preserve only for a powerful elite.

McClure's conspiratorial role in Kelly's assassination is an ironic final placement and homecoming for the necropolitan stasis symbolized by the filiative locale. Notably, Victor's mother 'often recalled Billy McClure's final words that soon she would always be able to find Victor when she wanted him' (225). Moreover, when Victor is shot, both his stylized posturing, and the cinematic prose in which it is rendered so effectively in the novel, break down. Although Victor desires to construct a cartography of action and expression choreographing 'like in a film' (230), he loses his capacity to control and, significantly, to perceive all the events leading to his death:

> But nothing was right. He wanted them to be serious-minded men who shouted out a warning. He wanted words full of allure and danger to shout back. Never take me alive. The rifle fire had a flat industrial sound. Victor knew the moves. Struggle to raise the gun. Clutch the breast and lean down forward in anguish. His face hit the pavement. He did not see one of the men leave cover and walk over to him and put his foot in his neck and shoot him through the back of the head with a snub-nose revolver. There were no words, got him at last. No last rueful gangster smile, goodbye world (230).

Thus the text returns the ideologeme of Victor Kelly, stripped of its aestheticization, to the necropolis of the tribal map, and illustrates the cultural and social function of such urban representations. Dermot McCarthy comments that 'what makes Victor so powerful and disturbing a figure is the sense that he represents both the past and the future. He is a character based on history and yet a fiction drawn from imagination, a signifier without significance except as a sign of our times, a simulacrum of a past that has yet to be' (148). In broad agreement, I am positing that the ideologeme of Victor Kelly allegorizes the late capitalist ordering of urban space, the strategic function of the tribal place in the occlusion of the totality.[21] Similarly, in Maurice Leitch's *Silver's City* (which is in many respects an important precursor of *Resurrection Man*, given its rehearsal of one man's attempt to name and map the city in accordance with a tribal geography that is invalidated by social change), the carceral city is not to be understood as a mimetic reflection of Belfast itself. Although Silver muses, when turning himself

---

[21] Whilst I am not denying that within the dominant identarian or sectarian politics of the North many working-class agents may utilize the tribal map as defined by Irish culture to relate to place and one another, I am insisting that the ultimate determinant in producing and maintaining the tribal place is the global process of late capitalism, which is not only the sign but the referent of our times.

in, because imprisonment is his existential condition – 'that would be his sentence, for the city made you pay for your dreams' (181) – he is rather incarcerated not by Belfast itself but by his naming of it, by the tribal, working-class geography encoded in his character.

The cinematism of both *Resurrection Man* and *Silver's City* highlights the importance of film as a form in the experience of (post)modernity in cities.[22] For Williams, the city vision is 'a continual dramatisation', and there is a fundamental correlation between the 'fragmentary experience' as perceptual condition and film as the medium of intrinsic movement: 'there is indeed a direct relation between the motion picture, especially in its development of cutting and montage, and the characteristic movement of an observer in the close and miscellaneous environment of the streets' (1973, 242).[23] The reification and dislocation of historical experience is continually figured as a cinematic unreality. In *Lies of Silence*, for example, Michael Dillon finds that his removal from the bourgeois stability of his personal life and implication in a terrorist plot 'was like a scene in a film. He was not part of this film. It was not part of his life' (229). The eponymous Silver in Leitch's novel is depicted as having 'a name from any one of a dozen old movies. The resemblance was laughable' (99), whilst Victor Kelly's highly stylized posturing is gleaned from gangster films. These affected identities and the reifications of (post)modernity in urban experience signal the dissolution of the filiative bond to place.

Jameson posits that the attempt to invent new and elaborate formal strategies, with which to circumvent the dilemmas of modernity and postmodernism, will emerge 'in forms that inscribe a new sense of the absent global colonial system on the very syntax of poetic language itself, a new play of absence and presence that at its most simplified will be haunted by the erotic and be tattooed with foreign place names, and at its most intense will involve the invention of remarkable new languages and forms' (1988a, 349-350). Just as Kelly's name itself effects a hybridization and a displacement, it is perhaps worth considering that Belfast's street names, continually evoked to structure tribal representations of place, actually bespeak the return of the repressed of precisely such new languages produced by the globalization of capital, for, more often than not, they signify the outpost of empire, networks of world economy, a global experience of violence and disruption: 'The city itself has withdrawn into its placenames. Palestine Street. Balaclava Street. The names of captured ports, lost battles, forgotten outposts held against inner darkness. There is a sense of collapsed trade and accumulate decline.

---

[22] Particularly instructive is David B. Clarke, ed. *The Cinematic City* (London: Routledge, 1997).

[23] Similarly, Benjamin considers film to be the paradigmatic mode of the experience of modernity: 'in film perception in the form of shock exemplifies itself as a formal principle'. 'Im Film kommt die chockförmige Wahrnehmung als formales Prinzip zur Geltung' (*GS*, I. 631).

In its names alone the city holds commerce with itself, a furtive levying of tariffs in the shadow' (McNamee, 3-4).[24]

Perhaps the most forceful embodiment of Jameson's new languages and forms is produced by Ian McDonald's science fiction thriller, *Sacrifice of Fools*, in which the Shian aliens transported to Northern Ireland take over the Shipyard, and its evocation of Belfast's industrial and imperial past, as their home:

> The two huge construction cranes stand over the new Nation. Symbol of the city, once. You could see them from everywhere. Two fuck-yous from the Protestant work ethic. But it was already dying then. Like the pyramids: monumental epics of engineering are symptoms of the end game. Engines rust, winding gears seize tight. You can still see them from all over the city. Cost too much to pull them down. Now lander 769 fills the dry dock between them, where one hundred years ago the *Oceanic* and the *Titanic* were built side by side. And the tall, lithe, androgynous creatures that the hard-men welders and caulkers couldn't begin to imagine slip through their cutting sheds and plating yards (71).

This effusion of late capitalist or postmodern hybridity is thus seen to threaten and dismantle the social dominants (masculinity, Protestantism, industrial production) encoded in the Shipyard as social symbol:

> In the few years since the doors of 769 opened and the Shian came out, they've made Queen's Island the capital of Outsider Ireland. A city within a city ... it might not be so bad if they had levelled the lot and built from the ground up, but the way they've recycled the old sheds and hangars and fused them with their own sinuous architecture feels like a corpse dressed and polished for a wake, or one of those sci-fi films ... where they take dead cops and patch them together with technology and send them with big guns out to bust crime (71-72).

This production of 'a city within a city', which subsumes the industrial heart of Belfast, characterizes the postmodern city itself and the politics and repressions of its spatializations. To return to Benjamin, the postmodern city is putatively the total arcade, its mapping now a celebratory intoxication of total *flânerie* without social or historical referent, through which class, labour and modes of production are cognitively and spatially expelled. This revivification of the city as 'corpse' should also alert us to the limits of the social possibilities of postmodernism, through its perpetuation of specific (working-class) territories of the city as necropolis, here reworked by their commodification, stylization and technologicalization. Moreover, this alien trespass also on one level allegorizes the perceived imposition of late capitalism into the North for a confused dominant culture. The supposed radicalism of such a 'deterritorialization', to employ Deleuze and Guattari's term, is therefore questionable, given that the contradictory logic of capitalism itself lurches systematically from processes of de- and re-territorialization. That is,

---

[24] Benjamin reveals that 'the city, through its street names, is a linguistic cosmos'. 'Die Stadt ist durch die Straßennamen ein sprachlicher Kosmos' (*GS* V. 650). The reinscription of this secret text is the goal of making the city *scriptible*.

capitalism de- and re-territorializes the family, religion, the nation, and of course ultimately itself as total system, and there is nothing emancipatory *per se* in this procedure. It then follows that there is no inherent liberation in a postmodern fiction. To this end, Laura Pelaschiar posits:

> Initially portrayed as home to alienation, confusion and violence in the more conservative and pessimistic depictions of the nineteen seventies and nineteen eighties, in the nineteen nineties Belfast has gradually become a new, fertile urban location, no longer a place from which escape is necessary, but rather a laboratory for opportunities, a post-modern place depicted as *the* only space where it is possible to build and articulate a (post)national conscience, the only location for any possible encyclopaedic, multivoiced and multi-ethnic development of Northern society (2000, 117).

This chapter has attempted to evince that the urban alternative to the intimate national space is not the preserve of postmodernism.[25] In fact, the postmodern city would repress as many historical materials as the *rusticative* mapping. Given the necroscopic gaze structuring the *repressive* representation of Belfast, therefore, the following formulation is possible: a postmodern Belfast is a post-mortem Belfast. That is, the postmodern everycity is not the overcoming of previous hellish representations of the city but rather their outcome, the ultimate cognitive banishment of the mortified stasis projected upon the working class. And if I began this chapter by stressing the portioning of Belfast as private, intimate communities in accordance with the *rusticative* ideologies of Irish Nationalism and Unionism, then late capitalism should also alert us to the dangers of another kind of privatized space – that of capital and commerce. What is evident is that the working class suffer a double disadvantage in terms of these two interlacing kinds of private space: ghettoized by the sectarian notion of self-contained, homogenous communities that has driven the urban planning strategy of Belfast's development and also ever further excluded by the recent gentrification of the city centre with its emphasis on that other kind of private space, commercial private ownership. It is therefore testament to the radical potential of the thriller's urban mappings that it repoliticizes both of these privatized, mystificatory spaces by permitting us to chart the city as a criminalized and total network of power relations.

In anticipating my next chapter on gender, McDonald's text is also illustrative in that its liminal hybridity and sexual transgression finally dissipate as Belfast becomes the social embodiment of the *femme fatale*: 'She is some queen bitch, this city, he thinks. She's ugly, she's small, she's mean, she treats you like shit, but you can't leave her, you keep coming back to her. She fucks you like nothing else. She's not even faithful, she fucks everyone who comes to her' (284). Comparably, in Leitch's *Silver's City*, Belfast is reduced to malign female presence for the

---

[25] A welcome and historically precise intervention in the critical debate over the new postmodern Northern novel is afforded by Richard Kirkland's 'Bourgeois Redemptions: The Fictions of Glenn Patterson and Robert McLiam Wilson' in Liam Harte and Michael Parker, eds. *Contemporary Irish Fiction: Themes, Tropes, Theories*. London: Macmillan, 2000. 213-231.

eponymous character: 'He thought of the city and the street-lamps lighting one by one, his city, the city that had made him what he was. Old and cynical begetter, it watched its sons come, it watched them go. Despite dreams, he had been brought back down to the level of its streets, as he always knew he would' (Leitch, 180-181). If we return to Barthes' definition of the city as the encounter with the other, the gendered implications of such mappings suggest modes of symbolic containment that attempt the dissolution of urban dialectics. It is an attempt to recodify the *unheimlich* apparition of class and social forces. Indeed, it is notable that Freud himself deploys gender as a means of occluding the utilization of the uncanny as a powerful social and historical force. Freud maintains that the female genitals are the ultimate *unheimlich* place, the entrance to the former *heim* of all human beings. In light of this mode of symbolic containment, it is significant that the Kelly family in Mornin's *All Our Fault* lack a mother. Under this formulation, the city itself stands as the absent mother for the family, the cause and enactment of their being lost, the dissolution of the filiative social co-ordinate. The recourse to gender as a mode of symbolic containment, however, prepares the ground for my next two chapters, wherein the struggle between the *repressive* and *redemptive* modalities of the thriller is developed toward the political centre of the form.

Chapter 4

'A Man Could Get Lost':
Constructions of Gender

'Down these mean streets a man must go who is ... neither tarnished nor afraid.
The detective in this kind of story must be such a man. He is the hero, he is
everything. He must be a complete man and a common man and yet a
universal man'.
Raymond Chandler, *The Simple Art of Murder*

Peter Humm and Paul Stigant evocatively suggest that 'popular fiction ties genre to gender with a tight pink or blue knot' (84). Yet it is crucial to appreciate that this metaphor of bold colour-coding institutes itself through a tautological reliance on broader social stereotyping, which demarcates ideal, internally-secure polarities of gendered identification. In analysing the culturally-constructed attachments of gender, the market, and the popular text and subject, may these bows not unravel? What historical shadows lie between their ideal tones? For the thriller is conventionally regarded as a constitutively masculine genre. Gender, in this case, functions as an effort to stabilize genre and its conflictual historical materials. Therefore, just as this book has questioned the relation of the popular text to the 'popular', positioning it not as an organic attachment but rather as the hegemonic production of an optimal subject, so the construction of gender facilitates the uncovering of the interstitial and contradictory mechanics of that dominant popular subject. The relation of the thriller to a complexity of masculinities and femininities pursues a Gramscian transformism through contradictory social materials in constructing dominant gendered positionings within the popular subject.[1]

Consequently, to evoke the characterization of the hero in crime fiction, which forms the epigraph of this chapter, Chandler's everyman as the sole, configural subject of the crime form must be undercut. He is not everything: a consummate

---

[1] Eileen Morgan asserts that the gendered limitations of the gangster and crime genres construct a fascination with conflicted masculinity, which extensively privileges male experience and ultimately seeks to make the divisions of a period comprehensible and acceptable to an audience (1998, 29). I wish to concur that the thriller can offer a site for staging masculinities but also to add these are by no means stable and are defeated by the historical conditions, which they seek to naturalize. Furthermore, the form also stages femininities, as with the parallel couples in *The Psalm Killer*, and the parallel females in Gordon Stevens' *Provo*.

masculinity is not commemorated as formal self-presence in the thriller. This everyman gets lost on the mean streets, submerged in the confrontation with other detectives, conspirators, criminals, men and women. For crime fiction is integrally a continual negotiation with otherness, with the secret or repressed.[2] In short, crime fiction provides a terrain for renegotiating social co-ordinates, not least masculinity, and adapting to new historical and social circumstances. Thus, Megarry, in Eugene McEldowney's *A Stone of the Heart*, articulates a pervasive diffusion of the ordered subjective locus in the forsaken pathways of gendered identities: 'It's as if the signposts have been changed. A man could get lost. At least in the old days, I knew where I stood' (1995, 94). It is this sense of masculinity in crisis and its usage of femininity as a space to inscribe social fears that I wish to bring to bear on this chapter, without, I hope, recapitulating the conventional account of the genre as securely male. The challenge is to distinguish hegemonic subjective constructions from totally pervasive or unitary generic imperatives. For example, Christine Gledhill posits that 'in the mainstream thriller the investigative structure presupposes a male hero in search of the truth about an event that either has already happened or is about to come to completion ... the plots of the thriller/detective story offer a world of action defined in male terms; the locales, the situations, iconography, violence are conventions connoting the male sphere' (E. Ann Kaplan, ed. 14). Gledhill continues, in tracing female stereotypes, that 'frequently the female figure exists as a crucial feature within the dangerous criminal world which the hero struggles with in the course of the investigation, and as often as not constitutes the central problem in the unraveling of truth. Thus the place of the female figure in the puzzle which the hero has to solve often displaces solution of the crime as the object of the plot' (E. Ann Kaplan, ed. 15). My analysis would differ from Gledhill's schema in seeking to undermine the notion of thriller as a teleologically masculine reaffirmation of order. Instead the form is precisely the dislocation of such a residual ideology; an insecure negotiation with new social co-ordinates by a range of social subjects for which the female figure becomes a mystificatory fetish for a hegemonic masculinity in construction. The representation of women in the thriller attests, not so much to the ability of a secure male subject to position women in a direct analogue of social subordination, but rather, and more optimistically, that such

---

[2] Laura Mulvey draws the following comparison with reference to the topographic liminality of crime fiction: 'it is tempting to see the detective story as the myth or legend of the newly constituted industrial cities that had grown up *outside* order. The nether world of the city, seething with bars, prostitutes and criminals, also the uncontrollable presence of the working class, could provide a mythic terrain for scenarios of adventure and constitute a modern space of liminality similar to the no man's land through which the ancient or folk-tale heroes embarked on a linear journey outside the city space, the journey of the urban detective is a descent into a hidden world of what is repressed by bourgeois morality and respectability to decode and decipher signs and restore order through the process of reason' (1989, 187).

representations are *sinthomes*[3] or historical symptoms masking the fracture of that masculine subject.

Therefore, a sense of masculinity as itself conflicted and in process, especially under the hegemonic reconfigurations of late capitalism, undermines a reduction of the thriller to pure, masculinist surveillance of objectified and criminalized femininity – for this is precisely the ideological intention of the dominant form that would mask its own historical contradiction. To this end, Sally Munt styles the hard-boiled hero as 'the controlled centre surrounded by chaos, and an effective reading must involve identification with this mediator of action, truth, and finally pleasure and relief through closure' (1). Hence, for Munt, the form is 'iconically masculine' (1). It is worth considering that this is buying into the ideology of conventional detective fiction rather than questioning its production.

Indeed, much work on crime fiction and masculinity tends to look through the dominant subject model without looking at it. For example, Tony Davies regards the male gaze of the thriller as a paradigmatic erotics of surveillance: 'in thrillers, men pursue, hide, threaten, fight, kill; but more than anything, they *look*. The timbre of the look will vary, from the apparently casual sizing up of a colleague or adversary to the charged climactic stare that passes, at the moment of truth, between hero and villain. But more than fist or weapon, the true medium of exchange and authentic instrument of male combat, rivalry and conquest is the eye' (1989, 118). Davies continues that 'looking, in these situations, has less to do with seeing than with dominating' (1989, 118).[4] The fetishistic absorption of this gaze indicates that there are other more utopian and indeed repressed subjectivities in the thriller. For the fetish is constructed precisely to produce an image or object, which serves designedly to mystify the material conditions of its own production, that which it stands in place of, that which it would repress. In short, the standard mechanism of male subject and female object construes a fetish designed to deny its referent, the historical complexity of gender subjectivities at variance with the dominant.[5]

An emphasis on the Gramscian transformism of the popular subject, which wills the utopian reinscription of the social materials with which this hegemonic

---

[3] Lacan uses the punning neologism, *le sinthome*, in place of *le symptome*, to reinforce his thesis that woman is the symptom of man: that is, a support of the subject's consistency yet also a point of radical inconsistency, a coded figuration which reveals the fracture of the Real. I am using the Lacanian *sinthome* in the context of the political unconscious, suggesting here that gender is one mode of symbolic containment by which the *repressive* modality seeks to negotiate History. See Lacan, *Le Séminaire. Livre XI*. Paris: Éditions du Seuil, 1978.

[4] Here, then, is the standard power-knowledge-pleasure cartography structuring the erotics of surveillance outlined in my introductory chapter.

[5] Munt interestingly transposes her formulation of crime fiction as conventionally masculine erotics of surveillance onto a model of the reputed male gaze of film: 'The fact that the detective transferred so easily on to film resulted from his position in fiction as reified spectacle, his knowing, evaluative gaze centred the text for consumption by a subservient reader/viewer' (1). Is there not a tension here between a location of the male detective as subject and centre of the gaze but also as reified spectacle?

subject must grapple, necessitates an account of the conflicting femininities and masculinities, which the optimal or projected subject of such texts seeks to both configure and repress. Nonetheless, in addition to contrariness, the concept of a hegemonic subject most obviously entails structures of dominance and optimal modalities of surveillance. Here Laura Mulvey's much-debated essay, 'Visual Pleasure and Narrative Cinema', is germane, particularly in light of Munt's correlation of crime fiction's social cartography and dominant modes of cinematic spectatorship. Mulvey's account of a specific kind of 'masculinisation' (1989, 37) of the viewing subject provides a broad model for contextualizing the hegemonic structuration of conflicting subjects in the thriller.[6] Moore's *Lies of Silence* offers a paradigmatic instance of such process. The conventional blurring of sex, violence and masculine power is conveyed by the following scene, in which terrorists have taken the Dillons hostage: 'The gunman leaned forward in his chair, holding the revolver between his thighs, pointing it at Moira like some reptilian penis. Blinking his small eyes, he stared her up and down, from her sandalled feet to her long bare legs, her slender body, her pale face, her long, dark, tumbled hair. It was a stare so overtly sexual that Dillon, watching, stiffened and sat tense' (47). This is a neat encapsulation of the standard sexual politics of the genre. In the last sentence of the passage, Dillon, through his attachment to the dominant scopics of the terrorist, is permitted access to the gaze, to a suggested sexual arousal, and to a positioning – however 'tense' or insecure. (Indeed, the anxiety of this position goes to the heart of the dialectic of masterful pleasure and anxiety structuring the thrills of the genre, which I shall detail in my next chapter).

However, whilst relaying a dominant masculine gaze, Mulvey's model must not produce a homogenous male gaze, for this, as indicated earlier, is part of the structural ideology through which a male focalization supposedly defines itself in relation to an objectified female.[7] This actually distracts us from the consideration of masculinity, which is then viewed as not merely dominant, but unitary, settled or even normative. So the hegemonic power of a specific definition of masculinity depends upon a denial of its self-contradiction that is instigated by its self-projection as monolithic and transhistorically unremitting. The fundamental representational or discursive point to be made here, in view of our established context of the gaze and the fetishized object masking the production of the former, is that the whole aim of a hegemonic project is to achieve ideological

---

[6] Mulvey's essay is frequently criticized for its reductivism, as in David Rodowick 'The Difficulty of Difference' *Wide Angle* 5;1. 1982. 4-15. However, perhaps the best re-adaption, the subtlety of which I am bringing to bear upon the hegemonic construction of the subject, is provided by Mulvey herself as 'Afterthoughts on "Visual Pleasure and Narrative Cinema" Inspired by King Vidor's *Duel in the Sun*'. 1989. 29-38.

[7] Moreover, Mary Anne Doane comments, with reference to feminism and the gaze, that 'feminist film criticism has consistently demonstrated that, in the classical Hollywood cinema, the woman is deprived of a gaze, deprived of subjectivity and repeatedly transformed into the object of masculine scopophiliac desire. Yet, women would seem to be perfect spectators, culturally positioned as they are outside the arena of history, politics, production – "looking on"'. (163).

transparency.[8] There is consequently a need to transcode a model of masculinity that would be consummately invisible and thereby pervasively defining. For such an ideological process not only wills the power of normative definition, but also, through that normativity, places itself beyond definition. So masculinity as normative, and in fact also *nominative* in configuring a gendered semiotic in accordance with the subject, not only posits femininity as the object under scrutiny in disguising its own material production but also thus seeks to repress other, variant or conflictive masculinities in addition to female sexualities.

On that point, there is an interesting example of a male on male gaze in Kate O'Riordan's *Involved*, in which the terrorist, Eamon, proves his steely determination by outstaring an informer. Notably, in the following passage, Eamon's gaze is immediately positioned in terms of knowledge and closure and its power ultimately culminates in the total scrutability of the objectified informer: 'he always knew in the end. It was in a man's gaze, in his stance, in the sweat that glistened on his brow at the moment of confrontation and that almost imperceptible spark of relief at the back of the petrified glazed eyes. The traitor's percipience as he tumbled toward inevitable exposure' (7). Moreover, the informer significantly occupies a feminine space under this dominant male gaze: 'He threw himself into the armchair usually occupied by his wife' (8). The refractive power of Eamon's dominant masculine gaze reflects through the informer's son and his view of his father under Eamon's interrogation: 'he groaned with relief and shame. The boy's eyes burned through him. Questioning, questioning, questioning' (13). Here, then, a discursively transparent dominant form of masculinity is empowered through the subordination and interrogation of other positions.[9]

The directing of scopic violence onto other forms of masculinity necessitates a circumspection as to the absolutism of Anne Cranny-Francis's point that violence in the thriller is solely 'an expression of misogyny, a fictional recompense to the conservative male reader for the growing autonomy of women in the real world. Its other component is helplessness, the impotence of the individual in the face of institutionalized corruption given fictional expression and resolution in the vigilante violence of the male detective' (1990, 168). The stratification of masculinities through such scopic violence indicates there are variant forms of desire operative in the thriller, none of which offer unitary identifications of male or female positioning with the projected reading subject, and which actually sit in tension with one another. Nevertheless, in retaining a sense of the hegemonic ideology of masculinity in the form, Steve Neale has commented that 'Where women are investigated, men are tested. Masculinity, as an ideal at least, is implicitly known. Femininity is, by contrast, a mystery This is one of the reasons

---

[8] Such a representational mystification helps explicate Stallybrass and White's point that 'what is *socially* peripheral is so frequently *symbolically* central' (5).

[9] Similarly, Leamus, in Stewart Binnie's *Across the Water*, loves guns because 'anyone was yours to command when he knew he was in your sights, no matter how strong his physique, how great his wealth, how immeasurable his influence' (cited in Rolston 1996, 405). The dominant gaze and central phallic symbol thus coalesce in relegating other specific forms of masculine power.

why the representation of masculinity, both inside and outside the cinema, has been so rarely discussed' (1992, 286). Whilst this is a succinct account of the form's recourse to an eternally mysterious femininity, it is worth asking, as Kirkham and Thumim do (1993, 11), whether being investigated and being tested are mutually exclusive. Furthermore, should an analysis not solicit exactly what kind of historical change this ideology of knowable masculinity and unfathomable femininity is designed to repress? Increasingly, particularly given the thriller's late capitalist referent, masculinities are made mysterious, anxious, powerless, even criminalized by the form. Masculinities are stratified through codes of violence, professionalism and so on, but it is the loss of an immutable, *a priori* model of masculinity that necessitates violence for the nonhegemonic in attempting to construct a *dominante* or nonconsensual mobilization. Violence is not inherently masculine but rather reveals the coercive, *dominante* aspect of a certain hegemonic kind of manliness that attests paradoxically to its attenuation.[10] So violence and physicality are indubitably components of a certain kind of warrior masculinity. But there is a more nuanced point to be made here since, as Roger Bromley asserts, violence is part of the processes that produce conventional masculinity and is not simply an expression of it. Thus, for Bromley, violence divides masculinities from each other and is seen as generated, at some levels, by role and performance anxieties (1989, 115).

Moreover, the overly macho figures peppering the 'Troubles' thriller, such as Andrew Lane's heroes in *Forgive the Executioner* and *The Ulsterman*, actually attest to the failure of masculinity, its crisis. Barbara Creed remarks of muscular bodies on screen, which resemble 'an anthropomorphised phallus, a phallus with muscles ... they are simulacra of an exaggerated masculinity, the original completely lost to sight, a casualty of the failure of the paternal signifier and the current crisis in master narratives' (65) (cited in Messent, ed. 228). In terms of the thriller's social gaze, the increasing amount of male figures, appearing as objects and not just gazers, intimates that masculinity needs to be made visible due to the supposed 'feminization' of labour discussed in my second chapter. It must reinscribe itself in the symbolic interstices of late capitalist culture because it can no longer be taken for granted as the given against which the feminine (or indeed subordinate masculinities) might be defined or displayed. Such increased visibility of masculinity is of course also centrally tied to the hegemonic breakdown of its dominant modes and the consequent loss of discursive transparency and nominativity.

---

[10] This correlation of masculinity and violence is not exhaustive and does not seek to eschew Rosalind Coward's (however overly deterministic) point that male readers enjoy stories 'preoccupied with putting the male body through all sorts of ordeals ... which are ultimately survived'. *Female Desire: Women's Sexuality Today*. London: Paladin, 1984. 189.

Given this Lacanian focus on the gaze, it is also worth considering that the ideal is something to which the subject is never adequate.[11] For instance, although Frank Krutnik contends that 'the "tough" thriller seems to be driven by challenges to the mutually reinforcing regimes of masculine cultural authority and masculine psychic stability' (xiii), he also concedes that 'the *noir* "tough" thrillers reveal an obsession with male figures who are both internally divided and alienated from the culturally permissible (or ideal) parameters of masculine identity, desire and achievement' (xiii). If we return to my epigraph from Chandler, it is worth determining whether a 'complete', 'common' and 'universal' man are not contradictory ideological enterprises, the site of an unobtainable desire. As a result, we are not dealing with the formal enactment of an ideal given, with a mere reflection of dominance, but rather precisely with the active reproduction, recodification and indeed collapse of forms of hegemonic masculinity.

Accordingly, in deliberating the optimal reading subject, there can be no simple or unproblematic identification between text and reader, male or female, with, if you like, the 'ideal ego' produced in such a mechanism. Perhaps the most succinct demonstration of the construction of such an ideal reading subject by the thriller's erotics of surveillance is provided by Susan Crossland's *Dangerous Games*. The following love scene involves the political columnist, Hugo Carroll, and Lisa Tabor, an aide to an American political lobbyist: 'They both looked at her in the mirror ... both of them watched him looking over her shoulder at this nymphlike creature standing half naked before him. The nymph stood naked in the mirror, innocent and desiring, yielding to him alone' (117-118). Here is a neat encapsulation of Mulvey's account of the masculinization of female subjectivity by the dominant. But such identification with an ideal ego is in no way unproblematic, as intimated by this continual reliance on the necessary fantasy space of the mirror and its determinate misrecognitions and oversights. Doubtless, the overriding function of such scopic mechanisms is to negate female subjectivity *per se*. This is conveyed, for example, by the intertwining of sex and violence in McNamee's *Resurrection Man*, through the character of Victor Kelly, whose powerful subjecthood and consummate scopic violence reifies, repositions and erases the subjectivity of his lovers: 'Victor could have any woman he wanted. Click his fingers. But the women only lasted one or two nights. They'd look into his face when they were alone with him and get frightened. Looking into Victor's blue eyes when you were fucking was like watching a televised account of your own death, a disconsolate epic' (11). However, this dominant subjectivity and its concentration on reinscribing female subjectivity is designedly intended to disguise the fact that Victor's masculinity is also profoundly alienated and reified by the inaccessibility of a stable and accessible identity (and I shall also consider this dislocation below in relation to Irish masculinity).

Consequently, when Janey Place asserts that the *noir* thriller 'is a male fantasy' (E. Ann Kaplan, ed. 35), it is important not only to undercut the absolutism of this

---

[11] A consummate survey of the problematics of the gaze is afforded by Martin Jay's *Downcast Eyes: The Denigration of Vision in Twentieth-Century French Thought*. London: U of California P, 1993.

statement by analysing thrillers by women or dealing primarily with forms of feminine subjectivity, but also, when considering masculinity, to ascertain precisely what forms of subject are produced by such fantasy and which are displaced. Place accurately states that the *noir* form is one in which a woman is defined by her sexuality. Given the importance of the placement of women to patriarchy, their displacement, i.e. within the supposedly masculine arena of the thriller, disturbs that system or worldview, so that the *noir* thriller is based on the exposure and then destruction of the sexual, manipulating woman. Ensuingly, the conventional ideology of the thriller, in which female characters enter the masculine preserve of action and adventure, precipitates and allegorizes a wider consideration of the entry of women into the social itself and their displacement within its hegemonic subjectivities. I want to suggest that such forms of displacement afflict not only femininity in the thriller but also serve to mystify the historical alienation of masculinity. E. Ann Kaplan posits that noir '*expresses* alienation, locates its cause squarely in the excesses of female sexuality ("natural" consequences of women's independence), and punishes that excess in order to re-place it within the patriarchal order' ('Introduction', 3).

Hence, the more fantastical and even ridiculous depictions of women within this representational economy, as typified by the representation of Republican volunteers in Ned Nicholl's *No More Leprechauns*. Therein Kathleen strips naked to attack the hero Danny with her karate skills: 'she held her hands out in front of her breasts, her right hand edged towards him, the left hand shaped like a claw ... her claw-like hand gripped his throat, her nails bit into flesh and her hand closed around his windpipe' (252). There is a serious point to be made here however. If the dominant ideology of patriarchy denies women subjectivity, historical or political agency, and sexuality, then any expression or staging of these attributes can only be thus according to the dominant discourse, can only be dehumanized, threatening and terrifying. So when Kathleen Gregory Klein comments that 'in a general way, all novels featuring women private eyes could be described as parodies' (173), she presupposes an authentically masculine presence or formal immanence that is actually displaced by the very historical conditions that produced the thriller. Accepting the surface ideology of mainstream texts, Klein posits that 'the imperatives of the genre overwhelm the political implications of the novel' (227), thereby denying any subversion of gendered absolutes. Undercutting this sense of an irresistibly dominant masculinity, Yvonne Tasker (1993) posits that masculinity in late capitalism is now either comic and ironic or alienated and bleak; it has become harder to maintain an unproblematical masculine physicality (as evidenced by Colin Bateman's heroes).

The correlation of the thriller with an assertive masculinity draws upon one of the form's residual generic sedimentations in adventure fiction. Nonetheless, what confronts this formally symbolic legacy of masculine adventure and its knowable, physically expressive identity in the thriller is the era of the state – and this is of crucial significance to gender identities. For the easy consonance between masculinity and violence, which forms the basis of various critiques not only of the thriller but also the Northern Irish conflict itself is disrupted by an appraisal of the state. Perhaps the most mechanistic example of biologic accounts of violence is

Robin Morgan's *The Demon Lover: On the Sexuality of Terrorism*. Although she claims to be circumventing biological determinism, Morgan maintains that 'history is a record of most women *acting peaceably*, and of most men *acting belligerently* – to a point where the capacity for belligerence is regarded as an essential ingredient of manhood and the proclivity for conciliation is thought largely a quality of women' (27). Morgan theorizes 'the deadly hero' and 'the redeeming ecstasy of tragic death' by asserting that 'the hero already lives as a dead man. As a dead man he is fearless, because as a dead man he is unconquerable by any life force' (63). This masculine death cult in turn explicates the representational violence necessarily foisted upon female characters in the thriller: 'because she represents life, she is the ultimate destroyer of what he values most – death' (70). Possibly the most formulaic rendering of this gender polarization is supplied by Mildred Downey Moxon's *Too Long a Sacrifice*, which combines the thriller form with a bizarre historical fantasy structure. In the text a husband and wife are sent as a punishment from mythical Ireland to 1970s Belfast. The dust cover sets the scene:

> Ancient Ireland. Tadgh the bard and Maire, his magical wife are spirited away by the Old Ones, counters in an age-long and inscrutable game.Today. In modern Belfast a resurrected Maire represents Summer, and the forces of peace; a materialised Tadgh leads the powers of Winter, the advocates of blood and terror. In the ensuing conflict, Life opposes Death, and the Hate Beast gibbers over all ...

Maire tells Republican women: 'you disgrace your nation and your sex' (238). Conspicuously, gender is deployed as a means of naturalizing the conflict.[12] Such biologicism informs Morgan's contention that terrorism is 'the state of man': 'far from being a threat to the State, terrorism is the means by which men under patriarchy judge one another fit to succeed' (130). I want to indicate the formal antinomy between this transcendental, almost metaphysical *state* of naturally violent masculinity and the *state* as the most concrete form of the social itself, entailing classes, genders, races, complex historical affiliations and conflicts. The function of crime as cognitive mapping destabilizes an ideology of masculine formal immanence by suggesting that masculinity is continually redefined in the supercession of the power of the organic by the power of the state.

One means by which the 'Troubles' thriller attempts to provide a mode of symbolic containment for dissipating the utopian function of considering the state is *exactly* by recourse to this (other immemorial) state of masculinity. By way of exemplification, David Glover interestingly takes issue with Dennis Porter's assertion that sexuality and criminality are mutually exclusive terms since 'a detective novel may excite on the level of its manifest content of violence without

---

[12] Reducing the conflict to male impulse or disorder, refutes its entire socio-historical context, and, as Bill Rolston notes, with regard to the conventional psychotic male: 'in the absence of other political men with whom they can be compared, the effect is not only that they appear as real, but that their narrowness and psychopathology serve as the *total* explanation of the Irish conflict – it derives from men, violent men, especially violent republican men' (1996, 405).

any necessary allusion to a latent sexual signified' (Porter 1981, 111). Heroes and heroines, Glover maintains, are obviously gendered identities, to which their capacity for action, including their response to violence, is closely linked. Glover considers the thriller form not only a celebration of risk-taking and aggression but also a male victory over the threat of castration, assertion of dominance, control and invulnerability, and the denial of sexual ambiguity. Glover makes the following periodization:

> the centralization of the state and its monopoly of armed force entailed a disciplining of the male body through moral and political constraints upon the earlier, less stable forms of male violence. Aesthetically, these changes were sublimated into the literary codes of chivalrous romance with their stress upon personal honour and heroic virtue. Fantasies of adventure rooted in this manly ethic of performance have been amongst the principal carriers of an ideological version of masculinity fixated upon exceptional uses of physical violence, the skilled management of the body under conditions of pressure, and upon the reconciliation of these means with some personal or social ideal. Yet as the official face of organized violence has become increasingly more and more technocratic, rendering heroism increasingly redundant, the continuing reinvention of the male adventure story has come under pressure, perhaps best exemplified by the complex desperation of the Rambo books and films with their remorseless stripping-back of the self to an inviolable bedrock and their noticeable ambivalence towards advanced weaponry and modern chains of command (76-77).

What I am arguing is that the contested fabric of the Northern State and the exoticization of Northern Ireland in the international thriller provide a renewed though compensatory testing ground, a desiring space, for this rogue masculinity. In other words, the contemporary representation of the North is skewed by its allegorical usage in gesturing yearningly back to an imagined terrain of masculine adventure that is structurally undermined in the contemporary thriller.

Nonetheless, in stressing the utopian function of the thriller's contemplation of the late capitalist state, this form of cognitive mapping is certainly amenable to feminist adaptation. Munt argues that 'despite commonsensical attempts to gender the detective novel as masculine, it could also be argued that whilst the form undoubtedly can foreground masculine and misogynistic structures, there is also an argument for the form being fundamentally friendly to feminists' (191). Following Palmer's claim that 'the basic apparatus of the thriller can accommodate more or less any set of political beliefs, precisely because they constitute only a superficial layer' (67), Munt continues: 'Perhaps it is more efficacious to examine those specific cliches imbuing crime fiction which, possibly *within an overall conformity*, can be appropriated by feminists for political ends' (197). Rather than conformity, my criterion is hegemony and the struggle of conflictive materials in the thriller form. For Munt tends to limit the feminist potentiality of the genre by placing feminine authority as a mere reversal of the norm, which produces a subversive yet transitory and masquerading subject: 'As the feminist author expresses her own fantasies of justice, her reader temporarily and figuratively gains membership to the law-making elite. By synthesizing the construction "hero" with "Woman", writers have been able to project fantasy images of independence and strength to counteract the prevailing fictional construct of woman-as-adjunct-to-man' (197).

Munt further posits that 'traditional crime fiction exonerates society by apportioning blame on to an individual. Feminist crime fiction makes guilt collective and social, and the need for change structural' (198). Again this formulation tends toward an acceptance of the surface ideology of earlier forms of crime fiction and overestimates the inherence of radicalism in feminisms, especially considering the mechanistic substitutions of the above passage. Nevertheless, Munt saliently suggests the potentialities of the conspiratorial ideologeme and its usurpation of the ideology of the single, resolvable crime:

> The conspiracy theory, also so necessary to the thriller structure, fits in perfectly with many feminists' suspicion of institutional power, seen as circumscribing female autonomy through diverse and devious means. The act of reading is a skilled deciphering of 'plots', so that the crime can be publicized. The thriller hero is a liberal fantasy antipathetic to state bureaucracy and authoritarianism, and can thus be adapted by the feminist to incriminate its agents and representatives (198).

However, given Munt's recognition that '[a] genre is a dynamic paradigm, dependent on definitions which change over time, a cultural code in which meanings are consistently contested' (201), her assertion that the figure of hero can only be feminized through parody by women writers is questionable (Munt, 204). For this recapitulates the idea of an authentic masculine core in the thriller, which my emphasis of the antinomies of form strives to undermine. Whilst Munt's account of crime fiction is perhaps the most thorough and engaged study of the form, her conclusion tends to suggest that subversion in the thriller as a self-contained structure comes from 'without', from attachment to other, equally internally consistent social narrative forms: 'Its mutability as a genre rests with its ability to combine elements of other forms such as realism and satire which have their roots in a radical sensibility. The peculiar attraction of a crime novel is its ability to appease sometimes contradictory desires, which presumably can placate the feminine and provoke the feminist in all of us' (207).

In particular, I wish to expose the antinomic displacement of a knowable, expressively physical masculinity in the thriller form and its tracing of institutional and social power. David Glover postulates that, in the moral relativism of the hard-boiled tradition, the hero's own code of ethics exists in tension with the social order: 'cut adrift from any code but his own, violence serves as the *telos* of action for the thriller's hero, that moment when he is tested and thereby comes to know himself most truly' (76). What is at stake, Glover maintains, is a refiguring of the physicality of violence and symbolic possession of the means of violence, through which male agency is staged as self-determined, active and brutal. This definition of masculinity is itself reproductive of a specific ideological model of society that is increasingly eroded in the thriller. In illuminating the problematics of a physically expressive masculinity and wider social power, Richard Dyer points out that, since only men have penises, the phallus is by no means just an arbitrarily chosen symbol of power. Nonetheless, this leads to the greatest instability of the male image: 'the penis isn't a patch on the phallus, it can never live up to its mystique. Hence, the excessive even hysterical quality of so much masculine imagery ... Like so much about masculinity, images of men, founded on such multiple instabilities, are such a strain' (1992, 276). Such profound and formative anxieties with this form of masculinity are revealed in Shaun Clarke's *Red Hand*. The text's hero, Peter Moore, is an archetypal model of the independent masculinity of physical immanence outlined by Glover, who regards his girlfriends thus: 'He had treated them all decently, or, at least as best he could, but his lifestyle was the kind that few women could understand, let alone live with, and he couldn't help that. A man either gave in ... to his women ... or he gave up for good' (1998, 10). However, his confrontation with the stock and 'beautifully deadly' (1998, 27) *femme fatale*, Patricia Monaghan, is the site of a profound anxiety. Having been raped by a terrorist gang with a gun, Monaghan finds the actual no comparison in satiating her desires. For her dismissal of physically expressive masculinity, the character is finally eliminated and her body mutilated in the text's close.

The detachment of the male body from the social symbolism of power has been adumbrated in earlier chapters in the treatment of the distinction between the hardman and the gunman and the crisis in a knowable masculinity and concomitant community. Late capitalism marks a profound dissolution of personalized, expressive manhood not only in relation to the state but also because of perceived feminization of labour and recodification of the family. Russell Celyn Jones's *Soldiers and Innocents* articulates the dislocation of traditional working-class masculinity. Its plot follows Captain Evan Price, who, after ten years elite service in Northern Ireland, deserts and kidnaps his five-year-old son. Significantly, given the conventionally established context of the masculine gaze and feminized object, his wife Celia is 'out of the picture. It's just me and the boy' (18). Price nostalgically flees to the Wales of his childhood: 'machismo was like a caste in those valleys: there was nothing a man could do to shake it off' (112). This new experience of parenting disrupts an ingrained traditional masculinity: 'In his experience, all men were the amateur parent in a marriage, if they were lucky enough to get to play parent at all. In Evan's world the men went to war or to train for war while the women raised the children single-handed' (29).

In light of the deployment of the North as a *desiring space* for dominant subjects in crisis, the text notably uses Belfast as a projection of these new treacherous times for male identity: '[h]e had to take each day as it came, manoeuvring away from where he'd recently been, navigating into his future by dead reckoning, walking backwards like a squaddy on the Ardoyne Road. With a pistol in his trouser pocket, Evan stepped out of the boat onto the jetty' (30). The recourse to a compensatory and powerfully violent phallic symbol to mitigate the historical trauma is telling in this scene. The passage is followed by the ensuing attempt to transcend the male body and its historical fracture as cultural signifier under such socioeconomic conditions: '[a]t 5am, still unable to sleep, he stripped off his clothes and stood naked in front of a full-length mirror behind a door, straining to see beyond himself, far into the distance beyond the image, to an Eden of non-conscious delights' (31). Price wakes in the morning 'without a stitch of clothing to cover himself': as he seeks to see beyond his body's fracture, the reader is impelled by this Lacanian scene to imagine it with the dispensation that it remains a fantasy for the optimal reading self. The text also elicits something of the historical reinscription of the *femme fatale*. Price's wife is depicted as troublingly more masculine than the contemporary male: 'She was taller than Evan by one inch, and in trousers often seemed more like a man than a man did' (41). Her character unfolds in stock, almost parodic, *femme fatale* manner.[13] After kidnapping his son, Price declares he is saving the boy from this malign female presence: 'she kills all the men she marries. Only now is she suffering like a woman whose child has been slaughtered' (91). This act of revenge and salvation is actually therefore a means of rationalizing economic conditions, wherein women have increasingly entered the workplace and men are incrementally more involved in parenting and the home. Notably, however, Price's wife is not a disruptive presence in the text as with the traditional *femme fatale*. She never appears as a character but is only recollected through Price's memories and is in many ways the absent cause of the text. This retrospective nostalgia intimates that the social change and increasing independence of women – for which the *femme fatale* stood as fearfully alluring figure from the inception of the *noir* thriller – has now come into being, that the horror has already happened and that new sites of gender relations and stereotypes remain yet to be imagined.

The masculine subject is unable to configure the conflicting stereotypes of femininity and make them cohere – Celia was a military nurse, an interesting confluence of the dangerous and the caring. We are told that 'Terence was born and she changed. Mothering mellowed her, tenderised her', but that 'by the time Terence reached three, Celia had stitched up her future. She and the boy were to be a unit isolated from the rest of the world. Unfortunately for Evan, he was part of the rest of the world' (42). Price is assisted by his friend Colin, who is in the ambulance service and thus in many ways operates as a parallel or surrogate Celia, constantly telling Evan how to care for the boy. So the text actually seeks to develop a new masculinity, no less alienated nor homosocial than the traditional dominant, but which does attempt to harness the demands of a new historical moment.

However, the text ends pessimistically with Price's arrest at his father's funeral – the symbolic erasure of the paternal signifier and the intervention of the state undermining the violently individualistic and adventurous masculine self mortified in the text:

> When Evan had been away in the military he had heard of a sexual revolution outside. He heard that women were in office, and fathers were bouncing their

---

[13] The text informs: 'Celia's tragic legacy was that she killed her first husband in a car crash and her second husband never recovered from a mental breakdown ... Celia didn't need a gun to kill, although she did learn how to fire Evan's weapons on the ranges in Aldershot. It was a thrill for her to empty a whole clip of 7.62mm rounds through an SLR, an event she always wanted to follow by sex' (41).

children on their knees. None of this had touched him. This was one revolution the army never fought. Society evolved, but its army remained a static metaphor for manhood in its most rigid and malevolent form. Soldiers are dinosaurs of the times (115).

Therefore, the only mitigation against this pessimism, is the adaptive, feminized masculinity of Colin, standing beyond the filiative security of the patriarchal family.[14]

It is perhaps instructive to turn to Irish masculinity to further dissolve the hegemonic attachments of masculinity. Not because there is something inherently peculiar about it but rather because it is nonhegemonic, particularly within the vast historical discourses which have used it either to subordinate or empower the Irish as a whole. Irish masculinity thus offers a way of foregrounding ideological frameworks that would conventionally achieve representational transparency. Therefore, the conventional problematization of the unstable, troubled construction of Irish masculinity demands attention. In examining the perceived need to formulate a stable masculinity, which is not so much peculiar as non-hegemonic, we can witness a dominant Irish masculinity moving from deterritorialized to reterritorializing subject. What must be stressed here is that we are not dealing with some unitary national problematic of masculinity but rather with the construction of a specifically dominant subjectivity in Ireland through recourse to the gendered discourse of a particular national-colonial model, which is actually intended to subordinate alternative gender identities. Indeed, regarding Irish masculinity as given yet displaced in a colonial discourse of power, which was itself gendered as a means of naturalizing historical relationalities, once more mistakes an ideology for that which it would repress or resolve.

Perhaps the most commonly cited account of the national-colonial model – a kind of gendered rite of passage for the dominant national subject – is provided by Ashis Nandy's *The Intimate Enemy* and its linkage of defeat and emasculation (10). Nandy asserts that:

> Only the victims of a culture of hyper-masculinity, adulthood, historicism, objectivism, and hyperrationality protect themselves by simultaneously conforming to the stereotype of the rulers, by over-stressing those aspects of the self which they share with the powerful, and by protecting in the corner of their heart a secret defiance which reduces to absurdity the victor's concept of the defeated and his unspoken belief that he is morally and culturally superior to his subjects, caught on the wrong side of history (100).

---

[14] Similarly, in McNab's *Remote Control*, the SAS hero, Nick Stone, is left alone on the run with the daughter of his murdered colleague and family, so that a fantasy of the perfect family, which has been necessarily eradicated in reality, functions as a filiative allegory through which a new kind of masculinity is developed capable of not only dealing with threats to a physically expressive masculinity in the thriller plot but also with this newly perceived 'feminisation' (53).

In one sense, therefore, the thriller form itself could be viewed as a specific cultural constellation of this hyperbolic affinity and psychic compensation. Moreover, the thriller, and the relation of Irish female writers to it, seemingly tenders itself as a specific instance of the general discursive formation identified by Christine St. Peter: 'What we discover in the North is how difficult it has been for Northern women to insert their "voices" into the extravagantly militarized "masculine" discourses that still predominate, even in the present peace process that affects all Northerners' (2). One problem with the dichotomization of colonial masculinity and feminized Ireland is that it produces a mechanistic account of oppression that actually assumes the gendering of imperial ideology. For example, Anne Owens Weekes contends that the entire Irish population shares the position of women in the metropolitan centre: 'colonization ... makes female both country and people' (15). Are the recurrent ambiguities in Irish masculinity reducible to this uncomplicated paradigm? It is telling that even the most seemingly patriarchal figure in recent Irish fiction, Moran, in John McGahern's *Amongst Women*, has his masculinity undercut by, and indeed feminized by, the Marian allusion of the novel's title. An interesting equivalent in the thriller is to be found in Leitch's *Silver's City*. Even the apparently hypermasculine paramilitary, Ned Galloway, adopts an ambiguous identity at the very moment that he is assuming a putatively secure warrior masculinity whilst waiting for a female associate of Silver: 'Taking up a handful of lipsticks and thinner pencils, he began covering his face with stripes and whorls, until the result seemed not far removed from a work of art. He lay on the bed giggling, thinking of her face when she opened the door and saw his warpaint' (155). An authentic masculine power is here vitiated not only by its feminization but also by the emphasis on the artificial stylization implicit in such gendering. It is this stylization – rather than a simplistic feminization of a given masculinity – which echoes throughout the 'Troubles' thriller and exhorts the destabilization of the colonial model of gender. To accept the inescapability of that model as the only cause of troubled Irish masculinities suggests that Irish males are all equally in thrall to the colonial father, all reclaiming an immemorial masculinity of hyperbolic emulation. Thus, Irish masculinity is ambiguously gendered or potentially conflictive only because it both colludes with patriarchy – that is, its dominance within Ireland itself – and yet is also subject to the arrogations of patriarchy due to a national subordination to the British state. For this model, and in particular its post-colonial *telos*, returns us to the conventional discursive transparency of masculinity discussed above: there endures the sense of masculinity as intuitively defined, a stable masculinity derogated by colonization and reinstated by that post-colonial *telos*.

In other words, the gendering of colonial discourse is more than just an ideological mechanics simplifying profound historical complexity. It is rather a normative, natural set of relationships and stages through which both masculinity and femininity as already-defined and agreed concepts must pass.[15] By contrast, I am suggesting the simultaneous hierarchization and suppression of other forms of

---

[15] Such a model is typified by Declan Kiberd's chapter on 'Fathers and Sons' in *Inventing Ireland: The Literature of the Modern Nation*. London: Jonathan Cape, 1995. 380-394.

masculinity by the dominant or sanctioned version. What is evident, in a text such as *Resurrection Man*, is that Victor Kelly does not intuitively or unaffectedly know how to behave as a man, but rather attempts to act like a man across a range of adopted identities.[16] The silence of his father, as noted in my third chapter, allegorizes a filiative breakdown within Unionism and its ideology of paternalism, into which void popular culture offers a series of potential models. This kind of dissolution is in no way reducible to a purely reactionary terror and may unfold what Adrian Frazer terms 'a richness in the possibilities of masculinity' (1997, 11). Though in accessing the viability of divergent models it is salient to bear in mind Foucault's censure that '"sexuality" is far more of a positive product of power than power was ever repression of sexuality' (1980, 120). Nevertheless, Ken Worpole, in tracing the popularity of the emergent hard-boiled American thriller in England, comments that 'many working-class readers, particularly men, found American writing so much more accessible in style and subject matter in comparison to the classical formalism of the English novel of suburban manners – and murders' (1983a, 37). Does the 'Troubles' thriller also fill a specific void for gritty, masculine class experience denied by the High Cultural legacy of the Revival imbuing both Irish Nationalism and Unionism? Worpole further asserts that 'the "tough-guy" vernacular style of writing, is very much the narrative style which many working-class *male* writers adopt as the appropriate register and syntax for writing about contemporary class experience' (1983a, 47). So, for Worpole, the world in which the vernacular flourishes is city life, which is seen as a semi-independent, relatively autonomous realm of men within their culture of work and social relationships, wherein working-class women are traditionally excluded from this world. However, as discussed in my second chapter in relation to the populist militarism of SAS thrillers, the supposed feminization of labour and the market under late capitalism has dissolved this public, masculine arena and filiative authority.

Given the centrality of the family to filiative models of ideological production, the thriller itself, from its trekking the mendacious, mean streets to its confrontation with the state presents filiation with a structural antinomy. Sylvia Harvey asserts that the thriller frustrates the fulfillment of desire or establishment of ideological equilibrium in the institution of the family (E. Ann Kaplan, ed. 23). Harvey observes how the family serves to legitimate and naturalize established values of competitive, repressive and hierarchical relationships, thereby rendering existing social relations acceptable and valid:

> If we can say that familial *entities* are the ideological fictions brought into being by family relations, then the absence of these *relations*, which are by definition

---

[16] Further contextualization is suggested by Frank Mort's account of how within late capitalism men are sold images which rupture the traditional icons of masculinity. They are stimulated to look at themselves, and other men, as objects of consumer desire (194). Slavoj Žižek asserts, in Lacanian terms, that the gaze marks the point from which the viewing subject is already gazed at: that is, the gaze as object prevents the subject from looking from a safe, objective distance (Wright and Wright, eds. 1999. 15).

normal in capitalist society, creates a vacuum that ideology abhors. This terrible absence of family relations allows for the production of the *seeds* of counter-ideologies. The absence or disfigurement of the family both calls attention to its own lack and to its own deformity, and may be seen to encourage the consideration of alternative institutions for the reproduction of social life. Despite the ritual punishment of acts of transgression, the vitality with which these acts are endowed produces an excess of meaning which cannot finally be contained. Narrative resolutions cannot recuperate their subversive significance (E. Ann Kaplan, ed. 33).

By way of exemplifying that female writers are not inherently subversive, this filiative disintegration also informs Sarah Michaels' *Summary Justice*.[17] The text's RUC hero, Somerville, whose family is killed by the IRA, embarks on a rogue revenge mission. This process entails a reconstituted conventional loner masculinity, as when he turns down a relationship with a girl in Botanic Hotel in an exemplary Lacanian moment of refusing relation to the woman: 'Somerville hadn't wanted to hurt her feelings. She had been keen to help, but he couldn't risk any kind of relationship, however brief' (126). What this hypermasculinity and its elevated alienation is designed to disguise through woman as psychic symptom is the dissolution of filiation, which now appears as a kind of Unionist family romance or allegorical fragment. Seemingly in keeping with Robin Morgan's account of the male death cult, Somerville declares: 'I decided to die the day the remaining pieces of my family were buried. You can't kill me' (259). Therefore, as filiative authority dissolves – for the patriarchal codes of both Irish Nationalism and Unionism, but here with specific reference to the latter – the family as ideological symbol is no longer the site of male power and is actually faced with powerlessness within the state formation itself.

Furthermore, in accordance with Paulina Palmer's circumspection towards the radicalism of heterosexual female thriller writers (cf. 1997), it is notable that the elements of the state who attempt to impede Somerville's revenge are part of a conspiracy most notably criminalized by its homosexuality, which here – rather than femininity – is the deranged sexuality. The violence in the text is male on male, for as the filiative model ruptures, an attempt to reformulate a hegemonic masculinity requires the need to deal with other men through violence as an economy of meaning. Yet this relation, together with the alienated hypermasculinity of Somerville, also raises the spectre of homoerotic or homosocial desire. Such desire of course forms the core of patriarchal systems, but is projected onto the degraded state establishment, which has undermined the dominance of this previously intuitive masculine power and its discursive production. The recurrent association of homosexuality with state corruption in the 'Troubles' thriller perhaps attests to the recoil of organic constructions of gender from the redefinition of the state. Éibhear Walshe uses Nandy's thesis on the profoundly gendered colonial relation to suggest that the homosexual as transgendered, 'pretend' woman and the lesbian as unsexed or pretend man are

---

[17] In a familiar concession to the marketing of the form as masculine, Sarah Michaels publishes as S.J. Michaels.

acutely threatening and unsettling identities within any postcolonial culture: 'for a nation "coming of age", the lesbian and gay sensibility must be edited out, shut up' (5). I am asserting here that the state-approved gendering of identity is by no means assured and that the structural contradiction of organic, filiative forms of sexual identity in the modern state actually produces the kind of politics operative in *Summary Justice*.

The attempt to negotiate a dominant masculinity from a degraded and homosexualized state and society complements the conventional recourse to the fear of a feminized establishment. In Baker's *Inheritance*, Dorothy Taylor, the Chief Constable of the new Police Service of Northern Ireland, is termed 'a woman on the way up' (103), who stands allegorically as the female authority figure of a state conspiracy. There is an elision of father and son as she tries to seduce McCallan into the conspiracy:

> There was always the possibility, of course, that what she saw in him was a chance to make up for something which she had not been able to fulfil with Bob McCallan. She was almost stretched out in the chair and he knew that if he put down his glass and went to her she would not resist him. It was there in her eyes, both an invitation and a challenge, and to his discomfort he felt himself beginning to become aroused (144-145).

What this patrilineal anxiety and desire conflating in the female *sinthome* attempts to mask is the demotion of the patriarchal signifier and its certainties. For McCallan finds out that his father was a murderer embroiled in the conspiracy: 'everything that he had held dear throughout his life, right from childhood, had been stripped away. There were no certainties anymore, no assumptions. Nothing was what it appeared to be; everything was a lie' (297). In attempting to comprehend this uncertainty, the *repressive* modality of the text therefore utilizes an immemorialized female object through which to counteract a historical disaffiliation within masculinity. There is a curious Lacanian dream in the text, wherein the women in McCallan's life simultaneously coalesce and transpose: 'The moment he woke he remembered the dream. In it, Ann and Julia had merged into one person, then separated and merged again so that when he was talking to one, she became the other' (201). All women and their treachery are thereby reduced into a single *sinthome*, a necessary nightmare or fantasy structure to bolster McCallan's waking consciousness. This *sinthome* contains two conventional though seemingly contradictory stereotypes of femininity. One is obviously the already discussed *femme fatale*, a model supersaturated in the text in the figure of Laura. When McCallan discovers her plot, he ruminates upon himself: 'And you – you have screwed her. He knew how exciting it had felt. The touch of her skin. Her scent. Her heat. Her mouth on him. But now there was the agony of his guilt stabbing inside, a knife being twisted. He remembered the incident in the car, too. She had been torturing him, playing with him, all part of the punishment' (296-297). In addition to this corrupting, fearfully alluring figure is woman as bearer of social ill in a different sense, as passive victim. For example, McCallan visits an Ulster Museum Troubles exhibition and is fascinated by a sculpture of a woman in an explosion: 'McCallan wondered why the sculptor had chosen a woman as the subject rather than a man. Was it because they seemed more helpless, more vulnerable? He remembered it being said once that they were the real victims of the Troubles, the wives and the mothers who had to live with the pain' (208).

What is the function of these seemingly contradictory female stereotypes? There is a telling conflation of the two ideologemes in Henry Porter's *Remembrance Day*. Even though Constantine Lindow helps an injured girl after a bomb blast in London, he subsequently has the following dream:

> Lindow was in the street again, making love to the girl. He cradled her head as they rocked together; his hands were filled with bunches of her hair. He could smell the perfume rising from her and feel the undulating movement of her body. Then he slid from her, appalled. He looked down at the blood that swelled in her midriff, an unstoppable flow that came from the wound. There were other people in the street, standing just behind him. He heard them cluck with disapproval. He wanted to say that he hadn't done this thing, but then he couldn't be sure that he had not driven the wound into this girl (19).

This blurring indicates that the purpose of both ideologemes is the empowerment of a masculine subject in a discourse that must either regulate or protect its feminine object. With reference to Irish masculinity, then, this gendered subject within the thriller in a sense conjoins with a colonial model in subjugating women. For example, Elizabeth Butler Cullingford notes that: 'Images of women that originated as the projections of male anxieties and aggression are used to validate the need to control and subordinate the female sex' (65). Thus, the national project, in constructing a hegemonic subject, may have resort to such a production of masculinity in the thriller, in a confirmation of Meaney's Nandian thesis on the feminization of colonization and the subsequent imposition and observance of strictly differentiated gender roles: 'Women in these conditions become guarantors of their men's status, bearers of national honour and the scapegoats of national identity. They are not merely transformed into symbols of the nation, they become the territory over which power is exercised' (1991, 7).

But care also needs to be exercised. The sense of the female object as *sinthome* seemingly confirms Ailbhe Smyth's Irish feminist point: 'Essentially vacuous, receptacle without individual identity, mute spectacle, silent cipher, the symbolic female figure is incapable of *conferring* meaning' (9). However, there is something too simplistic in her post-colonial dichotomies through which this cipher is discursively assembled: 'The liberation of state implies male role shift from that of Slave to Master, Margin to Centre, Other to Self. Women, powerless under patriarchy, are maintained as Other of the ex-Other, colonised of the post-colonised' (10). I am seeking to demonstrate that the confrontation with the state in the thriller defeats not only organic ideologies such as the Englishness of Thatcherism, or Irish Nationalism or Unionism, but also the organic construction of a unitary masculinity. Immemorialized gender positioning assists the dehistoricization of this subject in construction. The cognitive mapping of crime as the class consciousness of the 'objective traitor' intimates that to reduce the thriller to sheer, exalted masculine alienation is actually to activate one of the genre's primary *repressive* modalities of symbolic containment.

With the entry of the subject into History through crime narrative, I also wish to consider to what extent 'Troubles' thrillers by women reach beyond the empty receptacle incapable of conferring meaning. In doing so, it is noteworthy that the mainstream gender discourse of coloniality further skews the representation of the actual historical involvement of women in political and emancipatory projects in Ireland and also erases the historical specifics of oppression. Hence, there is a somewhat mechanistic gender discourse informing Carol Coulter's emancipatory anti-imperialist narrative: 'Given the oppressively masculine nature of the colonial state which ruled Ireland (as well as Britain itself and the other colonies in the British Empire), it was perhaps inevitable that women would play a major role in the struggle to overthrow it, and that the battle of women for the vote and other rights gave strength and depth to the nationalist enterprise' (1993, 19). Such an analysis confirms the discursive slippage of the colonial paradigm by eliding the subjugation of supposedly sectional interests such as feminism in the production of the hegemonic national subject and its self-obsessed identity politics.

The thriller form often yields depictions of women as, to borrow a term from Margaret Ward's exemplary study, 'unmanageable revolutionaries'. For example, in K.T. McCaffery's *Revenge*, after Susan Furlong is raped by a high profile businessman with Fianna Fáil connections, she ends up in a psychiatric hospital where she meets an old Republican volunteer Bernadette Maxwell. Interestingly Maxwell's nickname is Joan of Arc, an attempt to contain this display of female agency in an archetypal or mythic paradigm, which combines with the codification of such political activism in a psychiatric ward as sheer madness, as psychic aberration, in indicating the repressed history of women's involvement in Irish politics. Again it is worth contemplating that for dominant discursive formations which purposively deny female agency, any expression of the latter, whether political or sexual, can only appear within the semiotic of that system as aberrant and alterior. In other words, female sexuality in thrillers that collude with dominant national cultures can only be expressed as perversity.

How, then, can female thriller writers attempt to articulate a new and challenging system of gender representation in the 'Troubles' thriller and indeed culture more generally? The majority of texts written by women tend to combine elements of the thriller with the romance form. This interaction of sociolects reaffirms the gender imperatives of the market but it also bespeaks something of the social symbolism of narrative form. With regard to the fantastic structure, my analysis of the political unconscious has sought to elucidate that for dominant subjects the fantasy is often to be uncovered as a vehicle of repression or coterminous expression of anxiety, whilst for nonhegemonic or suppressed subjects fantasy is often the articulation of desire. The political unconscious elaborates that if fantasy is traditionally considered to be something that has not occurred in reality, then we could equally posit that reality, in the strongest sense of History itself, is something that has not occurred, at a conscious level at least, in the fantasy (i.e. the literary text as imaginary resolution to the *a priori* historical problematic that is non-representationally outside it). I do not wish to assume that romance relates only to designated feminine genres, as I have striven to uncover utopian imaginations and spaces of desire stretching across national identities, state formations, class or the city, in addition to gender.

In this regard, there is an interesting formal confluence in Peter Burden's *Warrior's Son*, published by the New English Library, which, as discussed in my second chapter, set about the recuperation of a hard-edged masculinity during the English interregnum. The text's timeframe offers a romance at the heart of this period that also permits the synchronic ordering of the New English library's 'Troubles' output. Published in 1990, the text's plot runs from 1976 to the late eighties. Its hero, much more a romance hero than a hardboiled one, is the aristocrat and former SAS soldier, Edward Leominster, who revives the family stud despite his father's reservations about his playboy lifestyle. The text is imbued with the elegiac tone of much New Right discourse on aristocratic decline and also similarly seeks to eventually override this flux. One of Leominster's many lovers comments that 'she had not thought it possible that anyone existed who so fulfilled her notion of an ideal man' (101). His masculinity is the site of the old and the new, a point of suture for the fracture in the English Right during the emergence of Thatcherism from the interregnum: 'He had himself developed a code of human ethics which could have been, and frequently were, confused with old-fashioned social notions of honour and duty' (175). Similarly: 'under such a typical English exterior, there's a distinctly un-Conservative attitude' (253). Despite an IRA plot to assassinate himself and the Prince of Wales, and the plotting of an Arab Sheik against him, Leominster manages to breed a Derby winner. And all this after his original horse, Warrior, is kidnapped, leading him to race Warrior's son, War Lord. For when the latter is beaten by the Arab's horse in the Derby it transpires that it is actually the kidnapped Warrior – proof that good breeding comes through in the end! There is also an interesting point here about the breakdown of patrilineal masculinity, for masculinity in the text goes to the heart of the New Right's own guilt about its legitimacy within Toryism. Although Edward is able to defy his father and pursue his racing dream, opening up a space of desire, the fulfilment of this dream – Warrior beating its son, War Lord – actually restores an order of patriarchal superiority and law to harness and legitimize the transgression of the son. In other words, the text's romance is the erasure of the sins of the son and the continuation of filiative continuity despite its avowed and actual historical disruption.

With this generic affinity and conflict in mind, I wish to examine to what extent the thriller may offer women writers a more oppositional form in which to remap their societies and reinscribe desire in History in a more subversive sense. The ascertainment of the feminist deployment of the thriller as a relay of inequality in society, however, demands the following acknowledgement: that the gendered colonial binary impairs the radicalism of this enterprise, through the recourse to a unitary national victimhood which actually overwrites the concrete historical subordination of women. For example, Brian McIlroy has commented, in relation to cinema, that in representations of the security forces:

> Policewomen are noticeably missing in most contemporary films dealing with the RUC. Perhaps filmmakers and writers feel their presence weakens the frame they hang around the picture of Northern Ireland: male, Protestant security forces exploiting and repressing female, Catholic civilians, including feminist Republican activists ... To be sure, the presence of numbers of policewomen do nothing to subvert patriarchal structures, but they do complicate the rather simplistic accusations of misogyny at the root of Protestant policing (1993, 103).[18]

The most notable counter is Petit's *The Psalm Killer*, which parallels the relationship between the serial killer, Candlestick, and his female manipulator, and Detective Inspector Cross and the female officer, Westerby. The text does attempt to offer an insight into the problematics of being a female police officer and of the position of women in Northern Irish society. However, this is mitigated by the heavy gothicization of the text, wherein Westerby often seems displaced in a dehistoricized malaise like her almost namesake, Lucy Westenra, in Stoker's *Dracula*. There are continually drawn equivalences between the conflict itself and domestic violence, as when Westerby interviews a woman whose abusive husband is long departed but: 'even with him gone, she still seemed curiously resigned to its inevitability' (252). This kind of account of both the conflict itself and violence against women is inflected with a mythic fatalism, as with Candlestick's comment: 'Violence had a sacred momentum, like going with a woman' (161). Violence transcends its historical context and is conflated into a seemingly unknowable and primordial psychosexual provenance.

A case in point is the scene in which Candlestick and his *femme fatale* manipulator, who has just killed the UDA leader Tommy Herron in his car, have sex while the corpse lies in the boot: 'he listened to her orgasm being wrenched from her in a series of grunting moans, and watched her face screw up with pleasure or pain, he couldn't tell. Christ, he thought, the whole thing was far more violent than the murder of Tommy Herron' (11). On one level, therefore, the text could be read as an attempt to address the inequality of women in society, to imbricate oppression such as domestic violence within a wider social context of state institutions and political structures. Nonetheless, this ready consonance of masculinity and violence removes the former from any historical context into a transcendental realm of psychosexual promptings, which, in a moment of telling ideological transference, facilitates the projection and reversal of this now immemorialized violence onto the paradigmatic dehistoriced *sinthome*, the horror of woman. The text's close withdraws from its confrontation with state formation and social inequality, with the difficulties facing Westerby's career and the violence she uncovers against other women, into the pervasive fear of precisely such an 'active', independent woman who must be removed from her economic and historical context:

> The more Westerby tried to imagine this woman the more she grew sure that the killings – for all their apparent sense of purpose – were after all sexually driven

---

[18] Blair McMahon's *Nights in Armour*, an Ulster Society publication depicting the RUC in the thriller form, is an obvious but by no means especially liberating counterexample.

> and had a sexual trigger ... she grew to believe that the woman in Candlestick's life was not passive but active, perhaps even the architect of their plan. Candlestick had written of himself that he was only the instrument. The killing and the fucking went hand in hand, she was sure, but she could not say why. Westerby felt this sexual itch herself, an almost uncontrollable desire that ambushed her when she least expected it. What demons, she wondered, had been unleashed in her (Petit, 632).

Therefore, the text's depiction of Westerby's position within the state does on one level achieve the feminist perspective articulated by Kimberly J. Dilley: 'Women's police novels explore legal contradictions. They illustrate women's position under the law' (59). The ubiquity of violence and abuse affirm Dilley's discernment that 'according to the woman police detectives, order and justice are not just a matter of removing the one who disrupted the status quo. The status quo is not a safe or equitable place for women' (91). However, as indicated, this insight is then collapsed into the most rudimentary gender mechanics of the standard thriller. How far do texts by female authors further this kind of insight into the displacement of women in society? As I have suggested above, the few 'Troubles' thrillers written by women tend to combine the form with elements of romance. How does the historical desire encoded in this form either enhance or impair the feminist potentialities identified by Dilley?

In making a case for the feminist potential dialectically ingrained with the more ideological formal levels of romance, Tania Modleski asserts that self-aggrandizement is a male mode:

> There are no doubt a number of reasons why female protagonists and female popular fiction cannot claim for themselves the kind of status male heroes and texts so often claim. This kind of aggrandizement, occurring both in fiction and in criticism, would appear to be a masculine code, traceable, at least in part, to the male oedipal conflict. This conflict, it is important to note, is resolved at the expense of woman and necessitates her devaluation. For the male gains access to culture and the symbolic first by perceiving the 'lack' of the once all-powerful mother and then by identifying with the 'superior' male, the father (12).

Modleski continues that 'at the end of a majority of popular narratives the woman is disfigured, dead, or at the very least, domesticated. And *her* downfall is anything *but* tragic' (12). Undoubtedly, this is often true but what of a text such as Petit's *The Psalm Killer* in which it is Candlestick and Cross who die, leaving us with the parallel females in the text? Similarly, Maureen T. Reddy posits that in the classic crime novel there is movement from disorder or violation of order to order, a reassuring rite of passage that is not only desirable but also possible in banishing disruptive social elements. This form, for Reddy, includes the acceptance of a masculine authority figure who is alone capable of explaining the world satisfactorily (5). The subversion of feminist crime fiction, therefore, Reddy continues resides in the destabilization of this putatively masculine mode: 'like gothic and sensation novels, feminist crime fiction displaces the traditionally central male consciousness, offering instead a woman-centred world view' (149).

This kind of analysis again mistakes the surface ideology of the text for what it formally and historically achieves. The thriller signals the defeat by late capitalism – in the interest of which such texts are supposedly written – of the tenability of precisely such an ideological resolution.

The thriller reveals the disturbance of the hegemonic certainties of masculinity, the nation, class and state formation under earlier historical conditions. The account of the genre as an almost orgasmically end-orientated, masculine form thus needs to be undercut. The demise of the possibility of this very ideology is attested by a scene in Colm Connolly's *The Pact*, between the IRA captain, Tommy Cahill, and his lover: '[n]ow the gentleness had gone or was totally submerged in the urgency to consume by climax, a pointless race of ejaculation and, with no victor, an ultimate feeling of futility. The frustration with, and growing irritation of the IRA campaign and his impatience with its leadership were threshed in the pliable moistness, but never relieved' (49). Here the state formation dissolves into the irresolubility of the conflict, which in turn, itself bespeaks a crisis in masculinity.

With this dispensation in mind – that the real subversive potential of the crime narrative for oppositional subjects resides not in the disruption of an ideology that has already fallen apart historically but in the investigation of the aporia of that fracture as a means of mapping the social itself – what opportunities are offered by the thriller and its interaction with romance for female subjects? Reddy's periodization draws a correspondence between the rise of sensation fiction, at a time when women were overturning the male publishing monopoly by founding presses, journal and magazines, and the advent of feminist crime fiction in the twentieth century, when there is an increase in feminist journals, presses, scholarship and a wider influence of feminist thought on society and culture more generally:

> Blending the themes of gothic and sensation fiction with the methods of detective fiction, feminist writers have created female heroes who challenge received wisdom about women's role and novels that subvert genre conventions. Feminist crime novels, far from being mere escapist literature or isolated, peculiar experiments in an essentially masculine preserve, participate in the larger feminist project of redefining and redistributing power, joining a long and valuable tradition of women's fiction (Reddy, 149).

This intercession of the fantastic accords with Modleski's proposal, in relation to the readerly angst, fear, suspense produced by gothic novels, that such texts provide a release for women's feelings of estrangement, disorientation, and paranoia, given the causal function of social alienation for such feeling. As to the specific configuration of the fantastic in romance form, Janice A. Radway postulates that romance satiates the needs of women as a function of their dependent status *as woman* and their acceptance of marriage as the only way towards female fulfilment. But the active process of romance reading, for Radway, also originates in a very real dissatisfaction and embodies a valid, if limited, protest:

While the act of romance reading is used by women as a means of partial protest against the role prescribed for them by the culture, the discourse itself actively insists upon the desirability, naturalness, and benefits of that role by portraying it not as the imposed necessity that it is but as a freely designed, personally controlled, individual choice. When the mythic ending of the romance undercuts the realism of the novelistic rendering of an individual woman's story, this literary form reaffirms its founding culture's belief that women are valuable not for their unique personal qualities but for their biological sameness and ability to perform that essential role of maintaining and reconstituting others (208).

What is notable about the confluence of the romance form with the 'Troubles' thriller is the role of the family. As discussed in my third chapter, both Irish Nationalism and Unionism, as foundationally filiative ideologies of organic intimacy, struggle to constitute a properly public realm in relation to the state or the city. Therefore, there is no ready correspondence between the public/private or male/female and the formal symbolism of the thriller and the romance. Romance narratives can express a dissatisfaction with filiation that articulates a wider interrogation of the dominant ideologies in Ireland, and for which the entry into the social in the form of the thriller provides a discursive forum. Yet the 'Love Across the Barricades' subgenre does also function more regressively, as in the work of Joan Lingard, to obscure an examination of the state by naturalizing sectarianism as thwarted communitarian reconciliation. In other words, as Lingard's protagonists themselves disclose by recurrently leaving the North, the communitarian romance defers both the consolidation and the overthrow of the Northern state as contested apparatus by denying its power structures.[19]

In O'Riordan's somewhat mechanistic *Involved*, a romance plot is pitted against thriller, in expressing a female dissatisfaction with the power structures of a Republican family. For the romantic involvement of the text's heroine, Kitty Fitzgerald, with Danny O'Neill entails social and political involvement (120). Although the plot articulates a salvational bourgeois concern for Danny's soul, at a formal level the thriller form is necessitated by the incapacity of the filiative ideologeme to map this romantic desire, as Fitzgerald is impelled from the intimacy of the home into the public realm of the streets and affiliation with other women and the social itself. In spite of that, the text also recapitulates the collapse of accounts of the conflict into psychosexual disorder that ultimately corrupts the overly previous romantic desire contained in the text, as in the description of Danny's elder brother, Eamon, on his way to threaten an informer: 'he approached the house slowly. The erection swelled between his legs' (5).

Linda Anderson has written several texts, which also combine the thriller with the romance form, the most symptomatically entitled of which is *Cuckoo*, as her texts deal with displaced, unsettled women and the destabilization of filiation. In

---

[19] Thus, the conventional 'national romance' by which nationally allegorized lovers unite across barriers of race or class in the consolidation of a specific state formation is problematized by the conflict over the Northern state itself. See Doris Sommer, *Foundational Fictions: The National Romances of Latin America*. Berkeley: U of Berkeley P, 1991. Sommer's framework is expertly compared to the North by Joe Cleary (1996).

To Stay Alive, Rosaleen expresses her dissatisfaction with Belfast and her husband Dan by sleeping with a British soldier, whom she subsequently witnesses searching her husband on the street: 'This vision of her husband stooped and dwarfed before that soldier, so easily victorious, upright and important, gave her a primitive surge of joy that made her weak and dizzy. She wanted to disown the feeling. Disown herself' (1984, 50). Here, a feminine desire is expressed by its gaze upon the stratification of two masculinities: namely, the demotion of an Irish filiative model by a phallic colonial form. However, she then reconsiders: '[h]ow dare he demean her husband before her eyes? He was their enemy. He felt nothing but contempt. He thought he could do what he pleased to their bodies. He had abused both of them. She ran over to Dan. She felt more bound to him by what had happened than by their marriage' (1984, 50) Again Rosaleen hails colonial discourse in feminizing her defeated husband, and the incident significantly culminates in the re-establishment of the filiative bond between husband and wife. In a way, then, the thriller form on one level functions as an escape from the boredom of family life for Rosaleen but ultimately her encounter with the social precipitates a withdrawal into the filiative ideologeme and the attenuation of desire for social change and improvement.

The radical credentials of the few 'Troubles' thrillers written by metropolitan feminists are also often thrown into contradiction and hampered by the uncritically monolithic gendering of victimhood in colonial discourse. Jane McLoughlin's *Coincidence*, which is published by Virago, is an example of a feminist attempt to combine a number of generic materials with a 'Troubles' backdrop. The dust jacket proclaims: '*Coincidence* is at once a thriller, a romance and a polemic in which the story of kidnapping, mutilation and imprisonment is played out behind the screen of the ordinariness of everyday life in Ireland'. The text's heroine, Kitty Lawrence, nee O'Shea, travels to Ireland where she is mistaken for another Kitty O'Shea intending to donate a million dollars to the IRA.[20] This plot device permits the text to introduce a number of terrorist characters as background and vicarious thrill for the rather hackneyed politics of the text. In supposedly giving an insight into the suffering of Irish women, we are introduced to the IRA volunteers, Liam O'Tomas and his lover Niamh, whose love-making is described through Niamh's point of view (again with colonial discourse deployed to discredit Irish masculinity):

> He could easily be a Brit, she thought. An undercover man. If he hits me once too often, I'll shop him and his dirty talk, treating me like a whore. God, wouldn't that be something if I did. Him up here mounting me like a dog in the road, and all the time I'd know the boys were waiting for him downstairs to march him off to a ditch somewhere. That would be something for a woman to know that was coming to her lover while he was rummaging at her like a great hound from behind, all cock and gasping for breath (31).

However, the text's feminist credentials are further undermined by the following scene – which would not be out of place in a New English Library text – wherein

---

[20] There is also of course an evocation of Parnell's Kitty O'Shea.

Niamh returns to the gratefully abused, feminine position of the most reactionary politics of the crime form: '[t]hey moved together like true lovers for some time, with Liam giving her some sweet loving strokes that made her feel all so full of love. Then he was banging and thumping against her backside like a good belting and there was no time and no breath, and then the lights exploded in her head and the were no words' (30-31). Such supposed feminine traits confirm Liam's view that: 'All women were fascinated by violence. They all wanted to know if he had ever killed and if he ever had, had he killed up close with a knife or a gun or with his bare hands. Sometimes he invented some nice stories for Niamh and watched her eyes cloud over full of shuddering violent thoughts as he whispered to her, that always turned them on' (33). Strikingly, the female gaze in this passage is again inhibited by a sexualized subordination to male violence and agency.

The limitations of *Coincidence* and its utilization of the North as backdrop, are emphatically confirmed by the text's self-referential attempt to display the emancipated independence of its heroine, Kitty: 'In books, she thought, it's always the demon male who awakens the woman, but that was because in the past, men wrote those books. In real life, it was the dried stick of a man who was awakened, when he ran up against a piece of hot female stuff who wasn't afraid to take what she wanted' (55-56). The action in the novel continues when Kitty is kidnapped again by 'another gang of Irish murderers. They were different, but the same' (146). This reactivation of identity and difference, this disavowal of concrete social dynamics, typifies the text's usage of the North as *sinthome*, as desiring space in a manner no less risible than the British New Right texts discussed in my second chapter.

A more interesting affiliation between metropolitan feminism and the 'Troubles' thriller is furnished by Valerie Miner's *Blood Sisters*. It is the story of two cousins – the daughters of Irish sisters – one of whom is in the Women's liberation movement, the other in the IRA. The cousins, both named Elizabeth, are known as Liz and Beth and described as 'mirror images' (88). This duality and effacement of individuality obviously seeks to subvert the selfhood produced by conventional crime fiction. Even so, there are no easy feminist readings of the emancipatory politics of women writing crime fiction, as evidenced by the racism informing the spurious feminist disdain in Liz's journey through London to Beth's house: 'The bus was packed now. Irish-looking men next to each other, stupefied from the fumes of their own beery breath and sweat' (13). The thriller form provides a mode for both cousins to map their position in society, revealing a tension between feminism and nationalism in their divergent attempts to explain women's unequal position. Beth initially opines: 'Why couldn't Liz realise that women had nationalities too? Maybe it was because she was American. Who would want to identify with America? This barmaid, here, was as much Irish as she was a woman. An Irish woman. You can't split yourself in two' (23). Beth nevertheless becomes increasingly involved in Liz's feminist groups, leading to an argument with her IRA boyfriend: 'I told him that he was exploiting women with some of his attitudes ... much the same way that England holds down the Irish'

(54). Again this is a very mechanistic use of the gendered discourse of colonialism in explaining social oppression.[21]

The text is littered with references to Maud Gonne and Countess Markievicz, and the grandmother of the cousins was Elizabeth O'Brien, a fictionalized activist in the Irish Women's Council. The text attempts to conjoin this repressed tradition of female Irish Nationalism and contemporary feminism. Ultimately, however, Beth injures herself with a bomb that kills her mother. Liz consequently decides to write a book about Beth and her mother, Gerry, and her own mother Polly and herself that is self-referentially entitled 'blood sisters' (206). Sally Munt locates the subversive potential in *Blood Sisters* in the opposition of female connectivity and affiliation to individuation:

> Our moral sympathy is engaged, not with a single hero, but with the complex social and political involvements of all the Flannigan family women ... these women are in active opposition to the state – Beth is manipulated by her Provisional IRA cell-group into bombing Whitehall, her mother's employer. Gerry is secretly working late to raise money for their Irish holiday; Beth breaks into her office just as the faulty bomb explodes (63).

Munt further asserts that 'through associating this violence with the male impulse – Liz's brother is maimed by mishandling a bomb, Beth is blackmailed by ex-boyfriend Bruce into the Whitehall plant – Miner advocates the non-violent struggle which formed the centre of the pacifistic feminism of the early 1980s. The family unit is blown apart' (63). The text resists closure, it resists both the defeat and the fulfilment of desire: 'It should not end here. It did not make sense. It could not end here. "We're all on the edge of breaking through", she had told Polly. "You and Gerry are finally coming together after all that time. Beth and I are doing well on the book. We are going back to Ireland together' (204). To this end, Munt posits: 'Their shocked solitary inadequacy is imposed by the state. Beth will be imprisoned for many years, and Liz is left to the isolation of authorship. She will write, significantly, of Irish women, and the Irish struggle, and their words will be their weapon, locating this ending within the vision for feminist publishing which generated the massive surge of creativity in feminist culture in the 1970s and 1980s' (63).

To an extent, then, the text utilizes the thriller form to trace the social impediments and forces reined against female attachment and political advancement. Yet it does so in a rather precious bourgeois manner that idealizes a particular kind of Irish Nationalism, which functions allochronically to refute concrete historical struggle. Miner's text accords with Maggie Humm's postulation that 'women detectives may share the marginality of their male peers, an

---

[21] Congressman Peter T. King's Irish-American *Terrible Beauty* is dedicated to 'the Republican Women of Ireland'. With reference to Neil Jordan's *The Crying Game*, Marilyn Reizbaum comments: 'the nationalist impulse to mirror the colonizer's (albeit mythic) standard of strength and unity, to be "hardmen" – this being the qualifying description, in all its resonant glory, of the IRA soldier – ironically underlies the need to dismiss/dominate the feminine' (1994, 24).

ambiguous relation to class or status, but in feminist writing the marginal is glorified' (Bloom, ed. 1990, 238). But there is nothing inherently subversive, nor politically enabling for that matter, in marginality. The thriller is the site of a range of alienated, marginal subjects, including masculinities, who may utilize crime to espouse a reactionary politics or alternatively may engage it as a utopian means of re-arranging the totality of social forces into a pattern that may be resisted.

Nevertheless, Miner's *Blood Sisters* and its oppositional solidarity against the state is perhaps one of the few 'Troubles' thrillers that strives to attest to Rosalind Coward and Linda Semple's claim that

> crime involves the disruption of normalities, and detective fiction is often the consequence of these disruptions. While detective fiction is of course explicitly about the restoration of law, it is important to remember that it is also crucially about the breaking of the law, and about transgression of the normal rules ... Women who, in real life, are less often criminals than victims, are clearly drawn to a genre dealing with transgression of the law (51).

Coward and Semple continue: 'women's concerns, far from being alien to this genre, are often the very stuff of the crime novel – violence, sexual violence, conflict between individuals and authority, the conflict between men and women. That such potentially radical concerns have often been at the heart of the form should therefore lead to no surprise that the form can be used specifically for radical ends' (54). Such radicalism is impaired by dealing with violence and social conflict as a biologically male disorder in which misguided women may share. It delimits the utopian mapping of the state formation in the thriller, the political kernel of which my concluding chapter shall endeavour to uncover.

Chapter 5

'It's Not for the Likes of Us to Philosophize': The Pleasure and Politics of Thrills, or, Towards a Political Aesthetics

'We moderns, we half-barbarians. We are in the midst of our bliss only when we are most in danger. The only stimulus that tickles us is the infinite, the immeasurable'.
Friedrich Nietzsche, *Beyond Good and Evil*

Whence is derived the pleasure of the thriller? Wherein lies the pleasure of its thrills? By producing a mechanics of pleasure from uncovering the seemingly interminable reaches of the state, the thriller, especially its conspiratorial mode, could be seen to accomplish the unleashing of a desire, a revolutionary desire, to chart and interpret our societies. As discussed above, conspiracy proffers a Jamesonian production of the missing psychology of the political unconscious and its transcription of the local to the global, a means by which the absent totality of social relations may be figured as a connective network of crime. Therefore, the thrill at the political centre of the genre, the confrontation of human consciousness with the spectral reaches of the late capitalist state, even as they engulf the human subject, offers a paradigmatic modality of the experience of (post)modernity itself:

> To be modern is to live a life of paradox and contradiction. It is to be overpowered by the immense bureaucratic organizations that have the power to control and often destroy all communities, values, lives: and yet to be undeterred in our determination to face these forces, to fight to change our world and make it our own. It is to be both revolutionary and conservative: alive to new possibilities for experience and adventure, frightened by the nihilistic depths to which so may modern adventures lead, longing to create and to hold on to something real even as everything melts (Berman, 14).

The contradictions of this modern consciousness encode the dialectical interplay of the ideological and the utopian modalities of popular fiction. However, given the problematics of this contradictory consciousness, it is important to interrogate the strategic seams of the thriller's social cartography. In the very process of mapping the vast apparatuses of the late capitalist state, the *repressive* modality recodifies this desire, effecting the dissipation of desire as a revolutionary historical force into an aesthetics of defeat, the indulgence of a pleasure in our own powerlessness. So the form provides the thrill of glimpsing, however fleetingly, the seemingly unfigurable social totality, yet its *repressive* modality withdraws from the transformative contemplation of this elevated instance. It produces pleasure in the radical alienation of revolutionary desire. Indeed, such alienation is indicative of the commodification of pleasure itself.

The imbrication of the 'Troubles' thriller's characters in the state apparatus, and their disablement in the face of its complex might, attest to the diminution of human agency and transformative desire. For example, Jack McCallan, in Baker's *Inheritance*, is told in the cover-up at the text's closure: 'We've seen how thin the fabric of this place is, how easily that can be damaged. It is a delicate equilibrium and we cannot allow Northern Ireland and its future prosperity to be affected any further' (335). Such embroilment in the mechanics of the state seems to confirm irresistible, Foucauldian circularity of power in contemporary society. Foucault's sense of power as productive does admittedly intimate how the thriller produces a series of aesthetic fulfilments. This grasp of the productive aspect of power is salient in an era wherein consumer capitalism and its postmodern cultural artifacts install a politics of pleasure out of the very conditions of the global power. Thus, in M.S. Power's *The Killing of Yesterday's Children*, when Colonel Maddox tells the RUC officer Asher that 'it's not for the likes of us to philosophize' (200), both characters stand as instruments of a power, which encompasses them and their society but which they seemingly cannot resist, or even at the very least, consciously begin to deliberate politically. Such myopic debilitation alerts us to the limitations of a Foucauldian analysis of power, wherein there is no human consciousness to alter or mobilize, for there is nothing beyond power and its productions of truth. Our own detective work in the political unconscious, however, affirms that there is an ultimate sociopolitical horizon to be realized, that it is possible to theorize and engage through praxis a sense of the complex totality of social relations which comprise our societies. A Foucauldian analysis, of the characters pinioned in the 'Troubles' thriller's network of supersaturated cover-up and conspiracy, ultimately offers only a series of discontinuous and self-enclosed discursive units producing their own limited truths. For example, Crawford's *Fall When Hit* closes with the proviso that 'there are a thousand cans of worms. We just opened one of them' (300).[1]

Thus, the journalist in Esler's *Loyalties* resignedly accepts the official government cover-up and its structuring of 'the botched up bits of reality into a coherent whole ... It was as good a story as any other. It was not true, but something to believe which might be better than any truth. For the moment at least'

---

[1] Aijaz Ahmad perceptively interrogates Foucauldian genealogy in the following manner: 'this history without system origins, human subjects or collective sites is nevertheless a history of all-encompassing Power, which is wielded by no-one and *cannot* be resisted, because there is nothing outside the fabrications of Power – perhaps *ought not* to be resisted because it is not only repressive but also profoundly productive. History, in other words, is not open to change, only to narrativization. Resistance can only be provisional, personal, local, micro, and pessimistic in advance' (130-131).

(438-439). The conspiracy becomes only one rehearsal of a sequestered pattern, a compensatory talisman, amidst an incomprehensible deluge of discourses of equally provisional, indeterminable viability. The protagonists in the 'Troubles' thriller, therefore, and the pleasures they induce, provide allegories of the celebration within late capitalism by postmodernism of the commodified consciousness. The schizophrenic simulacrum eulogized by Foucault or Deleuze and Guatarri, whilst more self-consciously postmodernist, nevertheless shares its historical referent with the *repressive* conspiracy in producing an aesthetics of bewilderment, which diminishes the revolutionary impetus of desire in History. The task for a Marxist aesthetic, therefore, is not the rejection of pleasure as sheer distraction in itself, but rather the reinscription and reformulation of such pleasure in unfolding a truly revolutionary and utopian inventory of desire in the 'Troubles' thriller.

It is the 'invisible hand' dreamed of by Adam Smith, the logic of capital itself, which ultimately stands as the conspiratorial totality apparently defeating the agency of the thriller's protagonists. As Jameson observes:

> Market ideology assures us that human beings make a mess of it when they try to control their destinies ('socialism is impossible') and that we are fortunate in possessing an interpersonal mechanism – the market – which can substitute for human hubris and planning and replace human decisions altogether. We only need to keep it clean and well oiled, and it now – like the monarch so many centuries ago – will see to us and keep us in line (1991, 273).

There is something subversive, no matter how reactionary the intentional authorial politics may be, about the attempt to lend textual figuration in the form of the thriller to social materials, which are avowedly secret and covert. Thus, a Marxist restructuration of the pleasure of the thriller must overdetermine the utopian modality which offers, in however evanescent or pessimistic a manner, a cartography of the social totality, and force the text's contradictory structural urges into a productive formal rupture. In establishing a transformative articulation of desire, Jameson notably adapts the Burkean thematization of the Beautiful and the Sublime to construct a politics of pleasure pertinent to the thriller's cognitive mappings. The Beautiful is grounded in the self-sufficient experience of small-scale objects in their own right, in keeping with the splintered and atomized consciousness of the idealized schizophrenic or the thriller's *repressive* subsumption by bewilderment at the differentiality of power. The Sublime, on the other hand, entails the pleasures of fear, or rather the aesthetic appropriation of pain as fear in a dual focus, which Jameson productively formulates as allegorical: 'the sublime takes its object as the pretext and the occasion for the intuition through it and beyond it of sheer unfigurable force itself, sheer power, that which stuns the imagination in the most literal sense' (1988b, Vol.2, 72).

This projective aesthetic offers a means of circumventing the defeatism of a Foucauldian circularity of power and of transfiguring Barthesian jouissance through historical agency in the form of the utopian reading practice of the totality:

the immense culture of the simulacrum whose experience, whether we like it or not, constitutes a whole series of daily ecstasies and punctual fits of *jouissance* or schizophrenic dissolutions ... may appropriately, one would think, be interpreted as so many unconscious points of contact with that equally unfigurable and unimaginable thing, the multinational apparatus, the great suprapersonal system of a late capitalist technology (Jameson 1988b, Vol.2, 73).

Jameson's model assists the dialecticizing of Barthes' binary evaluation between *the text of pleasure* and *the text of jouissance*, between, respectively, 'a comfortable practice of reading' and a text 'that imposes a state of loss, the text that discomforts' (1975, 14). Barthes' schema fundamentally opposes the pleasure in the popular text with jouissance in the canonical or classic text. For Barthes, only the 'anachronic' reader is sufficiently and critically positioned to be able to read both the high and the low: 'he [sic] enjoys the consistency of his selfhood (that is his pleasure) and seeks its loss (that is his bliss). He is a subject split twice over, doubly perverse' (1975, 14). The dialectical model stands against both this hierarchized situation of the text and its possibilities, and indeed, this celebrated, schizoid subject pointing playfully but importunately to the dilating purview of the academic under the deluge of potential textual objects divested by the culturalism of postmodernism. In relation to the thriller, the allegorical aesthetic of pleasure as praxis collapses Barthes' dichotomy through the grasp of the genre and the politics of its conspiratorial form as a dialectical regulation of convention and a sublime sense of loss or unfigurability. Hence the importance of a Marxist aesthetic: 'this dual, or "allegorical", focus is indeed what makes for both the uniqueness and the difficulties of Marxism in general as a conception of revolutionary transformation. The dialectic is in itself this dual obligation to invent ways of writing the here-and-now of the immediate situation with the totalizing logic of the global or Utopian one' (Jameson 1988b, Vol.2, 73).

Scott McCracken links popular fiction with transgression in affirming that 'transgression always plays a part in our enjoyment. To transgress means to violate or infringe, to go beyond certain bounds' (155). The politics of such pleasures are divulged in the transcoding of differential materials. Ultimately Marxism provides the theoretical framework through which to transcode disparate historical and formal materials into a totalized context. As discussed in my last chapter, the utopian mapping of the conspiratorial text is delimited by a series of overarching symbolic codes, which seam its desire. Thus, to take gender as a prime example, an analysis of the *sinthome* illustrates that masculinity is not the authentic core of crime fiction but is rather a mode of symbolic containment masking the political centre of the form. Put another way, the thriller is not inherently reactionary or pessimistic but more tenuously constructs specific symbolic codes designed to subtend the *redemptive* reading. This chapter will dissect the formal withdrawal from confronting the social totality into *repressive* nodes of pleasure in the following forms: the recoil into an immemorial masculinity producing a sublime thrill in the appropriation of the fear of female sexuality as single, recurrent crime; the political pessimism of the state and the late capitalist system as irresoluble complexity; Northern Ireland as the site of the anxious thrill of pure, unresolved otherness, as exoticized terrain, through which the conflict itself is then viewed as unsolvable. The enactment of these stereotypes, both as sources of pleasure and anxiety and as codes of and representational enclosure, intimates that such codes instigate the production of a dominant or optimal readership or *destinataire* for the 'Troubles' thriller.

Therefore, the entreaty by Colonel Maddox in Power's *The Killing of Yesterday's Children* against philosophizing upon one's placement in the thrills and action of the North is itself suggestive of the aesthetic sought by the *repressive* modality of the text. The ideological imperatives of the text seek to foreclose the utopian mapping of the conspiracy through the recourse to a more paranoid, compensatory series of fantasies. In place of a class allegorical ranging of social forces into a totalized pattern appears a terrain of phantasmal otherness: whether this be class, gender or an immersion in the alterity of the North itself. I want to counterpose the pleasure of the paranoid fantasy and its construction of totality with the confrontation of the individual subject with the totality in the conspiratorial ideologeme.

On a Lacanian note, the paranoid story implies the existence of an 'Other of the Other', a hidden subject who co-ordinates the great Other (the symbolic order, the social) and produces an effect of meaning through a senseless contingency, beyond the conscious intention of the speaking subject. This 'Other of the Other' is the Other of paranoia, the totalized whole who speaks through us without our knowing it. As Žižek observes:

> The paranoid construction enables us to escape the fact that 'the Other does not exist' (Lacan) – that it does not exist as a consistent, closed order – to escape the blind, contingent automatism, the constitutive stupidity of the symbolic order ... When faced with such a paranoid construction, we must not forget Freud's warning and mistake it for the 'illness' itself: the paranoid construction is, on the contrary, an attempt to heal ourselves, to pull ourselves out of the real 'illness', the 'end of the world,' the breakdown of the symbolic universe, by means of this substitute formation (Žižek, 1991, 18-19).

The North as sheer alterity, the gothicized working class, and the figure of the feminine all function as substitute formations regulated by the Big Other fantasy of Panopticon 'law and order' imbuing the conventional treatment of the thriller. They negate the active reading process constructing the social subject through the *lines of desire* encoded in the thriller's mapping of crime. By not philosophizing on our predicament, by finding gratification in the fantasy of the Big Other's instruction, we are indeed, to return to E.P. Thompson's critique of Althusser, only the *träger* of ulterior structural determinations. For example, in Petit's *The Psalm Killer*, Candlestick considers the position of himself and his co-agent thus: 'He knew nothing except for a suspicion that she, like he, had secret masters. Whether they were the same as his he had no idea' (3). Hence, the *repressive* modality wills a disabling of human intent cognate with Thompson's formulation of Althusserian History a 'process programmed within a structure, an orrery turned by a hidden hand' (295). However, as outlined in my introduction, a grasp of how the crime form can also instigate a Brechtian narrative entry into the catastrophic mystery of the social permits the dialectical formulation of History as an experience of exigency and desire. Succinctly, it facilitates the wrestling of a class subject and narrative from the fantasy of the Big Other.

The task is to ascertain how utopian pleasure may be circumscribed or indeed transcribed by more anxiously engendered gratifications. With regard to gender and symbolic containment, a political aesthetics may be elaborated from the surrogacy of the Lacanian Real as itself a gendered mode of symbolic containment for History and the social totality allegorized by the crime narrative.[2] My previous chapter attempted not only to analyse the displacement of female subjectivity in the thriller but also to stress the need to regard masculinity as problematical, to question the idea that a unitary and given male is always the subject and in control of textual focalization. In order to produce an aesthetic that socializes the Lacanian Real, I shall propose a reciprocal desideratum to confute the hegemonic masculine forms discursively structuring the mainstream ideologies of both the thriller and psychoanalysis.

Accordingly, Steve Neale pertinently questions psychoanalysis as 'the identification of a discourse that is finally masculine' (1992, 48). Neale's analysis provides a methodology for undercutting the seaming of History by the Real of the hegemonically gendered subject in the thriller. By interrogating the central phallus/penis relation of both distinction and oscillation by which psychoanalysis is bounded, Neale affirms that 'the vision, any vision, is constructed, not given; appealing to its certainty, psychoanalysis can only repeat the ideological impasse of the natural, the mythical representation of things' (1992, 50).[3] Neale continues that 'when psychoanalysis produces woman, the woman, as not-all, it falls short, remains locked in a static assignation. It is not the woman who is not-all but psychoanalysis, which is what the latter has been so generally unwilling to grasp. Psychoanalysis discovers and ceaselessly fails – in its theory – the unconscious, and that failure is history, the social relations of production, classes, sexes' (1992, 55). That is, psychoanalysis attempts to override the history of the subject, the specification of its production and division in the symbolic, by locating that conflict securely beyond History as defined by the transcendental and privileged signifier of the phallus.

In short, psychoanalysis naturalizes its own formative fetishization. The whole ideological task of the eroticization of castration and its production of symbolic

---

[2] In offering a Marxist reinscription of the Lacanian Real, I would advocate that the importance of Lacan to theories of the subject resides in his emphasis upon the latter as the site of conflicting states of being and becoming, of risk and instability rather than fixity. Subjectivity is not a direct reflection of real gender relations but is rather a process of representation encumbered with specific hegemonic and social assignments.

[3] There is in Lacan, as with the conventional ideological designations of the thriller, a unquestioned imagining of the feminine, which, in psychoanalysis, demarcates an annexing of the biological and the psychological that runs somewhat contrary to psychoanalysis' avowed commitment to addressing the splitting of the subject and ultimately produces a transhistorically secure dominant.

division is the transposition of difference onto male and female as defined by the 'normal' fetish discursively enthroned by the penis-phallus. Namely, as Neale discloses, the configuration of 'the relation of men, women and desire in a particular economy of representation, that of disavowal, the recognition and refusal of lack; the difference of the woman is the visibility of the man, the assured perspective, the form of exchange; with woman's representation as *the* lack, *the* difference, the point or erotic return of "a certain mystery", the veil of truth' (1992, 74). Thus, for psychoanalysis, sexual difference is the Real resisting symbolization, which stands in the place of History in my political aesthetics. So psychoanalysis seeks to efface its own historical production – the historical fracture of the patriarchal bourgeois family and its attendant social authority which its discourse has been unable to think beyond – by naturalizing its own primary fetish and dominant subject. Broadly speaking, there is a similar point of erotic return in the thriller in the figure of the feminine, which equally seeks to stand in the place of the social totality itself and proffer a mode of symbolic containment and pleasure within a putatively assured masculine vantage point through which to disavow History itself.

The substitution of the erotic return of feminine criminality for the unconscious figuration of the social totality in the thriller seeks to disclaim the utopian symbolism of the form by attempting to wrestle from a range of formal and historical debris the ideology of the single, resolvable crime. For Barthes, the pleasure of the text is perhaps a subversive but comfortably pluralistic rendering of the dialogic. It abolishes what he terms *logical contradiction* through an acceptance of illogicality and incongruity, so as to entail the 'cohabitation of languages *working side by side*: the pleasure of the text is a sanctioned Babel' (3-4). The recourse to gender, and in particular femininity, as a final unveiling of pleasure attempts to revivify aesthetically the Golden Age ideology of the resolvable crime and undercuts the more sublime thrill of the form.

The mode of symbolic containment structuring the transposition of the utopian mapping of the social with the detected feminine is perhaps best theorized by David Lodge's parodic Morris Zapp and his thesis on 'Textuality as Striptease' in *Small World*: 'The reader plays with himself as the text plays upon him, plays upon his curiosity, desire, as a striptease dancer plays upon her audience's curiosity and desire ... The dancer teases the audience, as the text teases its readers, with the promise of an ultimate revelation that is inevitably postponed' (26). The enthused Zapp links the desire of obsessive reading to the mother/womb: 'To read is to surrender oneself to an endless displacement of curiosity and desire from one sentence to another, from one action to another, from one level to another. The text unveils itself before itself, but never allows itself to be possessed; and instead of striving to possess it we should take pleasure in its teasing' (27). Barthes' own essay, 'Striptease', articulates the fundamental contradiction of striptease: 'Woman is desexualized at the very moment when she is stripped naked. We may therefore say that we are dealing in a sense with a spectacle based on fear, or rather the pretence of fear, as if eroticism here went no further than a sort of delicious terror, whose ritual signs have only to be announced to evoke at once the idea of sex and its conjuration' (1993, 84). This sense of the striptease as 'mystifying spectacle' is cognate with the thriller's emplotment of the feminine, which ultimately aims 'at establishing the woman *right from the start* as an object in disguise' (Barthes 1993, 84). Thus, Barthes' account of the 'magical decor' (1993, 85) of the striptease and its 'meticulous exorcism of sex' (1993, 86) allegorizes the thriller's deployment of the feminine as *sinthome*, which not only denies both sexuality and political agency to women, but also serves finally as fetishized object masking the exorcism of the social from such a dynamic of anxious pleasure.

The political and aesthetic function of the figure of the feminine for a dominant subject is conveyed by McDonald's *Sacrifice of Fools* and Baker's *Inheritance*. McDonald's science fiction thriller, *Sacrifice of Fools*, imagines a Northern Ireland in 2001 which becomes home for 100,000 Shian aliens, eight million of whom have arrived on earth from outer space. The purpose, we are told, of sending some of these aliens to Northern Ireland is an effort in social engineering designed to circumvent the historic pattern of bipolarization. It is an indictment of the 'Troubles' thriller's disavowal of human agency in the North that even this most utopian of texts can only contemplate the imposition of a third, tribalized homogeneity in to the North as a means of social transformation. In Raymond Williams's conceptualization of utopian visions, it is certainly not the radical 'willed transformation' (1980, 196), whereby a new society is brought about through human effort and struggle. It is rather an example of 'the externally altered world' (1980, 196), which suggests that Northern Ireland can only be reformed through unsolicited impositions or natural events. Nonetheless, in however degraded a form, the deployment of an alternative consciousness through which to circumvent both Irish Nationalism and Unionism does actuate a utopian class allegory. As a series of brutal murders begin to occur, the conspiratorial mapping becomes the repository of a class awareness, which confronts the social totality as a number of leading religious and political figures are implicated in sordid underworld activity. However, the text then withdraws from its utopian confrontation of the totality of social forces and relationships as it transpires that the killings were actually the deranged acts of an adolescent female alien during the Shian mating season. Here, then, the text recoils from its subversive interrogation of the legitimacy of the social order into the dwelling upon the single crime, the recondite riddle, of female sexuality.

A similar textual dynamic occurs in Baker's *Inheritance*, which, as discussed in my third chapter, does map the Northern State as criminal conspiracy. However, McCallan eventually becomes implicated in a cover-up, which seeks to limit the potential damage of his discoveries by blaming the daughter of one of the conspiracy's victims for all the murders and social disturbance. The use of gender here crystallizes the dialectical negotiations of ideology and utopia, as the *repressive* modality provides a structure of symbolic containment, which attempts to foreclose the utopian contemplation of the social totality through recourse to an immemorial masculinity confronting the crime of femininity. In short, the sublime thrill, at once fearful and redemptive, of approaching the unfigurable force of the collectivity in all its complexity, becomes, for the text's optimal reading self, ahistorically reducible to, or underwritten by, the equally fearful and desirous masculine decipherment of an eternally mysterious female sexuality. The figure of the feminine is the final embodiment and transposition of social upheaval, represented as the death of the father, returning to the text through the gendered subject the ideology of the single, eradicable crime: 'There had been enough slaughter. It had to stop now and there was only one way it could: he had to kill her. She was here somewhere, the woman who had done all this, who had murdered his father and would have killed him too. He felt a surge of excitement. She was so deadly. And so close' (329). There is almost a Kristevan abjection in the thrilling pleasure engendered by this most intimate and deadly horror, disclosing not otherness but rather the function such a figure has in repressing historical materials that actually constitute the text.

The establishment cover-up supplied to McCallan at the level of content is enacted as a formal aesthetic: 'We've already told the world that we've no idea who this woman was but that it certainly seems as if she was acting alone. If you've studied the papers, you'll see there are all sorts of theories now, that she was some sort of psychopath, a mad anarchist perhaps, with a hatred of the police, capitalism, God knows what. I think it will go down as an extraordinary and unexplained episode, like an earthquake or a flood, unpredictable and unrepeatable, one of life's mysteries' (335-336). This passage contains a profound moment of ideological countermand that is symptomatic of the redrawing of a utopian aesthetic by the gendered mode of symbolic containment. The figure of the feminine as consummate mystery becomes a centripetal point of aesthetic focalization, and, in doing so, replaces the concrete mapping of the legal apparatus, the state and police, and of course capitalism itself – all of which lapse into spurious supposition before this confounding presence that is paradoxically a seductive nullity. Gender, specifically the ideology of an immemorialized masculinity and female *sinthome*, thus functions to perpetuate aesthetically the historically impossible: that is, the withdrawal of the cognitive mapping of the criminal totality into the ideology of the single, isolate crime (femininity).

The production of an immemorialized masculine subject around the reiterative enigma of the North, and its distillation in the figure of the feminine, are typified by the work of Jack Higgins. In *Confessional*, the assassin, Mikhail Kelly, who plans to assassinate the Pope during a visit to England in 1982, has three women in his life: Tanya Voroninova, the Russian agent he wronged as a child; Morag, a Scottish girl with whom he gets involved and saves from a brutal family life in redeeming himself though hampering his mission; and Susan Calder, the British agent who shoots him in front of the Pope. We are informed: 'Strange – the most important people in his life were women and in the end they were the death of him' (1985, 256). This elision of concrete female identity in the *sinthome* is demonstrated by Higgins' *The Savage Day*. The hero of the first person narrative, Simon Vaughan, is initially informed of the rape of the IRA volunteer, Norah Murphy, by B-Specials: 'It occurred to me then, and not for the first time, that there were occasions when I despaired of humanity. And yet there was no sense of personal involvement and any pity I felt was not so much for Norah Murphy as for that wretched, frightened little girl in the backyard of that house in Belfast so many years ago' (1972, 85). Vaughan here identifies with an idealized, historically displaced femininity designed to erase any contextual expression of female or Irish

Republican agency as encoded in Norah. Furthermore, it is the masculine character of Vaughan, who is placed as guarantor and protector of this idealized femininity, which is degraded by female agency. Similarly, in *Drink with the Devil*, Kathleen Ryan, a Loyalist paramilitary wanting to destroy the Peace Process, harbours such bitterness because she was raped by Catholics in her youth, but Dillon realizes 'how truly mad she had become' (1996, 310).

Norah is subsequently kidnapped as the niece of an IRA leader considered too soft by hardline elements and is burned on the face with a poker by Republican Frank Barry during her ordeal. Again Vaughan is prompted to righteous indignation: 'I was thinking of Norah, remembering the stink of her flesh burning, considering with some care exactly how I was going to give it to him when the time came' (1972, 142). Norah functions as the cultural and gendered object upon which Vaughan's privileged manhood is constructed against the indiscretion of Irish forms. It then transpires that the branding was a trick and that Norah was in league with Frank Barry, who supplied her with painkillers. Nora finally kills the idealist Binnie Gallagher, whom Vaughan respects, but her escape is thwarted as Vaughan has rigged her boat with explosives: 'I gazed down at the dark waters, searching for some sign of Norah Murphy, the merest hint that she had existed, but found none. Then I turned and walked away through the rain' (1972, 223). Such erasure is a classic Lacanian moment, wherein woman does not exist in the sense that the figure of the feminine is a representational symptom, intimating that our own detective work is the assemblage of the signs around this absence.

The aesthetic role of the *sinthome* and its ideological foreclosure of the utopian figuration of the totality are confirmed by Higgins' *Angel of Death*. The combination of masculine anxiety and desire in the contradictory feminine figurations of the text's title is reinforced by the character of Grace Browning – an interestingly ambiguous name that conflates figurations of the feminine as angelically good and simultaneously violently emulous of phallic power and violence. Browning is an assassin for the 30th January group, along with a KGB aristocrat and his gay Tory lover. So once more femininity is not the only producer of sexual and social fear in a thriller. On the run after a failed attempt to assassinate a US senator involved in the Peace Process, Browning flees to her KGB handler and tells him: 'you helped create me ... An Angel of Death was what you wanted and that's what you got' (1995, 268). Eventually she is tracked down and killed, Ferguson commenting: 'she'd nowhere else to go' (1995, 273). Such representational and formal imperatives indicate that the figure of the feminine has nothing to do with an 'actual' engagement with depicting women but is rather a textual space into which historical fears and longings are impelled. Browning was also an actress and before she is killed Dillon tells her 'this isn't stage six at MGM, Grace, it's for real. It's not a script any longer', to which she replies 'oh yes it is – it's my script' (1995, 273). In a sense, this is strikingly true, it is her script if it is acknowledged that here woman stands as an object of representational containment for the inexorable, prior subtext of History, a laceral script to be decoded.

How, then, does this figure of the feminine seek aesthetically and ideologically to deflect the utopian narrative desire of the thriller to map the social as a total network of crime? Peter Brooks holds the conventional crime narrative to be a paradigmatic model of Barthes' *hermeneutic* code of narrative enigma and answer, as opposed to the *proairetic* code of actions and adventure: 'The clearest example of the hermeneutic code would no doubt be the detective story, in that everything in the story's structure, and its temporality, depends on the resolution of enigma. Plot, then, might be thought of as an 'overcoding' of the proairetic by the hermeneutic, the latter structuring the discrete elements of the former into larger interpretative wholes, working out their play of meaning and significance' (Brooks, 18). In the era of the thriller, there is a diffusion of codes and a resultant dissolution of the hermeneutic at the level of content. This ensures that a final answering of enigma is impossible, but formally, in my utopian reading, an unconscious collective effort is made to imagine the consummate mystery of the late capitalism itself. Therefore, theories of narrative desire focusing upon a single, resolved enigma are recapitulating an older form of narrative into a dehistoricized gender aesthetic.

Brooks also cites Lacan in stating that the bar separating signifier from signified is the bar of repression, indicating the inaccessibility of the true signified (the object of unconscious desire). Consequently, for Brooks, discourse becomes the interconnection of signifiers one with another in a signifying chain where meaning (in the sense of access to the meaning of unconscious desire) does not consist in any single link of the chain, yet through which meaning nonetheless insists. Hence, the capacity of language to mean something other than what it says. This, I would argue, parallels the more properly historical remit of the political unconscious, and, indeed, withdraws from the latter in offering immemorialized sexual relations as the site of this pressure. Brooks asserts that 'if narrative desire keeps moving us forward, it is because narrative metonymy can never quite speak its name' (56). Gender becomes a Lacanian mode for containing such desire: woman as *sinthome*, as that which resists symbolization, stands as the final discursive signpost of an ideology spiralling a vertiginous pathway to its historical oblivion. The utilization of the erotic return of the feminine as the symbolic containment of that which cannot speak its name is conveyed by the representation of the Brighton bomber as female in Power's *A Darkness in the Eye*.[4] The bomber is the site of a symbolically recodified desire standing in place of historical desire, in an occlusion of History. Although she is described as the 'mastermind' (175) behind the Brighton Bomb, she is unnamable, and is referred to variously as 'that damn woman' (168), 'that damned, accursed woman' (161), 'a silly bitch' (161).[5] Here the figure of the feminine and its return of 'a certain mystery' simplify profound historical rupture, constructing a narrative pathway and pleasure around it. Lacan comments that 'the enigmas that desire poses to any "natural philosophy", its frenzy miming the abyss of the infinite, the intimate collusion in which it envelops the pleasure of knowing and that of dominating with pleasure, belongs to

---

[4] The actual Brighton bomber, Patrick Magee, who was sentenced to fifty years imprisonment for his part in the attempt to assassinate Thatcher, is author of the brilliant survey *Gangsters or Guerrillas?: Representations of Irish Republicans in Troubles Fiction.* Belfast: Beyond the Pale, 2001.

[5] Indeed, one of her own fellow volunteers comments: 'I don't even know your name' (165).

no other derangement of instinct than its being caught on the rails – eternally extended toward the *desire of something else* – of metonymy' (1977a, 518). Against the Nietzschean nihilism of this abyssal infinitude of bourgeois decline, crime functions metonymically within the *redemptive* modality of the thriller and finally returns the part to its whole, the local crime to the social as total mystery. By contrast, the trajectory of the erotic return of the feminine and indeed the more general exoticization of the North is precisely a reverse mechanism of pleasure and anxiety, the retreat from the whole to the fetishized object, the masking of the absent cause in the local site. Therefore, the ideological mechanisms of a *repressive* aesthetic must be distinguished from that which it would recant. Brooks maintains that 'narratives portray the motors of desire that drive and consume their plots, and they also lay bare the nature of narration as a form of human desire: the need to tell as a primary human drive that seeks to seduce and to subjugate the listener, to implicate him in the thrust of a desire that can never quite speak its name – never quite come to the point – but that insists on speaking over and over again its movement toward that name' (61). But ultimately History is 'that name', for which this seemingly nonrepresentable sign, figured as the feminine, is itself a caret.

In assessing how such an aesthetic seeks to reorder historical materials, the unnamable woman spectrally haunting Power's *A Darkness in the Eye* notably provides one of the most profound moments of ideological conflation in the 'Troubles' thriller, eliding the North as feminized otherness and the terrible figure of the female terrorist. What precise acts of political and historical projection and repression does such a mode of symbolic containment seek to achieve? Jayne Steel has noted the proximity of fear and desire in representations of female terrorists in British texts, prompting Steel to cleverly coin the neologism Vampira: 'Though they are shaped and characterized by a variety of popular genres of fiction, representations of female members of the PIRA share, metaphorically, the seductive and deadly qualities of Gothic vampires, draining the will and feeding off the blood of British soldiers and citizens' (274). What is noteworthy in Power's text is that the unnamable Republican woman stands in the place of another figure of the feminine, that of Thatcher herself, who was of course the target of the Brighton Bomb, but is even more absently present in the text. Steel's analysis elucidates the formal politics of this terrorist figure of the feminine standing in the place of another gendered historical trauma:

> In the 1980s it was Thatcher who became 'the boldest and most unmanageable revolutionary', tearing up the post-war social consensus, waging a pitiless war against every form of resistance. In film, fiction and the press, Vampira images flourished under the reign of Thatcher. Operating according to the Moebial structure of the law that enables it to operate, ideologically, in the very image of its antithesis, Thatcher's unmanageable, charismatic, transgressive 'lawlessness' paradoxically held together a highly authoritarian, right-wing regime. Similarly, in the propaganda war between the British government and the PIRA, Vampira can be seen to have been recruited to fuel the abject fear and hatred of woman (including Thatcher herself), that characterized Britain under the reign of the first woman Prime Minister, and to use that fear and hatred to galvanise Britain's

terrorised subjects to endorse and enjoy the violence deployed not just against Irish Republicanism but against 'the enemy within' in whatever form it took (282-283).

The figure of Thatcher as consummate and absent embodiment of the *sinthome* reinforces the sense that such figurations must be denaturalized in unfolding the historical problematics that they both repress and resolve.

The North itself as fetishized *topos* also performs fundamental ideological groundwork in the *repressive* effort gratifyingly to mask historical pressures, which have divested the ideological framing of earlier forms of detective narrative. By way of contextualization, Žižek utilizes an instructive Lacanian deployment of the Greek word *ate*, which harnesses an ambiguity denoting, simultaneously, the horrifying limit that can never be reached, and the *space beyond it*. In stressing the primacy of the limit over the space, Žižek asserts that we do not have two spheres, that of reality and of pure fantasy, divided by a certain limit, but rather just reality and its limit, the void around which it is structured. As a result, the fantasy space is secondary, it materializes a certain limit or changes the *impossible* into the *prohibited*. Thus, the limit marks a certain fundamental impossibility while its beyond is prohibited: 'we therefore have the formula of the mysterious reversal of horror into bliss: by means of it the *impossible limit* changes into the *forbidden place*' (Žižek, Copjec ed. 1993, 216). Comparably, the erotic return of the feminine, or the North as fetishized *topos*, function as such a limit, which seeks to arrogate the properly utopian social transgression of the *redemptive* modality of the form. Žižek elaborates that

> the logic of this reversal is that of the transmutation of the real into the symbolic: the impossible-real changes into an object of symbolic prohibition. The paradox (and perhaps the very function of the prohibition as such) consists in the fact that, as soon as it is conceived as prohibited, the impossible-real changes into something *possible*, that is into something that cannot be reached not because of its inherent impossibility but simply because access to it is hindered by the external barrier of a prohibition (Copjec, ed. 1993, 216-217).

This mechanism, then, may be rewritten as an ideological complex structuring the recodification of History (for which the Lacanian Real is itself a limit) in the guise of the aberrations of the working-class, women, or the North as sheer alterity, all of which are precariously patrolled by an erotics of surveillance situating pleasure in the prohibitions of the *repressive* modality. The trespass of these reactionary frontiers, into the forbidden space beyond *ate* by a dominant subject, is constituted by the transmutation of historical impossibility into compensatory representational production. That is, the reversal of the impossible limit into the prohibited space eludes a confrontation of the Real (the totality as encoded in the conspiratorial ideologeme) as impossible for strictly such reactionary mappings.

Moreover, as Žižek recognizes, one of the fundamental mechanisms of ideological licitness is that we legitimize the existing order by presenting it as the realization of a fantasy that is not ours but the Other's (Copjec, ed. 217). In other words, the utopian mapping of the conspiracy dissolves into the paranoid dream of the Big Other and its disabling of human agency. Thus, in Gill's *McGarr and the Method of Descartes* conspiracy becomes not the toppling but the maintenance of the social as a fantasy power structure: 'The complete story was one that would not be told. How could it? The charges, if provable, would bring down two governments and even further confound the problems of the North, if that was possible' (1985, 289). It is this more socialized sense of the Real, which facilitates an understanding of how the paranoid fantasies of the thriller form support the representation of the 'Reality' of Northern Ireland in the genre as compensatory fantasy structures.

Rather than regarding the Real as some primordial existential dilemma, therefore, I wish to rewrite the Lacanian formula by proposing the foreclosure of History as the Real by the modes of symbolic containment exercised by the *repressive* modality. To this end, Steve Neale asserts:

> Both the detective genre and the thriller inscribe the spectating subject as caught up in a particular version of epistemophilia, always engaging it to be 'satisfied', to be given the answer to the riddle. In other words, always engaging it in terms of the structure of fetishism. This is not by accident: disavowal and the desire to know are in fact always co-extensive, with epistemophilia being constantly displaced in order to preserve the fissure supporting/necessitating the fetish. Indeed it might be argued that fetishism itself is the product of the articulation of both these instances together, that it is a structure founded upon the modalities of the epistemophilic drive: the desire to know *and* disavowal, together, articulate a desire to know something else, a substitute for what in fact is at stake. The process of finding out is thus represented in relation to that which one wishes to avoid knowing. What is specific to the detective film and the thriller is the fact that this co-extensiveness is persistently demonstrated though never exposed to the fissure supporting it. It is not a matter of identifying or of finding the 'fetish' incarnated in any given clue, or in the last piece that makes the jigsaw 'fit', restoring a complete picture. On the contrary, it is the jigsaw puzzle itself, the story of the crime that represents the structure of fetishism, the process of its institution and elaboration binding the spectator into the structure of (split) belief. In the detective and thriller genres, this story functions to restore 'law and order' in an overt and literal way: what 'fills the gap', what sutures the wound that the crime both represents and opens up, is, precisely, a narrative scarred by red herrings (1996, 42-43).

For Neale, voyeurism, exhibitionism and fetishism are the formative components of a genre that consists of the elaboration of a narrative under the sign of these three drives. Is this exegesis not strictly the *repressive* modality of the text? Voyeurism, because we are spectating through the fantasy narrative of the Big Other, and fetishism, because this partial object stands in place of the absent totality. For, against this formulation of the crime narrative as a totalized structure of fetishism supporting 'law and order', the *redemptive* modality of the text deploys crime, laid down as a gauntlet, as a complex network offering a narrative entry into precisely what is disavowed in the caret of the fetish. It is unsurprising that the figure of the feminine should obsessively be this caret masking the absent cause of History itself, given that the central Freudian fetish, which is itself a discursively ingrained structure of fetishism, is the mother's 'penis'. Freud's account of this formative absence as paradoxically absent yet also present in the form of the fetish – 'the horror of castration has set a memorial to itself in the creation of this substitute' (1984, 353) – provides a methodology, impaired by the limitations of psychoanalysis and its naturalized laws, which may be expanded to indicate how the substitute crime, for the "law and order" fantasy of the Big Other, disavows the recovery of the social itself as total crime. The iterative terrain of the North as produced by the thriller instigates a circuitous desire to know which is really a disavowal and circumvention of a more properly historical desire.

The conventional psychoanalytical account of popular reading pleasure would emphasize such repetition as a universal condition.[6] Daniel Gunn posits that repetition and return are fundamental to crime fiction, not only for writers but also for readers who compulsively consume one novel after another, so that there are two formal levels of repetition: 'does repetition point towards some original movement of unity or always towards division and loss?' (5). In addition, Jameson considers the popular text 'sheer repetition' (1992b, 20). However, in dealing with a vast popular cultural body of texts producing an image of the North as interminably traumatic, it is tempting to consider the particular inflection such a discursive formation grants Walter Benjamin's remark that 'the idea of eternal recurrence transforms historical events into mass-produced articles' (1985, 36). What, then, is the historical context of this repetition, this production of an attenuated desire within overarching structures of commodification and exoticization, not to say fetishism? From a Lacanian perspective, fantasy designates the subject's apparently 'impossible' relation to *a*, the object-cause of its desire. Desire is therefore not something given but has to be constructed, so that the realization of desire does not consist in its being fulfilled or fully satisfied but rather forms an alignment with the reproduction of desire as such.[7]

---

[6] A Lacanian position would claim that the real purpose of the *drive* is not its goal (full satisfaction) but rather that its ultimate aim is reproduce itself as drive, return to its circular path, so that the real source of enjoyment is the repetitive movement of this closed circuit in a codification of desire that putatively finds its popular cultural apotheosis in the thriller form. Lacan posits: '[i]f the drive may be satisfied without attaining what, from the point-of-view of a biological totalization of function, would be the satisfaction of its end of reproduction, it is because it is a partial drive, and its aim is simply this return into circuit' (1977b. 179).

[7] For a Lacanian, *objet petit a* is exactly the surplus, the elusive make-believe through which we find pleasure in the trivia of everyday existence, a fantasy space, a screen for the projection of our desires. Žižek observes: '[t]he paradox of desire is that it posits retroactively its own cause, i.e., the *objet a* is an object that can be perceived only by a gaze "distorted" by desire, an object that *does not exist* for an "objective" gaze. In other words, the object *a* is always, *by definition*, perceived in a distorted way, because outside this distortion, "in itself", *it does not exist*, since it *is nothing but* the embodiment, the materialization of this very distortion, of this surplus of confusion and perturbation introduced by desire into so-called "objective reality". The *object a* is "objectively" nothing, though, viewed from a certain perspective, it assumes the shape of "something"' (1991, 12).

The recognition that desire is its interpretation reformulates the utopian desire to map our societies and denaturalizes this continually disappointing desire. Desire is the very force which compels us to progress from one signifier to another in the hope of attaining the ultimate signifier that would fix the meaning of the preceding chain. For Žižek, the role of detective in the classic detective narrative is to dissolve the impasse of universalized guilt – namely, that during the course of the investigation anyone could be the murderer – by finally locating it in a single subject and thus exculpating all others. Therefore, Žižek maintains, the detective annihilates libidinal possibility, the 'inner' truth that everyone in the social microcosm might have been the murderer (i.e. that we are all murderers in the unconscious of our desire at the level of 'reality'). Thus, our desire is externalized in the scapegoat and we can desire without paying the price for it. However, Žižek continues, in the thriller era the detective loses distance that would enable him to analyse this false scene:

> In this case, then, it is the detective himself ... who undergoes a kind of 'loss of reality', who finds himself in a dreamlike world where it is never quite clear who is playing what game. And the person who embodies this deceitful character of the universe, its fundamental corruption, the person who lures the detective and plays him for a 'sucker', is as a rule the *femme fatale*, which is why the final 'settlement of accounts' usually consists in the detective's confrontation with her (1991, 63).

Firstly, I would question the rather typically pessimistic account of desire and its formal role as the total exhaustion of the genre. As noted in my introduction, the thriller makes explicit what was masked by the ideology of earlier detective fiction and remained its political unconscious – that is, that the whole of society is under investigation in such narratives – and one of its potentialities is the opening of that formal fissure to oppositional subjects remapping the social. It is specifically the desire-as-interpretation of the dominant detecting subject of the fantasy of 'law and order', which resists this utopian cognitive mapping and seeks to circumvent its exposition through circular disavowal. In the second instance, the figure of the feminine is proffered as a fetish object of continually remonitored finality to reject an immersion of the detective in the social and resurrect a false scene, upon which the interpretative desire of the dominant subject may be both grounded and limited. In other words, such desire appears so reiterative because it is an allochronic and deflective desire to re-stage the now historically impossible, transforming the present material conditions of its production into that 'impossible', that Real, which must be symbolically codified, redistributed in objects of fetish.

Žižck contends that the figure of the feminine bespeaks something of the limiting of desire: 'contrary to appearance, the *femme fatale* embodies a radical *ethical* attitude, that of 'not ceding one's desire', of persisting in it to the very end when its true nature as the death drive is revealed. It is the hero who, by rejecting the *femme fatale*, breaks with his ethical stance (1991, 63). I would here substitute, for this nihilistic death drive, the death of this specific subject in the face of History, in order to properly understand the ideological work done by the figure of the feminine:

> The destiny of the femme fatale in film noir, her final hysterical breakdown, exemplifies perfectly the Lacanian proposition that 'woman does not exist': she is nothing but 'the symptom of man', her power of fascination masks the void of her nonexistence, so that when she is finally rejected, her whole ontological consistency is dissolved. But precisely as nonexisitng, i.e., at the moment at which, through hysterical breakdown, she *assumes* her nonexistence, she constitutes herself as 'subject': what is waiting for her *beyond* hystericization is the death drive at its purest (Žižek 1991, 65).

In a parallel gesture, my own attempt to rewrite the figuration of Irish History as trauma, as hysterical *femme fatale*, wills the circumvention of this historical nonexistence and the return of the symptom to the historical constitution of the subject. With regard to the conventional feminist thesis on *film noir* – that the *femme fatale* presents a mortal threat to man's very identity as subject, so that by finally rejecting her he regains his sense of personal identity – Žižek asserts that this formulation contains a truth in a sense exactly opposite to the way it is usually understood:

> It is not Woman as object of fascination that causes us to lose our sense of judgement and moral attitude but, on the contrary, that which remains hidden beneath this fascinating mask and which appears once the masks fall out: the dimension of the pure subject fully assuming the death drive ... The real dimension of the threat is revealed when we 'traverse' the fantasy, when the coordinates of the fantasy space are lost via hysterical breakdown. In other words, what is really menacing about the femme fatale is not that she is fatal for *men* but that she presents a case of a 'pure', nonpathological subject fully assuming *her own* fate (1991, 66).

My own particular inflection is to elaborate that the female *sinthome* masks History in its purest textual form and, as an object in the face of this necessity, seeks to displace a historical subject properly assuming its fate.

Another sign of the forestalling of utopian desire in the 'Troubles' thriller is boredom. For all the pleasure of thrills and the aesthetics I have attempted to elaborate, it is amazing how fundamentally boring many of these texts actually are. In particular, Tom Clancy and many of the SAS texts have protracted operational and technical descriptions, which are readily skimmed by the reading subject. This reading manoeuvre accords with Barthes' concept of *tmesis* and its active disregard of the integrity of text, wherein one can skip passages not at the level of surface but at the moment of consumption so that the author cannot predict *tmesis* or choose 'what will not be read' (1976, 11). I would wish to rewrite boredom in more formal terms however. How may boredom be theorized in this manner? For Barthes, boredom is associable with the populist text of pleasure rather than the text of bliss, so that boredom may be viewed as a reassuring and comforting reading practice:

> Text of pleasure: the text that contents, fills, grants euphoria; the text that comes from culture and does not break with it, is linked to a *comfortable* practice of reading. Text of bliss: the text that imposes a state of loss, the text that discomforts (perhaps to the point of even boredom), unsettles the reader's historical, cultural,

psychological assumptions, the consistency of his tastes, values, memories, brings to a crisis his relation with language (1976, 14).

In a way, boredom affirms a Žižekean aesthetic wherein the utopian mapping of the thriller is finally dissolved into the Big Other's fantasy of 'law and order': 'how can we take pleasure in a *reported* pleasure (boredom of all narratives of dreams, of parties) ... I can make myself its voyeur: I observe clandestinely the pleasure of others, I enter perversion' (Barthes 1976, 17). In other words, the fetishized object, the voyeurism of the cover-up in the name of the 'invisible hand', literally perverts the utopian relay of the social as total crime and our subjective, narrative relation to it. Barthes maintains that 'pleasure can be expressed in words, bliss cannot ... with the writer of bliss (and his reader) begins the untenable text, the impossible text' (1976, 21-22). I would revise this point by suggesting that the unconscious collective mapping of the totality is rather an impossible text for the modes of symbolic containment returning the reading subject to the female *sinthome*, the fetishized *topos* of the North, the dream of the Big Other. Barthes sets the following conundrum:

> boredom is not simple. We do not escape boredom (with a work, a text) with a gesture of impatience or rejection. Just as a gesture of impatience or rejection. Just as the pleasure of the text supposes a whole indirect production, so boredom cannot presume it is entitled to any spontaneity ... Boredom is not far from bliss, it is bliss seen from the shores of pleasure (1976, 25-26).

I want to suggest that boredom is actually the formal site of utopian longing. Benjamin posits that boredom is 'an index of participation in the collective sleep' but also affirms that 'boredom is always the outer surface of unconscious happenings'.[8] Boredom, therefore, can be codified as an impatience with the fantasy of the Big Other, the 'collective sleep', and is thus the anticipation of historical awakening. But Benjamin also posits 'we experience boredom when we do not know what we are waiting for'.[9] Thus, it is the task of the *redemptive* modality of the text to recognize, in Benjamin's terms, 'the dream as itself a dream. It is in this moment that the historian undertakes the task of dream interpretation'.[10] For Benjamin the dreaming collectivity 'finds its expression in the dream and its meaning in awakening'.[11] In short, our detective work in the political unconscious interrogates the expression of imaginary resolutions to historical problematics in the thriller through the reinscription of utopian meaning and possibility in the interpretation and awakening, the subjective entry into historical agency.

---

[8] 'Langeweile – als Index für die Teilnahme am Schlaf des Kollektivs' (*GS* V. 164); 'Langeweile ist immer die Außenseite des unbewußten Geschehens' (*GS* V. 1006).

[9] 'Langeweile haben wir, wenn wir nicht wissen, worauf wir warten' (*GS* V. 161).

[10] 'Die Menschheit, die Augen sich reibend, gerade dieses Traumbild als solches erkennt. In diesem Augenblick ist es, daß der Historiker an ihm die Aufgabe der Traumdeteutung übernimmt' (*GS* V. 580).

[11] 'Sie finden im Traum ihren Ausdruck und im Erwachen ihre Deutung' (*GS* V. 496).

Similarly, Ernest Mandel asserts that the sensations of tedium, monotony, and boredom are a manifestation of a deeper anxiety. For Mandel, there are two pathways by which the subject may defeat boredom: namely, to either become productive and thereby happy, or alternately to escape its manifestations – the latter being the average person's pursuit of amusement and distraction. I wish here to dialecticize these polarities, to trace productively, if you like, the utopian dimension of the popular text and refute the detailing of its social function as sheer escapism whilst not losing sight of its ideological underpinnings. In a further moment of ideological conflation in the 'Troubles' thriller, boredom readily collapses into the standard Irish historical paradigm. Seamus Deane asserts that both Irish writing and writing on Ireland are deeply involved with 'the experience of boredom' (1997, 156).[12] Deane observes: 'the repeated re-emergence of Ireland as an object of the scrutiny of others. These others need not be foreigners. They are often the Irish themselves, endlessly engaged with the problematic of Ireland-as-such; endlessly entrapped between representing it as a quaint other to imperial normality, or as a radical otherness for which no canonical system of representation is sufficient' (1997, 156). As the historical objects of others (most notably the Big Other) in the *repressive* modality of the thriller, the challenge therefore in this study is to have rewritten the historical catastrophe identified by Brecht, to resituate ourselves and these texts as specific, subjective placings in and towards History itself.

Perhaps the persistence of boredom in Irish writing attest to the limited visions of both Irish Nationalism and Unionism, the national construction of each standing outside its own narrative coherence, due to Partition and the implosion of Britishness respectively, yet still pursuing longingly its *telos*? It is History that disrupts the mythic narrative of both ideologies, whose stagnation exemplifies the 'homogeneous, empty time' identified by Benjamin and astutely applied to the national imaginary by Benedict Anderson. Indeed, in tracing the formal disintegration of the national maps of Irish Nationalism and Unionism in the thriller, Anderson has commented that 'it is the magic of nationalism to turn chance into destiny' (12). The magic of such an ideology resides in the production of political expression not only out of an immemorial past but also a limitless future. So where nationalism would turn chance into destiny, the utopian modality of the crime narrative performs a more determinate social mapping that throws the former into irresoluble fracture, by turning chance into concrete conjunction both spatially and historically.

---

[12] In *Resurrection Man*, we are informed that 'Ryan noticed how newspapers and television were developing a familiar and comforting vocabulary to deal with violence. Sentences which could be read easily off the page. It involved repetition of key phrases. Atrocity reports began to achieve the pure level of a chant. It was no longer about conveying information. It was about focusing the mind inwards, attending to the durable rhythyms of violence' (McNamee, 58). Deane comments in *Civilians and Barbarians* that discourse on the North is deadened by a 'sense of exhaustion' (14). I am arguing in this conclusion that ultimately what are exhausted by the dynamic of History are the representational delimitations and ideological codes masking the complexity of the North.

Another point to be made here is that temporality is central to the experience of boredom, that boredom is not a mythic seclusion but actually the anticipation, or indeed fear, of historical return. The narrative entry into History, formulated by the Brechtian sense of historical catastrophe discussed in my introduction, intimates that crime fiction can proffer a modality whereby we can think beyond our being the objects of History. Deane postulates that 'boredom is both a symptom and a technique of repression, both in its psychic and political forms ... Paradoxically, the representation of boredom also involves an intensification of the rhetorical strategies which are needed to create a text that is, simultaneously, driven towards completeness and dispersed amidst fragmentary incoherences' (1997, 168). The *repressive* modality drives towards a completeness that is as ideologically unsound as the single, resolvable crime of the Golden Age of the crime form. It is a completeness based on the reputed total regulation of the figure of the feminine, the North as sheer alterity, which actually seeks incompleteness and delimitation through the relay to such fetish objects. The utopian modality of the text takes 'fragmentary incoherences' and politically transforms them through networks of crime into figurations of the totality.

So in terms of where the political aesthetics of the crime form finally lay, therefore, Mandel interestingly considers the ultimately determining instance of the crime fiction as performing an 'integrative function' (122) within bourgeois society. Nonetheless, Mandel recognizes in late capitalism an increasing interpenetration between the police, informers, and criminals, and an increasing symbiosis of crime, big business and the reinforced state, in move from the Manichean representation of society. Mandel comments:

> While the criminal was generally not treated any more sympathetically than before, the established order itself gradually became more and more ambiguous, more and more closely identified with shady methods, corruption, compromises on basic values. What was initially true for hostile foreign states in the spy story now increasingly became true for the writer's own state too. Law and order ceased to be absolutely Good: they became relative, ambiguous, dubious. The individual fighter against crime – whether private eye or honest cop – ceased to be a self-confident, 'positive' hero from the bourgeois point of view. They became almost tragic figures, operating within the framework and in the service of an Establishment in which they believed less and less, which they even began to hate and despise (122).

Thus, Mandel concludes, crime fiction is no longer integrative with respect to bourgeois society but is now 'disintegrative'. However, Mandel still contends that its subversion is limited to individual revolt against the prevalent bourgeois values. Such a revolt is doomed to fail, for Mandel, it is 'the labour of Sisyphus' (124): i.e., eliminate one agent of corruption and ten more will appear. Only collective revolt has transformative potential and this, he maintains, has nothing to do with thrillers. In resolving the interplay between the *repressive* and *redemptive* modalities, I wish to contest Mandel's reading by suggesting that the thriller form contains what I shall term *phantasms of the collectivity*. This dialectical phrasing hopes to capture the ideological and utopian in the thriller. Firstly, to suggest that the form, in its more reactionary, Panopticon mappings, offers the spectre of the social totality within the parameters of the dominant subject. Which is to say, we are presented with the dominant subject's fear of the collective, which is then recodified into the regulation of the female *sinthome*, the gothicized working class, the North as fetish. Yet *phantasms of the collectivity* is also intended to intimate the recoding of that repressed totality by the collective itself as a recoverable utopian structure within the text. That is, the crime form presents us with the utopian desires of the collective self; with the speculative figuration of the social totality as a narrative entry into History.

Thus, I hope to avoid the pessimism of Mandel's otherwise positive appreciation of crime fiction's return to what he sees as a primordial pattern of the outlaw hero, attesting to a growing scepticism about law and order and the state itself. Mandel follows Eric Hobsbawm (cf. 1985) in suggesting that the former rebels were rebels with a cause, the fight against injustice, torture, absolutism, corruption, for personal freedom and formal equality, whereas the noble bandits of today are without a cause, disillusioned and cynical. Mandel asserts that even when they know what they are fighting against, they have no idea what they are fighting for, and that ultimately their banditry contains a rather ominous idealization of private vengeance and vigilante violence. Hence, Mandel concludes of the form:

> The history of the crime story is a social history, for it appears intertwined with the history of bourgeois society itself. If the question is asked why it should be reflected in the history of a specific literary genre, the answer is: because the history of bourgeois society is also that of property and the negation of property, in other words, crime; because the history of bourgeois society is also the growing, explosive contradiction between individual needs or passions and mechanically imposed patterns of social conformism; because bourgeois society in and of itself breeds crime, originates in crime, and leads to crime; perhaps because bourgeois society is, when all is said and done, a criminal society (135).

There have been numerous attacks on Mandel's thesis, and Marxism more generally, as being overly reductive. Nonetheless, whilst I have intended to show that the form is inherently more subversive than Mandel will allow, the Marxist model alerts us that we are dealing with dominant and conflictual social practice, social agents, social forms, and that there is always an *ultimately determining instance* to a text. It is finally the sense of capitalism as a total mystery or crime, which is the ultimately determining instance of the 'Troubles' thriller. This has become increasingly evident in the post-ceasefire period, wherein the modes of symbolic containment proffered by the figure of the terrorist and its reactivation of a host of national stereotypes has begun to unravel, hopefully allowing the more utopian impulses of the form more expression. That is, the historical modification and undermining of the dominant modes of symbolic containment in the 'Troubles' thriller can be further undermined in the utopian transcoding of Mandel's lone Sisyphus-figure in a class allegorical manner.

With regard to the dissipation of such stereotyping and their increased historical impossibility, it is symptomatic that Colin Bateman's comedic thrillers should emerge in the post-ceasefire period. Whilst the thriller has always lent itself to parody from 'without', such as the work of John Morrow, it is telling that Bateman is now enabled to write successfully and securely from 'within' the genre. To this end, Marx once commented that 'History is thorough and passes through many stages when she carries a worn-out form to burial. The last stage of a world-historical form is its comedy' (1977, 66). In Bateman's texts, the old stereotypes are still deployed but are overdetermined, and that discursive overdetermination is itself prompted by the overflow of the ultimate textual determination, that of History itself, which throws such attachments into irony and parody. In short, the 'Troubles' thriller, as with the Cold War thriller before it, is forced to contemplate its own demise but also its perpetuation. As it runs out of sustainable modes of symbolic containment through which to scramble its confrontation with the ultimate crime of capitalism itself, the thriller must somewhat fatalistically pursue this formative mystery, that it would also repress, as a means of prolonging its own historical function. Succinctly, when the 'Troubles' thriller exhausts its reactionary modes of symbolic containment it must finally reveal its radical core: the criminalization of the capitalist state formation itself. A succinct example of this point is provided by Clarke's *Underworld*. In the text an SAS soldier is sent to post-Peace Process Belfast to 'neutralize' six warring Republican gangs. Each of these gangs, who are fighting over control of the city, allegorize the various stereotypes foisted upon the figure of the terrorist, such as the psychopath, the idealist, the gangster and so on, as each gang is led by one these types.[13] It is the inexorable force of History which ensures that all the gangs are eliminated until only the capitalist gangsters remain, providing a neat instance of the increased historical impossibility of some of the 'Troubles' thriller's ideological baggage and the more distilled confrontation with its historical referent.

Another SAS text, McNab's *Remote Control*, is also pertinent here. The text's conspiracy involves the Gibraltar killings and a murky world of US and British intelligence operations. The text's title itself, and the manner in which its hero, Nick Stone, is initially manipulated, intimate the need for cognitive mapping in order to reinscribe the detached local instance with the bigger picture. Stone is told it is all about 'business' and British industry (1998, 475). Thus, Stone's confrontation with capitalism as a global conspiracy provides an explanation for a conflict previously described in sedimented terms of tribalism, psychopathology, atavism, sheer evil, an explanation which positions Stone and the organization for whom he worked with a totalized criminal pattern:

> I knew now why McCann, Farrell and Savage had to die. Enniskillen. The backlash against PIRA. People signing books of condolence. Irish-Americans stopping their donations. There must have been a real danger of dialogue and reconciliation. Simmonds and his mates couldn't have that. They had to create martyrs to keep the pot boiling.

---

[13] For a survey of these stereotypes, see Alan Titley's 'Rough Rug-Headed Kerns: The Irish Gunman in the Popular Novel'. *Eire-Ireland* Vol.15, No.4, 1980. 15-38.

> And me? I was probably just a very small glitch in a well-oiled machine. Come to that, Northern Ireland was probably only one item among many in their company accounts. For all I knew, these guys also provoked killings and riots in Hebron, stirred up Croats and Serbs, and even got Kennedy killed because he wanted to stop the Vietnam War (500-501).

Furthermore, in *The Psalm Killer* there is a fascinating imposition of the serial killer form onto the sectarian 'Troubles' forms. The novel's plot centres on an attempt in the 1990s to show how senseless all the killing has been through a spree of even more senseless serial killings involving two agents from the 1970s. This is an effort, so typical of late capitalism, to solve historical problems by ignoring them, a move towards a postmodern Northern Ireland. Michael Dibdin comments that 'every era has an emblematic transgression which addresses its intimate fears and fantasies ... the cult crime in recent years has been serial killing – a death which says a lot about the lives we lead' (7). The serial killer figure which has become such a cultural obsession of late – why is this obsession so potent? Well, given that a British Prime Minister, Margaret Thatcher, once claimed that 'there is no such thing as society' (cited by MacLauglin 1997, 136), I would offer the following explanation. We foist on to the figure of the serial killer all our anxieties about our society itself, about its dominant trends and ultimate values. If the serial killer is defined as asocial, lacking in emotional ties to others, a loner and an enigma gesturing to the social fracture of our times, then we can locate the figure within the alienated individualization of consumer capitalism. (We can go further, however, when we consider that the attributes that I have just ascribed to the serial killer – asociality, lacking emotional ties to others, solitariness – are all simultaneously characteristics of the detective too). The *repressive* desire of *The Psalm Killer* and its illusion of a criminal pattern that is really a mystificatory seriality dissipates the text's commendable *redemptive* figuration of the British state, and goes to the heart of the late capitalist regulation and reordering of sectarianism and the state in contemporary Northern Ireland.

So finally, then, where lies the radicalism of the thriller in such historical conditions? Stephen Knight asserts, in broad agreement with my own analysis, that 'crime fiction can be an instrument of political justice' (Bell, ed. 1990, 186):

> There is of necessity a certain element of radical critique built into the pattern of the most conservative writers, because, in order to realise fully a threat that will engage the fears of the audience and so create a pattern that can produce a truly consoling resolution, the text must first dramatise some genuine historical fear and possibility; that is, it must speak with a partly radical voice and realise some aspect of the actual social relations of a period (Bell, ed. 1990, 175).

Mutatis mutandis, I have attempted to show in my analysis of the conspiratorial mapping that if a society is to be threatened then we would first have to know what that society (as a totality) is to realize our fears. But this very ranging of the totality is itself an experience of desire, the resolution of a mystery. Thus, there is a dialectic of anxiety and desire, and the utopian trajectory resides in the fact that we have to know precisely what interests are being threatened in the form. On one level, uncovering these interests attests to our powerlessness in accordance with Mandel's thesis. Yet at another level this distance is firstly a signal that we are not included in the functioning of our societies and the operation of power. This prompts the utopian attempt to comprehend the criminalized pattern of these forces in a crime narrative that overrides the Panopticon subject's defence of 'law and order' and actually enacts an oppositional subjective entry in the prior mystery of History. In brief, a subtle transcoding of the conspiratorial mapping occurs: the conspiracy as local threat to the established order is radically transcribed, as the established order itself becomes the total conspiracy threatening the political subject.

Hence, grasping such a social cartography as a figuration of the objective traitor mitigates the pessimism of Mandel's hero and its singular exegesis. In effect, the passive reading is inherently contained by, and encoded in, the *repressive* modality whilst the *redemptive* figuration requires an active, counterhegemonic reading.[14] The *repressive* mechanics offers the content level of the text as itself a cover story, if you will. That is, the official cover-up handed to so many protagonists in the thriller allegorizes the *ideological suture* of the *repressive* modality as itself a failed cover-up etched in the ideology of form. A utopian reading apprehends the textual figuration of the dominant ideology *in flagrante delicto* and textualizes what it would seek to cover-up or suture. In effect, the textual effort at ideological closure is paradoxically a profound disclosure of historical fracture. To return to Benjamin, by interpreting formal terror of the 'Troubles' thriller, we truly are both detectives and conspirators, mapping the social and willing its transformation. Jameson crystallizes the utopian subject in the conspiratorial ideologeme which traduces Mandel's Sisyphus:

> the narrative cannot but remain allegorical, since the object it attempts to represent
> – namely, the social totality itself – is not an empirical entity and cannot be made
> to materialize as such in front of the individual viewer. In effect, the new figure
> we are here asked to supply continues to suggest something other than itself, in the
> occurrence of a conspiracy that is in reality a (class) war (1992a, 45-46).

By developing a political aesthetics, this chapter has attempted to uncover a Žižekean '*jouis-sense*' (Wright and Wright, eds. 1999, 17), or meaning in enjoyment. For a Lacanian method, the symptom exists as a residue of enjoyment beyond meaning, resisting symbolization, and the ultimate utopian moment of psychoanalysis is the analytical identification with the symptom as the ethical, speculative subject of desire. A political aesthetics of the thriller wills an identification with the historical symptoms textualized in the political unconscious with the aim of imaginatively re-constructing a historical subject, and hence of circumventing our placement as mere *träger* or objects of History. The text then

---

[14] A comparable contextualization is proposed by Stuart Hall's analysis of the double movement of containment and resistance in popular culture. 'Notes on Deconstructing the Popular' in Raphael Samuel, ed. *People's History and Socialist Theory* (London: Routledge and Kegan Paul, 1981). 227-240.

offers a space in which to articulate the *phantasms of the collectivity*, the speculative imagining of the social in a necessarily narrative form. The class allegorical disposition of both the oppositional and the hegemonic subject in relation to the absent totality is suggested by Žižek:

> class struggle is 'real' in the strict Lacanian sense: a 'hitch', an impediment which gives rise to ever-new symbolizations by means of which one endeavours to integrate and domesticate it (the corporatist translation-displacement of class struggle into the organic articulation of the 'members' of the 'social body', for example), but which simultaneously condemns these endeavours to ultimate failure. Class struggle is none other than the name for the unfathomable limit that cannot be objectified, located within the social totality. Or – to put it in yet another way – 'class struggle' designates the point with regard to which 'there is no metalanguage': in so far as every position within the social totality is ultimately overdetermined by class struggle, no neutral place is excluded from the dynamics of class struggle from which it would be possible to locate class struggle within the social totality (Wright and Wright, eds. 1999, 75).

Hence, even when the thriller's protagonists are seemingly pinioned by political institutions of the state and the Panopticon fantasy, such placements nevertheless evidence vectors through which to produce a necessarily narrative framework reformulating the prior Brechtian catastrophe of History. It is the task of our own conspiratorial detective work in the political unconscious to restructure the pleasure of the thriller in overdetermining the *redemptive* modality, which offers us, in however evanescent or pessimistic a manner, a concretely subjective cartography of the social totality, in order to force the text's contradictory imperatives into productive formal rupture. For, despite the often reactionary and fantastic conspiracies imagined by the *repressive* imaginary – its Soviet-sponsored plots, conniving homosexual aristocrats, insidious Arab extremists, deranged female characters, or even, as we have seen, alien invaders – the putatively ungraspable and penumbral conspiracy, which ultimately foreshadows and obsessively stalks these texts is none other than the seemingly vast inscrutable logic of the global conspiracy of global capitalism itself. And in contrast to a popular will to end sectarian conflict, the state-sponsored aspects of the Peace Process – extending British 'Third Way' capitalism westwards and the Celtic Tiger northwards through the promotion of private finance and the exclusion of the poor from public life – aim at establishing a wishy-washy and market-driven postmodern pluralism that actually serves to mask the real divides in our society (socio-economic ones), divides that threaten ultimately to remove power from people completely. So in a social context wherein not only the conflict but also the peace are conducted by covert elites apparently beyond public accountability, the utopian mode of the thriller has a politically vital role to play in unmasking the shadowy mechanics of contemporary capitalism and undermining the legitimacy of the state formation.

Appendix A

Travelling With Crime Novels

Walter Benjamin
Translated by Aaron Kelly and Martin Harvey

On the train, very few people read books which they have in their shelves at home, preferring to buy what presents itself to them at the last minute. They mistrust the effect of carefully laid out volumes, and rightly so. Besides, they think it important perhaps to make their purchase specifically at the carriage, colourfully decked out with bunting, on the asphalt of the platform. After all, everyone knows the cult that is here invoked. Everyone has at one time reached for the hoisted, swaying books, not so much out of the pleasure of reading than with the dark sense of doing something which placates the gods of the railway. One knows the coins which one devotes to this offertory box commend one to the mercy of the boiler-god which blazes through the night, the smoke-naiads which romp above the train and the judder-demon who is master of all lullabies. One knows them all from dreams, knows too the succession of mythic trials and dangers which commends itself to the zeitgeist as the 'railway journey', an unfathomable flight across the sleeping thresholds of time and space over which it moves, from the famous 'too late' of those left behind – the archetype of all loss – to the solitude of the compartment, the fear of missing one's connection, and the horror pulling into the unrecognised station. One feels unsuspectingly entangled in a giant machine and one recognizes in oneself the speechless witness of the struggle between the Gods of railways and stations.

Likes are cured by likes. Deadening one fear with another is our salvation. Between the freshly cut pages of crime novels one seeks the idle or, if you like, virgin feelings of trepidation which could help us overcome the archaic ones of the journey. In this way we may go so far as being frivolous and make Sven Elvestad along with his friend Asbjörn Krag, or Frank Heller and Mr Collins, our travelling companions. But this smart company is not to everyone's taste. Perhaps, in honour of the timetable, one would like a more precise companion, such as Leo Perutz, who wrote the powerfully rhythmic and syncopated stories whose stations one speeds through, watch in hand, like little provincial towns along the route. Or someone who summons up more understanding for the uncertainty of the future one is travelling towards, for the unsolved puzzles left behind: then one will travel with Gaston Leroux and, over the *Phantom of the Opera* and the *Perfume of the Lady in Black*, soon feel like a passenger of the *Ghost Train* which raced through German theatres last year. Or just think of Sherlock Holmes and his friend

Watson—how they would know to bring out the eerie secret of a dusty second-class compartment, both of them as passengers immersed in silence, the one behind the screen of a newspaper, the other behind a curtain of smoke-clouds. It is possible too that all these ghostly figures dissolve into thin air in front of the picture which emerges before us out of the unforgettable crime novels of A.K. Green, as a portrait of their author. One has to imagine her as an old lady in a bonnet, who is just as familiar with the intricate relationships of her heroes as with the huge, creaking closets in one of which, according to the British saying, every family has a skeleton. Her short stories are just as long as the Gotthard Tunnel and her great novels *Behind Closed Doors* and *The Affair Next Door* blossom in the purple compartment light like dame's violets.

So much for what reading does for the traveller. But what does the journey not do for the reader? When else is one so engrossed in reading and so certain to feel one's own existence blended with that of the protagonist? Is reader's body not the weaver's shuttle which, to the rhythm of the wheels, tirelessly shoots through the thread his hero's book of destiny? People did not read in the stagecoach, and you do not read in the car. Reading on a journey goes together with rail travel just like stopping in train stations. It is well known that many train stations are like cathedrals. However, we wish to thank the gaudily coloured little altars on wheels, chased past the train by a yelling acolyte of curiosity, absentmindedness and sensation, when – snuggled up for a few hours with the countryside flying by as in a fluttering scarf – we feel the shiver of excitement and the rhythms of the wheels run down our spine.

Appendix B

On the Popularity of the Crime Novel

Bertolt Brecht
Translated by Aaron Kelly and Martin Harvey

Undoubtedly the crime novel displays all the characteristics of a flourishing genre of literature. It is true that it scarcely appears in the periodic 'bestseller' polls, and that does not by any means have to be because it does not count as 'literature'. It is more likely that the broad masses really still prefer the psychological novel and that the crime novel is only chosen by a community of cognoscenti which, although strong in number, is not overwhelming. For these people, however, reading crime novels has assumed the character and strength of a habit. It is an intellectual habit. Reading psychological (or shall we say literary) novels cannot be called an intellectual activity with the same certainty, for the psychological (literary) novel discloses itself to the reader by essentially different operations than logical thought. The crime novel is about logical thought and demands such logical thought from the reader. It is close to the crossword puzzle in that respect.

Correspondingly it has a formula and displays its strength in variation thereof. No crime writer would hesitate in the slightest to have his murder occur in the library of a Lord's country estate, although that is highly unoriginal. Characters are seldom changed and there are only very few motives for the murder. A good crime writer does not invest a lot of talent or thought in either the creation of new characters or in the discovery of new motives for the deed. That is not what matters. Whoever exclaims, 'always the same!', when he notes that a tenth of all murders take place in a vicarage has not understood the crime novel. He could just as well exclaim, 'always the same!' in the theatre the moment the curtain goes up. The originality lies in other things. Indeed, the fact that one feature of the crime novel is the variation of more or less fixed elements even grants the whole genre its aesthetic benchmark. It is one of the characteristics of a sophisticated genre of literature. Incidentally, the cry of 'always the same' by someone not in the know is based on the same error as the white man's opinion that all blacks look the same. There is a plethora of formulas for the crime novel, all that is important is that they are formulas.

Like the world itself, the crime novel too is ruled by the British. The code of the British crime novel is the richest and most unified. It enjoys the most stringent of rules and these are elaborated into good critical essays. The Americans have far weaker formulas and, from the British point of view, are guilty of hankering for originality. Their murders happen continuously, like an epidemic. Occasionally their novels sink to the level of a thriller, that is, the thrill is no longer a spiritual one, it is only a purely nervous one.

A good British crime novel is above all fair. It shows moral strength. It is a matter of honour to 'play the game'. The reader is not deceived – all the material is presented to him before the detective solves the puzzle. He is put in a position to tackle the solution himself. It is astonishing how the basic pattern of a good crime novel is reminiscent of the working method of physicists. First of all, certain facts are noted. There is a body. The watch is smashed and shows two o'clock. The housekeeper has a healthy aunt. The sky was overcast that night. And so on and so on. Then, hypotheses are put forward that can correspond with these facts. The accumulation of new facts or the invalidation of facts already noted forces one to look for a new hypothesis. With the conclusion comes the test of the hypothesis: the experiment. If the hypothesis is right, then the murderer has to appear in this place at this time on the strength of this reasoning. What is crucial is that the action is not developed from the characters, but the characters from the action. The people are seen conducting themselves, but in fragments. Their motives are unclear and have to be logically deduced. The decisive factor in their actions is assumed to be their interests – indeed, almost exclusively their financial interests. One searches for them. One can see the convergence with the scientific point of view and the enormous difference from the introspectively psychological novel. In comparison it is far less important that scientific methods are depicted in the crime novel and that medicine, chemistry and mechanics play a major role. The crime writer's entire method of composition is influenced by science. We can mention here that a clear schism between subjective and objective psychology can be seen in the modern literary novel too, in Joyce, Döblin and Dos Passos, and such trends crop up even in the most recent American Verism, although here it is probably a matter of retrospective narrative forms. Of course one has to remain free of aesthetic judgements in order to see the link between these highly complicated works of Joyce, Döblin and Dos Passos and the crime novel of Sayers, Freeman and Rhode. If one sees the connection then one recognizes that, despite all its primitiveness (not just of the aesthetic kind), the crime novel meets the needs of people of a scientific age even more than the works of the avant-garde.

Admittedly, when discussing the popularity of the crime novel, we must give a great deal of attention to the reader's appetite for adventurous happenings, simple excitement and so on, which the crime novel satisfies. It is enjoyable just to see people *act*, to witness actions with actual consequences that are ascertainable straightaway. The people in crime novels do not just leave traces in the souls of their fellow men, but also in their bodies and in the garden soil in front of the library. The literary novel and real life stand here on one side, the crime novel, a special excerpt of real life, on the other. In real life people seldom find that they leave traces, certainly as long as they do not turn to crime and the police discover these traces. The life of the atomized masses and the collectivized individual of our time passes without trace. The crime novel offers certain surrogates here.

An adventure novel could hardly be written in any other way than as crime novel: in our society adventures are criminal. But the intellectual enjoyment comes from the *mental task* which the crime novel sets the detective and the reader. First of all the talent for observation is given a field on which it can play. The event which has taken place is assembled out of the changes to the appearance of the scene; the battle is reconstructed from the battlefield. The unexpected plays a role. We have to discover *inconsistencies*. The surgeon has callused hands, the floor is dry although the window is open and it has been raining; the butler was awake but he did not hear the gunshot. Then the witnesses' statements are critically scrutinized: this is a lie, that is a mistake. In the latter case we watch, as it were, through instruments which measure inaccurately and have to gauge the extent of the deviation. This process of making observations, drawing conclusions and thus coming to a decision gives us all kinds of satisfaction, if only because everyday life seldom grants us such an effective process of thought and because usually many obstacles appear in the way between observation and conclusion, as well as between conclusion and decision. In most cases we are not in a position to make use of our observations at all – whether we make them or not has no influence on the course of our social relations. We are neither master of our conclusions nor master of our decisions.

In a crime novel we are served up precisely measured-out periods of life – isolated, marked out little complexes of occurrences in which the causality functions satisfactorily. This makes for pleasurable thinking. Let us take a simple example, this time from the history of crime, not the novel. The murder was carried out by means of coal gas. There are two possible culprits. One of them has an alibi for midnight, the other for the morning. The solution is deduced from the presence of a pair of dead flies on the window ledge. Therefore the murder occurred in the morning: the flies were at the bright window – in such a way questions regarding our so complicated life can really be *decided*. An unknown murder victim is also identified through gratifying conclusions on a demarcated field of investigation. By means of exact observations the victim's social, and indeed geographical, position is established. The little things found on him slowly obtain their own biography. His dental bridge was made by this and that dentist. But even before that is ascertained one knows that, at least at the time he had the bridgework done, his financial circumstances must have been good, for it is an expensive bridge.

The group of suspects is also small. Their behaviour can be observed precisely and subjected to small tests. The investigator (detective and reader) is in an atmosphere oddly free of convention. The roguish baron as well as the lifelong, loyal servant or the seventy-year-old aunt *can* be the culprit. No cabinet minister is free from suspicion. The decision is made whether he killed one of his fellow men in a zone where only motive and opportunity operate. We take pleasure in the way the crime writer leads us to rational judgements by forcing us to abandon our prejudices. In order to do so he has to master the art of seduction. He must equip the people involved in the murder with both unsympathetic as well as attractive features. He must provoke our prejudices. The benevolent old botanist *can't* be the murderer, he has us exclaim. A gardener with two previous convictions for poaching is capable of anything, he has us sigh. He misleads us through his *portrayal of character*.

Warned a thousand times (from reading a thousand crime novels) we forget once more that only motive and opportunity are decisive. It is merely social circumstances which make the crime possible or necessary: they violate the character just as they formed it. Of course the murderer is an evil person, but to discover that we have to pin the murder on him. The crime novel does not offer a more direct way to uncover his morals. And so it remains in tracking down the causal connection. Specifying the causality of human actions is the main intellectual pleasure that the crime novel affords us.

Everywhere in our everyday lives we undoubtedly come across the difficulties physicists have in the area of causality – but not in the crime novel. As with physicists in certain areas, we have in our everyday life, in so far as it concerns social situations, to rely on a *statistical* causality. In all existential questions, perhaps with the exception of the most primitive ones, we have to make do with probability estimates. Whether knowledge of this or that will get us this or that post can, at best, be probable. We are not even capable of establishing clear motives for our own decisions, let alone those of others. The opportunities which present themselves to us are extremely indistinct, veiled, blurred. The law of causality functions at most only up to a certain point. In the crime novel it works once again. A few tricks remove the sources of disturbance. The field of view is skilfully restricted. And the deductions are made in retrospect, from the catastrophe. Thus we arrive at a position which is of course very favourable to speculation. At the same time we can use a process of thought which our life has developed in us. We have arrived at a fundamental point in our small examination into why the intellectual operations which the crime novel enables us to undertake are so exceedingly popular in our time.

We gain our knowledge of life in a catastrophic form. It is from catastrophes that we have to infer the manner in which our social formation functions. Through reflection, we must deduce the 'inside story' of crises, depressions, revolutions, and wars. We already sense from reading the newspapers (but also bills, letters of dismissal, call-up papers and so forth) that somebody must have done something for the evident catastrophe to have taken place. So what then has been done and by whom? Behind the reported events, we suspect other occurrences about which we are not told. These are the *real* occurrences. If we knew these incidents, we would understand. Only History can inform us about these real occurrences – insofar as the protagonists have not succeeded in keeping them completely secret. History is written *after* catastrophes. The basic situation in which intellectuals find themselves – that they are objects and not subjects of history – forms the thought processes which they can apply with enjoyment in the crime story. Existence depends upon unknown factors. 'Something must have happened', 'something is brewing', 'a situation has arisen' – this is what they feel, and the mind goes out on patrol. But enlightenment only comes, if at all, after the catastrophe. The murder has happened. What was brewing beforehand? What sort of situation had arisen? Well, it is perhaps possible to deduce. This point may not be the crucial one, it is possibly only one of many points. The popularity of the crime novel has many causes. However, this reason seems at least to me to be one of the most interesting.

But the characters are very roughly depicted, the motives for the action are blatant, the events crude, everything, especially the interlacing of the plot, is so improbable, there is much too much coincidence; an unsophisticated mind is at work. There is no point in disputing that the depiction of the characters is mostly superficial. What is said about them is mostly just as much as the reader needs to understand their actions; the establishing of the character before the reader generally happens feature by feature; there is a continual link with behaviour. This and that person is vindictive and for that reason writes the letter, or this and that letter is written by a vindictive person: who is the vindictive person? The reader takes part in the building of the character as a dutiful activity; it is an unveiling which must of necessity be done. And since this mostly results in disadvantages for the pursued, the person whose character is to be depicted, he only divulges the traits of his character very reluctantly. He does not just express himself, he comes up with traits, he falsifies: he deliberately disrupts the experiment. Think again of modern physics. The object being observed is changed through observation. Such outstanding achievements of literary psychology (outstanding achievements because, from the point of view of modern scientific psychology, the novel's depiction of man is completely antiquated) are, in the crime novel, an immediate result of the fact that here life is conceived of and figured as working life. Sometimes even creations of a higher kind can be found. Poe's chess player, Conan Doyle's Sherlock Holmes and Chesterton's Father Brown.

Bibliography

Primary Texts

Aalben, Patrick. *The Grab*. London: Robert Hale. 1977.

Adams, James. *Taking the Tunnel*. London: Michael Joseph, 1993.

Adams, Patrick. *Everything Can be Okay*. Los Angeles: Amber, 1979.

Anderson, Linda. *Cuckoo*. London: Futura, 1984.

— . *To Stay Alive*. London: The Bodley Head, 1986.

Anthony, Evelyn. *A Place to Hide*. New York: Putnam, 1987.

Armstrong, Campbell. *Jig*. London: Hodder and Stoughton, 1987.

Asher, Michael. *Shoot to Kill: A Soldier's Journey Through Violence*. London: Penguin, 1991.

Atwater, James D. *Time Bomb*. Feltham: Hamlyn, 1979.

Aylott, Bob. *Cry for Tomorrow*. London: Everest, 1973.

Baker, Keith. *Inheritance*. London: Headline, 1996.

Ball, Brian. *Keegan: The No-Option Contract*. London: Arthur Baker, 1975.

Ballinger, W.A. *The Green Grassy Slopes*. London: Corgi, 1969.

Barlow, James. *Both Your Houses*. London: Pan, 1973.

Barnacle, Hugo. *Day One*. London: Quartet Books, 1998.

Bateman, Colin. *Cycle of Violence*. London: Harper Collins, 1995a.

— . *Divorcing Jack*. London: Harper Collins, 1995b.

— . *Of Wee Sweetie Mice and Men*. London: Harper Collins, 1996.

— . *Empire State*. London: Harper Collins, 1997.

Beckett, Mary. *Give Them Stones*. London: Bloomsbury, 1987.

Bennett, Ronan. *Overthrown by Strangers*. London: Penguin, 1993.

— . *The Second Prison*. London: Penguin, 1992.

Binnie, Stewart. *Across the Water*. London: Alison, 1979.

Blain, Sean. *The Java Man*. London: Michael Joseph, 1995.

Blake, Philippa. *Looking Out*. Sevenoaks, Kent: Coronet Books, 1989.

Braddon, Russell. *The Progress of Private Lillyworth*. London: Michael Joseph, 1971.

Bradford, Roy. *The Last Ditch*. Belfast: The Blackstaff P, 1981.

Bradby, Tom. *Shadow Dancer*. London: Bantam P, 1998.

Brady, John. *Unholy Ground*. London: Constable, 1989.

— . *A Stone of the Heart*. London: Penguin, 1990.

Breslin, Jimmy. *World Without End, Amen*. London: Hutchinson, 1974.

Brewster, David. *The Heart's Grown Brutal*. London: Angus and Robertson, 1972.

Brian, Sam. *Winter's Return*. Lurgan: Ulster Society, 1996.

Bringle, Mary. *Death of an Unknown Man*. London: Collins, 1986.

— . *The Man in Moss Coloured Trousers*. New York: Doubleday, 1987.

Broderick, John. *The Fugitives*. London: Pan, 1976.

Brown, George. *Ringmain*. London: Arrow, 1992.

Bruce, Paul. *The Nemesis File*. London: Blake, 1995.

Burdon, Peter. *Warrior's Son*. London: New English Library, 1990.

Burns, Richard. *Why Diamond Had to Die*. London: Bloomsbury, 1989.

Byrne, Robert. *The Tunnel*. London: Michael Joseph, 1977.

Cannon, Elliott. *Stand By to Shoot*. London: Robert Hale, 1973.

Carrick, James. *With O'Leary in the Grave*. London: Heineman, 1971.

Carroll, James. *Madonna Red*. London: Coronet, 1978.

Carson, Ciaran. *Belfast Confetti*. Newcastle Upon Tyne: Bloodaxe, 1990.

Carter, Peter. *Under Goliath*. London: Oxford U P, 1977.

Case, Jim. *Belfast Blitz*. New York: Warner Books, 1987.

Casey, Kevin. *Dreams of Revenge*. London: Faber, 1977.

Caulfield, Max. *The Black City*. London: Ace Books, 1959. (1952).

Cawley, Robert. *Friend or Foe?* London: Sphere, 1977.

— . *Shockwave*. London: Sphere, 1979.

Celyn Jones, Russell. *Soldiers and Innocents*. London ; Jonathan Cape, 1990.

Chapman, John. *City War*. London: Robert Hale, 1979.

Charles, Robert. *The Hour of the Wolf*. New York: Pinnacle, 1974.

— . *The Scream of a Dove*. London: New English Library, 1979.

Clancy, Ambrose. *Blind Pilot*. Harmondsworth: Penguin, 1980.

Clancy, Tom. *Patriot Games*. London: Harper Collins, 1988.

Clarke, A.F.N. *Contact*. London: Pan, 1984. (1983).

Clarke, Shaun. *Soldier E – SAS: Sniper Fire in Belfast*. Maidstone: 22 Books, 1993.

— . *Underworld*. London: Coronet, 1997.

— . *Red Hand*. London: Coronet, 1998.

Cleary, Jon. *Peter's Pence*. New York: Pyramid, 1975.

Clifford, Francis. *Drummer in the Dark*. London: Collins, 1974.

Collins, Michael. *The Meat Eaters*. London: Jonathan Cape, 1992.

— . *Emerald Underground*. London: Phoenix House, 1998.

Connolly, Colm. *The Pact*. London: Andre Deutsch, 1980.

Connolly, Ray. *News Death*. London: Collins, 1978.

Coogan, Patrick. *The General*. London: Sinclair-Stevens, 1993.

Cottrell, Roger. *The Orpheus Programme*. London: Minerva P, 1994.

Countryman Jr., Albert J. *The Streets of Derry*. Palmyra, NJ: Countryman Publishing, 1986.

Courts, Johnson. *Collusion*. London: Minerva, 1995.

Cowell, John. *The Begrudgers*. Dublin: The O'Brien P, 1978.

Crawford, Richard. *Fall When Hit*. London: Mandarin, 1993.

— . *The Minstrel Boy*. London: Mandarin, 1995

Crawford, Robert. *Whip Hand*. London: Constable, 1972.

Cregan, Conor. *With Extreme Prejudice*. London: Coronet Books, 1994.

Crossland, Susan. *Dangerous Games*. London: Weidenfeld and Nicolson, 1991.

Cunningham, Peter. *Who Trespass Against Us*. London: Arrow, 1993.

Daly, Ita. *All Fall Down*. London: Bloomsbury, 1992.

Daniel, James. *They Told Me You Were Dead*. London: Pan, 1994.

Davies, Murray. *The Drumbeat of Jimmy Sands*. London: Harper Collins, 1999.

de Mille, Nelson. *Cathedral*. London: Granada, 1981.

de St Jorre, John and Brian Shakespeare. *The Patriot Game*. London: Coronet, 1973.

Dickinson, Peter. *The Green Gene*. London: Hodder and Stoughton, 1973.

Dillon, Martin. *The Serpent's Tail*. London: Fourth Estate, 1996.

Doherty, Angela. *Constant Friends*. London: Orion, 1993.

Donnelly, Joe. *The Shee*. London: Century, 1992.

Dowling, Kevin. *Interface: Ireland*. London: Barrie and Jenkins, 1979.

Downey Broxon, Mildred. *Too Long A Sacrifice*. London: Futura, 1983.

Driscoll, Peter. *In Connection with Kilshaw*. London: MacDonald, 1974.

Duffaud, Briege. *A Wreath upon the Dead*. Dublin: Poolbeg, 1993.

Dunne, Colin. *Rat Catcher*. London: Secker and Warburg, 1985.

Dunne, Lee. *Ringleader*. Glasgow: The Molendinar P, 1981.

Easterman, Daniel. *Day of Wrath*. London: Harper Collins, 1995.

Emerson, Sally. *Firechild*. London: Michael Joseph, 1987.

Esler, Gavin. *Loyalties*. London: Headline, 1990.

— . *The Blood Brother*. London: Harper Collins, 1996.

Faulkner, Tom. *The Machiavellian Legacy*. Sussex: The Book Guild, 1994.

Feeney, John. *Worm Friday*. Dun Laoghaire: Anna Livia, 1974.

Finlay, Fergus. *A Cruel Trade*. London: Andre Deutsch, 1990.

Flannery, Sean. *Kilo Option*. New York: Forge, 1996.

Foxall, P.A. *Inspector Derben's War*. London: Robert Hale, 1976.

— . *Inspector Derben and the Widow Maker*. London: Robert Hale, 1977.

Franklin, Max. *Hennessy*. London: Futura, 1975.

Gadney, Reg. *Just When We Are Safest*. London: Faber, 1995.

Gallie, Menna. *You're Welcome to Ulster!* London: Victor Gollancz, 1970.

Gaynor, Chris. *Conduct Unbecoming*. London: Citron P, 1998.

Gibson, Tom. *A Wild Hope*. London: Robert Hale, 1983.

Gilbert, Michael. *Trouble*. London: Harper and Row, 1987.

Gill, Bartholomew. *McGarr at the Dublin Horse Show*. London: Robert Hale, 1975.

— . *McGarr and the Method of Descartes*. Harmondsworth: Penguin, 1985.

— . *McGarr and the P. M. of Belgrave Square*. Harmondsworth: Penguin, 1986.

Green, F.L. *Odd Man Out*. London: Cardinal, 1991 (1945).

Gross, Ken. *Hell Bent*. New York: Doherty Associates, 1992.

Hale, John. *Lover's and Heretics*. London: Victor Gollancz, 1976.

Hammett, Dashiell. *The Four Great Novels*. London: Picador, 1982.

Hamill, Desmond. *Bitter Orange*. London: Hutchinson, 1979.

Hanley, Clifford. *Prissy*. London: Collins, 1978.

Hanley, David. *In Guilt and in Glory*. London: Hutchinson, 1979.

Harcourt, Palma. *A Sleep of Spies*. London: Collins, 1979.

Harriott, Ted. *No Sanctuary*. London: Secker and Warburg, 1983.

Hawke, Christopher. *For Campaign Service*. London: Corgi, 1979.

Hayward, David. *The Provo Link*. London: Robert Hale, 1979.

Healy, Dermot. *Fighting with Shadows*. London: Allison and Busby, 1984.

Healy, Shay. *Green Card Blues*. Dublin: The O'Brien P, 1994.

Hegarty, David. *Short Storm*. Cork: Emperor, 1991.

Hegarty, Walter. *The Price of Chips*. London: Davis-Poynter, 1973.

Herron, Shaun. *Through the Darky and Hairy Wood*. London: Jonathan Cape, 1973a.

— . *The Whore Mother*. London: Jonathan Cape, 1973b.

Higgins, George V. *The Patriot Game*. London: Secker and Warburg, 1982.

Higgins, Jack. *The Savage Day*. London: Collins, 1972.

— . *A Prayer for the Dying*. London: Collins, 1973.

— . *Solo*. London: London: Collins, 1980.

— . *Touch the Devil*. London: Collins, 1982.

— . *Confessional*. London: Collins, 1985.

— . *Eye of the Storm*. London: Chapmans, 1992.

— . *Angel of Death*. London: Michael Joseph, 1995.

— . *Drink with the Devil*. London: Michael Joseph, 1996.

Hill, Nikki. *Death Grows on You*. London ; Michael Joseph, 1990.

Hogan, Desmond. *A New Shirt*. London: Faber and Faber, 1987.

Holland, Jack. *The Prisoner's Wife*. London: Robert Hale, 1982.
— . *Walking Corpses*. Dublin: Torc, 1994.
Holloway, Rupert. *The Terrorist Conspiracy*. Lewes, Sussex: The Book Guild,1982.
Howlett, John. *Orange*. London: Hutchinson, 1985.
Hugo, Richard. *Last Judgement*. London: Macmillan, 1984.
Hurd, Douglas. *Vote to Kill*. London: Collins, 1975.
Hurley, Graham. *Reaper*. London: Pan, 1992.
Hutson, Shaun. *Renegades*. London: Sphere, 1991.
— . *White Ghost*. London: Little, 1994.
— . *Knife Edge*. London: Warner, 1998.
Hynes, James. *The Wild Colonial Boy*. New York: Washington Square P, 1990.
Ingoldby, Grace. *Across the Water*. London: Michael Joseph, 1985.
Jacks, Oliver. *Assassination Day*. London: Coronet, 1978.
James, Evelyn. *Taking the Forbidden Road*. Holywood: The Third House, 1991.
Joyce, Joe. *Off the Record*. London: Heinemann, 1989.
— . *The Trigger Man*. London: Mandarin, 1990.
Judd, Alan. *A Breed of Heroes*. London: Fontana, 1985.
Kebbe, Jonathan. *The Armalite Maiden*. London: Mandarin, 1991.
Kelly, James. *The Marrow from the Bone*. Bailieboro: Kelly Kane Ltd., 1987.
Kennedy, James. *Armed and Dangerous*. London: Heinemann, 1996.
Kenyon, Michael. *A Sorry State*. London: Collins, 1974.
Kerrigan, Philip. *Dead Ground*. London: Macmillan, 1985.
Kiely, Benedict. *Nothing Happens in Carrickmacross*. London: Methuen, 1986.
— . *Proxopera*. London: Methuen, 1988.
Kiely, David M. *The Angel Tapes*. Belfast: The Blackstaff P, 1997.
King, Peter T. *Terrible Beauty*. Boulder, Colorado: Roberts Reinhart, 1999.
Kippax, Fank. *Other People's Blood*. London: Harper Collins, 1992.
Lane, Andrew. *Forgive the Executioner*. London: New English Library, 1978.
— . *The Ulsterman*. London: New English Library, 1979.
Langley, Bob. *Death Stalk*. London: Michael Joseph, 1977.
— . *The War of the Running Fox*. London: Routledge, 1978.
Larkin, Philip. *Collected Poems*. Ed and intro. Anthony Thwaite. London: Faber, 1988.
Lauder, Peter. *Noble Lord*. London: Fontana, 1986.
Leather, Stephen. *The Chinaman*. London: Coronet, 1993.
— . *The Long Shot*. London: Hodder and Stoughton, 1994.
— . *The Double Tap*. London: Hodder and Stoughton, 1996.
Leinster, Colin. *The Outsider*. London: New English Library, 1980.
Leitch, Maurice. *Silver's City*. London: Abacus, 1983. (1981).
Leland, Mary. *Approaching Priests*. London: Sinclair-Stevenson, 1991.
Leslie, Peter. *The Extremists*. London: New English Library, 1970.
Lingard, Joan. *The Lord on Our Side*. London: Hodder and Stoughton,1970a.
— . *The Twelfth of July*. London: Hamish Hamilton, 1970b.
— . *Across the Barricades*. London: Hamish Hamilton, 1972.
— . *Into Exile*. London: Hamish Hamilton, 1973.
— . *The Guilty Party*. London: Hamish Hamilton, 1987.
— . *A Proper Place*. London: Pengiun, 1988.
— . *Dark Shadows*. London: Puffin, 1998.
Lund, James. *The Ultimate*. London: John Caulder, 1976.
MacKenzie, Lee. *Hadleigh*. London: New English Library, 1970.
MacLaverty, Bernard. *Cal*. London: Penguin, 1984.

Mann, Paul. *The Traitor's Contract*. New York: Knightsbridge, 1991.
Manning, Kitty. *The Between People*. Dublin: Attic P, 1990.
Maxim, John. *Haven*. New York: Avon, 1997.
May, Naomi. *Troubles*. London: John Caulder, 1976.
McBratney, Sam. *Mark Time*. London: Abelard, 1976.
McCabe, Eugene. *Victims: A Tale from Fermanagh*. Dublin: The Mercier P, 1976.
McCaffrey, K.T. *Revenge*. Dublin: Mercier P, 1999.
McCallion, Harry. *Killing Zone*. London: Bloomsbury, 1995.
McCartan, Domominc. *Operation Emerald*. London: Pluto P, 1985.
McCarthy, Thomas. *Without Power*. Dublin: Poolbeg P, 1991.
McCarty, Nick. *Spearhead*. London: Arrow, 1978.
McCaughren, Tom. *Rainbows of the Moon*. Dublin: Anvil, 1989.
McDonald, Ian. *Sacrifice of Fools*. London: Victor Gollancz, 1996.
McEldowney, Eugene. *A Kind of Homecoming*. London: Heinemann, 1994.
— . *A Stone of the Heart*. London: Heinemann, 1995.
— . *The Sad Case of Harpo Higgins*. London: Heinemann, 1996.
— . *Murder at Piper's Gate*. London: Arrow, 1998.
McGartland, Martin. *Fifty Dead Men Walking*. London: Blake, 1997.
McGeough, Gerry. *Defenders*. Monaghan: Seesya P, 1998.
McKeon, James. *Operation Pontiff*. Cork: Acorn P, 1994.
McLoughlin, Jane. *Coincidence*. London: Virago, 1992.
McMahon, Blair. *Nights in Armour*. Lurgan: Ulster Society, 1993.
McNab, Andy. *Immediate Action*. London: Corgi, 1996.
— . *Remote Control*. London: Corgi, 1998.
McNamara, Michael. *The Dancing Floor*. London: Allen, 1979.
— . *The Sovereign Solution*. London: Star, 1980.
McNamee, Eoin. *Resurrection Man*. London: Picador, 1994.
Meenan, Hugo. *No Time for Love*. Dingle: Brandon, 1987.
Melville-Ross, Andrew. *Shaw's War*. London: Sphere Books, 1989.
Michaels, S.J. *Summary Justice*. London: Pan Books, 1988.
— . *Dieback*. London: Pan Books, 1991.
Miner, Valerie. *Blood Sisters*. London: Methuen, 1988.
Mitchell, Julie. *Sunday Afternoons*. London: Viking, 1988.
Moore, Brian. *The Lonely Passion of Judith Hearne*. London: Paladin, 1988.
— . *Lies of Silence*. London: Vintage, 1992.
Mornin, Daniel. *All Our Fault*. London: Arrow, 1996.
Morrison, Danny. *The Wrong Man*. Dublin: Mercier P, 1997.
Morrow, John. *The Confessions of Proinsias O'Toole*. Belfast: The Blackstaff P, 1977.
Murphy, Sean. *Foreign Chains*. Belfast: AIP, 1996.
Nelson, Walter. *The Minstrel Code*. London: New English Library, 1980.
Neville, Pauline. *Peggy*. London: Arcadia, 1999.
Newmann, Christopher. *The Devil's Own*. London: Bantam Books, 1997.
Newman, G.F. *The Testing Ground*. London: Michael Joseph, 1987.
Nicholl, Ned. *No More Leprechauns*. London: New English Library, 1973.
Nolan, Frederick. *Designated Assassin*. London: Arrow, 1991.
North, Michael. *Mission to Ulster*. London: Dennis Dobson, 1981.
O'Connor, Brian. *The One-Shot War*. New York: Ballantine Books, 1980.
O'Donovan, Uinsin. *Rag Shadows*. Ballinasloe: Cillenna, 1980.
O'Flaherty, Liam. *The Informer*. London: Jonathan Cape, 1925.
O'Neill, Edward. *The Rotterdam Delivery*. London: Victor Gollancz, 1975.

O'Reilly, Victor. *Games of the Hangman*. London: Headline, 1992.
— . *Games of Vengeance*. London: Headline, 1994.
O'Riordan, Kate. *Involved*. London: Flamingo, 1995.
O'Rourke, T.S. *Ganglands*. Dublin: Breffni, 1996.
Ould, Chris. *A Kind Of Sleep*. London: Andre Deutsch, 1986.
Parkes, Rogre. *Riot*. London: Collins, 1986.
Paul, William. *Seasons of Revenge*. London: Futura, 1985.
Perry, Ritchie. *Dead End*. London: Collins, 1977.
Petit, Chris. *The Psalm Killer*. London: Macmillan, 1996.
Pincher, Chapman. *The Eye of the Tornado*. London: Michael Joseph, 1976.
Porter, Henry. *Remembrance Day*. London: Orion, 1999.
Porter, R.W. *Kiss and Kill*. London: Robert Hale, 1981.
Power, M.S. *The Killing of Yesterday's Children*. London: Chatto and Windus, 1985.
— . *Lonely the Man Without Heroes*. London: William Heinemann, 1986.
— . *A Darkness in the Eye*. London: William Heinemann, 1987.
— . *Come the Executioner*. London: Hamish Hamilton, 1991.
Prior, Allan. *Her Majesty's Secret Agent*. London: Grafton, 1986.
Quigley, Patrick. *Borderland*. Dingle: Brandon: 1994.
Rankin, Ian. *Mortal Causes*. London: Orion, 1994.
Ransley, Peter. *The Price*. London: Corgi, 1984.
Renwick, Aly. *Last Night Another Soldier*. London: Information on Ireland, 1989.
Rice, David. *Blood Guilt*. Belfast: The Blackstaff P, 1994.
Roberts, Jan. *A Blood Affair*. London: Harper Colllins, 1991.
Royce, Kenneth. *A Wild Justice*. London: Coronet, 1993.
Ryan, Chris. *Stand By, Stand By*. London: Century, 1996.
Seaman, Donald. *The Bomb That Could Lip-Read*. London: Futura, 1975.
— . *The Committee*. London: Hamish Hamilton, 1977.
Seymour, Gerald. *Harry's Game*. Glasgow: Fontana Collins, 1975.
— . *The Glory Boys*. London: Collins, 1976.
— . *The Contract*. London: Collins, 1980.
— . *Field of Blood*. London: Collins, 1985.
— . *The Journeyman Tailor*. London: Harvill, 1992.
Shah, Eddy. *Fallen Angels*. London: Doubleday, 1994.
Shannon, James. *A Game of Soldiers*. London: Sphere, 1985.
Shea, Michael. *Spin Doctor*. London: Harper Collins, 1995.
Shelley, Mike. *The Last Private Eye in Belfast*. Belfast: Domino Books, 1984.
Sherman, Eileen. *Victor's Place*. Edison, New Jersey: Cornerstone P, 1989.
— . *The Divided Heart*. London: Warner, 1997.
Shriver, Lionel. *Ordinary Decent Criminals*. London: Harper Collins, 1992.
Silva, Daniel. *The Marching Season*. London: Weidenfeld and Nicolson, 1999.
Sinclair, Dennis. *The Third Force*. London: Corgi, 1976.
Smith, Murray. *The Devil's Juggler*. London: Michael Joseph, 1993.
Smith, Surrey. *A Gun for Delilah*. London: Robert Hale, 1979.
Stevens, Gordon. *Provo*. London: Harper Collins, 1993.
St James, Ian. *The Killing Anniversary*. London: Heinemann, 1984.
Strong, Terence. *Whisper Who Dares*. London: Coronet, 1982.
— . *Stalking Horse*. London: Hodder and Stoughton, 1993.
— . *The Tick Tock Man*. London: Mandarin, 1995 (1994).
Target, George W. *The Patriots*. London: Duckworth, 1974.
Thompson, David. *Broken English*. New York: Henry Holt, 1987.

Toman, Edward. *Shambles Corner*. London: Flamingo, 1993.
Urch, Marion. *Violent Shadows*. London: Headline, 1996.
Uris, Leon. *Trinity*. London: Andre Deutsch, 1976.
Valentine, Deborah. *Fine Distinctions*. London: Victor Gollancz, 1991.
Van Greenaway, Peter. *Suffer! The Little Children*. London: Victor Gollancz, 1976.
Weston, Simon and Patrick Hill. *Cause of Death*. Rochester, Kent: 22 Books, 1995.
White, Stuart. *The Shamrock Boy*. London: Bodley Head, 1990.
Young, Sylvester. *What Goes Around*. London: BlackAmber, 1999.

Secondary Sources

Adair, Tom. 'The Fictional Face of Belfast'. *Linen Hall Review*. 3; 4. Winter 1986. 10-12.
Adams, James et al, eds. *Ambush: The War Between the SAS and the IRA*. London: Pan, 1988.
Adams, J.R.R. *The Printed Word and the Common Man: Popular Culture in Ulster 1700-1900*. Belfast: Institute for Irish Studies, 1987.
Adamson, Ian. *Cruthin: The Ancient Kindred*. Newtownards: Nosmada Books, 1974.
— . *The Identity of Ulster: The Land, the Language and the People*. Belfast: W and G Baird, 1982.
— . *The Ulster People: Ancient, Medieval and Modern*. Bangor: Pretani P, 1991.
Adonis, Andrew and Tim Hames, eds. *A Conservative Revolution? The Thatcher-Reagan Decade in Perspective*. Manchester: Manchester U P, 1994.
Adorno, Theodor and Max Horkheimer. *Dialectic of Enlightenment*. Trans. John Cumming. London: Allen Lane, 1973.
Agnew, John. *Place and Politics: The Geographical Mediation of State and Society*. Boston: Allen and Unwin, 1987.
— , ed. *Political Geography: A Reader*. London: Arnold, 1997.
Ahmad, Aijaz. *In Theory: Classes, Nations, Literatures*. London: Verso, 1992.
Alexander, Yonah and Alan O'Day, eds. *Terrorism in Ireland*. London: Croom Helm, 1984.
— , eds. *Ireland's Terrorist Dilemma*. Dordcut: Martinus Nijhoff, 1986.
— , eds. *Ireland's Terrorist Trauma: Interdisciplinary Perspectives*. London: Harvester Wheatsheaf, 1989.
—, eds. *The Irish Terrorism Experience*. Aldershot: Dartmouth, 1991.
Allen, John et al, eds. *Unsettling Cities*. London: Routledge, 1999.
Althusser, Louis. *For Marx*. Trans. B. Brewster. London: Verso, 1979.
— . *Essays on Ideology*. London: Verso, 1993.
Altinal, Savkar. 'M.S. Power's *Come the Executioner*'. *TLS*. 4622. 1 Nov 1991. 21.
Anderson, Benedict. *Imagined Communities: Reflections on the Origin and Spread of Nationalism*. Revised and extended edition. London: Verso, 1991.
Anderson, James and Ian Shuttleworth. 'Sectarian Readings of Sectarianism: Interpreting the Northern Ireland Census'. *The Irish Review* 16, Autumn / Winter 1994. 74-93.
Anderson, Perry. *English Questions*. London: Verso, 1992a.
— . *A Zone of Engagement*. London: Verso, 1992b.
Anthias, Floya and Nira Yuval-Davis. *Racialized Boundaries: Race, Nation, Gender, Colour and Class and the Anti-Racist Struggle*. London: Routledge, 1992.
Arthur, Paul and Keith Jeffery. *Northern Ireland since 1968*. Oxford: Blackwell, 1996.
Aughey, Arthur. *Under Siege: Ulster Unionism and the Anglo-Irish Agreement*. Belfast: The Blackstaff P, 1989.
Bailey, Brian. *The Resurrection Men*. London: Macdonald, 1991.

Bakhtin, M.M. *The Dialogic Imagination: Four Essays*. Ed. Michael Holquist. Trans. Caryl Emerson and Michael Holquist. Austin: U of Texas P, 1981.

Baker, Keith. 'Reporting the Conflict' in McLoone, ed. 118-126.

Balibar, Etienne and Immanuel Wallerstein. *Race, Nation, Class: Ambiguous Identities*. London: Verso, 1991.

Ballard, J.G. 'Fictions of Every Kind'. Vale, V. and Andrea Jono eds. *Re/Search* 8-9. A Special Issue on J.G Ballard. 1984. 98-100.

——. 'Introduction'. *Crash*. London: Paladin, 1990.

Bardon, Jonathan and David Burnett. *Belfast: A Pocket History*. Belfast: The Blackstaff P, 1996.

Barthes, Roland. *Writing Degree Zero*. Trans. Annette Lavers and Colin Smyth. New York: Hill and Wang, 1967.

——. *The Pleasure of the Text*. Trans. Richard Miller. London: Jonathan Cape, 1976.

——. 'Semiology and the Urban' in Gottdiener and Lagopoulos, eds. 1986. 87-98.

——. 'From Work to Text' in Rick Rylance, ed. *Debating Texts*. Milton Keynes: Open UP, 1987. 117-122.

——. *S/Z*. Trans. Richard Miller. Oxford: Basil Blackwell, 1990. (1975).

——. 'The Reality Effect' in Furst, ed. 1992. 135-141.

——. *Mythologies*. Trans. Annette Lavers. London: Vintage, 1993. (1957).

Barrett, Michele. *Women's Oppression Today*. London: NLB, 1980.

Baudrillard, Jean. *The Mirror of Production*. Trans. Mark Poster. St Louis: Telos, 1975.

——. *Selected Writings*. Ed. Mark Poster. Cambridge: Polity P, 1988.

——. *Simulations*. trans. Paul Foss et al. New York: Semiotext(e), 1983.

Beckett, J.C. and R.E. Glasscock, eds. *Belfast: The Origin and Growth of An Industrial City*. London: B.B.C., 1967.

Bell, Daniel. *The End of Ideology*. Cambridge, Massachusetts: Harvard U P, 1988.

Bell, Ian A. ed. *Peripheral Visions: Images of Nationhood in Contemporary British Fiction*. Cardiff: U of Wales P, 1995.

Bell, Ian A. and Graham Daldry, eds. *Watching the Detectives: Essays on Crime Fiction*. London: Macmillan, 1990.

Bell, J. Bowyer. 'The Chroniclers of Violence: The Troubles in Northern Ireland Interpreted'. *Éire-Ireland* 7 ; 1. 1972. 28-38.

——. 'The Troubles As Trash'. *Hibernia* 20 Jan 1978. 22.

——. *The Secret Army: The IRA 1916-1979*. Swords: Poolbeg, 1990.

Belsey, Catherine. 'Deconstructing the Text: Sherlock Holmes' in Bennett, ed. 1990. 277-285.

Bender, Barbara. 'Introduction' to Bender, ed. *Landscape: Politics and Perspectives*. Oxford: Berg, 1993. 1-17.

Benjamin, Walter. *Gesammelte Schriften*. 7 Vols. Ed. Rolf Tiedemann and Hermann Schweppenhaueser. Frankfurt: Suhrkamp Verlag, 1972-89.

——. *Charles Baudelaire: A Lyric Poet in the Era of High Capitalism*. Trans. Harry Zorn. London: New Left Books, 1973.

——. *The Origin of German Tragic Drama*. Trans. John Osborne. Intro. George Steiner. London: NLB, 1977.

——. *Understanding Brecht*. Trans. Anna Bostock. Intro. Stanley Mitchell. London: Verso, 1983.

——. 'Central Park'. Trans. Lloyd Spencer. *New German Critique* 34. 1985. 32-58.

——. *Illuminations*. Ed. and intro. Hannah Arendt. Trans. Harry Zorn. London: Fontana, 1992a.

— . *One-Way Street and Other Writings*. Intro. Susan Sontag. Trans. Edmund Jephcott and Kingsley Shorter. London: Verso, 1992b.

— . *The Arcades Project*. Trans. Howard Eiland and Kevin McLaughlin. London: Belknap P of Harvard U P, 1999.

Bennett, Ronan. 'An Irish Answer'. *The Guardian*. 16 July 1994. 6.

Bennett, Tony. *Formalism and Marxism*. London: Methuen, 1979.

— . 'Introduction: Detective Fiction' in Bennett, ed. 1990. 211-219.

— . 'Introduction: Fictioning the Nation' in Bennett, ed. 1990. 61-68.

— . 'Introduction: Popular Fictions and Cultural Technologies' in Bennett, ed. 1990. 3-8.

— . 'Marxism and Popular Fiction' in Humm et al, eds. 237-265.

— , ed. *Popular Fiction: Technology, Ideology, Production, Reading*. London: Routledge, 1990.

— . *Culture: A Reformer's Science*. London: SAGE, 1998.

Bennett, Tony, Mercer, Colin and Janet Woollacott, eds. *Popular Culture and Social Relations*. Milton Keynes: Open U P, 1986.

Bennett, Tony and Janet Woollacott. *Bond and Beyond: The Political Career of a Popular Hero*. London: Macmillan, 1987.

Beresford Ellis, Peter. *A History of the Irish Working Class*. London: Pluto P, 1985.

Berger, Arthur Asa. *Popular Culture Genres: Theories and Texts*. London: SAGE, 1992.

Berger, Maurice. 'Visual Terrorism' in David Brown and Robert Merill, eds. *Violent Persuasions: the Politics and Imagery of Terrorism*. Washington: Bay P, 1993. 17-46.

Berman, Marshall. *All That is Solid Melts into Air: The Experience of Modernity*. London: Verso, 1983.

Bew, Paul. *Ideology and the Irish Question: Ulster Unionism and Irish Nationalism 1912-1916*. Oxford: Clarendon P, 1994.

Bew, Paul and Henry Patterson. *The British State and the Ulster Crisis: From Wilson to Thatcher*. London: Verso, 1990.

Bew, Paul, Peter Gibbon and Henry Patterson. *Northern Ireland 1921-1996: Political Forces and Social Classes*. London: Serif, 1996.

Bhabha, Homi K. ed. and intro. *Nation and Narration*. London: Routledge, 1990.

— . *The Location of Culture*. London: Routledge, 1994.

— . 'In a Spirit of Calm Violence' in Prakash, ed. 1995. 326-343.

Bishop, Patrick and Eamonn Mallie. *The Provisional IRA*. London: Heinemann, 1987.

Black, Joel. *The Aesthetics of Murder: A Study in Romantic Literature and Contemporary Culture*. London: The Johns Hopkins U P, 1991.

Bloom, Clive. 'Introduction: The Spy Thriller: A Genre Under Cover?' in Bloom, ed. 1990a. 1-11.

—, ed. *Spy Thrillers: From Buchan to le Carré*. London: Macmillan, 1990a.

—, ed. *Twentieth-Century Suspense: The Thriller Comes of Age*. London: Macmillan, 1990b.

— . *Cult Fiction: Popular Reading and Pulp Theory*. London: Macmillan, 1996.

Boal, Frederick W. 'Segregating and Mixing: Space and Residence in Belfast' in Boal, Frederick W. and Neville H. Douglas eds. *Integration and Division: Geographical Perspectives on the Northern Ireland Problem*. London: Academic P, 1982. 249-280.

Bolger, Dermot. 'Introduction' in Bolger, ed. *The Picador Book of Irish Contemporary Fiction*. London: Pan, 1993. vii-xxvi.

Bolger, Stephen Garrett. *The Irish Character in American Fiction, 1830-1860*. New York: Arno P, 1976.

Bonner, David. 'The United Kingdom's Response to Terrorism'. *Terrorism and Political Violence* 4 ; 4. Winter 1992.

Bouché, Elizabeth. 'No Big Thrill'. *Fortnight*. 312. Dec 1992. 46.

Boyce, George. 'Northern Ireland: A Place Apart?' in Hughes, ed. 13-26.

Boyd, Andrew. *The Rise of the Irish Trade Unions*. Belfast: Anvil, 1985.

Bradbury, Richard. 'Reading John le Carré' in Bloom, ed. 1990a. 130-139.

Brand, Dana. 'From the *Flâneur* to the Detective: Interpreting the City of Poe' in Bennett, 1990. 220-237.

Brecht, Bertold. 'Über die Popularität des Kriminalromans'. *Gesammelte Werke Vol.19. Schriften zur Literatur und Kunst*. Frankfurt am Main: Suhrkamp Verlag, 1967. 450-458.

Breen, Jon L. and Martin H. Greenberg, eds. *Synod of Sleuths: Essays on Judeo-Christian Detective Fiction*. London: The Scarecrow P, 1990.

Breuilly, John. *Nationalism and the State*. Manchester: Manchester U P, 1985.

Brienzo, Gary. 'Belfast: Bernard MacLaverty's Heart of Darkness' in Preston and Simpson Housley, eds. 17-28.

Brittan, Arthur. *The Privatised World*. London: Routledge and Kegan Paul, 1977.

Brod, Harry and Michael Kaufman, eds. *Theorizing Masculinites*. London: SAGE, 1994.

Bromley, Peter. 'The Gentry, Bourgeois Hegemony and Popular Fiction: *Rebecca* and *Rogue Male*' in Humm et al, eds. 151-172.

— . 'Rewriting the Masculine Script: The Novels of Joseph Hansen' in Longhurst, ed. 102-117.

Brooks, Peter. *Reading For the Plot: Design and Intention in Narrative*. London: Harvard U P, 1992.

Brown, Stephen. 'Crisis-Response and Retail Change in Belfast City Centre'. *Irish Geography* 19, 1986. 83-91.

Brown, Terence. 'Normalcy in Belfast'. *Irish Literary Supplement*. Fall, 1985. 7.

— . *Ireland's Literature: Selected Essays*. Gigginstown: The Lilliput P, 1988.

Brown, Joseph. 'The Literature of Violence: The Writer and Northern Ireland' in Sullivan and Wilson, eds. 154-168.

Brownmiller, Susan. *Against our Will: Men, Women and Rape*. London: Penguin, 1975.

Bruce, Steve. 'The Problem of "Pro-State" Terrorism: Loyalist Paramilitaries in Northern Ireland'. *Terrorism and Political Violence* 4; 1. Spring 1992a. 67-88.

— . *The Red Hand: Protestant Paramilitaries in Northern Ireland*. Oxford: Oxford U P, 1992b.

— . 'Loyalists in Northern Ireland: Further Thoughts on Pro-State Terror'. *Terrorism and Political Violence* 5; 4. Winter 1993. 252-265.

— . *The Edge of the Union: The Ulster Loyalist Political Vision*. Oxford: Oxford U P, 1994.

Buci-Glucksmann, Christine. 'State, Transition and Passive Revolution' in Mouffe, ed. 207-236.

Buckley, Anthony D. ed. *Symbols in Northern Ireland*. Belfast: Institute for Irish Studies, 1998.

Buckley, Marella. 'Sitting on Your Politics: The Irish Among the British and the Women Among the Irish' in MacLaughlin, ed. 94-133.

Buck-Morss, Susan. *The Origin of Negative Dialectics: Theodor Adorno, Walter Benjamin, and the Frankfurt Institute*. Hassocks, Sussex: The Harvester P, 1977.

— . *The Dialectics of Seeing: Walter Benjamin and the Arcades Project*. London: The MIT P, 1990.

— . 'Aesthetics and Anaesthetics: Walter Benjamin's Artwork Essay Reconsidered'. *October* 62, Fall 1992. 3-41

— . 'The City as Dreamworld and Catastrophe'. *October* 73, Summer 1995. 3-26.

Burnham, Clint. *The Jamesonian Unconscious: The Aesthetics of Marxist Theory*. London: Duke U P, 1995.

Burton, Frank. *The Politics of Legitimacy: Struggles in a Belfast Community*. London: Routledge and Kegan Paul, 1978.

Butler, David. 'The Trouble with Reporting Northern Ireland' in McLoone, ed. 127-135.

Byrne, Anne and Madeleine Leonard, eds. *Women and Irish Nationalism: A Sociological Reader*. Belfast: Beyond the Pale Publications, 1997.

Byrne, Sean. 'Conflict Regulation or Conflict Resolution: Third Party Intervention in the Northern Ireland Conflict – Prospects for Peace'. *Terrorism and Political Violence*. 7; 2 Summer 1995. 1-24.

Cahalan, James. *Great Hatred, Little Room: The Irish Historical Novel*. Dublin: Gill and Macmillan, 1983.

— . *The Irish Novel: A Critical History*. Dublin: Gill and Macmillan, 1988.

Cairns, David and Shaun Richards. "Woman' in the Discourse of Celticism: A Reading of *The Shadow of the Glen*.' *Canadian Journal of Irish Studies* 13; 1. 1987. 43-60.

— . *Writing Ireland: Colonialism, Nationalism and Culture*. Manchester: Manchester U P, 1988.

Cairns, Ed. *Caught in the Crossfire: Children and the Northern Ireland Conflict*. Belfast: The Appletree P, 1987.

Callinicos, Alex. *Against Postmodernism: A Marxist Critique*. Oxford: Polity P, 1992.

Campbell, Sue Ellen. 'The Detective Heroine and the Death of Her Hero'. *Modern Fiction Studies*. 29; 3. Autumn 1983. 497-510.

Cannadine, David. 'The Context, Performance and Meaning of Ritual: The British Monarchy and the 'Invention of Tradition', c. 1820-1977'. *Rituals of Royalty, Power and Ceremonial*. Cambridge: Cambridge U P, 1987. 100-165.

— . *Class in Britain*. London: Yale U P, 1998a.

— . *History in Our Time*. London: Yale U P, 1998b.

— . *The Decline and Fall of the British Aristocracy*. London: Yale U P, 1990.

— . *Aspects of Aristocracy: Grandeur and Decline in Modern Britain*. London: Yale U P, 1994.

Canaan, Joyce E. 'One Thing Leads to Another: Drinking, Fighting and Working-Class Masculinities' in Mac an Ghaill, ed. 114-125.

Carlton, David and Carlo Schaerf, eds. *Contemporary Terror: Studies in Sub-State Violence*. London: Macmillan, 1981.

Carter, Erica et al, eds. *Space and Place: Theories of Identity and Location*. London: Lawrence and Wishart, 1993.

Casey, John. 'One Nation: The Politics of Race'. *The Salisbury Review* 1; 1. Autumn 1982. 23-28.

Castells, Manuel. *The Urban Question: A Marxist Approach*. London: Edward Arnold, 1977.

— . 'European Cities, the Informational Society, and the Global Economy'. *New Left Review* 204. Mar / April 1994. 18-32.

Cawelti, John G. *Adventure, Mystery, and Romance: Formula Stories as Art and Popular Culture*. London: U of Chicago P, 1976.

Cerasini, Mark A. 'Tom Clancy's Fiction: The Birth of the Techno-Thriller' in Greenberg, ed. 5-55.

Chalk, Peter. 'The Liberal Democratic Response to Terrorism'. *Terrorism and Political Violence* 7; 4. Winter 1995. 10-44.

Chandler, Raymond. 'The Simple Art of Murder' (1944) in *Pearls Are a Nuisance*. Harmondsworth: Penguin, 1973. 181-199.

Chapman, Rowena and Jonathan Rutherford, eds. *Male Order: Unwrapping Masculinity*. London: Lawrence and Wishart, 1988.

Cheng, Vincent J. *Joyce, Race, and Empire*. Cambridge: Cambridge U P, 1995.

Chibnall, Steve and Robert Murphy, eds. *British Crime Cinema*. London: Routledge, 1999.

Ching-Liang Low, Gail. *White Skins / Black Masks: Representation and Colonialism*. London: Routledge, 1996.

Choay, Françoise. 'Urbanism and Semiology' in Gottdiemer and Lagopoulos, eds. 160-175.

Clarke, David B. *The Cinematic City*. London: Routledge, 1997.

Clayton, Pamela. *Enemies and Passing Friends: Settler Ideologies in Twentieth Century Ulster*. London: Pluto P, 1996.

Cleary, Joe. '"Fork-Tongued on the Border Bit": Partition and the Politics of Form in Contemporary Narratives of the Northern Irish Conflict'. *South Atlantic Quarterly* 95; 1. 1996. 227-276.

— . 'Domestic Troubles: Tragedy and the Northern Ireland Conflict'. *South Atlantic Quarterly* 98; 3. 1999. 501-537.

Cochrane, Fergal. 'Any Takers ? The Isolation of Northern Ireland'. *Political Studies* XLII 1994. 378-395.

— . *Unionist Politics and the Politics of Unionism Since the Anglo-Irish Agreement*. Cork: Cork U P, 1997.

Cohen, Philip. 'The Perversions of Inheritance' in Philip Cohen and Harwant S. Bains, eds. *Multi-Racist Britain*. Houndmills: Macmillan, 1988. 1-18.

Cohen-Almagor, Raphael. 'Liberalism and the Limits of Pluralism'. *Terrorism and Political Violence* 7; 2. Summer 1995. 25-48.

Cohen, Steven and Ina Rae Hark, eds. *Screening the Male: Exploring Masculinities in Hollywood Cinema*. London: Routledge, 1993.

Collins, Jim. *Uncommon Cultures: Popular Culture and Post-Modernism*. London: Routledge, 1989.

Collins, Timothy ed. *Decoding the Landscape*. London: Centre for Landscape Studies, 1994.

Collinson, David and Jeff Hearn. '"Men at Work": Multiple Masculinities / Multiple Workplaces' in Mac an Ghaill, ed. 61-76.

Connolly, James. *Selected Writings*. Ed. and intro. Peter Beresford Ellis. London: Pelican, 1981.

Copjec, Joan. 'Introduction' in Copjec, ed. 1993. vii-xii.

— . 'The Phenomenal Nonphenomenal: Private Space in *Film Noir*' in Copjec, ed. 167-197.

—, ed. *Shades of Noir: A Reader*. London: Verso, 1993.

Corcoran, Clodagh. *Pornography: The New Terrorism*. Dublin: Attic P, 1989.

Cornell, Jennifer C. '"The Other Community": Northern Ireland in British Television'. *New Hibernica Review* 1; 2. Summer 1997. 37-47.

Cornell, Neil. *The Literary Fantastic: From Gothic to Postmodernism*. London: Harvester Wheatsheaf, 1990.

Coulter, Carol. *Ireland: Between the First and the Third Worlds*. Dublin: Attic P, 1990.

— . *The Hidden Tradition: Feminism, Women and Nationalism in Ireland*. Cork: Cork U P, 1993.

— . 'Feminism and Nationalism in Ireland' in Miller, ed. 1998. 160-178.

Coulter, Colin. 'Class, Ethnicity and Political Identity in Northern Ireland'. *Irish Journal of Sociology* 4. 1994. 1-26.

— . 'Direct Rule and the Unionist Middle Classes' in English and Walker, eds. 1996. 169-191.

Coward, Rosalind. *Female Desire: Women's Sexuality Today*. London: Paladin, 1984.

Coward, Rosalind and Linda Semple. 'Tracking Down the Past: Women and Detective Fiction'. Helen Carr, ed. *From My Guy to Sci-Fi: Genre and Women's Writing in the Postmodern World*. London: Pandora P, 1989. 39-57.

Cowie, Elizabeth. '*Film Noir* and Women' in Copjec, ed. 1993. 121-165.

Cowling, Mark and Lawrence Wilde, eds. *Approaches to Marx*. Milton Keynes: Open U P, 1989.

Cowling, Maurice, ed. *Conservative Essays*. London: Cassell, 1978.

Craig, Cairns. *Out of History: Narrative Paradigms in Scottish and English Culture*. Edinburgh: Polygon, 1996.

Craig, Patricia. 'Introduction' to Patricia Craig, ed. *The Rattle of the North: An Anthology of Ulster Prose*. Belfast: The Blackstaff P, 1992. 1-12.

— . 'Introduction' to Craig, ed. *The Belfast Anthology*. Belfast: The Blackstaff P, 1999. vii-xvii.

Craig, Patricia and Mary Cadogan. *The Lady Investigates: Women Detectives and Spies in Fiction*. London: Victor Gollancz, 1981.

Cranny-Francis, Anne. 'Gender and Genre: Feminist Rewritings of Detective Fiction'. *Women's Studies International Forum*. 11; 1. 1988. 69-84.

— . *Feminist Fiction*. Cambridge: Polity P, 1990.

Crawford, Colin. *Defenders or Criminals? Loyalist Prisoners and Criminalisation*. Belfast: The Blackstaff P, 1999.

Crawford, Mairtín, ed. *Green Screen: The State of the Contemporary Irish Film Industry*. Supplement to *Fortnight* 379. June 1999.

Cresap, Steven. 'Sublime Politics: On the Uses of an Aesthetics of Terror'. *CLIO* 19; 2. 1990. 111-125.

Crick, Bernard. 'A Tale of Four Nations'. *Chapman* 67 Winter 1991-1992. 17-21.

Cronin, John. 'Ulster's Alarming Novels'. *Éire-Ireland* 4; 4. 1969. 27-34.

Crowley, Tony. 'Bakhtin and the History of Language' in Hirschkop and Shepherd, eds. 1989. 68-90.

— . *Language in History: Theories and Texts*. London: Routledge, 1996.

Cunningham, Francie. 'Writing in the Rag and Bone Shop of the Troubles'. *The Sunday Business Post* 11 Sept 1994. 26.

Curran, Joseph M. *Hibernian Green on the Silver Screen: The Irish and American Movies*. London: Greenwood P, 1989.

Curtin, Chris, Pauline Jackson and Barbara O'Connor, eds. *Gender in Irish Society*. Galway: Galway U P, 1987.

Curtin, Chris, Hastings Donnan and Thomas M. Wilson, eds. *Irish Urban Cultures*. Belfast: QUB, 1993.

Curtis, L.P. Jr. *Anglo-Saxons and Celts: A Study of Anti-Irish Prejudice in Victorian England*. Bridgeport, Connecticut: Conference on British Studies, 1968.

Curtis, Liz. *Ireland: The Propaganda War, The British Media and the 'Battle for Hearts and Minds'*. London: Pluto P, 1984a.

— . *Nothing but the Same Old Story: The Roots of Anti-Irish Racism*. London: Information on Ireland, 1984b.

— . 'Reporting Republican Violence' in Rolston and Miller, 1996. 309-328.

Cusack, Jim and Henry McDonald. *UVF*. Dublin: Poolbeg P, 1997.

Cusack, Jim and Max Taylor. 'The Resurgence of a Terrorist Organization: Part 1: The UDA, A Case Study'. *Terrorism and Political Violence* 5; 3 Autumn 1993. 1-27.

Davies, Tony. 'The Divided Gaze: Reflections on the Political Thriller' in Longhurst, ed. 1989. 118-135.

Davis, Brian. *The Thriller: The Suspense Film from 1946*. London: Studio Vista, 1973.

Davis, Mike. *City of Quartz: Excavating the Future in Los Angeles*. London: Verso, 1990.

Dawe, Gerald. *The Rest is History*. Newry: Abbey P, 1998.

Dawe, Gerald and Edna Longley eds. *Across a Roaring Hill: The Protestant Imagination in Modern Ireland. Essays in Honour of John Hewitt*. Belfast: The Blackstaff P, 1985.

Dawson, G.M. 'Defensive Planning in Belfast'. *Irish Geography* 17, 1984. 27-41.

Deane, Seamus. *Civilians and Barbarians*. Derry: Field Day, 1983.

——. *Heroic Styles: The Tradition of an Idea*. Derry: Field Day, 1984a.

——. 'Remembering the Irish Future'. *Crane Bag* 3; 1, 1984b. 81-92.

——. *Celtic Revivals: Essays in Modern Irish Literature 1880-1980*. London: Faber, 1985.

——. 'Introduction' to Terry Eagleton et al. *Nationalism, Colonialism and Literature*. Minneapolis: U of Minnesota P, 1990. 3-19.

——. 'General Introduction' to *The Field Day Anthology of Irish Writing*. Derry: Field Day, 1991. xix-xxvi.

——. 'Political Writings and Speeches 1900-1988' in *The Field Day Anthology* 3. 1991. 681-685.

——. *Strange Country: Modernity and Nationhood in Irish Writing since 1790*. Oxford: Clarendon P, 1997.

Debord, Guy. *Comments on the Society of the Spectacle*. Trans. Malcolm Imrie. London: Verso, 1990.

De Certeau, Michel. 'Practices of Spaces' in Marshall Blonsky, ed. *On Signs*. Oxford: Basil Blackwell, 1985. 122-145.

Deleuze, Gilles and Felix Guattari. *Anti-Oedipus*. Trans. R. Hurley et al. Intro. Michel Foucault. London: Athlone P, 1984.

——. *Kafka: Toward a Minor Literature*. Trans. Dana Polan. Minneapolis: U of Minneapolis P, 1986.

——. *A Thousand Plateaus*. Trans. and intro. Brian Massumi. London: Athlone P, 1988.

Denning, Michael. 'Licensed to Look: James Bond and the Heroism of Consumption' in Francis Mulhern, ed. and intro. *Contemporary Marxist Literary Criticism*. London: Longman, 1992. 211-229.

Deutsch, Karl W. *Nationalism and Social Communication: An Inquiry into the Foundations of Nationality*. Second Edition. Cambridge: MIT P, 1975.

Deutsch, Richard. '"Within Two Shadows": The Troubles in Ireland' in Patrick Rafroidi and Maurice Harmon, eds. *The Irish Novel in Our Time*. Lille: Lille U P, 1976. 131-154.

——. 'Fiction du Nord, Ou: Les Heroes sont Fatigues'. *Études Irlandaises* 8. Dec 1983. 380-381.

——. 'Au Nord, Rien du Nouveau'. *Études Irlandaises* 10. Dec 1985. 333-334.

——. 'Le Noir Sied à L'Ulster'. *Études Irlandaises* 11. 1986. 248-249.

Devlin, Paddy. *Yes We Have No Bananas: Outdoor Relief in Belfast 1920-39*. Belfast: The Blackstaff P, 1981.

Dibdin, Michael, ed. *The Picador Book of Crime Writing*. London: Picador, 1994.

Dilley, Kimberly J. *Busybodies, Meddlers, and Snoops: The Female Hero in Contemporary Women's Mysteries*. London: Greenwood P, 1998.

Dillon, Martin. *The Dirty War*. London: Hutchinson, 1988.

——. *The Shankill Butchers: A Case Study of Mass Murder*. London: Arrow, 1990.

——. *God and the Gun: The Church and Irish Terrorism*. London: Orion, 1997.

Doane, Mary Ann. 'Subjectivity and Desire: An(other) Way of Looking' in Easthope, ed. 1993. 162-178.

Docherty, Brian, ed. *American Crime Fiction: Studies in the Genre*. London: Macmillan, 1988.

Docker, John. *Postmodernism and Popular Culture*. Cambridge: Cambridge U P, 1994.

Doherty, Paul. 'Socio-Spatial Change in the Belfast Urban Area'. *Irish Geography* 21, 1988. 11-19.

Donovan, Stewart. 'Song and Suffering: A Survey of the Literature of the Northern Irish Conflict, 1969-89'. *Antigonish Review* 80. 1990. 145-161.

Doyle, David Noel and Owen Dudley Edwards, eds. *America and Ireland, 1776-1976: The American Identity and the Irish Connection*. London: Greenwood P, 1980.

Dunn, Seamus ed. *Facets of the Conflict in Northern Ireland*. London: Macmillan, 1995.

During, Simon. 'Literature: Nationalism's Other? The Case for Revision' in Bhabha, ed. 138-153.

Duytschaever, Joris and Geert Lernout eds. *History and Violence in Anglo-Irish Literature*. Amsterdam: Rodopi, 1988.

Dyer, Richard. 'Don't Look Now: The Male Pin-Up' in *Screen Reader*, 1992. 265-276.

Eagleton, Terry. *Criticism and Ideology: A Study in Marxist Literary Theory*. London: Verso, 1976.

— . *The Function of Criticism: From The Spectator to Post-Structuralism*. London: Verso, 1984.

— . *Nationalism, Irony and Commitment*. Derry: Field Day, 1988.

— , ed. *Raymond Williams: Critical Perspectives*. Cambridge: Polity P, 1989.

— . *The Ideology of the Aesthetic*. Oxford: Basil Blackwell, 1990.

— . *Heathcliff and the Great Hunger: Studies in Irish Culture*. London: Verso, 1995.

— . *The Illusions of Postmodernism*. Oxford: Blackwell, 1996.

— . 'The Ideology of Irish Studies'. *Bullán: An Irish Studies Journal*. 3; 1. Spring 1997. 5-14.

— . *Crazy John and the Bishop and Other Essays on Irish Culture*. Cork: Cork U P, 1998.

Easthope, Antony, ed. *Contemporary Film Theory*. London: Longmann, 1993.

Eco, Umbero. *The Role of the Reader: Explorations in the Semiotics of Texts*. London: Indiana U P, 1979.

Edgar, David. 'The Free and the Good' in Levitas, ed. 55-79.

Edge, Sarah. 'Representing Gender and National Identity' in Miller, ed. 1998. 211-227.

— . 'Feisty Colleens or Mother Ireland: Representations of Women in Irish Cinema' in Crawford, ed. *Fortnight* Supplement. 8-10.

Edley, Nigel and Margaret Wetherell. 'Masculinity, Power and Identity' in Mac an Ghaill, ed. 97-113.

English, Richard. '"Cultural Traditions" and Political Ambiguity'. *The Irish Review* 15. Spring 1994. 97-106.

English, Richard and Graham Walker, eds. *Unionism in Modern Ireland: New Perspectives on Politics and Culture*. Dublin: Gill and Macmillan, 1996.

Espey, David B. 'Imperialism and the Image of the White Hunter'. *Research Studies* 46; 1. March 1978. 12-19.

Eubank, William Lee. 'Does Democracy Encourage Terrorism?'. *Terrorism and Political Violence* 6; 4 Winter 1994. 417-434.

Evans, Eric J. *Thatcher and Thatcherism*. London: Routledge, 1997.

Evans, Geoffrey and Mary Duffy. 'Beyond the Sectarian Divide: The Social Bases and Political Consequences of Nationalist and Unionist Party Competition in Northern Ireland'. *British Journal of Political Science* 27. 1997. 47-81.

Evason, Eileen. *Against the Grain: The Contemporary Women's Movement in Northern Ireland*. Dublin: Attic P, 1991.

Eyler, Audrey S. and Robert F. Garratt. 'Preface' in Eyler and Garrat, eds. *The Uses of the Past: Essays on Irish Culture*. London: Associated U P, 1988. 7-9.

Fanning, Charles. *The Irish Voice in America: Irish-American Fiction from the 1760s to the 1980s*. Lexington: U of Kentucky P, 1990.

Farrell, Michael. *The Apparatus of Repression*. Derry: Field Day, 1986.

Feldmann, Allen. *Formations of Violence: The Narrative of the Body and Political Terror in Northern Ireland*. London: U of Chicago P, 1991.

Fennell, Desmond. *The Revision of Irish Nationalism*. Dublin: Open Air, 1989.

— . 'The Recent Birth and Checkered Career of "Rural Ireland"'. *New Hibernica Review* 1; 4. Winter 1997. 9-18.

Fentress, James. 'On the Good Use of Murder: Terrorism as a Social Identity'. *New Formations* 30. 1996-1997. 106-121.

Fine, Bob et al eds. *Capitalism and the Rule of Law: From Deviancy Theory to Marxism*. London: Hutchinson, 1979.

Fine, Bob and Robert Millar, eds. *Policing the Miners' Strike*. London: Lawrence and Wishart, 1985.

Finlayson, Alan. *Political Ideology and the Mythic Discourse of Nationalism*. Ph.D. Thesis, Queen's University Belfast, 1996.

— . 'Discourse and Contemporary Loyalist Identity' in Shirlow and McGovern, eds. 1997a. 72-94.

— . 'The Problem of "Culture" in Northern Ireland: A Critique of the Cultural Traditions Group'. *The Irish Review*. 20. Winter/Spring 1997b. 76-88.

Fisher, Paul. 'Zooming in on Danger Zones'. *The Guardian* 12 Jan 1995. G2. 24.

Fiske, John. *Reading the Popular*. London: Routledge, 1990.

Flanagan, Deidre. 'Belfast and the Place-Names Therein'. Trans. A.J. Hughes. *Ulster Folklife* 38. 1992. 79-97.

Flannigan-Saint-Aubin, Arthur. 'The Male Body and Literary Metaphors for Masculinity' in Brod and Kaufman, eds. 1994. 239-258.

Fleetwood, John. *The Irish Body Snatchers: A History of Body Snatching in Ireland*. Dublin: Tomar, 1988.

Foster, Hal. 'Armor Fou'. *October* 57, 1991. 65-98.

Foster, John Wilson. *Forces and Themes in Ulster Fiction*. Dublin: Gill and Macmillan, 1974.

— . *Colonial Consequences: Essays in Irish Literature and Culture*. Dublin: The Lilliput P, 1991.

Foucault, Michel. *The Archaeology of Knowledge*. London: Tavistock, 1972.

— . *Language, Counter-Memory, Practice: Selected Essays and Interviews*. Ed. and intro. Donald F. Bouchard. Trans. Donald F. Bouchard and Sherry Simon. Oxford: Basil Blackwell, 1977.

— . *Power / Knowledge: Selected Interviews and Other Writings, 1972-1977*. Ed. Colin Gordon. Trans Colin Gordon, John Mepham and Kate Soper. Brighton: Harvester Wheatsheaf, 1980.

— . *The History of Sexuality Volume One: An Introduction*. Trans. Robert Hurley. London: Penguin, 1990.

— . *Discipline and Punish: The Birth of the Prison*. Trans. Alan Sheridan. London: Penguin, 1991.

— . *The Use of Pleasure: The History of Sexuality Volume Two*. Trans. Robert Hurley. London: Penguin, 1992.

Fowler, Douglas. 'The Pleasures of Terror'. *Extrapolation* 28; 1. 1987. 75-86.

Franco, Jean. 'The Nation as Imagined Community' in H. Aram Veeser, ed. *The New Historicism*. London: Routledge, 1989.

Freud, Sigmund. *Beyond the Pleasure Principle. The Standard Edition of the Complete Psychological Works of Sigmund Freud Vol.18*. ed. James Strachey. London: Hogarth P, 1953-74.

— . *The Interpretation of Dreams. The Pelican Freud Library: Volume Four*. Trans. James Strachey. Ed. James Strachey and Alan Tyson. London: Pelican, 1976.

— . *On Sexuality: Three Essays in the Theory of Sexuality, and Other Works*. ed. Angela Richards. London: Penguin, 1984.

— . 'The Uncanny'. *Art and Literature: Jensen's 'Godiva', Leonardo da Vinci and Other Works. The Penguin Freud Library Vol. 14*. Trans. James Starkey. Ed. Albert Dickson. London: Penguin, 1990. 335-376.

Furst, Lillian R. ed. *Realism*. London: Longman, 1992.

Gaffikin, Frank and Mike Morrissey. *Northern Ireland: The Thatcher Years*. London: Zed Books, 1990.

—, eds. *City Visions: Imagining Place, Enfranchising People*. London: Pluto P, 1999.

Gamble, Andrew. 'Economic Decline and the Crisis of Legitimacy' in Graham and Prosser, eds. 22-35.

— . *The Free Economy and the Strong State*. Second Edition. London: Macmillan, 1994.

Gardiner, Judith Kegan. 'Mind Mother: Psychoanalysis and Feminism' in Greene and Kahn, eds. 113-145.

Garvin, Tom. 'The Return of History: Collective Myths and Modern Nationalisms'. *The Irish Review* 9, Autumn 1990. 16-30.

Geary, Ray and John Morrison. 'An Illustration of the Literary Approach to the Study of Law: The "Mysteries" Novel of the Nineteenth Century and the "Troubles" Thriller' in Norma Dawson et al, eds. *One Hundred and Fifty Years of Irish Law*. Belfast: SLS Legal Publications, 1996. 105-123.

Geddes, Patrick. 'Civics: as Applied Sociology' in Hellen E. Meller, ed. *The Ideal City*. Leicester: Leicester U P, 1979. 75-183.

Gellner, Ernst. *Nations and Nationalism*. Oxford: Basil Blackwell, 1983.

Geoghegan, Vincent. *Utopianism and Marxism*. London: Methuen, 1987.

Geraghty, Tony. *Who Dares Wins: The Story of the Special Air Service 1950-1980*. London: Arms and Armour P, 1980.

Gibbons, Luke. 'Framing History: Neil Jordan's *Michael Collins*'. *History Ireland* 5; 1. Spring 1997. 47-51.

— . 'Coming Out of Hibernation? The Myth of Modernity in Irish Culture' in Richard Kearney, ed. *Across the Frontiers: Ireland in the 1990s*. Dublin: Wolfhound P, 1988a. 205-218.

— . 'Romanticism, Realism and Irish Cinema' in Rockett, Gibbons and Hill, eds. 1998b.194-257.

— . *Transformations in Irish Culture*. Cork: Cork U P, 1996.

Gilbert, Michael. *Crime in Good Company*. London: Constable, 1959.

Gilbert, Paul. *Terrorism, Security and Nationality: An International Study in Applied Political Philosophy*. London: Routledge, 1994.

Gilbert, Sandra M. and Susan Gubar. *No Man's Land: The Place of the Woman Writer in the Twentieth Century. Vol.1. The War of the Words*. London: Yale U P1988.

— . *Vol.2 Sexchanges*. London: Yale U P, 1989.

— . *Vol.3 Letters from the Front*. London: Yale U P,1994.

Gilley, Sheridan. 'English Attitudes to the Irish in England 1789-1900' in Colin Holmes, ed. *Immigrants and Minorities in British Society*. London: George Allen and Unwin, 1978. 81-110.

Gilloch, Graeme. *Myth and Metropolis: Walter Benjamin and the City*. Cambridge: Polity P, 1996.

Gilmour, Ian. *Dancing with Dogma: Britain under Thatcherism*. London: Simon and Schuster, 1992.

Ginzburg, Carlo. 'Morelli, Freud and Sherlock Holmes: Clues and Scientific Method' in Bennett, ed. 252-276.

Girard, René. *Violence and the Sacred*. Trans. Patrick Gregory. Baltimore: The Johns Hopkins U P, 1977.

Gledhill, Christine. 'Genre and Gender: The Case of Soap Opera' in Hall, ed. 1997. 337-386.

Glover, David. 'The Stuff That Dreams are Made Of: Masculinity, Femininity and the Thriller' in Longhurst, ed. 1989. 67-83.

Goldring, Maurice. *Belfast: From Loyalty to Rebellion*. London: Lawrence and Wishart, 1991.

Goodby, John, 'Bhabha, the Post / Colonial and Glenn Patterson's *Burning Your Own*'. *Irish Studies Review* 17; 1. 1999. 65-71.

Goodman, Paul. 'The Future of the Family'. *The Salisbury Review* 10; 3. Mar 1992. 15-19.

Gottdiener, M. *The Social Production of Urban Space*. Austin: U of Texas P, 1985.

— . 'Culture, Ideology, and the Sign of the City' in Gottdiener and Lagopoulos, eds. 1986. 202-218.

Gottdiener, M. and Alexandros Ph. Lagopoulos, eds. *The City and the Sign: An Introduction to Urban Semiotics*. New York: Columbia U P, 1986.

Gracey, J. and P. Howard. 'Northern Ireland Political Literature 1968-1970: A Catalogue of the Collection in the Linen Hall Library'. *Irish Booklore* 1; 1. 1971. 44-82.

Graham, Brian. 'The Imagining of Place: Representation and Identity in Contemporary Ireland' in Brian Graham, ed. 192-212.

—, ed. *In Search of Ireland: A Cultural Geography*. London: Routledge, 1997.

— . 'Ireland and Irishness: Place, Culture and Identity' in Brian Graham, ed. 1997. 1-15.

— . 'Ulster: A Representation of Place yet to be Imagined' in Shirlow and McGovern, eds. 1997. 34-54.

Graham, Colin. '"Liminal Spaces": Post-Colonial Theories and Irish Culture'. *The Irish Review*. Autumn / Winter 1994. 29-43.

— . *Ideologies of Epic: Nation, Empire and Victorian Poetry*. Manchester: Manchester U P, 1998.

— . '"Maybe That's Just Blarney": Irish Culture and the Persistence of Authenticity' in Graham and Kirkland, eds. 1999, 7-28.

Graham, Colin and Richard Kirkland, eds. *Ireland and Cultural Theory: The Mechanics of Authenticity*. London: Macmillan, 1999.

Graham, Cosmo and Tony Prosser. 'Introduction: The Constitution and the New Conservatives' in Graham and Prosser, eds. 1-21.

—, eds. *Waiving the Rules: The Constitution under Thatcherism*. Milton Keynes: Open U P, 1988.

Gramsci, Antonio. *Selections from the Prison Notebooks*. Ed. and trans. Quintin Hoare and Geoffrey Nowell Smith. London: Lawrence and Wishart, 1996. (1973).

Grant, Patrick. *Breaking Enmities: Religion, Literature and Culture in Northern Ireland, 1967-97*. New York: St. Martin's P, 1999.

Gray, Breda. '(Dis)locating "Woman" and Women in Representations of Irish National Identity' in Byrne and Leonard, eds. 1997. 517-534.

— . 'Unmasking Irishness: Irish Women, the Irish Nation and the Irish Diaspora' in MacLaughlin, ed. 1997. 209-235.

Gray, W. Russel. 'Entropy, Energy, Empathy: *Blade Runner* and Detective Fiction' in Judith B. Kerman, ed. *Retrofitting 'Blade Runner' and Philip K. Dick's 'Do Androids Dream of Electric Sheep?'*. Ohio: Bowling Green U Popular P, 1991. 66-75.

Green, Martin. *Dreams of Adventure, Deeds of Empire*. London: Routledge, 1980.

Greenberg, Martin H. 'An Interview with Tom Clancy' in Greenberg, ed. 57-86.

— , ed. *The Tom Clancy Companion*. London: Fontana, 1992.

Greene, Gayle and Coppelia Kahn. *Making A Difference: Feminist Literary Criticism*. London: Methuen, 1985.

Grimes, Larry E. 'Stepsons of Sam: Re-Visions of the Hard-Boiled Detective Formula in Recent American Fiction'. *Modern Fiction Studies*. 29; 3. Autumn 1983. 535-544.

Grossberg, Lawrence. 'On Postmodernism and Articulation: An Interview with Stuart Hall' in Morley and Chen, eds. 131-150.

Grosz, Elizabeth. *Jacques Lacan: A Feminist Introduction*. London: Routledge, 1990.

Guattari, Felix. *Molecular Revolution*. Harmondsworth: Penguin, 1984.

Guelke, Adrian. *The Age of Terrorism and the International Political System*. London: I.B. Tauris, 1995.

— . 'Paramilitiaries, Republicans and Loyalists' in Dunn ed. 114-130.

Guelke, Adrian and Jim Smyth. 'The Ballot Bomb: Terrorism and the Electoral Process in Northern Ireland'. *Terrorism and Political Violence* 4; 2. Summer 1992. 103-124.

Guetti, James. 'Aggressive Reading: Detective Fiction and Realistic Narrative' in J.K. Van Dover, ed. *The Critical Response to Raymond Chandler*. London: Greenwood P, 1995. 139-144.

Guibernau, Montserrat. *Nationalisms: The Nation-State and Nationalism in the Twentieth Century*. Cambridge: Polity P, 1996.

Gunn, Daniel. *Psychoanalysis and Fiction*. Cambridge: Cambridge U P, 1988.

Gutterman, David S. 'Postmodernism and the Interrogation of Masculinity' in Brod and Kaufman, eds. 1994. 219-238.

Hadden, Peter. *Troubled Times: The National Question in Ireland*. Belfast: Herald Books, 1995.

Hadfield, Andrew and John McVeagh, eds. *Strangers to That Land: British Perceptions of Ireland from the Reformation to the Famine*. Gerrards Cross: Colin Smythe, 1984.

Hall, Stuart. 'Notes on Deconstructing "the Popular"' in Raphael Samuel, ed. *People's History and Socialist Theory*. London: Routledge and Kegan Paul, 1981. 227-240.

— . *The Hard Road to Renewal: Thatcherism and the Crisis of the Left*. London: Verso, 1988.

— . 'Encoding, Decoding' in Simon During, ed. *The Cultural Studies Reader*. London: Routledge, 1993. 90-103.

— . 'For Allon White: Metaphors of Transformation' in Morley and Chen, eds. 1996a. 287-305.

— . 'The Meaning of New Times' in Morley and Chen, eds. 1996b. 223-237.

— , ed. *Representation: Cultural Representations and Signifying Practices*. London: SAGE, 1997.

— . 'The Work of Representation' in Hall ed. 1997. 15-74.

Hall, Stuart et al. *Policing the Crisis: Mugging, The State, and Law and Order*. London: Macmillan, 1978.

Hall, Stuart and Bram Gieben, eds. *Formations of Modernity*. Cambridge: Polity P, 1992.

Hall, Stuart, David Held and Tony McGrew, eds. *Modernity and Its Futures*. Cambridge: Polity P, 1992.

Hall, Stuart and Martin Jacques, eds. *The Politics of Thatcherism*. London: Lawrence and Wishart, 1983.

Hamilton, Cynthia S. *Western and Hard-Boiled Detective Fiction in America: From High Noon to Midnight.* London: Macmillan, 1987.

Haraway, Donna. *Simians, Cyborgs, and Women: The Reinvention of Nature.* London: Routledge, 1991.

Harmon, Maurice, ed. *The Irish Writer and the City.* Gerrards Cross: Colin Smythe, 1984.

Harris, David. *From Class Struggle to the Politics of Pleasure: The Effects of Gramscianism on Cultural Studies.* London: Routledge, 1992.

Harris, Robin, ed. *The Collected Speeches of Margaret Thatcher.* London: Harper Collins, 1997.

Harte, Liam and Michael Parker, eds. *Contemporary Irish Fiction: Themes, Tropes, Theories.* London: Macmillan, 2000.

Harvey, David. *Consciousness and the Urban Experience.* Oxford: Basil Blackwell, 1985a.

— . *The Urbanization of Capital.* Oxford: Basil Blackwell, 1985b.

— . *The Condition of Postmodernity: An Inquiry into the Origins of Cultural Change.* Oxford: Basil Blackwell, 1990.

Harvie, Christopher. 'Garron Top to Caer Gybi: Images of the Inland Sea'. *The Irish Review* 19. Spring / Summer 1996. 44-61.

Haslam, Richard. '"The Pose Arranged and Lingered Over": Visualizing the "Troubles"' in Harte and Parker, eds. 2000. 192-212.

Haut, Woody. *Pulp Culture: Hardboiled Fiction and the Cold War.* London: Serpent's Tail, 1995.

— . *Neon Noir: Contemporary American Crime Fiction.* London: Serpent's Tail, 1999.

Hawkins, Harriet. *Classics and Trash: Traditions and Taboos in High Literature and Popular Modern Genres.* London: Harvester Wheatsheaf, 1990.

Haywood, Christian and Mairtín Mac an Ghaill. 'Schooling Masculinities' in Mac an Ghaill, ed. 50-60.

Haywood, Ian. *Working-Class Fiction: From Chartism to 'Trainspotting'.* Plymouth: Northcote House, 1997.

Hazelkorn, Ellen. 'Why is There No Socialism in Ireland? Theoretical Problems of Irish Marxism'. *Science and Society* 53; 2. Summer 1989. 136-164.

Heaney, Seamus. 'Delirium of the Brave'. *The Listener* 27 Nov 1969. 757-759.

— . 'Correspondences: Emigrants and Inner Exiles' in Richard Kearney, ed. *Migrations: The Irish at Home and Abroad.* Dublin: Wolfhound P, 1990. 21-31.

Hearn, Jeff. 'Is Masculinity Dead? A Critique of the Concept of Masculinity / Masculinities' in Mac an Ghaill, ed. 202-217.

Hearn, Jeff and David L. Coliinson. 'Theorizing Unities and Differences Between Men and Between Masculinities' in Brod and Kaufman, eds. 1994. 97-118.

Hennessey, Rosemary and Rajeswari Mohan. 'The Construction of Woman in Three Popular Texts of Empire' in Williams and Chrisman, eds. 462-479.

Hepburn, A.C. *A Past Apart: Studies in the History of Catholic Belfast 1850-1950.* Belfast: Ulster Historical Society, 1996.

Heskin, Ken. *Northern Ireland: A Psychological Analysis.* Dublin: Gill and Macmillan, 1980.

Heward, Christine. 'Masculinities and Families' in Mac an Ghaill, ed. 35-49.

Higgins, Michael D. 'Culture and Exile: The Global Irish'. *New Hibernica Review* 1; 3. Fall 1997. 9-22.

Hill, John. . 'Images of Violence' in Rockett, Gibbons and Hill, eds. 1988. 147-193.

— . 'Hidden Agenda: Politics and the Thriller'. *Circa* 57, May-June, 1991. 37-41.

— . 'Allegorizing the Nation: British Gangster Films of the 1980s' in Chibnall and Murphy, eds. 1999. 160-171.

Hill-Collins, Patricia. *Black Feminist Thought: Knowledge, Consciousness and the Politics of Empowerment*. London: Harper Collins, 1990.

Foster, Hirsch. *The Dark Side of the Screen: Film Noir*. New York: Da Capo, 1981.

Hirsch, Gordon. '*Frankenstein*, Detective Fiction, and *Jekyll and Hyde*' in William Veeder and Gordon Hirsch, eds. *Dr. Jekyll and Mr. Hyde: After One Hundred Years*. London: U of Chicago P, 1988. 223-246.

Hirschkop, Ken and David Shepherd, eds. *Bakhtin and Cultural Theory*. Manchester: Manchester U P, 1989.

Hobsbawm, Eric J. 'Falklands Fallout' in Hall and Jacques, eds. 1983. 257-270.

— . *Bandits*. Harmondsworth: Penguin, 1985.

— . *Nations and Nationalism since 1780: Programme, Myth, Reality*. Cambridge: Cambridge U P, 1990.

Hoch, Paul. *White Hero Black Mask: Racism, Sexism and the Mask of Masculinity*. London: Pluto P, 1979.

Hoggart, Richard. *The Uses of Literacy: Aspects of Working-Class Life with Special Reference to Publications and Entertainments*. London: Penguin, 1991. (1957).

Holland, Jack. 'Covering the Northern Crisis: The U.S. Press and Northern Ireland' in Rolston and Miller, eds. 377-402.

Holmes, Richard. *Firing Line*. London: Jonathan Cape, 1985.

Hooks, Bell. *Yearning: Race, Gender and Cultural Politics*. London: Turnaround, 1991.

Howell, David. *A Lost Left: Three Studies in Socialism and Nationalism*. Manchester: Manchester U P, 1986.

Hubly, Erlene. 'The Formula Challenged: The Novels of P.D. James'. *Modern Fiction Studies*. 29; 3. Autumn 1983. 511-521.

Hughes, Eamonn. ''It Seems History is to Blame': *Ulysses* and Cultural History'. *Ideas and Production* 6. 1987. 100-115.

— . 'Introduction: Northern Ireland – Border Country' in Eamonn Hughes, ed. *Culture and Politics in Northern Ireland 1960-1990*. Milton Keynes: Open U P, 1991. 1-12.

— . 'Lancelot's Position: The Fiction of Irish-Britain' in A. Robert Lee, ed. *Other Britain, Other British: Contemporary Multicultural Fiction*. London: Pluto P, 1995. 142-160.

— . 'Listening and Telling'. *The Irish Review* 19, Spring/Summer 1996a. 146-151.

— . '"Town of Shadows": Representations of Belfast in Recent Fiction'. *Religion and Literature* 28; 2-3. Summer / Autumn 1996b. 141-160.

— . 'Belfastards and Derriers'. *The Irish Review*. 20. Winter/Spring 1997. 151-57.

— . ''Could Anyone Write It?': Place in Tom Paulin's Poetry' in Graham and Kirkland, eds. 1999. 162-192.

— . 'Forgeting the Future'. *The Irish Review* 25. Winter/Spring 1999-2000. 1-15.

Humm, Maggie. 'Feminist Detective Fiction' in Bloom, ed. 1990b. 237-254.

Humm, Peter and Paul Stigant. 'The Masculine Fiction of William McIlvanney' in Longhurst, ed. 1989. 84-101.

Humm, Peter et al, eds. *Popular Fictions: Essays in Literature and History*. London: Methuen, 1986.

Hutcheon, Linda. *A Poetics of Postmodernism: History, Theory, Fiction*. London: Routledge, 1988.

Hutchinson, John and Anthony D. Smith. 'Introduction' to Hutchinson and Smith, eds. *Nationalism*. Oxford: Oxford U P, 1994. 3-13.

Hutchinson, Wesley. '*Resurrection Man* d'Eoin McNamee: Decrire L'Espace de Belfast'. *Études Irlandaises* 23; 1. Spring 1998. 101-113.

Hutton, Sean and Paul Stewart, eds. *Ireland's Histories: Aspects of State, Society and Ideology*. London: Routledge, 1991.

Hutton, Will. *The State We're In*. New and Revised Edition. London: Vintage, 1996.

Ignatieff, Michael. *Blood and Belonging: Journeys in the New Nationalism*. London: Chatto and Windus, 1993.

Jackson, Rosemary. *Fantasy: The Literature of Subversion*. London: Routledge, 1988.

James, P.D. 'Murder, Mystery and Morality'. *The Salisbury Review* 9; 1. Sept 1990. 10-14.

Jameson, Frederic. 'On Raymond Chandler'. *Southern Review* 6 ; 3 1970. 624-650.

— . *The Prison-House of Language: A Critical Account of Structuralism and Russian Formalism*. Princeton: Princeton U P, 1972.

— . *Marxism and Form: Twentieth-Century Dialectical Theories of Literature*. Princeton: Princeton U P, 1974.

— . *Fables of Aggression: Wyndham Lewis, the Modernist as Fascist*. London: U of California P, 1979a.

— . 'Reification and Utopia in Mass Culture'. *Social Text* 1, Winter 1979b. 130-148.

— . '*Ulysses* in History' in W.J. McCormack and Alistair Stead. eds. *James Joyce and Modern Literature*. London: Routledge, 1982. 126-141.

— . *Sartre: The Origins of a Style*. New edition with Afterword. New York: Columbia U P, 1984. (1961).

— . 'Third World Literature in the Era of Late Capitalism'. *Social Text*. 15, Fall 1986. 65-88.

— . 'Cognitive Mapping' in Cary Nelson and Lawrence Greenberg, eds. *Marxism and the Interpretation of Culture*. Chicago: U of Illinois P, 1988a. 347-360.

— . *The Ideologies of Theory: Essays 1971-1986. Volume One: Situations of Theory*. London: Routledge, 1988b.

— . *The Ideologies of Theory: Essays 1971-1986. Volume Two: The Syntax of History*. London: Routledge, 1988b.

— . *Modernism and Imperialism*. Derry: Field Day, 1988c.

— . *Late Marxism: Adorno, or, the Persistence of the Dialectic*. London: Verso, 1990.

— . *Postmodernism, Or, The Cultural Logic of Late Capitalism*. London: Verso, 1991.

— . *The Geopolitical Aesthetic: Cinema and Space in the World System*. London: BFI Publishing, 1992a.

— . *Signatures of the Visible*. London: Routledge, 1992b.

— . 'The Synoptic Chandler' in Copjec, ed. 1993. 33-56.

— . *The Seeds of Time*. New York: Columbia U P, 1994.

— . 'An Unfinished Project'. *London Review of Books* 17; 15. 3 Aug 1995. 8-9.

— . *The Political Unconscious: Narrative as a Socially Symbolic Act*. London: Routledge, 1996.

— . *Brecht and Method*. London: Verso, 1998.

JanMohamed, Abdul R. 'The Economy of Manichean Allegory: The Function of Racial Difference in Colonialist Literature'. *Critical Inquiry* 12. Autumn 1985. 59-87.

Jarman, Neil. 'Troubled Images: The Iconography of Loyalism'. *Critique of Anthropology* 12; 2. 1992. 133-165.

— . 'Intersecting Belfast' in Bender, ed. 1993. 107-138.

— . *Material Conflicts: Parades and Visual Displays in Northern Ireland*. Oxford: Berg, 1997.

Jay, Martin. *Downcast Eyes: The Denigration of Vision in Twentieth-Century French Thought*. London: U of California P, 1993.

Jeffery, Keith. 'Losing Sight of the Enemy'. *TLS* 4574. 30 Nov-6 Dec, 1990. 1300.

Jeffery, Keith and Eunan O'Halpin. 'Ireland in Spy Fiction' in Wark, K. ed. *Intelligence and National Security* 5; 4. Oct 1990. A Special Issue on Spy Fiction, Spy Films and Real Intelligence. 92-116.

Jenkins, Peter. *Mrs. Thatcher's Revolution: The Ending of the Socialist Era*. London: Jonathan Cape, 1987.

Jenkins, William D. *The Adventure of the Detected Detective: Sherlock Holmes in James Joyce's Finnegans Wake*. London: Greenwood P, 1998.

Jennings, Michael W. *Dialectical Images: Walter Benjamin's Theory of Literary Criticism*. London: Cornell U P, 1987.

Joannon, Pierre. 'Nord'. *Études Irlandaises* 12; 2. 1987. 383-384.

Johnson, Toni O'Brien and David Cairns eds. *Gender in Irish Writing*. Milton Keynes: Open U P, 1991.

Johnstone, Robert and Bill Kirk. *Images of Belfast*. Belfast: The Blackstaff P, 1983.

Jones, Dudley. 'The Great Crime? The Spy Fiction of Len Deighton' in Bloom, ed. 1990a. 100-112.

Jones, Emrys. *A Social Geography of Belfast*. London: Oxford U P, 1960.

Jordin, Martin. 'Contemporary Futures: The Analysis of Science Fiction' in Pawling, ed. 50-75.

Joyce, Simon. 'Resisting Arrest / Arresting Resistance: Crime Fiction, Cultural Studies, and the Turn to History'. *Criticism* 32; 2. Spring 1995. 309-335.

Kaplan, E. Ann, ed. *Women in Film Noir*. Revised Edition. London: BFI, 1996.

Kaplan, Cora. 'Pandora's Box: Subjectivity, Class and Sexuality in Socialist Feminist Criticism' in Greene and Kahn, eds. 146-176.

Kaplan, Giselda. 'Feminism and Nationalism: The European Case' in West, ed. 3-40.

Kaufman, Michael. 'Men, Feminism, and Men's Contradictory Experience of Power' in Brod and Kaufman, eds. 1994. 142-163.

Kearney, Richard. *Transitions: Narratives in Modern Irish Culture*. Manchester: Manchester U P, 1988.

— . *Postnationalist Ireland: Politics, Culture, Philosophy*. London: Routledge, 1997.

Kellas, James G. *The Politics of Nationalism and Ethnicity*. London: Macmillan, 1991.

Kiberd, Declan. 'The Moral Superiority of Rural Villages'. *The Irish Times* 9 Dec 1986.

— . *Inventing Ireland: the Literature of the Modern Nation*. London: Jonathan Cape, 1995.

Kimmel, Michael S. 'Masculinity as Homophobia: Fear, Shame, and Silence in the Construction of Gender Identity' in Brod and Kaufman, eds. 1994. 119-141.

Kirkham, Pat and Janet Thumim, eds. *You Tarzan: Masculinity, Movies and Men*. London: Lawrence and Wishart, 1993.

— , eds. *Me Jane: Masculinity, Movies and Women*. London: Lawrence and Wishart, 1995.

Kirkland, Richard. *Literature and Culture in Northern Ireland Since 1966: Moments of Danger*. London: Longmann, 1996.

— . 'Bourgeois Redemptions: The Fictions of Glenn Patterson and Robert McLiam Wilson' in Harte and Parker, eds. 2000. 232-254.

Klein, Kathleen Gregory. *The Woman Detective: Gender and Genre*. Ohio: Bowling Green State, 1985.

Knight, Stephen. *Form and Ideology in Crime Fiction*. London: Macmillan, 1980.

— . 'Radical Thrillers' in Bell and Daldry, eds. 1990. 172-187.

Koenig, Marianne. Review of *Silver's City*. *Irish University Review* 12; 2. 1982. 243-245.

Kristeva, Julia. *Powers of Horror: An Essay on Abjection*. Trans. Leon S. Roudiez. New York: Columbia U P, 1982.

— . *Nations without Nationalism*. Trans. Leon S. Roudiez. New York: Columbia U P, 1993.

Krieger, Joel. *Reagan, Thatcher, and the Politics of Decline*. Cambridge: Polity P, 1986.

Krutnick, Frank. *In a Lonely Street: Film Noir, Genre, Masculinity*. London: Routledge, 1991.

— . 'Something More than Night: Tales of the *Noir* City' in David B. Clarke, ed. 1997. 83-109.

Kuhn, Arnette. 'Women's Genres' in *Screen Reader*, 1992. 301-311.

Kuhn, Reinhard. *The Demon of Noontide: Ennui in Western Literature*. Princeton: Princeton U P, 1976.

Lacan, Jacques. *Écrits: A Selection*. Trans. Alan Sheridan. London: Tavistock P, 1977a.

— . *The Four Fundamental Concepts of Psychoanalysis*. London: Hogarth P, 1977b.

— . *Le Séminaire: Livre XI*. Paris: Éditions du Seuil, 1978.

Laclau, Ernesto. *Politics and Ideology in Marxist Theory*. London: NLB, 1977.

— . *New Reflections on the Revolution of Our Time*. London: Verso, 1990.

Landrum, Larry. *American Mystery and Detective Novels*. London: Greenwood P, 1999.

Landry, Donna and Gerald MacLean. *Materialist Feminisms*. Oxford: Blackwell, 1993.

Lapsley, Rob and Michael Westlake. 'From *Casablanca* to *Pretty Woman*: The Politics of Romance' in Easthope, ed. 1993. 179-203.

Laquer, Walter. *Terrorism*. London: Sphere, 1978.

Ledrut, Raymond. 'Speech and the Silence of the City' in Gottdiener and Lagopoulos, eds. 114-134.

Lee, Alison. *Realism and Power: Postmodern British Fiction*. London: Routledge, 1990.

Leerssen, Joep. 'Mimesis and Stereotype' in Leerssen and Spiering, eds. 1991. 165-175.

— . 'The Western Mirage: On the Celtic Chronotope in the European Imagination' in Collins ed. 1994. 1-11.

— . *Mere Irish and Fíor-Ghael: Studies in the Idea of Irish Nationality, Its Development and Literary Expression prior to the Nineteenth Century*. Second Edition. Cork: Cork U P, 1996a.

— . *Remembrance and Imagination: Patterns in the Historical and Literary Representation of Ireland in the Nineteenth Century*. Cork: Cork UP, 1996b.

— . '1798: The Recurrence of Violence and Two Conceptualizations of History'. *The Irish Review* 22. Summer 1998. 37-45.

Leerssen, Joep and Menno Spiering, eds. *National Identity: Symbol and Representation*. Amsterdam-Atlanta, GA: Rodopi, 1991.

Lehan, Richard. *The City in Literature: An Intellectual and Cultural History*. London: U of California P, 1998.

Leitch, Thomas. 'From Detective Story to Detective Novel'. *Modern Fiction Studies* 29; 3. Autumn 1983. 475-484.

Leith, Linda. 'Subverting the Sectarian Heritage: The Recent Novels of Northern Ireland'. *Canadian Journal of Irish Studies*. 18; 1. Dec 1992. 88-106.

Letwin, Shirley Robin. *The Anatomy of Thatcherism*. London: Fontana, 1992.

Levitas, Ruth. 'Competition and Compliance: The Utopias of the New Right' in Levitas, ed. 80-106.

— , ed. *The Ideology of the New Right*. Cambridge: Polity P, 1986.

— . 'Ideology and the New Right' in Levitas, ed. 1-24.

Levy, Diane Wolfe. 'City Signs: Toward a Definition of Urban Literature'. *Modern Fiction Studies* 24; 1 Spring 1978. 65-73.

Littlejohn, Gary, ed. *Power and the State*. London: Croom Helm, 1978.

Lloyd, David. *Nationalism and Minor Literature: James Clarence Mangan and the Emergence of Irish Cultural Nationalism*. London: U of California P, 1987.

— . *Anomalous States: Irish Writing and the Post-Colonial Moment*. Dublin: Lilliput P, 1993.

— . *Ireland After History*. Cork: Cork U P, 1999.

Lloyd, David and Paul Thomas. *Culture and the State*. London: Routledge, 1998.

Lodge, David. *Small World.* London: Penguin, 1985.

Löwy, Michael. 'Marxists and the National Question'. *New Left Review* 96 Mar-April 1976. 81-100.

Longhurst, Derek, ed. *Gender, Genre and Narrative Pleasure.* London: Unwin, 1989.

Longley, Edna. 'A Northern "Turn"?'. *The Irish Review* 15. Spring 1994a. 1-14.

— . *The Living Stream: Literature and Revisionism in Ireland.* Newcastle: Bloodaxe, 1994b.

— . 'On the Frontiers of Culture'. *The Guardian* 23 July 1994c. 17.

— . 'What Do Protestants Want?' *The Irish Review* 20. Winter/Spring 1997. 104-120.

Loughlin, James. *Ulster Unionism and British National Identity since 1885.* London: Pinter, 1995.

Luibheid, Eithne. 'Irish Immigrants in the United States' Racial System' in MacLaughlin, ed. 253-273.

Lukacs, Georg. *History and Class Consciousness: Studies in Marxist Dialectics.* Trans. Rodney Livingstone. London: Merlin P, 1971. (1968).

— . *The Theory of the Novel: A Historico-Philosophical Essay on the Forms of Great Epic Literature.* Trans. Anna Bostock. London: Merlin P, 1978. (1920).

— . *Essays on Realism.* Ed. and intro. Rodney Livingstone. Trans. David Fernbach. London: Lawrence and Wishart, 1980.

— . *The Historical Novel.* Trans. Hannah and Stanley Mitchell. London: Penguin, 1981. (1962).

Lynch, Kevin. *The Image of the City.* London: MIT P, 1975.

Lyotard, Jean-François. *The Postmodern Condition: A Report on Knowledge.* Trans. Geoff Bennington and Brian Massumi. Foreword by Frederic Jameson. Manchester: Manchester U P, 1996.

Mac an Ghaill, Mairtín, ed. *Understanding Masculinities: Social Relations and Cultural Arenas.* Buckingham: Open U P, 1996.

MacDonald, Michael. 'Blurring the Difference: The Politics of Identity in Northern Ireland' in Alexander and O'Day, eds. 57-80.

MacDonagh, Oliver. *States of Mind: A Study of the Anglo-Irish Conflict 1790-1980.* London: George Allen and Unwin, 1983.

Macherey, Pierre. *A Theory of Literary Production.* Trans. Geoffrey Wall. London: Routledge and Kegan Paul, 1978. (1966).

MacKenzie, John M. 'The Imperial Pioneer and Hunter and the British Masculine Stereotype in Late Victorian and Edwardian Times' in Mangan, J.A. and James Walvin, eds. *Manliness and Morality: Middle-Class Masculinity in Britain and America 1800-1940.* Manchester: Manchester U P, 1987. 176-198.

—, ed. *Imperialism and Popular Culture.* Manchester: Manchester U P, 1986.

MacKillop, James. 'Ulster Violence in Fiction' in Sullivan and Wilson eds. 131-153.

MacKinnon, Catharine A. 'Feminism, Marxism, Method, and the State: An Agenda for Theory'. *Signs* 7. Spring 1982. 515-544.

MacLaughlin, Jim. 'The Devaluation of "Nation" as "Home" and the De-Politicisation of Recent Irish Emigration' in MacLaughlin, ed. 179-208.

— . 'Introduction' in MacLaughlin, ed. 5-35.

— , ed. *Location and Dislocation in Contemporary Irish Society: Emigration and Irish Identities.* Cork: Cork U P, 1997.

— . 'The New Vanishing Irish: Social Characteristics of "New Wave" Irish Emigration' in MacLaughlin, ed. 133-157.

MacLoughlin, Adrian. *The City of Belfast.* Dublin: Swift Publications, 1982.

Magee, Pat. 'Do they Mean Us ?'. *The Guardian* 3 Sept 1997a. 12-13.

— . *Gangsters or Guerrillas? Representations of Irish Republicans in Troubles Fiction.* Belfast: Beyond the Pale, 2001.

— . 'The Quest for the Great Troubles Novel'. *The Captive Voice-An Glor Gafa* 8; 2. Spring 1997b. 8-9.

Maguire, W. A. *Belfast.* Keele: Keele U P, 1993.

Mahoney, Elisabeth. '"The People in Parentheses": Space under Pressure in the Post-modern City' in David B. Clarke, ed. 1997. 168-185.

Mandel, Ernest. *Delightful Murder: A Social History of the Crime Story.* London: Pluto P, 1984.

Marx, Karl. *Selected Writings.* Ed. and intro. David McLellan. Oxford: Oxford U P, 1977.

Marx, Karl and Frederick Engels. *The Communist Manifesto.* Intro. A.J.P. Taylor. Trans. Samuel Moore. London: Penguin, 1968 (1888).

Maxwell, D.E.S. 'Imagining the North: Violence and the Writers'. *Éire-Ireland* 8; 2. 1973. 91-107.

Mazzoleni, Donatella. 'The City and the Imaginary'. Trans. John Koumantarakis. In Carter, ed. 285-301.

McArdle, Patsy. *The Secret War: An Account of the Sinister Activities along the Border Involving Garda, RUC, British Army and the SAS.* Dublin: Mercier P, 1984.

McAuley, James W. 'Cuchullain and an RPG-7: The Ideology and Politics of the Ulster Defence Association' in Hughes, ed. 1991. 45-68.

— . '"Flying the One-Winged Bird": Ulster Unionism and the Peace Process' in Shirlow and McGovern, eds. 1997. 158-175.

McAuley, J.W. and P.J. McCormack. 'The Protestant Working Class and the State in Northern Ireland since 1930: A Problematic Relationship' in Hutton and Stewart, eds. 114-128.

McBride, Ian. 'Ulster and the British Problem' in English and Walker, eds. 1-18.

McCarthy, Conor. *Modernisation, Crisis and Culture in Ireland, 1969-1992.* Dublin: Four Courts P, 2000.

McCarthy, Dermot. 'Belfast Babel: Postmodern Lingo in Eoin McNamee's *Resurrection Man*'. *Irish University Review* 30; 1. Spring/Summer 2000. 132-148.

McCartney, Robert. *Liberty and Authority in Ireland.* Derry: Field Day, 1985.

McClintock, Anne. 'The Angel of Progress: Pitfalls of the Term "Postcolonialism"' in Francis Barker et al, eds. *Colonial Discourse / Postcolonial Theory.* Manchester: Manchester U P, 1994. 253-266.

McCracken, Scott. *Pulp: Reading Popular Fiction.* Manchester: Manchester U P, 1998.

McGarry, John and Brendan O'Leary. *Explaining Northern Ireland: Broken Images.* Oxford: Blackwell, 1995.

McGrory, Patrick J. *Law and the Constitution: Present Discontents.* Derry: Field Day, 1986.

McGuigan, Jim. *Cultural Populism.* London ; Routledge, 1992.

McIlroy, Brian. 'The Repression of Communities: Visual Representations of Northern Ireland During the Thatcher Years' in Lester Friedman, ed. *Fires Were Started: British Cinema and Thatcherism.* Minneapolis: U of Minneapolis P, 1993. 92-108.

— . *Shooting to Kill: Filmmaking and the 'Troubles' in Northern Ireland.* Trowbridge, Wiltshire: Flicks Books, 1998.

McIntosh, Gillian. *The Force of Culture: Unionist Identities in Twentieth-Century Ireland.* Cork: Cork U P, 1999.

McIvor, Basil. *Hope Deferred: Experiences of an Irish Unionist.* Belfast: The Blackstaff P, 1998.

McKay, Susan. *Northern Protestants: An Unsettled People.* Belfast: The Blackstaff P, 2000.

McLoone, Martin, ed. *Broadcasting in a Divided Community: Seventy Years of the BBC in Northern Ireland.* Belfast: The Institute of Irish Studies, 1996.

— . 'Drama Out of a Crisis: BBC Television Drama and the Northern Ireland Troubles' in McLoone, ed. 73-104.

McMinn, Joseph. 'Contemporary Novels on the "Troubles"'. *Études Irlandaises* 5. 1980. 113-121.

McNamee, Peter and Tom Lovett. *Working-Class Community in Northern Ireland.* Belfast: The Ulster People's College, 1987.

Meaney, Geraldine. *Sex and Nation: Women in Irish Culture and Politics.* Dublin: Attic P, 1991.

— . 'Sex and Nation: Women in Irish Culture and Politics' in A. Smyth, ed. *The Irish Women's Studies Reader.* Dublin: Attic P, 1993. 230-244.

Melmouth, John. 'A People's Provocations'. *TLS* 4391. 29 May 1987. 588.

Merry, Bruce. *Anatomy of the Spy Thriller.* Dublin: Gill and Macmillan, 1977.

Messent, Peter, ed. *Criminal Proceedings: The Contemporary American Crime Novel.* London: Pluto P, 1995.

Metress, Christopher. 'Living Degree Zero: Masculinity and the Threat of Desire in the *Roman Noir*' in Peter F. Murphy, ed. *Fictions of Masculinity: Crossing Cultures, Crossing Sexualities.* London: New York U P, 1994. 154-184.

Miller, David. *Don't Mention the War: Northern Ireland, Propaganda and the Media.* London: Pluto P, 1994.

— , ed. *Rethinking Northern Ireland: Culture, Ideology and Colonialism.* London: Longman, 1998.

Miller, David and Greg McLaughlin. 'Reporting the Peace in Ireland' in Rolston and Miller, eds. 421-439.

Miller, Jane. *Seductions: Studies in Reading and Culture.* London: Virago, 1990.

Miller, Kerby A. *Emigrants and Exiles: Ireland and the Irish Exodus to North America.* Oxford: Oxford U P, 1985.

Miller, Reuben. 'The Literature of Terrorism'. *Terrorism* 11; 1. 1988. 63-67.

Milton, Kay. 'Belfast: Whose City?' in Curtin et al, eds. 23-37.

Minne, Joris, Maurice Goldring and John Newsinger. 'A Few Troubles More'. *Irish Studies Review* 19. Summer 1997. 53-56.

Minogue, Kenneth and Michael Biddiss, eds. *Thatcherism: Personality and Politics.* London: Macmillan, 1987.

Modleski, Tania. *Loving with a Vengeance.* London: Anchor Books, 1982.

— . 'The Terror of Pleasure: The Contemporary Horror Film and Postmodern Theory' in Modleski, ed. *Studies in Entertainment: Critical Approaches to Mass Culture.* Indiana: Indiana U P, 1986. 155-166

Monaghan, David. 'John Le Carré and England: A Spy-Eye View'. *ModernFiction Studies.* 29; 3. Autumn 1983. 569-582.

Monk, Claire. 'From Underworld to Underclass: Crime and British Cinema in the 1990s' in Chibnall and Murphy, eds. 1999. 172-188.

Moretti, Franco. *Signs Taken for Wonders: Essays in the Sociology of Literary Forms.* Trans. Susan Fischer, David Forgacs and David Miller. London: Verso, 1988.

Morgan, Austen and Bob Purdie eds. *Ireland: Divided Nation, Divided Class.* London: Ink Links, 1980.

Morgan, David H.J. 'Theater of War: Combat, the Military and Masculinities' in Brod and Kaufman, eds. 1994. 165-182.

Morgan, Eileen. 'Ireland's Lost Action Hero: *Michael Collins*, A Secret History of Irish Cinema'. *New Hibernica Review* 2; 1. Spring 1998. 26-42.

Morgan, Robin. *The Demon Lover: On the Sexuality of Terrorism*. London: Mandarin, 1990.

Morgan, Valerie. 'Women and the Conflict in Northern Ireland' in O'Day, ed. 1995. 59-73.

Morgan, Valerie and Grace Fraser. 'Women and the Northern Ireland Conflict: Experiences and Responses' in Dunn ed. 81-96.

Morley, David and Kuan-Hsing Chen, eds. *Stuart Hall: Critical Dialogues in Cultural Studies*. London: Routledge, 1996.

Morris, Virginia B. 'Arsenic and Blue Lace: Sayer's Criminal Women'. *Modern Fiction Studies*. 29; 3. Autumn 1983. 485-495.

Motion, Andrew. *Philip Larkin: A Writer's Life*. London: Faber, 1993.

Mouffe, Chantal, ed. *Gramsci and Marxist Theory*. London: Routledge and Kegan Paul, 1979.

— . 'Hegemony and Ideology in Gramsci' in Mouffe, ed. 168-204.

Moxon-Browne, Edward. 'The Water and the Fish: Public Opinion and the Provisional IRA in Northern Ireland' in Wilkinson, ed. 1981. 41-72.

— . *Nation, Class and Creed in Northern Ireland*. Aldershot: Gower, 1983.

Moylan, Tony. *Demand the Impossible: Science Fiction and the Utopian Imagination*. London: Methuen, 1996.

Mulhern, Francis. *The Present Lasts a Long Time: Essays in Cultural Politics*. Cork: Cork U P, 1998.

Mulloy, Eanna. *Emergency Legislation: Dynasties of Coercion*. Derry: Field Day, 1986.

Mulvey, Laura. *Visual and Other Pleasures*. London: Macmillan, 1989.

— . *Fetishism and Curiosity*. Bloomington: Indiana U P, 1996.

Mumford, Lewis. *The City in History: Its Origins, Its Transformations, and Its Prospects*. London: Penguin, 1984. (1961).

Munck, Ronald. 'Class and Religion in Belfast: A Historical Perspective'. *Journal of Contemporary History* 20; 2. 1985. 241-259.

Munt, Sally R. *Murder by the Book? Feminism and the Crime Novel*. London: Routledge, 1994.

Murray, Raymond. *The SAS in Ireland*. Cork: Mercier P, 1990.

Murtagh, Brendan. 'Beyond the Hype: Targeting Social Deprivation in Belfast's Public Housing Estates' in Neill, Fitzsimons and Murtagh, eds. 185-208.

— . 'Image Making Versus Reality: Ethnic Division and the Planning Challenge of Belfast's Peacelines' in Neill, Fitzsimons and Murtagh, eds. 209-230.

Nairn, Tom. *The Break-Up of Britain: Crisis and Neo-Nationalism*. London: Verso, 1981.

— . 'Britain's Living Legacy' in Hall and Jacques eds. 1983. 281-288.

— . *Faces of Nationalism: Janus Revisited*. London: Verso, 1997.

Nandy, Ashis. *Exiled at Home*. Comprises *At The Edge of Psychology*, *The Intimate Enemy* and *Creating a Nationality*. Delhi: Oxford U P, 1998.

Nash, Catherine. 'Embodied Irishness: Gender, Sexuality and Irish Identities' in Brian Graham, ed. 1997. 108-127.

Nash, Walter. *Language in Popular Fiction*. London: Routledge, 1990.

Neale, Stephen. 'Difference' in *Screen Reader*, 1992. 47-106.

— . 'Masculinity as Spectacle' in *Screen Reader*, 1992. 276-287.

— . *Genre*. Chippenham: BFI Publishing, 1996.

Neill, William J.V. '"Lipstick on the Gorilla": Conflict Management, Urban Development and Image Making in Belfast' in Neill, Fitzsimons and Murtagh, eds. 50-76.

Neill, William J.V., Diana S. Fitzsimons and Brendan Murtagh, eds. *Reimagining the Pariah City: Urban Development in Belfast and Detroit*. Aldershot: Avebury, 1995.

Nelson, Dana. *National Manhood: Capitalist Citizenship and the Imagined Fraternity of Men*. Durham and London: Duke U P, 1998.

Nelson, Sarah. *Ulster's Uncertain Defenders: Protestant Political, Paramilitary and Community Groups and the Northern Ireland Conflict*. Belfast: Appletree P, 1984.

Nelson, William and Nancy Avery. 'Art Where You Least Expect It: Myth and Ritual in the Detective Series'. *Modern Fiction Studies*. 29; 3. Autumn 1983. 463-474.

Neve, Brian. 'Cinema, the Ceasefire and "the Troubles"'. *Irish Studies Review* 20, Autumn 1997. 2-8.

Newsinger, John. '"Do You Walk the Walk?": Aspects of Masculinity in Some Vietnam War Films' in Kirkham and Thumim, eds. 1993. 126-136.

— . 'Thatcher, Northern Ireland and *The Downing Street Years*'. *Irish Studies Review* 7. Summer 1994. 2-6.

— . 'Our Boys in the North'. *Irish Studies Review*. 16. Autumn 1996. 34-37.

— . *Dangerous Men: The SAS and Popular Culture*. London: Pluto P, 1997a.

— . '"The Gangrene in One Limb': Political Memoirs and the Troubles'. *Études Irlandaises* 22; 1. Spring 1997b. 187-207b.

Nic an tSaoir, Deirdre. 'The World of Make-Believe'. *An Phoblacht* Thursday, 16 Aug 1990. 13.

— . 'The Good, The Bad and the Ugly'. *An Phoblacht* Thursday, 11 Feb 1993. 8-9.

Nimni, Ephrain. *Marxism and Nationalism: Theoretical Origins of a Political Crisis*. London: Pluto P, 1991.

Nolan, Paul. 'Images of a Wild West'. *Fortnight* 311. Nov 1992. 42.

Nugent, Julie. 'The Remains of Empire: Conflicting Representations in Contemporary Film'. *Irish Studies Review* 7. Summer 1994. 23-27.

Oates, Joyce Carol. 'Imaginary Cities: America' in Michael C. Jaye and Ann Chalmers Watts, eds. *Literature and the American Urban Experience*. Manchester: Manchester U P, 1981.

O'Brien, George. 'Ireland 2000: A Very Short Story'. *The Irish Review* 11. Winter 1991-1992. 40-46.

— . 'The Big Elsewhere and the Wayward Hyphen: Further Gleanings from the Clarity Archive' in Eve Patten, ed. *Returning to Ourselves: Second Volume of Papers from the John Hewitt International Summer School*. Belfast: Lagan P, 1995. 217-226.

— . 'Introduction: Traditions and Transition in Contemporary Irish Fiction'. *Colby Quarterly* 31; 2. 1995. 5-22.

O'Brien, Peggy. 'The Irish-American Literary Connection' in Doyle and Edwards, eds. 261-278.

Ó Ceallaigh, Daltún. *Britain and Ireland: Sovereignty and Nationality*. Dublin: Leirmheas, 1996.

O'Connor, Fionnuala. *In Search of a State: Catholics in Northern Ireland*. Belfast: The Blackstaff P, 1993.

O'Day, Alan, ed. *Dimensions of Irish Terrorism*. Dartmouth: Aldershot, 1993.

—, ed. *Terrorism's Laboratory: The Case of Northern Ireland*. Dartmouth: Aldershot, 1995.

O'Dowd, Liam. 'Constituting Division, Impeding Agreement: The Neglected Role of British Nationalism in Northern Ireland' in James Anderson and James Goodman, eds. *Dis/Agreeing Ireland: Contexts, Obstacles, Hopes*. London: Pluto P, 1998. 108-125.

O'Dowd, Mary and Sabine Wichert, eds. *Chattel, Servant or Citizen: Women's Status in Church, State and Society*. Belfast: Institute of Irish Studies, 1995.

Olwig, Kenneth Robert. 'Sexual Cosmology: Nation and Landscape at the Conceptual Interstices of Nature and Culture; or What Does Landscape Really Mean?' in Bender, ed. 307-343.

O'Malley, Eoin. 'Reflections on Ireland's Economic Identity'. *Studies* 75; 300. Winter 1986. 477-86.

Onega, Susana and Jose Angel Garcia Landa eds. *Narratology*. London: Longman, 1996.

O'Neill, Kevin. 'Shooting to Thrill: Thirty Years of Irish "Troubles" Cinema' in Crawford, ed. *Fortnight* Supplement 10-11.

O'Sullivan, Patrick. *The Irish in the New Communities. The Irish World Wide: History, Heritage, Identity Vol.2*. London: London: U P, 1992.

— . *The Creative Migrant. The Irish World Wide: History, Heritage, Identity Vol. 3*. London: London U P, 1994.

— . *Irish Women and Irish Migration. The Irish World Wide: History, Heritage, Identity Vol.4*. London: Leicester U P, 1995.

O'Toole, Fintan. 'Going West: The Country Versus the City in Irish Writing'. *The Crane Bag* 12; 2. 1987. 111-116.

— . *A Mass for Jesse James: A Journey Through 1980s Ireland*. Dublin: Raven Arts P, 1990.

Black Hole, Green Card: The Disappearance of Ireland. Dublin: New Island Books, 1994.

Paisley, Rhonda. 'A Struggle About Identity, Loyalty, Government and, above all, Territory'. *Irish Times* 28 Oct 1993. 14.

Palmer, Jerry. *Thrillers: Genesis and Structure of a Popular Genre*. London: Edward Arnold, 1978.

— . 'Thrillers' in Pawling, ed. 1984. 76-98.

Palmer, Paulina, 'The Lesbian Thriller' in Messent, ed. 1997. 87-110.

Palmer, R. Barton. *Hollywood's Dark Cinema: The American Film Noir*. New York: Twayne, 1994.

Parker, Andrew. 'Sporting Masculinities: Gender Relations and the Body' in Mac an Ghaill, ed. 126-138.

Parker, Andrew et al, eds. *Nationalisms and Sexualities*. London: Routledge, 1992.

Parkinson, Alan. *Ulster Loyalism and the British Media*. Dublin: Four Courts P, 1998.

Paterson, Richard and Philip Schlesinger. 'State Heroes for the Eighties'. *Screen* 24; 3. 1983. 55-72.

Patten, Eve. 'Fiction in Conflict: Northern Ireland's Prodigal Novelists' in Bell, ed. 128-148.

Patterson, Glenn. 'Butcher's Tools'. *Fortnight* 331. Sept 1994. 43-44.

— . 'I am a Northern Irish Novelist' in Bell, ed. 1995. 149-152.

Patterson, Henry. *The Politics of Illusion: A Political History of the IRA*. London: Serif, 1997.

Paulin, Tom. *Ireland and the English Crisis*. Newcastle: Bloodaxe, 1984.

Pawling, Christopher. 'Introduction: Popular Fiction: Ideology or Utopia?' in Pawling, ed. 1-19

—, ed. *Popular Fiction and Social Change*. New York: St Martin's P, 1984.

Pease, Donald E. 'Introduction: National Narratives, Postnational Narration'. *Modern Fiction Studies* 43; 1. Spring 1997. 1-23.

Pelaschiar, Laura. *Writing the North: The Contemporary Novel in Northern Ireland*. Trieste: Edizioni Parnaso, 1998.

— . 'Transforming Belfast: The Evolving Role of the City in Northern Irish Fiction'. *Irish University Review* 30; 1. Spring/Summer 2000. 117-131.

Pettitt, Lance. 'Pigs and Provos, Prostitutes and Prejudice: Gay Representation in Irish Film, 1984-1995' in Walshe, ed. 1997. 252-284.

Phillips, Richard. *Mapping Men and Empire: A Geography of Adventure*. London: Routledge, 1997.

Phoenix, Eamonn. *Northern Nationalism: Nationalist Politics, Partition and the Catholic Minority in Northern Ireland 1890-1940*. Belfast: Ulster Historical Foundation, 1994.

Picciotto, Sol. 'The Theory of the State, Class Struggle and the Rule of Law' in Fine, ed. 164-177.

Pike, Burton. *The Image of the City in Modern Literature*. Princeton: Princeton U P, 1981.

Pocock, Douglas C.D. *Humanistic Geography and Literature: Essays on the Urban Experience of Place*. London: Croom Helm, 1981.

Poole, Michael A. 'In Search of Ethnicity in Ireland' in Brian Graham, ed. 1997. 128-147.

Porter, Dennis. *The Pursuit of Crime: Art and Ideology in Detective Fiction*. London: Yale U P, 1981.

— . 'Orientalism and its Problems' in Williams and Chrisman, eds. 1993. 150-161.

Porter, Dorothy. 'Imagining a City'. *Chapman* 63. Jan 1991. 42-50.

Porter, Norman. *Rethinking Unionism: An Alternative Vision for Northern Ireland*. New Updated Edition. Belfast: The Blackstaff P, 1998.

Poulantzas, Nicos. *Political Power and Social Classes*. Trans. Timothy O'Hagan. London: NLB, 1973.

— . *Classes in Contemporary Capitalism*. Trans. David Fernbach. London: NLB, 1974.

— . *State, Power, Socialism*. Trans. Patrick Camiller. London: NLB, 1978.

Prakash, Gyan. *After Colonialism: Imperial Histories and Postcolonial Displacements*. Princeton, NJ: Princeton U P, 1995.

Preston, Peter and Paul Simpson-Housley. 'Introduction: Writing the City' in Preston and Simpson-Housley, eds. 1-14.

—, eds. *Writing the City: Eden, Babylon and the New Jerusalem*. London: Routledge, 1994.

Priestman, Martin. *Detective Fiction and Literature: The Figure on the Carpet*. London: Macmillan, 1990.

Pykett, Lyn. 'Investigating Women: The Female Sleuth after Feminism' in Bell and Daldry, eds. 1990. 48-67.

Rader, Barbara A. and Howard G. Zettler, eds. *The Sleuth and the Scholar: Origins, Evolution, and Current Trends in Detective Fiction*. London: Greenwood P, 1988.

Radway, Janice A. *Reading the Romance: Women, Patriarchy, and Popular Literature*. London: U of North Carolina P, 1991 (1994).

Rajan, Gita and Radhika Mohanram. *Postcolonial Discourse and Changing Cultural Contexts*. London: Greenwood P, 1995.

Rechts, Albert. *Handbook to a Hypothetical City*. Gigginstown: The Lilliput P, 1986.

Reddy, Maureen T. *Sisters in Crime: Feminism and the Crime Novel*. New York: Continuum, 1988.

Rees, Merlyn. 'Terror in Ireland and Britain's Response' in Wilkinson, ed. 83-88.

Reilly, Wayne G. 'The Management of Political Violence in Quebec and Northern Ireland: A Comparison'. *Terrorism and Political Violence* 6; 1. Spring 1994. 44-61.

Reizbaum, Marilyn. 'Canonical Double Cross: Scottish and Irish Women's Writing' in Karen E. Lawrence ed. *Decolonizing Tradition: New Views of Twentieth-Century 'British' Literary Canons*. Urbana and Chicago: U of Illinois P, 1992. 165-190.

— . 'Not a Crying Game: The Feminist Appeal: Nationalism, Feminism and the Contemporary Literatures of Scotland and Ireland'. *Scotlands* 2, 1994. 24-31.

Rickard, John S. ed. *Irishness and (Post)Modernism*. London: Associated U P, 1994.

Robins, Kevin. 'Prisoners of the City: Whatever Could a Postmodern City Be?' in Carter, ed. 303-330.

Roche, Patrick J. and Brian Barton eds. *The Northern Ireland Question: Myth and Reality*. Aldershot: Avebury, 1991.

Rockett, Kevin. 'History, Politics and Irish Cinema' in Rockett, Gibbons and Hill. 1988. 3-144.

— . 'The Irish Migrant and Film' in O'Sullivan, ed. 1994. 170-191.

Rockett, Kevin, Luke Gibbons and John Hill. *Cinema and Ireland*. London: Routledge, 1988.

Rolston, Bill. 'Escaping From Belfast: Class, Ideology and Literature in Northern Ireland'. *Race and Class* 20 ; 1. 1978. 41-62.

— , ed. *The Media and Northern Ireland: Covering the Troubles*. London: Macmillan, 1991.

— . 'Gagging for It'. *Fortnight* 340, June 1995. 18-20.

— . 'Mothers, Whores and Villains: Images of Women in the Novels of the Northern Ireland Conflict' in Rolston and Miller, eds. 421-439.

Rolston, Bill and David Miller, eds. *War and Words: The Northern Ireland Media Reader*. Belfast: Beyond the Pale Publications, 1996.

Roper, Michael and John Tosh, eds. *Manful Assertions: Masculinities in Britain since 1800*. London: Routledge, 1991.

Roth, Marty. *Foul and Fair Play: Reading Genre in Classic Detective Fiction*. London: U of Georgia P, 1995.

Roulston, Carmel. 'Gender, Nation, Class: The Politics of Difference in Northern Ireland'. *Scottish Affairs* 18. Winter 1997a. 54-68.

— . 'Woman on the Margin: The Women's Movements in Northern Ireland, 1973-1995' in West, ed. 1997b. 41-58.

Rowbotham, Sheila et al. *Beyond the Fragments*. London: Merlin, 1979.

Ruddick, Sara. 'Pacifying the Forces: Drafting Women in the Interests of Peace'. *Signs* 8; 3. 1983. 470-531.

Ruthe, Holger. 'Terrorism in Ireland: A Theoretical Approach' in Siegmund-Schultze, ed. 52-56.

Rutherford, John. *Men's Silences: Predicaments in Masculinity*. London: Routledge, 1992.

Said, Edward. 'Permission to Narrate'. *London Review of Books*. 16-29 Feb 1984a. 13-17.

— . *The World, the Text, and the Critic*. London: Faber, 1984b.

— . *Yeats and Decolonization*. Derry: Field Day, 1988.

— . *Culture and Imperialism*. London: Vintage, 1994.

— . *Orientalism: Western Conceptions of the Orient*. Reprinted with a new afterword. London: Penguin, 1995.

Said, Edward and Raymond Williams. 'Media, Margins and Modernity', an Appendix to Williams's *The Politics of Modernism: Against the New Conformists*. London: Verso, 1989. 177-197.

Sailer, Susan Shaw, ed. *Representing Ireland: Gender, Class, Nationality*. Gainesville: U P of Florida, 1997.

Sales, Rosemary. 'Gender and Protestantism in Northern Ireland' in Shirlow and McGovern, eds. 1997a. 140-157.

— . *Women Divided: Gender, Religion and Politics in Northern Ireland*. London: Routledge, 1997b.

Samuel, Raphael. 'Mrs. Thatcher and Victorian Values'. *Island Stories: Unravelling Britain. Theatres of Memory Vol.2*. London: Verso, 1998. 330-348.

Sanderson, Wendy. 'Women, Cities and Identity: The Production and Consumption of Gendered Space in Belfast' in Byrne and Leonard, eds. 1997. 479-493.

Sandler, Todd. 'On the Relationship between Democracy and Terrorism'. *Terrorism and Political Violence* 7; 4. Winter 1995. 1-9.

Sartre, Jean-Paul. 'Des rats et des hommes'. *Situations* 4. Paris: Gallimard, 1964. 38-84.

— . *Critique of Dialectical Reason*. Ed. Jonathan Ree. Trans. Alan Sheridan-Smith. London: New Left Books, 1976.

Saruchanjan, Alla. 'The Ulster Crisis in Fiction' in Siegmund-Schultze, ed. 170-180.

Scanlan, Margaret. 'The Unbearable Present: Northern Ireland in Four Contemporary Novels'. *Études Irlandaises* 10, Dec 1985. 145-161.

— . 'An Acceptable Level of Violence: Women, Fiction and Northern Ireland' in Theo d'Haen and Jose Lanters, eds. *Troubled Histories, Troubled Fictions: Twentieth Century Anglo-Irish Prose*. Amsterdam: Rodopi, 1995. 159-172.

Schlesinger, Philip, Graham Murdock and Philip Elliott. *Televising 'Terrorism': Political Violence in Popular Culture*. London: Comedia, 1983.

Schmid, Alex P. 'The Response Problem as a Definition Problem'. *Terrorism and Political Violence* 4; 4. Winter 1992a. 7-13.

— . 'Terrorism and Democracy'. *Terrorism and Political Violence* 4; 4. Winter 1992b. 14-25.

Schwarzmantel, John. *Socialism and the Idea of the Nation*. London: Harvester Wheatsheaf, 1991.

Screen. The Sexual Subject: A Screen Reader in Sexuality. London: Routledge, 1992.

Scruton, Roger. 'Thinkers of the Left: E.P. Thompson'. *The Salisbury Review* 1; 1. Autumn 1982. 12-15.

— . *The Meaning of Conservatism*. Second Edition. London: Macmillan, 1984.

— . *The Philosopher on Dover Beach: Essays*. Manchester: Carcanet, 1990.

Seidel, Gill. 'Culture, Nation and "Race" in the British and French New Right' in Levitas, ed. 107-135.

Selzter, Mark. 'Serial Killers'. *Differences* 5; 1. 1993. 92-128.

Sennett, Richard. *The Uses of Disorder: Personal Identity and City Life*. London: Allen Lane/The Penguin P, 1970.

— . *The Fall of Public Man*. Cambridge: Cambridge U P, 1977.

— . *Flesh and Stone: The Body and the City in Western Civilization*. London: Faber, 1994.

Shadoian, J. *Dreams and Dead Ends: The American Gangster / Crime Film*. Cambridge, Mass: MIT P, 1977.

Sharratt, Bernard. *Reading Relations: Structures of Literary Production: A Dialectical Text/Book*. Brighton: The Harvester P, 1982.

Shannon, Catherine B. 'The Woman Writer as Historical Witness: Northern Ireland, 1969-1994' in Maryann Gianella Valiulis and Mary O'Dowd, eds. *Women and Irish History: Essays in Honour of Margaret MacCurtain*. Dublin: Wolfhound P, 1997. 239-259.

Shannon, James. *Violent Exclusion: The Depiction of Terrorism in Contemporary Northern Irish Writing*. Unpublished M.A. Diss. The Queen's University of Belfast, 1997.

Shearman, Hugh. *Northern Ireland: Its People, Resources, History and Government*. Belfast: HMSO, 1962.

— . *Northern Ireland*. Belfast: HMSO, 1968.

— . *Conflict in Northern Ireland. The Year Book of World Affairs Vol. 24*. 1970.

Shephard, Ben. 'Showbiz Imperialism: The Case of Peter Lobenula' in MacKenzie, ed. 94-112.

Shirlow, Peter and Mark McGovern. 'Counter-Insurgency, De-industrialisation and the Political Economy of Ulster Loyalism' in Shirlow and McGovern, eds. 176-198.

— . 'Introduction' in Shirlow and McGovern, eds. 1-15.

— , eds. *Who are 'the People'? Unionism, Protestantism and Loyalism in Northern Ireland*. London: Pluto P, 1997.

Dorothea Siegmund-Schultze, ed. *Irland: Gesellschaft und Kultur* 4. Halle-Wittenberg: Martin Luther U P, 1985.

Silvermann, Marylin. 'An Urban Place in Rural Ireland: An Historical Ethnography of Domination, 1841-1989' in Curtin et al, eds. 203-225.

Simmel, Georg. *On Individuality and Social Forms: Selected Writings*. Ed. and intro Donald N. Levine. London: U of Chicago P, 1971.

Simons, John. '*Real* Detectives and *Fictional* Criminals' in Bell and Daldry, eds. 84-96.

Sinfield, Alan. *Literature, Politics and Culture in Postwar Britain*. Oxford: Basil Blackwell, 1989.

Smith, Anthony D. *The Ethnic Origin of Nations*. Oxford: Basil Blackwell, 1986.

— . *Nations and Nationalism in a Global Era*. Oxford: Polity P, 1995.

Smyth, Damian. 'Being Unkind to Belfast'. *Fortnight* 325. Feb 1994. 43.

Smyth, Gerry. *The Novel and the Nation: Studies in the New Irish Fiction*. London: Pluto P, 1997.

— . *Decolonisation and Criticism: The Construction of Irish Literature*. London: Pluto P, 1998.

Smyth, Jim. 'Industrial Development and the Unmaking of the Irish Working Class' in Hutton and Stewart, eds. 1991a. 94-113.

— . 'Weasels in a Hole: Ideologies of the Irish Conflict' in Alexander and O'Day, eds. 1991b. 135-154.

Smythe, Ailbhe. 'The Floozie in the Jacuzzi'. *The Irish Review* 6. 1989. 7-24.

Sommer, Doris. *Foundational Fictions: The National Romances of Latin America*. Berkeley: U of Berkeley P, 1991.

Sorel, Georges. *Reflections on Violence*. Trans. T.E. Hulme. New York: B.W. Huebsch, 1914. New York: AMS P, 1975.

Spelman, Elizabeth. *Inessential Woman: Problems of Exclusion in Feminist Thought*. London: The Women's P, 1988.

Spicer, Andrew. 'The Emergence of the British Tough Guy: Stanley Baxter, Masculinity and the Crime Thriller' in Chobnall and Murphy, eds. 1999. 81-93.

Spiering, Menno. 'The Foreigness of Foreigners in some British Invasion Stories, with Special Reference to the Euro-Threat in *Apocalypse 2000*' in Leerssen and Spiering, eds. 93-107.

Spivak, Gayatri Chakravorty. 'Displacement and the Discourse of Woman' in Mark Krupnick, ed. *Displacement: Derrida and After*. Bloomington: Indiana U P, 1983. 169-195.

— . 'Can the Subaltern Speak?' in Cary Nelson and Lawrence Grossberg, eds. *Marxism and the Interpretation of Culture*. Chicago: U of Illinois P, 1988a. 271-313.

— . *In Other Worlds: Essays in Cultural Politics*. London: Routledge, 1988b.

— . *The Post-Colonial Critic: Interviews, Strategies, Dialogues*. Ed. Sarah Harasym. London: Routledge, 1990.

— . *Outside in the Teaching Machine*. London: Routledge, 1993.

Squier, Susan Merrill ed. *Women Writers and the City: Essays in Feminist Literary Criticism*. Knoxville: U of Tennessee P, 1984.

St. Peter, Christine. *Changing Ireland: Strategies in Contemporary Women's Fiction*. New York: St Martin's P, 2000.

Stacey, Jackie. *Star Gazing: Hollywood Cinema and Female Spectatorship*. London: Routledge, 1994.

Stallybrass, Peter and Allon White. *The Politics and Poetics of Transgression*. London: Methuen, 1986.

Stasiulis, Daiva and Nira Yuval-Davis, eds. *Unsettling Settler Societies: Articulations of Gender, Race, Ethnicity and Class*. London: SAGE, 1995.

Steel, Jayne. 'Vampira: Representations of the Irish Female Terrorist'. *Irish Studies Review* 16; 3. Dec 1998. 273-284.

Steele, Timothy. 'Matter and Mystery: Neglected Works and Background Materials of Detective Fiction'. *Modern Fiction Studies* 29; 3. Autumn 1983. 435-450.

Stegat, Holger. 'The Validity of Marx's Analysis: Northern Ireland 1969 to 1982' in Siegmund-Schultze, ed. 33-43.

Stewart, Bruce. '"Our Proper Dark": A Chapter of Conclusions' in Bruce Stewart, ed. *That Other World: The Supernatural and the Fantastic in Irish Literature and its Contexts Vol.2*. Gerrards Cross: Colin Smythe, 1998. 365-385.

Storey, Michael. '"Bewildered Chimes": Image, Voice and Structure in Recent Irish Fiction' in Dawe and Longley eds. 1985. 161-181.

— . 'Post-Colonialism and Stories of the Irish Troubles'. *New Hibernica Review* 2; 3. Autumn 1998. 63-77.

Storper, Michael and Richard Walker. *The Capitalist Imperative: Territory, Technology and Industrial Growth*. Oxford: Basil Blackwell, 1989.

Sullivan, Eileen A. and Harold A. Wilson eds. *Conflict in Ireland*. Gainesville, Florida: U of Florida P, 1976.

Sullivan, Larry E. and Lydia Cushman eds. *Pioneers, Passionate Ladies, and Private Eyes: Dime Novels, Series Books and Paperbacks*. London: The Haworth P, 1996.

Sutherland, John. *Fiction and the Fiction Industry*. London: Athlone P, 1978.

— . *Bestsellers: Popular Fiction of the 1970s*. London: Routledge and Kegan Paul, 1981.

— . *Where was Rebecca Shot? Puzzles, Curiosities and Conundrums in Modern Fiction*. London: Phoenix, 1999.

Svoboa, Frederic. 'The Snub-Nosed Mystique: Observations on the American Detective Hero'. *Modern Fiction Studies*. 29; 3. Autumn 1983. 557-568.

Symons, Julian. *The Detective Story in Britain*. London: Longmans, Green and Co, 1962. *Bloody Murder: From the Detective Story to the Crime Novel: A History*. London: Pan Books, 1992.

— . *Criminal Practices: Symons on Crime Writing 60s to 90s*. London: Macmillan, 1994.

Szelenyi, Ivan, ed. *Cities in Recession: Critical Responses to the Policies of the New Right*. London: SAGE, 1984.

Tabb, William K. and Larry Sawers, eds. *Marxism and the Metropolis: New Perspectives in Urban Political Economy*. New York: Oxford U P, 1978.

Tambling, Jeremy. *Narrative and Ideology*. Milton Keynes: Open U P, 1991.

Tasker, Yvonne. *Spectacular Bodies: Gender, Genre and the Action Cinema*. London: Routledge, 1993.

Teague, Paul, ed. *Beyond the Rhetoric: Politics, the Economy and Social Policy in Northern Ireland*. London: Lawrence and Wishart, 1987.

ten Tusscher, Tessa. 'Patriarchy, Capitalism and the New Right' in Judith Evans et al, eds. *Feminism and Political Theory*. London: SAGE, 1986. 66-84.

Thatcher, Margaret. *The Downing Street Years*. London: Harper Collins, 1995.

Thomas, Ronald R. 'Double Exposures: Arresting Images in *Bleak House* and *The House of the Seven Gables*'. *Novel: A Forum on Fiction* 31; 1. Fall 1997. 87-113.

Thompson, Denys, ed. *Discrimination and Popular Culture*. London: Penguin, 1970.

Thompson, E.P. *The Poverty of Theory and Other Essays*. London: Merlin, 1979.

Thompson, Spurgeon. 'The Commodification of Culture and Decolonisation in Northern Ireland'. *Irish Studies Review* 7; 1. 1999. 53-63.

Thurston, Richard. 'Are You Sittting Comfortably? Men's Storytelling, Masculinities, Prison Culture and Violence' in Mac an Ghaill, ed. 139-152.

Thwaite, Anthony. *Selected Letters of Philip Larkin*. London: Faber, 1992.

Titley, Alan. 'Rough Rug-Headed Kerns: The Irish Gunman in the Popular Novel'. *Éire-Ireland* 15; 4. 1980. 15-38.

Tittmar, H-g. 'Urban Terrorism: A Psychological Perspective'. *Terrorism and Political Violence* 4; 3. Autumn 1992. 64-71.

Tobin, R.B. 'Possibilities of Transformation: The Representation of Violence in Eoin McNamee's *Resurrection Man*'. *Writing Ulster* 6. 131-142.

Todd, Jennifer. 'History and Structure in Loyalist Ideology: The Possibilities of Ideological Change'. *Irish Journal of Sociology* 4. 1994. 67-79.

Todorov, Tzvetan. *The Poetics of Prose*. Trans. Richard Howard. Foreword Jonathan Culler. Oxford: Basil Blackwell, 1977.

Tomlinson, John. *Cultural Imperialism: A Critical Introduction*. London: Pinter, 1991.

Toolis, Kevin. *Rebel Hearts: Journeys within the IRA's Soul*. London: Picador, 1995.

Townshend, Charles. *Political Violence in Ireland: Government and Resistance since 1848*. Oxford: Clarendon, 1983.

Tugwell, Maurice. 'Politics and Propaganda of the Provisional IRA' in Wilkinson, ed. 13-40.

Urban, Mark. *Big Boys' Rules: The Secret Struggle against the IRA*. London: Faber, 1992.

Utley, T.E. 'The Significance of Mrs. Thatcher' in Cowling, ed. 1978. 41-51.

— . 'Almost the Whole Truth about Ulster'. *The Salisbury Review* 1; 2. Autumn 1982. 9-11.

Van Boheemen-Saaf, Christine. *Joyce, Derrida, Lacan, and the Trauma of History: Reading, Narrative and Postcolonialism*. Cambridge: Cambridge U P, 1999.

Various. 'Crime and Detection'. *TLS* 4079. 5 June 1981.

Voloshinov, V.N. *Marxism and the Philosophy of Language*. London: Seminar P, 1973.

Waites, Bernard, Tony Bennett and Graham Martin, eds. *Popular Culture: Past and Present*. London: Croom Helm, 1982.

Walby, Sylvia. *Theorizing Patriarchy*. Oxford: Blackwell, 1990.

Wallerstein, Immanuel. 'The Ideological Tensions of Capitalism: Universalism Versus Sexism and Racism' in Balibar and Wallerstein, 29-36.

Wallis, Roy et al. *No Surrender! Paisleyism and the Politics of Ethnic Identity in Northern Ireland*. Belfast: QUB, 1986.

Walshe, Éibhear. 'Introduction: Sex, Nation and Dissent' in Éibhear Walshe, ed. 1997. 1-15.

—, ed. *Sex, Nation and Dissent in Irish Writing*. Cork: Cork U P, 1997.

Walter, Bronwen. 'Contemporary Irish Settlement in London: Women's Worlds, Men's Worlds' in MacLaughlin, ed. 1997. 61-94.

— . 'Gendered Irishness in Britain: Changing Constructions' in Graham and Kirkland, eds. 1999. 77-98.

Ward, Margaret. *Unmanageable Revolutionaries*. London: Pluto P, 1983.

— . *The Missing Sex: Putting Women into Irish History*. Dublin: Attic P, 1991a.

— . 'The Women's Movement in the North of Ireland: Twenty Years On' in Hutton and Stewart, eds. 1991b. 149-163.

— . 'Irish Women and Nationalism'. *Irish Studies Review* 17. Winter 1996-97. 8-14.

— . 'Introduction: Feminism Constructs Nationalism' in West, ed. 1997. xi-xxxvi.

Watt, Stephen. 'The Politics of Bernard MacLaverty's *Cal*'. *Éire-Ireland* 28; 3. 1993. 130-146.

— . 'The Irish Invade America: Terrorism, Gender, and Assimilation'. *New Hibernica Review* 2 ; 2. Summer 1998. 9-27.

Weekes, Ann Owens. *Irish Women Writers: An Uncharted Tradition*. Lexington: U of Kentucky P, 1990.

West, Lois A. ed. *Feminist Nationalism*. London: Routledge, 1997.

West, Richard. 'At Grips with the Provos'. *TLS* 4179. 6 May 1983. 455.

Westwood, Sallie. '"Feckless Fathers": Masculinities and the British State' in Mac an Ghaill, ed. 21-34.

White, Robert W. 'British Violence and British Injustice in Undemocratic Northern Ireland'. *Terrorism and Political Violence* 4; 3. Autumn 1992. 117-119.

Whyte, John. *Interpreting Northern Ireland*. Foreword by Garret Fitzgerald. Oxford: Clarendon P, 1990.

Wichert, Sabine. *Northern Ireland since 1945*. London: Longman, 1991.

Wickham-Jones, Mark. 'Right Turn: A Revionist Account of the 1975 Conservative Party Leadership Election'. *20 Century British History* 8; 1. 1997. 74-89.

Wiener, Ralph. *The Rape and Plunder of the Shankill in Belfast*. Belfast: Nothems, 1976.

Wiles, Paul. 'Law, Order and the State' in Graham and Prosser, eds. 153-173.

Wilkinson, Paul, ed. *British Perspectives on Terrorism*. London: George Allen and Unwin, 1981.

Willemen, Paul. *Look and Frictions*. London: BFI, 1994.

Willet, Ralph. *The Naked City: Urban Crime Fiction in the USA*. Manchester: Manchester U P, 1996.

Williams, Patrick and Laura Chrisman, eds. *Colonial Discourse and Post-Colonial Theory: A Reader*. London: Harvester and Wheatsheaf, 1993.

Williams, Raymond. *Culture and Society 1870-1950*. London: Penguin, 1963.

— . *The Long Revolution*. London: Penguin, 1965.

— . *The Country and the City*. London: Chatto and Windus, 1973.

— . *Keywords: A Vocabulary of Culture and Society*. Glasgow: Fontana, 1976.

— . *Communications*. London: Penguin, 1977a.

— . *Marxism and Literature*. Oxford: Oxford U P, 1977b.

— . *Problems in Materialism and Culture*. London: Verso, 1980.

— . *Culture*. London: Fontana, 1986a.

— . 'The Uses of Cultural Theory'. *New Left Review*. 158. July/August 1986b. 19-51.

Williamson, Judith. *Consuming Passions: The Dynamics of Popular Culture*. London: Marion Boyars, 1988.

Willott, Sara and Christine Griffin. 'Men, Masculinity and the Challenge of Long Term Unemployment' in Mac an Ghaill, ed. 77-92.

Willmott, Peter. 'Urban Kinship Past and Present'. *Social Studies Review* Nov 1988. 44-46.

Wilson, Edgar. *A Very British Miracle: The Failure of Thatcherism*. London: Pluto P, 1992.

Wirth-Nesher, Hana. *City Codes: Reading the Modern Urban Novel*. Cambridge: Cambridge U P, 1996.

Wolfe, Peter. 'The Critics Did It'. *Modern Fiction Studies*. 29; 3. Autumn 1983. 389-433.

Wolin, Richard. *Walter Benjamin: An Aesthetic of Redemption*. London: U of California P, 1994.

Woodiwiss, Anthony. *Social Theory After Postmodernism: Rethinking Production, Law and Class*. London: Pluto P, 1990.

Worpole, Ken. 'The American Connection: The Masculine Style in Popular Fiction'. *New Left Review* 139. May-June 1983a. 79-84.

— . *Dockers and Detectives*. London: Verso, 1983b.

— . 'Mother to Legend (Or Going Underground): The London Novel' in Bell, ed. 1995. 181-193.

Wright, Elizabeth. *Feminism and Psychoanalysis: A Critical Dictionary*. Oxford: Blackwell, 1993.

Wright, Elizabeth and Edmond Wright, eds. *The Žižek Reader*. Oxford: Blackwell, 1999.

Wright, Frank. *Northern Ireland: A Comparative Analysis*. Dublin: Gill and Macmillan, 1988.

Wright, Joanne. 'Northern Ireland: A British Isles Security Complex'. *Terrorism and Political Violence* 5; 4. Winter 1993. 266-287.

Wright, Patrick. *On Living in an Old Country: The National Past in Contemporary Britain*. London: Verso, 1985.

— . *A Journey Through Ruins: The Last Days of London*. London: Radius, 1991.

Young, Lola. '"Nothing is as It Seems": Re-viewing *The Crying Game*' in Kirkham and Thumim, eds. 1995. 273-285.

— . *Fear of the Dark: 'Race', Gender and Sexuality in the Cinema*. London: Routledge, 1996.

Yuval-Davis, Nira. *Gender and Nation*. London: SAGE, 1997.

Zaretsky, Eli. *Capitalism, the Family, and Personal Life*. London: Harper Colophon Books, 1976.

Zerzan, John. *Elements of Refusal*. Seattle: Left Bank Books, 1988.

— . *Future Primitive and Other Essays*. New York: Autonomedia, 1994.

Žižek, Slavoj. *The Sublime Object of Ideology*. London: Verso, 1989.

— . *Looking Awry: An Introduction to Jacques Lacan through Popular Culture*. London: MIT P, 1991.

— . '"The Thing that Thinks": The Kantian Background of the *Noir* Subject' in Copjec, ed. 1993. 199-226.

Zubaidi, Sami. 'Theories of Nationalism' in Littlejohn, ed. 52-71.

Zwicker, Heather. 'Gendered Troubles: Refiguring "Woman" in Northern Ireland' In Kayann Short et al, eds. *Sexual Artifice: Persons, Images, Politics*. New York: New York U P, 1994. 198-220.

Index

Ahmad, Aijaz 12, 35
Althusser, Louis 2, 7, 8, 144
Anderson, Benedict 158
Anderson, Linda 135–6
Asher, Michael 98
Aughey, Arthur 72–3

Baker, Keith 77–9, 128–9, 141,
    147–8
Bakhtin, M.M. 86
Ballinger, W.A. 90–91
Barnacle, Hugo 56
Barthes, Roland 86, 97, 110, 143, 146–7,
    150, 156–7
Bateman, Colin 2, 5, 11, 79–81, 101,
    118, 160–161
    Cycle of Violence 79–80
    Divorcing Jack 2, 5, 11, 79–81, 101
    Of Wee Sweetie Mice and Men 80
Belfast 25, 48, 83–110
    representation of 25, 48, 83–110
Bell, J. Bowyer 26
Bender, Barbara 100
Benjamin, Walter, 1, 11, 16, 24, 25, 46–
    7, 86–8, 91–2, 102, 104, 108,
    154, 157, 158, 165–6
Bennett, Ronan 70–71
Bennett, Tony 9–10, 27
Berman, Marshall 63, 140
Bhabha, Homi K. 29, 31–2, 50–51
Bouché, Elizabeth 4
Bradford, Roy 72
Brand, Dana, 92
Brecht, Bertolt 6–7, 145, 158, 159, 164,
    167–171
Bromley, Roger 116
Brooks, Peter 150–151
Brown, Terence 63, 84

Burden, Peter 131

Carson, Ciaran 101
Castells, Manuel 87, 105–6
Caufield, Max 89–90
Chandler, Raymond 111, 117
Clancy, Tom 30, 53, 69–70, 156
Clarke, A.F.N. 48, 98
Clarke, Shaun 29, 44–5, 53–5, 56, 92,
    122, 161
    Red Hand 92, 122
    Underworld 44–5, 53–5, 56, 161
Connolly, Colm 134
Coulter, Carol 130
Coward, Rosalind 139
Craig, Cairns 31
Cranny-Francis, Anne 23, 115
Crawford, Robert 75–6, 95–6, 141
Creed, Barbara 116
crime genre 3–9, 15–23, 25, 26, 35–6,
    38–9, 41–2, 53–5, 81, 91–2,
    102–3, 109–110, 111–139, 140–
    164
    politics of 3–9, 15-23, 25, 26, 35–6,
    38–9, 90–91, 102–3, 140–164
    representation of gender in 25, 41–2,
    53–5, 81, 109–110, 111–139,
    143–157
Crossland, Susan 117
Cullingford, Elizabeth Butler 129
Curtis, Liz 26, 29, 49

Davies, Murray 42
Davies, Tony 113
Davis, Mike 94
Deane, Seamus 35, 158–9
Deleuze, Gilles 142
Dibdin, Michael 162

Dickinson, Peter 32–3, 47–8
Dilley, Kimberly J. 133
Dyer, Richard 121–122

Eagleton, Terry 10–11, 62–3, 78
Easterman, Daniel 60
English Nationalism 24, 26–56, 131
    and the New Right 24, 27, 33, 35–56
Esler, Gavin 141–2

Feldmann, Alan 98–9, 101
Finlayson, Alan 14
Forster, E.M. 96
Foster John Wilson 83
Foucault, Michel 3, 27–8, 34–5, 141, 142
Frazer, Adrian 126
Freud, Sigmund 95, 110, 154

Gibbons, Luke 26–7, 85
Gill, Bartholomew 67, 153
Gledhill, Christine 112
Glover, David 119–120, 121–2
Gottdiener, M. 87, 89
Graham, Colin 59
Gramsci, Antonio 9, 27–8, 34, 43, 111, 113
Green, F.L. 15, 89
Gunn, Daniel 154

Hall, Stuart 34, 35, 45
Hammett, Dashiell 11, 83, 90–91
Harvey, Sylvia 126–7
Hawke, Christopher 28, 30
Heaney, Seamus 81, 83–4, 86, 94, 104
Herron, Shaun 60–2
Higgins, George V. 69
Higgins, Jack 6, 60, 148–9
    Angel of Death 149
    Confessional 148–9
    Drink with the Devil 149
    The Eagle Has Landed 6
    Touch the Devil 6
Hobsbaum, Eric 160

Hughes, Eamonn 30, 49, 68–9, 70, 80–81, 86, 87, 93, 99
Humm, Maggie, 138–9
Hurd, Douglas 36, 49
Hutton, Will 52

Irish Nationalism 15, 22–3, 24, 36, 57–71, 81–2, 83–6, 91–3, 94–5, 96–7, 99–102, 105 –6, 109–110, 129, 135, 139, 158

James, P.D. 38
Jameson, Fredric 2–3, 5, 7–9, 11–14, 22, 30, 38–9, 59–60, 102–3, 107, 140, 142–3
Jarman, Neil 91
Jones, Russell Celyn 122–4

Kaplan E. Ann 118
Kebbe, Jonathan 3
Kiberd, Declan 31, 35, 125
Kiely, Benedict, 16–22, 25
Kirkland, Richard 34, 109
Klein, Kathleen Gregory 118
Knight, Stephen 5, 162
Kristeva, Julia 24
Krutnik, Frank 117

Lacan, Jacques 14, 113, 117, 123, 128, 144, 145, 150–151, 153, 154, 163
Lane, Andrew 40, 46, 49, 51, 116
Larkin, Philip 36–7
Leather, Stephen 52
Leerssen, Joep 1, 46, 56, 58–9, 60–61
Leitch, Maurice 106–7, 109–110, 125
Lingard, Joan 135
Lloyd, David 9, 10
Lodge, David 146
Longley, Edna 2, 57, 85, 96
Luibheid, Eithne 69
Lund, James 33–4
Lynch, Kevin 103

McCabe, Eugene 16–22
McCaffery, K.T. 130
McCracken, Scott 9, 143
McDonald, Ian 9, 107–9, 147
McEldowney, Eugene, 112
McGahern, John 125
McGeough, Gerry 66–9
MacGill, Patrick 62
Macherey, Pierre 8, 29
McIlroy, Brian 131–2
MacLaverty, Bernard 64–6
McLavery, Michael 84
McLaughlin, Jane 136–7
McLaughlin, Jim 68
McMahon, Blair 71–2, 132
McNab, Andy 15, 51, 124, 161–2
    Immediate Action 15
    Remote Control 51, 124, 161–2
McNamee, Eoin 73–5, 78, 88, 96–8, 117, 126
    Resurrection Man 73–5, 78, 88, 96–8, 117, 126
Mandel, Ernest 158, 159–160, 163
Marx, Karl, 8, 161
Mazzoleni, Donatella 99
Meaney, Geraldine 129
Michaels, S.J. 75–7, 127–8
Miller, Kerby 68
Miner, Valerie 137–9
Modleski, Tania 133–4
Moore, Brian 1, 63–4, 93–5, 104, 107, 114
Moretti, Franco 3, 103
Morgan, Robin 119
Mornin, Daniel 94–5, 110
Moxon, Mildred Downey 119
Mulhern, Francis 73, 77
Mulvey, Laura 112, 113–114
Mumford, Lewis 100, 102
Munt, Sally 113–114, 120–121, 138

Nairn, Tom 12
Nandy, Ashis 124–5, 129
Neale, Steve 115–116, 145–6, 153–4

Nietzsche, Friedrich 140, 151
Nelson, Walter, 37–8, 52, 55
Newman, G.F. 55–6
Newsinger, John 37, 41
Nicholl, Ned 118

O'Connor Fionnuala 64
O'Dowd, Liam 50
O'Flaherty, Liam 15
O'Reilly, Victor 60
O'Riordan, Kate 115, 135

Palmer, Jerry 4, 16, 120
Palmer, Paulina 127
Patterson, Glenn 87, 97, 98
Pelaschiar, Laura 21, 109
Perry, Ritchie 46
Petit, Chris 24, 31, 50, 88, 132–3, 144, 162
    The Psalm Killer 24, 31, 50, 88, 132–3, 144, 162
Pincher, Chapman 39
Pike, Burton 101
Place, Janey 117–118
Porter, Dennis 20, 27, 119–120
Porter, Henry 129
Power, M.S. 6, 141, 144, 150, 151

Radaway, Janice A. 134–5
Reid, Forrest 96
Reddy, Maureen T. 133–4

Said, Edward 15, 27–8, 30–31, 34
St Peter, Christine 125
Sartre, Jean-Paul 23
SAS 40–56, 126, 131, 156
Scanlan, Margaret 3, 65
Semple, Linda 139
Sennett, Richard 81–82
Seymour, Gerald 2, 30, 42, 45, 48–9, 86, 91, 100–101
    The Glory Boys, 48
    Harry's Game 2, 42, 49, 86, 91, 100–101

The Journeyman Tailor 30, 45, 49
Shah, Eddy 42, 88
Shearman, Hugh 84
Smith, Adam 142
Smyth, Ailbhe 129
Smyth, Gerry 102
Spivak, Gayatri 29
Stallybrass, Peter 98
Steel, Jayne 151–2
Stevens, Gordon 49, 52
Strong, Terence 39, 40–41

Tasker, Yvonne 118
Thatcher, Margaret 36, 39, 40, 44, 52, 151–2, 162
Thatcherism 35–56, 129, 131, 162
Thompson, E.P. 7, 144

Unionism 15, 22–3, 24, 50–51, 57–64, 71–82, 83–6, 91–3, 95–7, 99–102, 105–6, 109 –110, 129, 135, 158
Uris, Leon 66

Walshe, Éibhear 127–8
Ward, Margaret 130
Weekes, Anne Ownes 125
White, Allon 98
Willet, Ralph 86
Williams, Raymond 3, 13, 20, 34, 86, 87, 91, 104, 107, 147
Wirth-Nesher, Hana 103
Worpole, Ken 102, 126
Wright, Patrick 44, 46–7, 96

Žižek, Slavoj 144, 152–3, 154–7, 163–4